LoveLess

Volume 8

HAMBURG // LONDON // LOS ANGELES // TOKYO

Loveless Volume 8
Created by Yun Kouga

Translation - Ray Yoshimoto
English Adaptation - Christine Boylan
Copy Editor - Nikhil Burman
Retouch and Lettering - Star Print Brokers
Production Artist - Michael Paolilli
Graphic Designer - Monalisa De Asis

Editor - Lillian Diaz-Przybyl
Digital Imaging Manager - Chris Buford
Pre-Production Supervisor - Vicente Rivera, Jr.
Production Specialist - Lucas Rivera
Managing Editor - Vy Nguyen
Art Director - Al-Insan Lashley
Editor-in-Chief - Rob Tokar
Publisher - Mike Kiley
President and C.O.O. - John Parker
C.E.O. and Chief Creative Officer - Stu Levy

A  Manga

TOKYOPOP and  are trademarks or registered trademarks of TOKYOPOP Inc.

TOKYOPOP Inc.
5900 Wilshire Blvd. Suite 2000
Los Angeles, CA 90036

E-mail: info@TOKYOPOP.com
Come visit us online at www.TOKYOPOP.com

ISBN: 978-1-4278-1302-2

First TOKYOPOP printing: September 2008
10 9 8 7 6 5 4 3 2 1
Printed in the USA

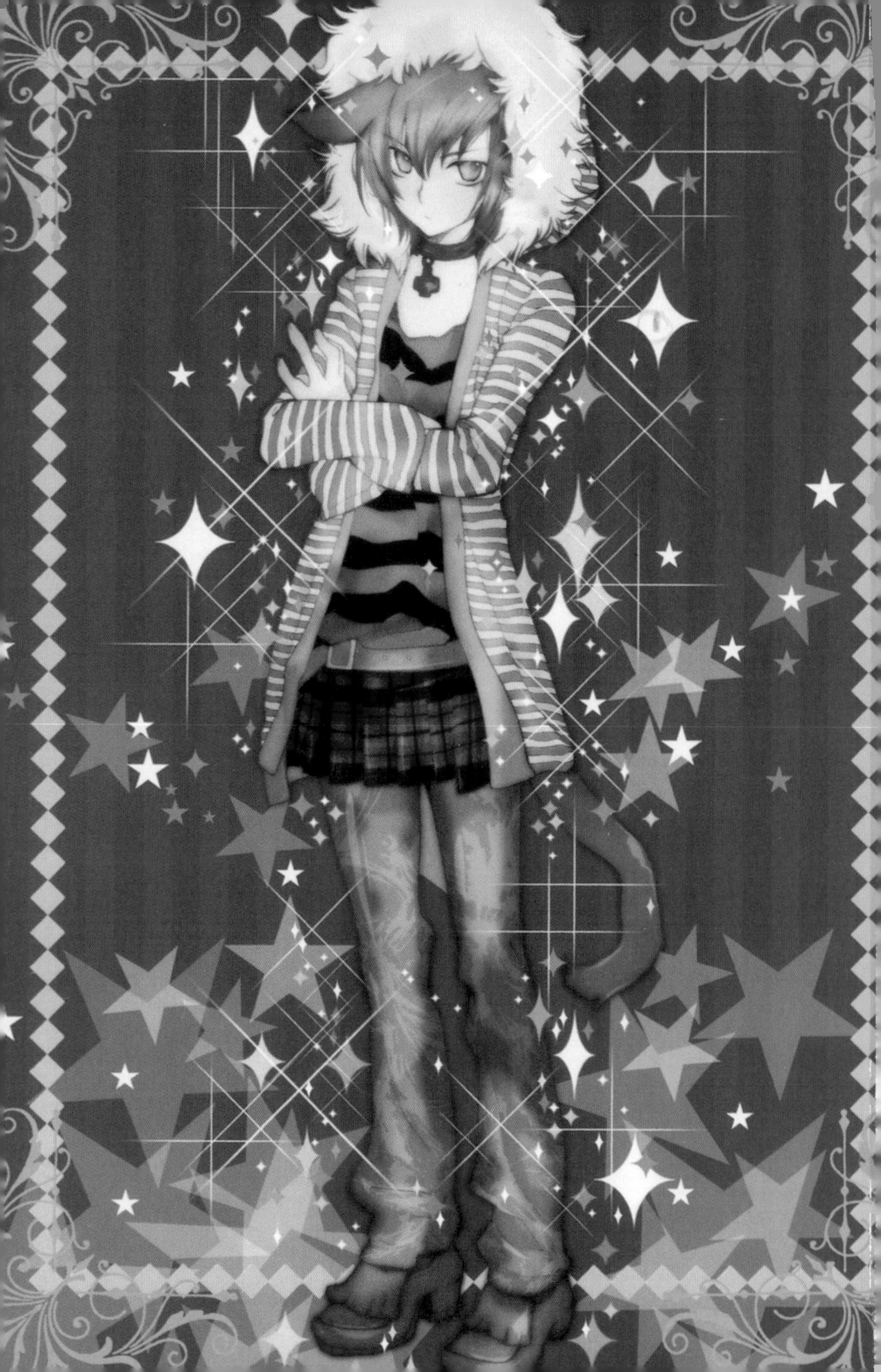

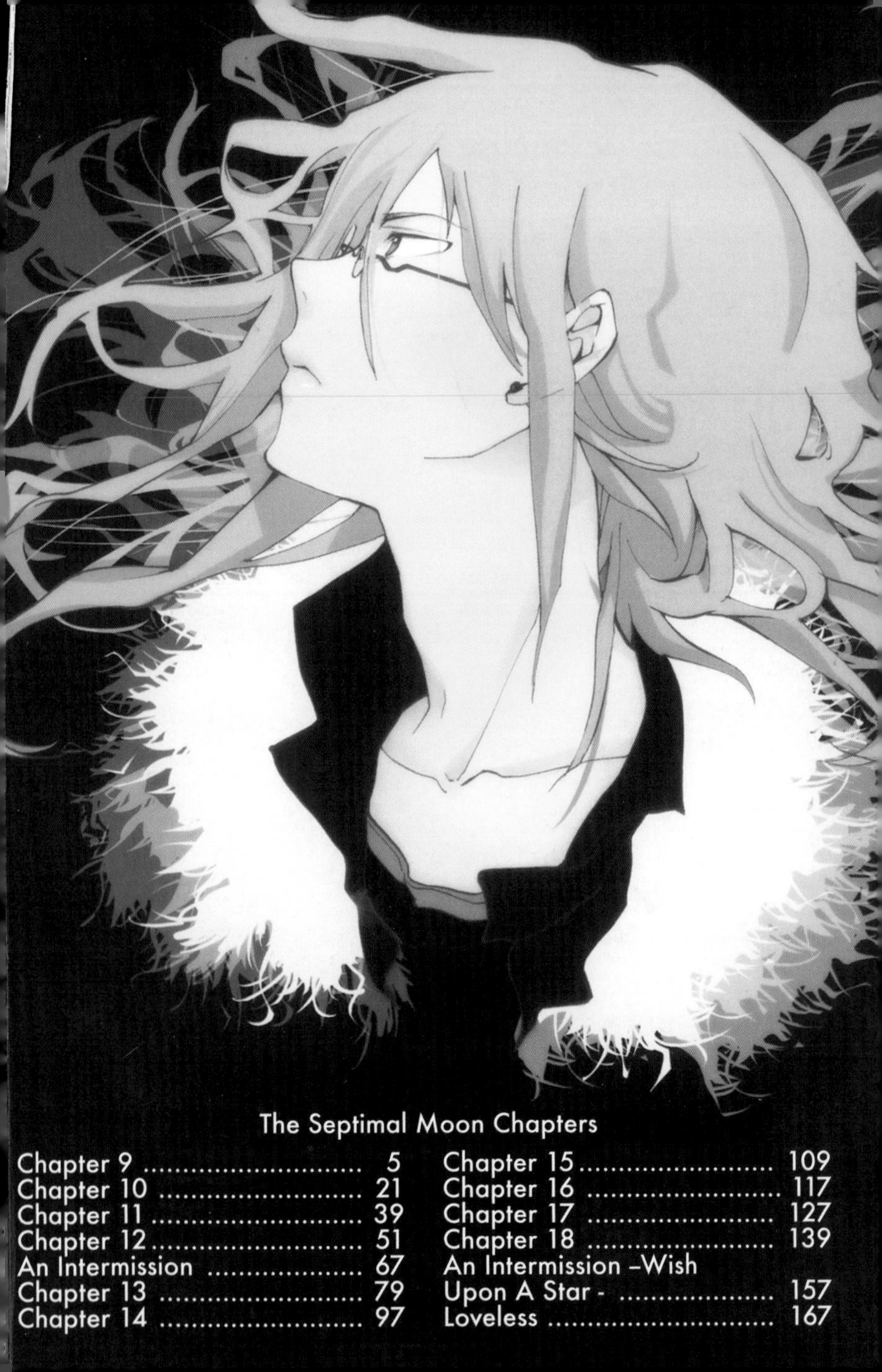

The Septimal Moon Chapters

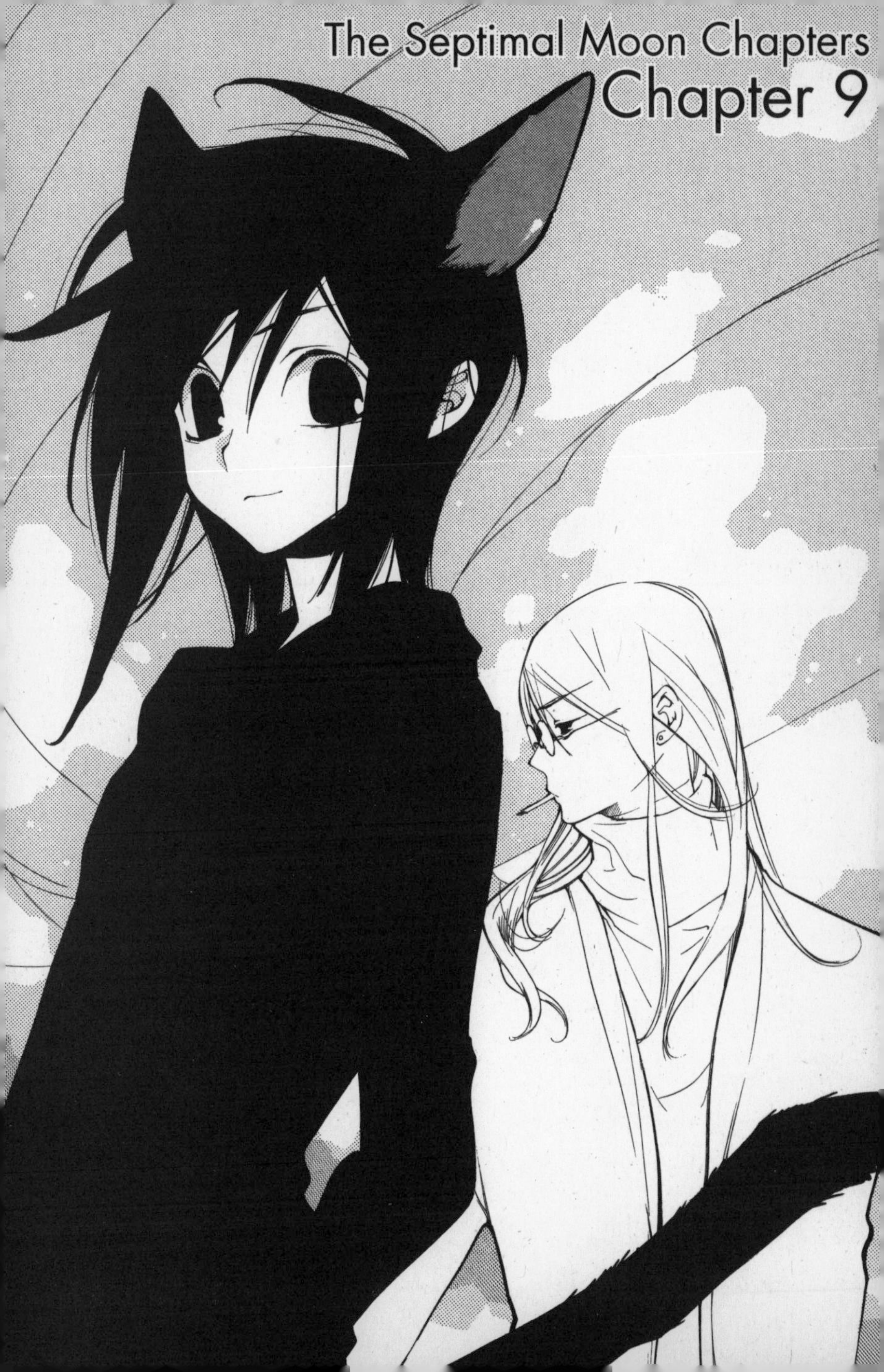
The Septimal Moon Chapters
Chapter 9

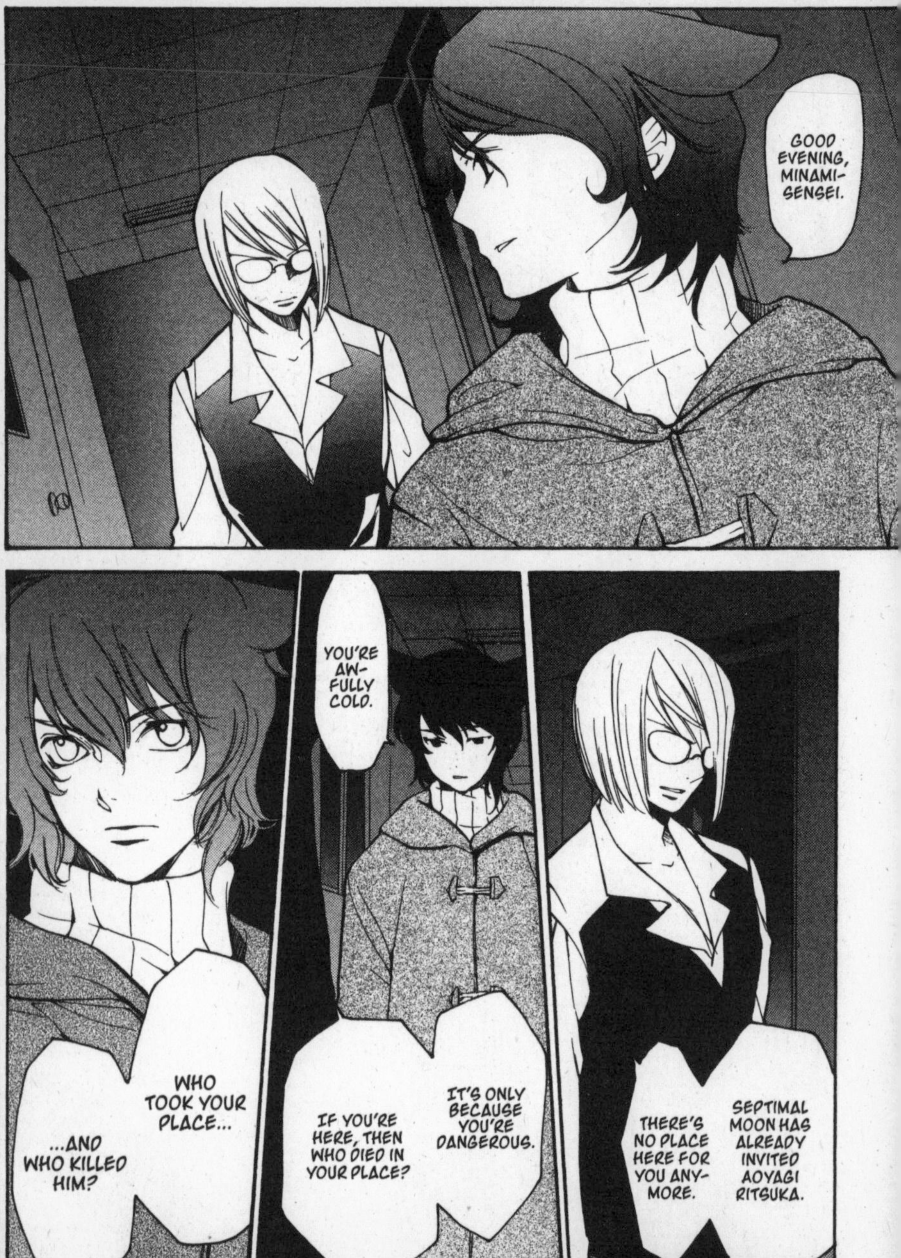
GOOD EVENING, MINAMI-SENSEI.
SEPTIMAL MOON HAS ALREADY INVITED AOYAGI RITSUKA.
THERE'S NO PLACE HERE FOR YOU ANY-MORE.
YOU'RE AW-FULLY COLD.
IT'S ONLY BECAUSE YOU'RE DANGEROUS.
IF YOU'RE HERE, THEN WHO DIED IN YOUR PLACE?
WHO TOOK YOUR PLACE...
...AND WHO KILLED HIM?

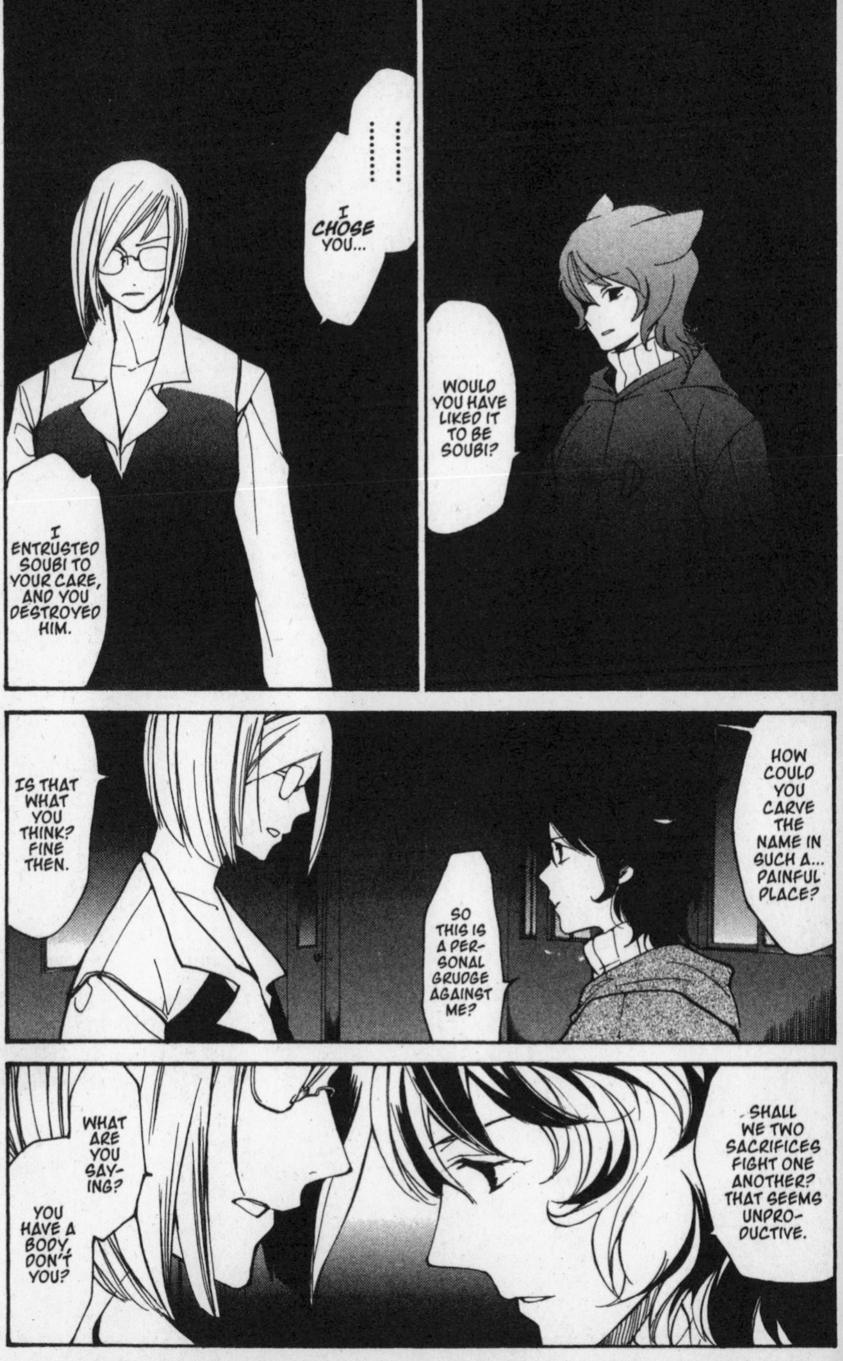
WOULD YOU HAVE LIKED IT TO BE SOUBI?
......
I CHOSE YOU...
I ENTRUSTED SOUBI TO YOUR CARE, AND YOU DESTROYED HIM.
HOW COULD YOU CARVE THE NAME IN SUCH A... PAINFUL PLACE?
SO THIS IS A PERSONAL GRUDGE AGAINST ME?
IS THAT WHAT YOU THINK? FINE THEN.
SHALL WE TWO SACRIFICES FIGHT ONE ANOTHER? THAT SEEMS UNPRODUCTIVE.
WHAT ARE YOU SAYING?
YOU HAVE A BODY, DON'T YOU?

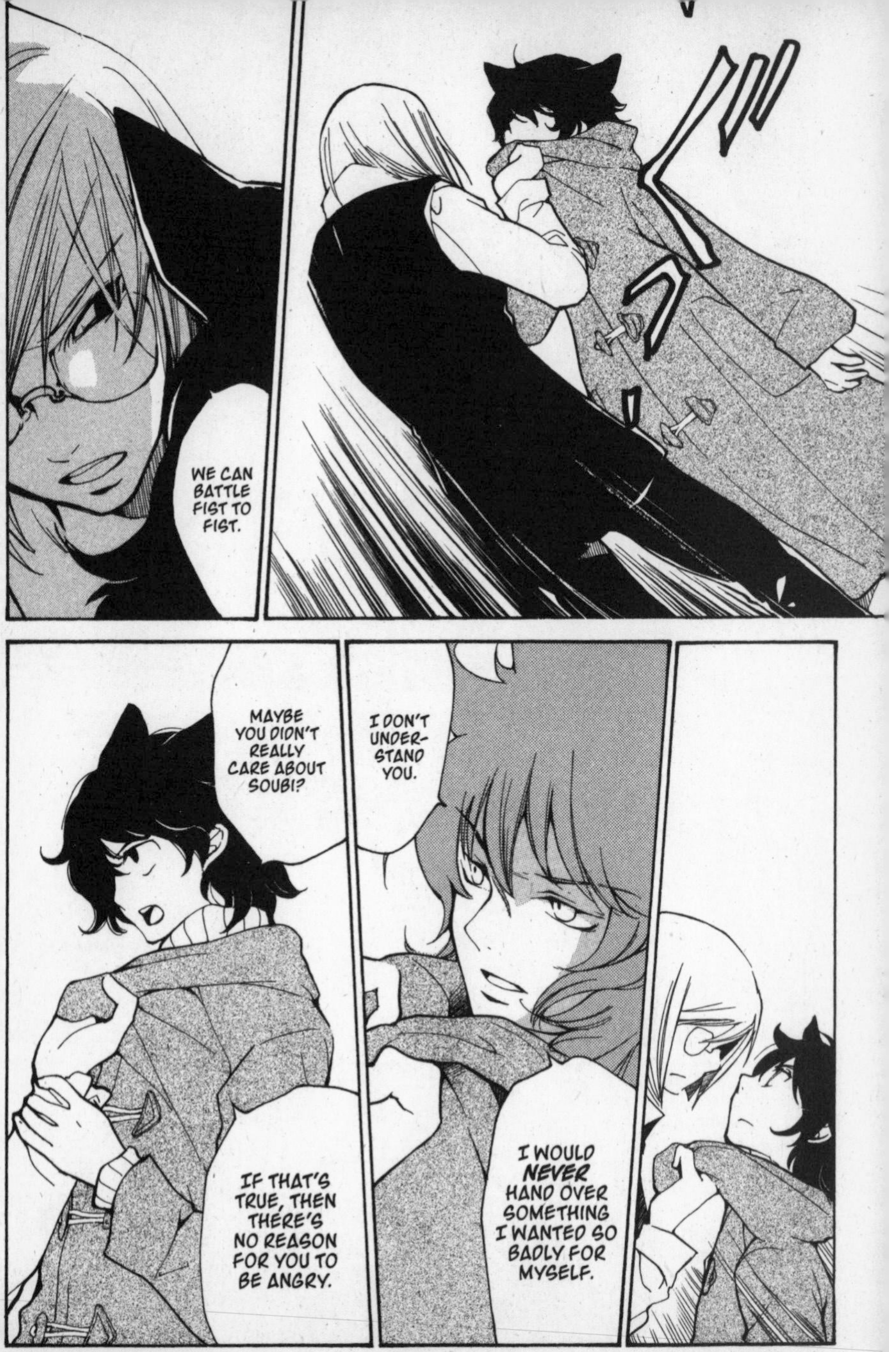
WE CAN BATTLE FIST TO FIST.
I DON'T UNDER-STAND YOU.
I WOULD NEVER HAND OVER SOMETHING I WANTED SO BADLY FOR MYSELF.
MAYBE YOU DIDN'T REALLY CARE ABOUT SOUBI?
IF THAT'S TRUE, THEN THERE'S NO REASON FOR YOU TO BE ANGRY.

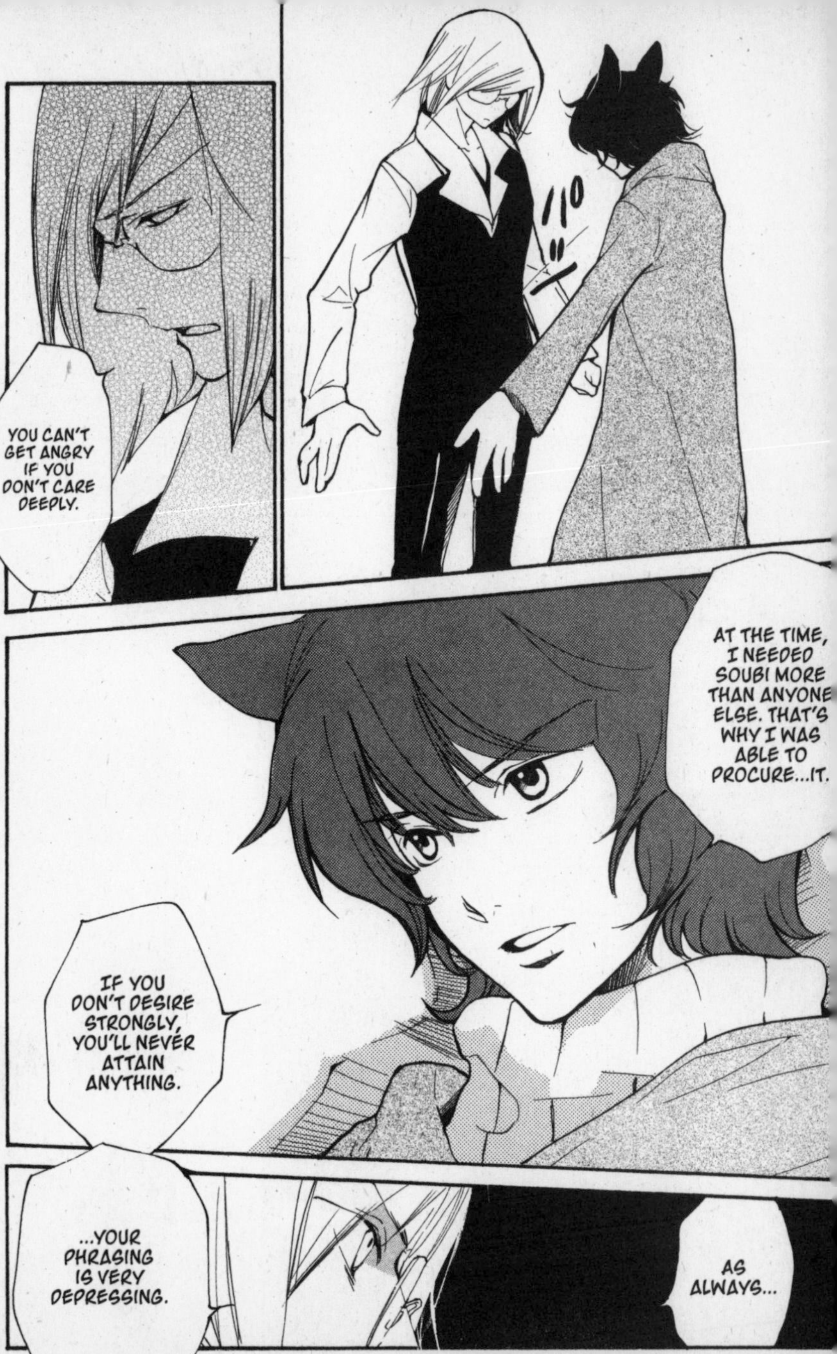
YOU CAN'T GET ANGRY IF YOU DON'T CARE DEEPLY.
AT THE TIME, I NEEDED SOUBI MORE THAN ANYONE ELSE. THAT'S WHY I WAS ABLE TO PROCURE...IT.
IF YOU DON'T DESIRE STRONGLY, YOU'LL NEVER ATTAIN ANYTHING.
AS ALWAYS...
...YOUR PHRASING IS VERY DEPRESSING.

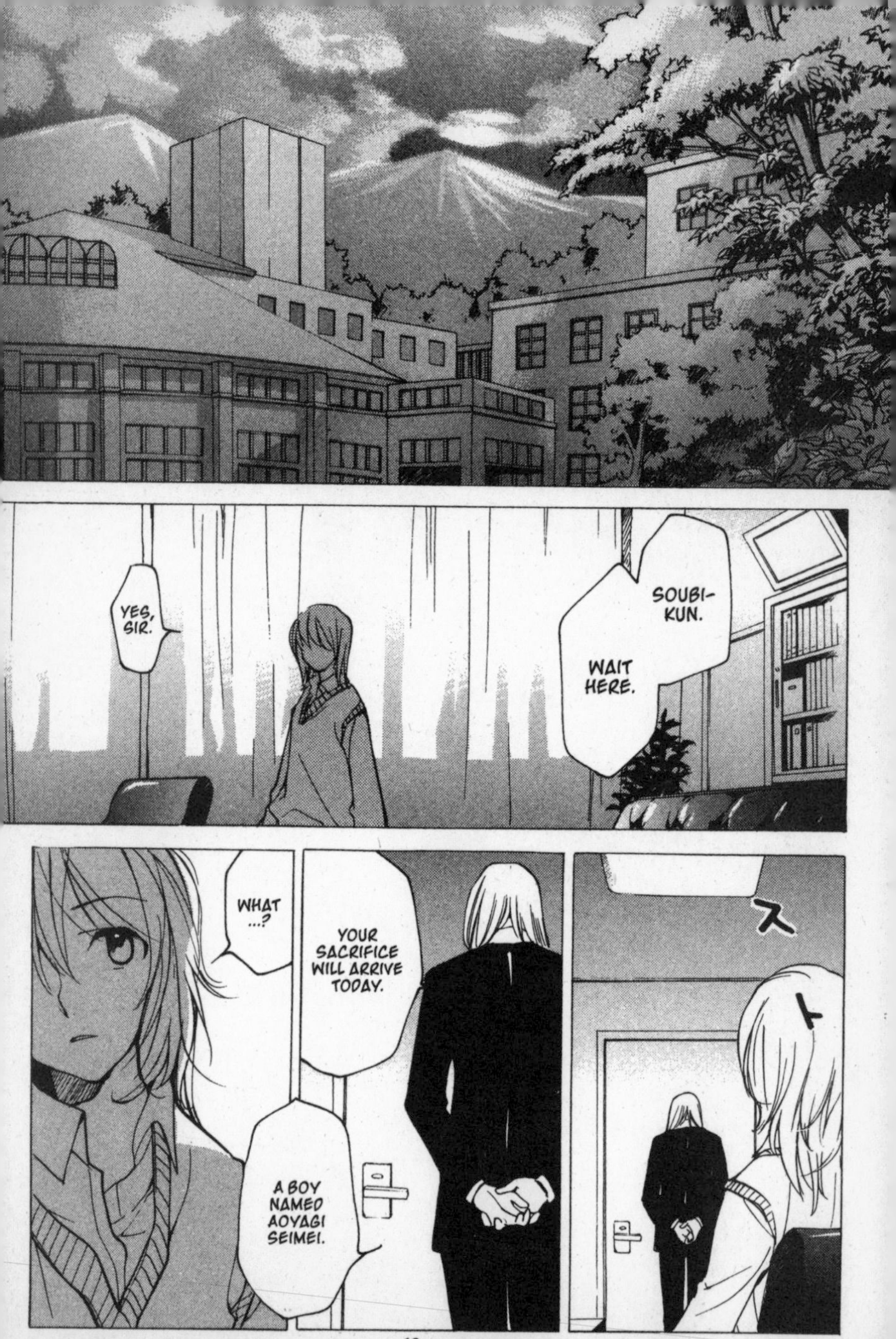
SOUBI-KUN.
WAIT HERE.
YES, SIR.
ス
ト
YOUR SACRIFICE WILL ARRIVE TODAY.
A BOY NAMED AOYAGI SEIMEI.
WHAT ...?

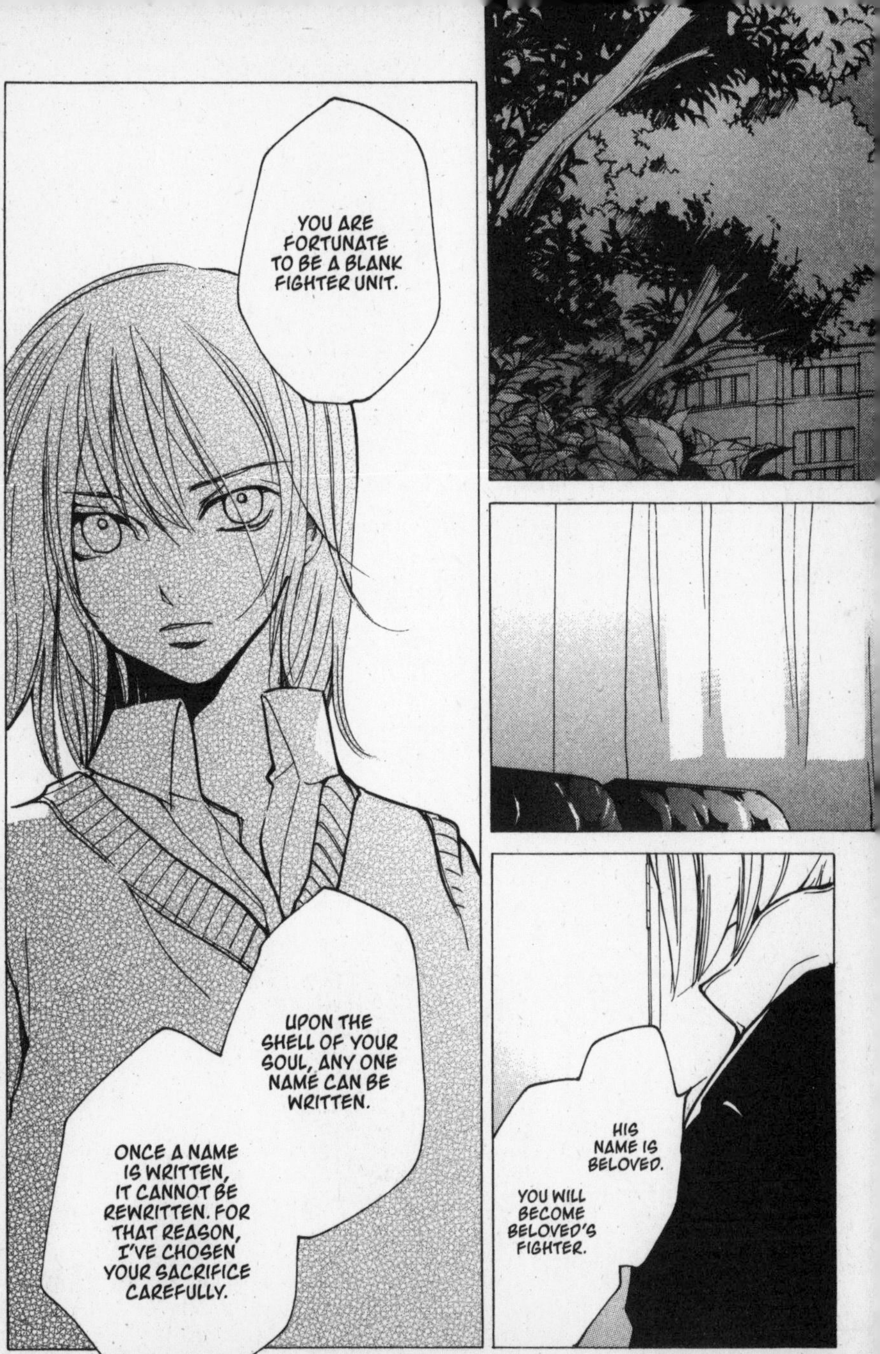
HIS NAME IS BELOVED.
YOU WILL BECOME BELOVED'S FIGHTER.
YOU ARE FORTUNATE TO BE A BLANK FIGHTER UNIT.
UPON THE SHELL OF YOUR SOUL, ANY ONE NAME CAN BE WRITTEN.
ONCE A NAME IS WRITTEN, IT CANNOT BE REWRITTEN. FOR THAT REASON, I'VE CHOSEN YOUR SACRIFICE CAREFULLY.

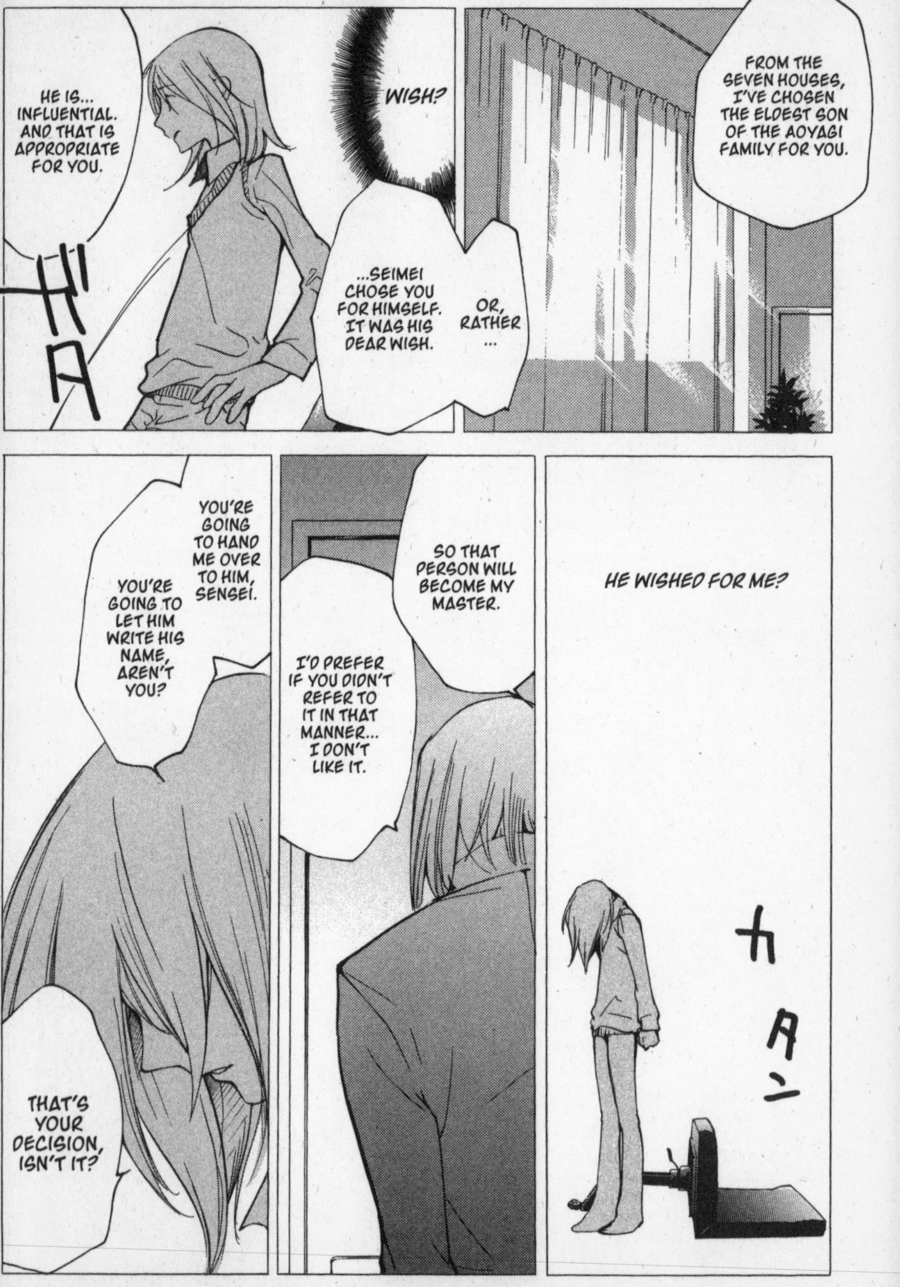
FROM THE SEVEN HOUSES, I'VE CHOSEN THE ELDEST SON OF THE AOYAGI FAMILY FOR YOU.
HE IS... INFLUENTIAL. AND THAT IS APPROPRIATE FOR YOU.
OR, RATHER ...
...SEIMEI CHOSE YOU FOR HIMSELF. IT WAS HIS DEAR WISH.
WISH?
ガタ
HE WISHED FOR ME?
カタン
SO THAT PERSON WILL BECOME MY MASTER.
I'D PREFER IF YOU DIDN'T REFER TO IT IN THAT MANNER... I DON'T LIKE IT.
YOU'RE GOING TO HAND ME OVER TO HIM, SENSEI.
YOU'RE GOING TO LET HIM WRITE HIS NAME, AREN'T YOU?
THAT'S YOUR DECISION, ISN'T IT?

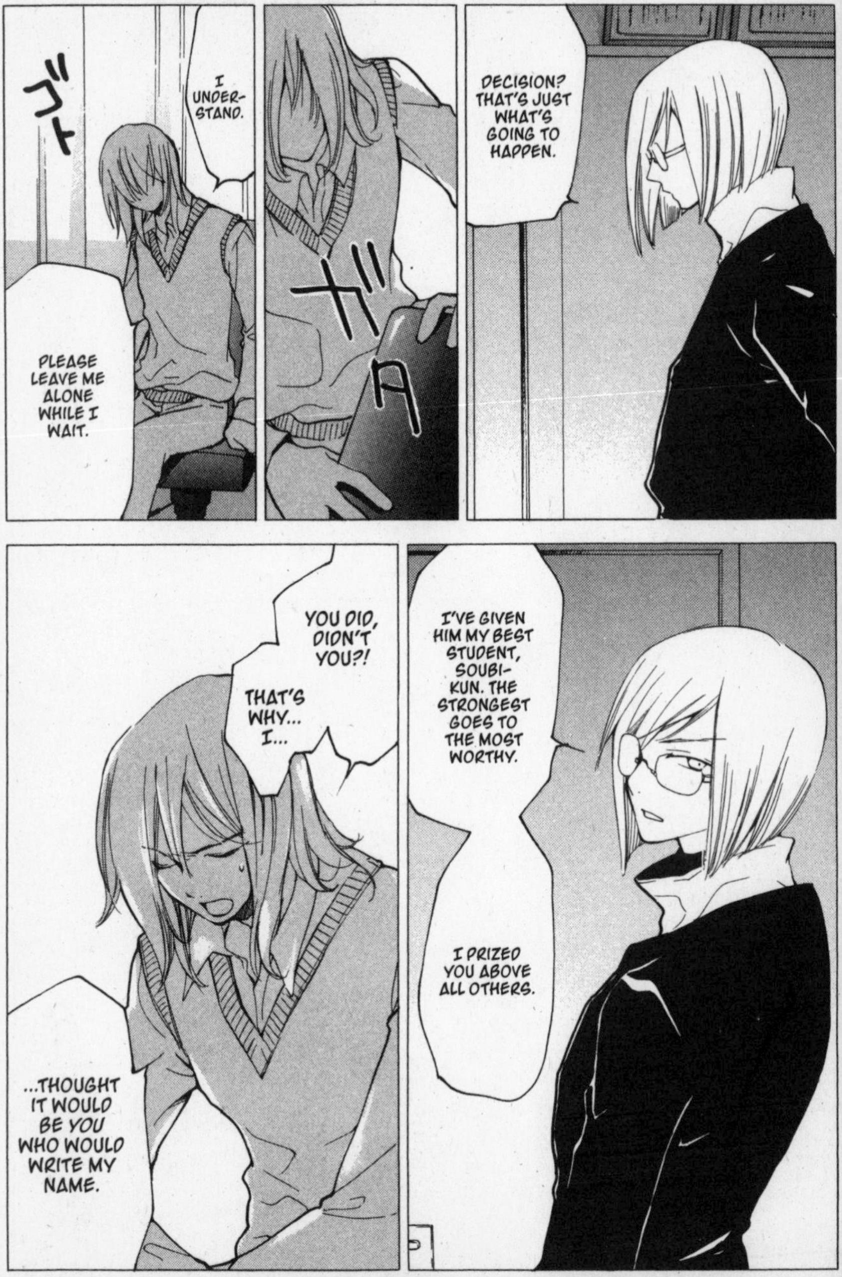
DECISION? THAT'S JUST WHAT'S GOING TO HAPPEN.
ガタ
ゴト
I UNDER-STAND.
PLEASE LEAVE ME ALONE WHILE I WAIT.
I'VE GIVEN HIM MY BEST STUDENT, SOUBI-KUN. THE STRONGEST GOES TO THE MOST WORTHY.
I PRIZED YOU ABOVE ALL OTHERS.
YOU DID, DIDN'T YOU?!
THAT'S WHY... I...
...THOUGHT IT WOULD BE *YOU* WHO WOULD WRITE MY NAME.

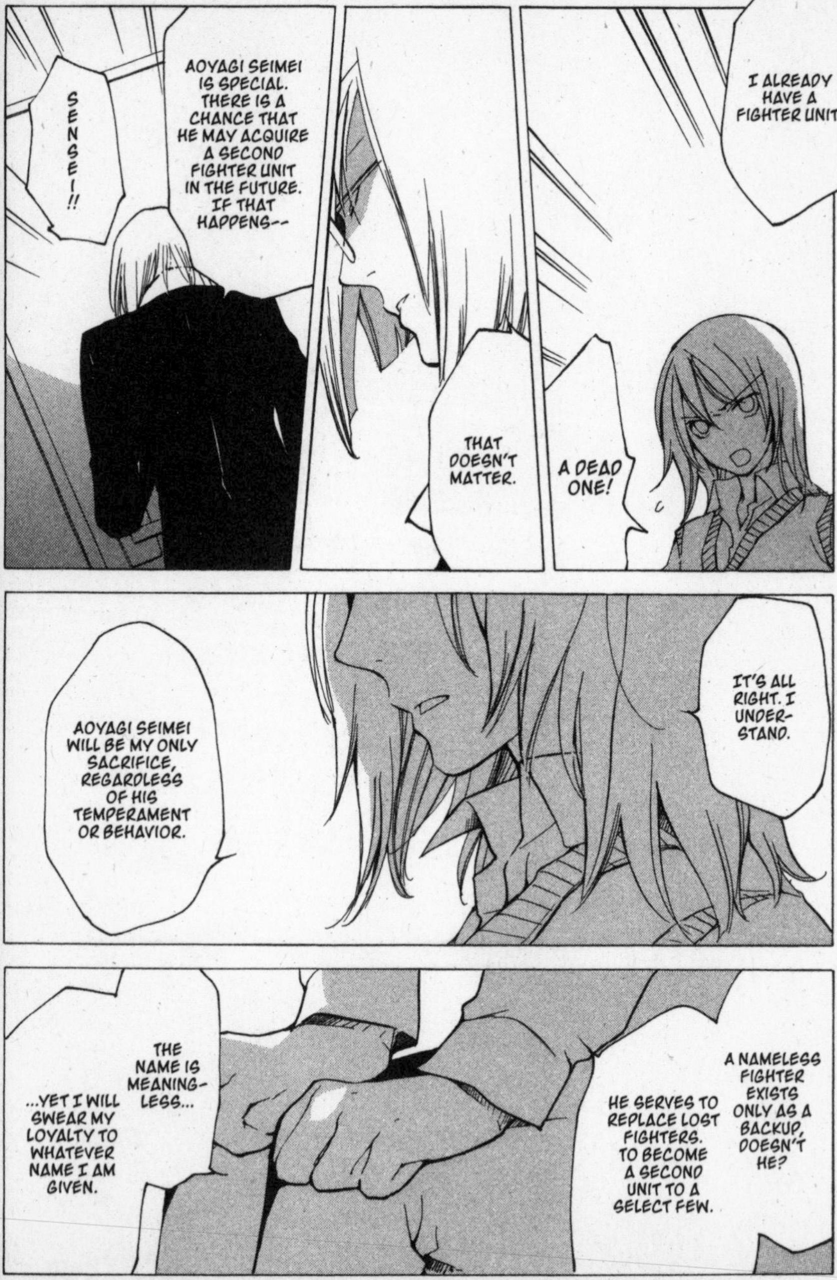
I ALREADY HAVE A FIGHTER UNIT.
A DEAD ONE!
THAT DOESN'T MATTER.
AOYAGI SEIMEI IS SPECIAL. THERE IS A CHANCE THAT HE MAY ACQUIRE A SECOND FIGHTER UNIT IN THE FUTURE. IF THAT HAPPENS--
SENSEI!!
IT'S ALL RIGHT. I UNDER-STAND.
AOYAGI SEIMEI WILL BE MY ONLY SACRIFICE, REGARDLESS OF HIS TEMPERAMENT OR BEHAVIOR.
A NAMELESS FIGHTER EXISTS ONLY AS A BACKUP, DOESN'T HE?
HE SERVES TO REPLACE LOST FIGHTERS. TO BECOME A SECOND UNIT TO A SELECT FEW.
THE NAME IS MEANING-LESS...
...YET I WILL SWEAR MY LOYALTY TO WHATEVER NAME I AM GIVEN.

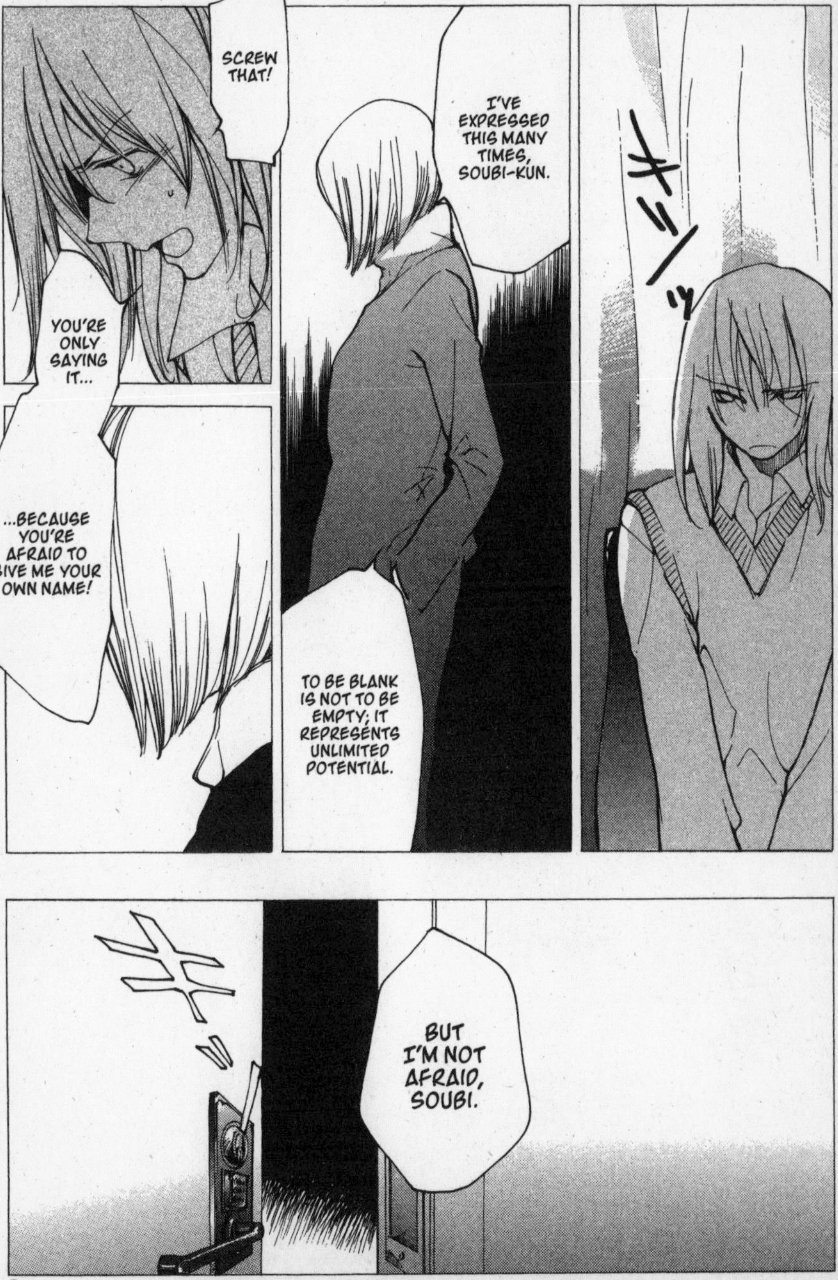
I'VE EXPRESSED THIS MANY TIMES, SOUBI-KUN.
TO BE BLANK IS NOT TO BE EMPTY; IT REPRESENTS UNLIMITED POTENTIAL.
SCREW THAT!
YOU'RE ONLY SAYING IT...
...BECAUSE YOU'RE AFRAID TO GIVE ME YOUR OWN NAME!
BUT I'M NOT AFRAID, SOUBI.

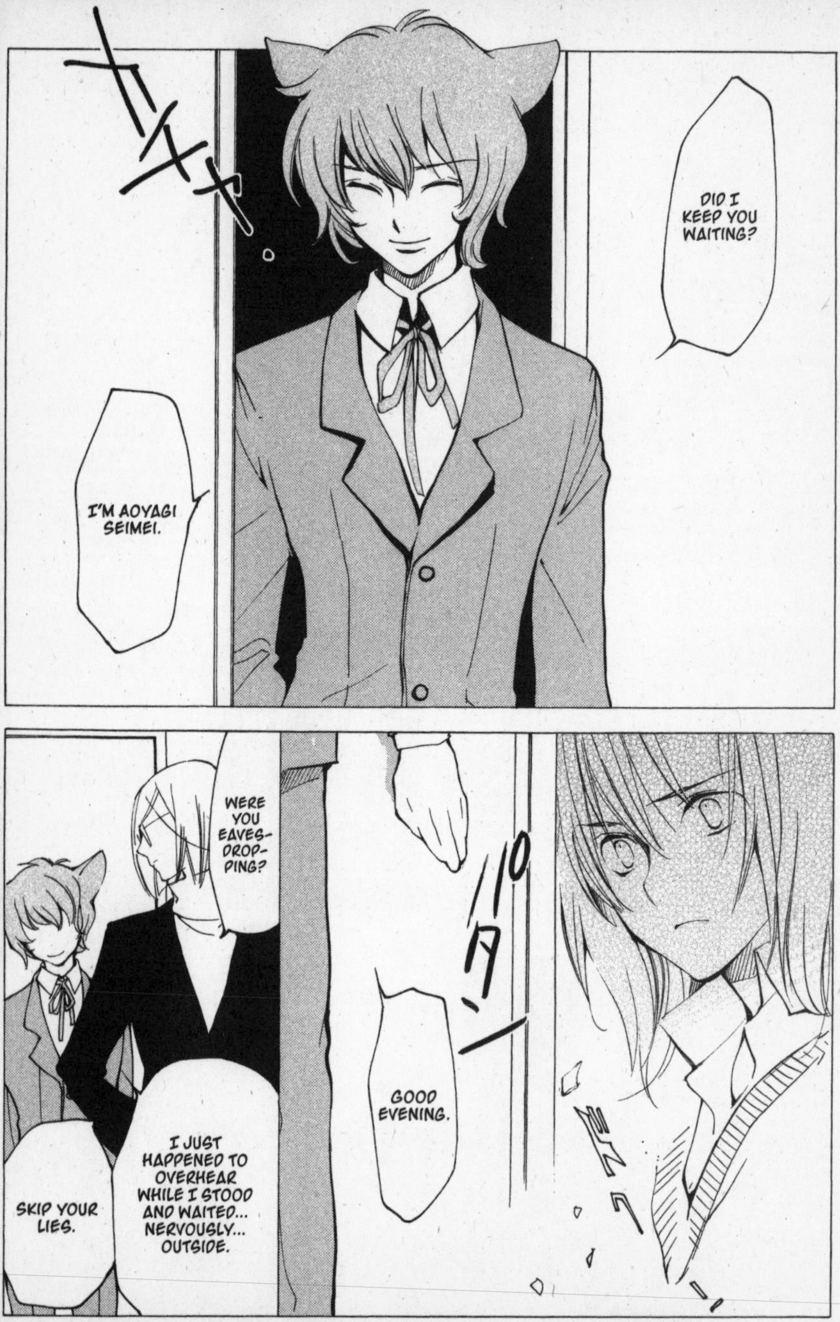
DID I KEEP YOU WAITING?
I'M AOYAGI SEIMEI.
GOOD EVENING.
WERE YOU EAVES-DROPPING?
I JUST HAPPENED TO OVERHEAR WHILE I STOOD AND WAITED... NERVOUSLY... OUTSIDE.
SKIP YOUR LIES.

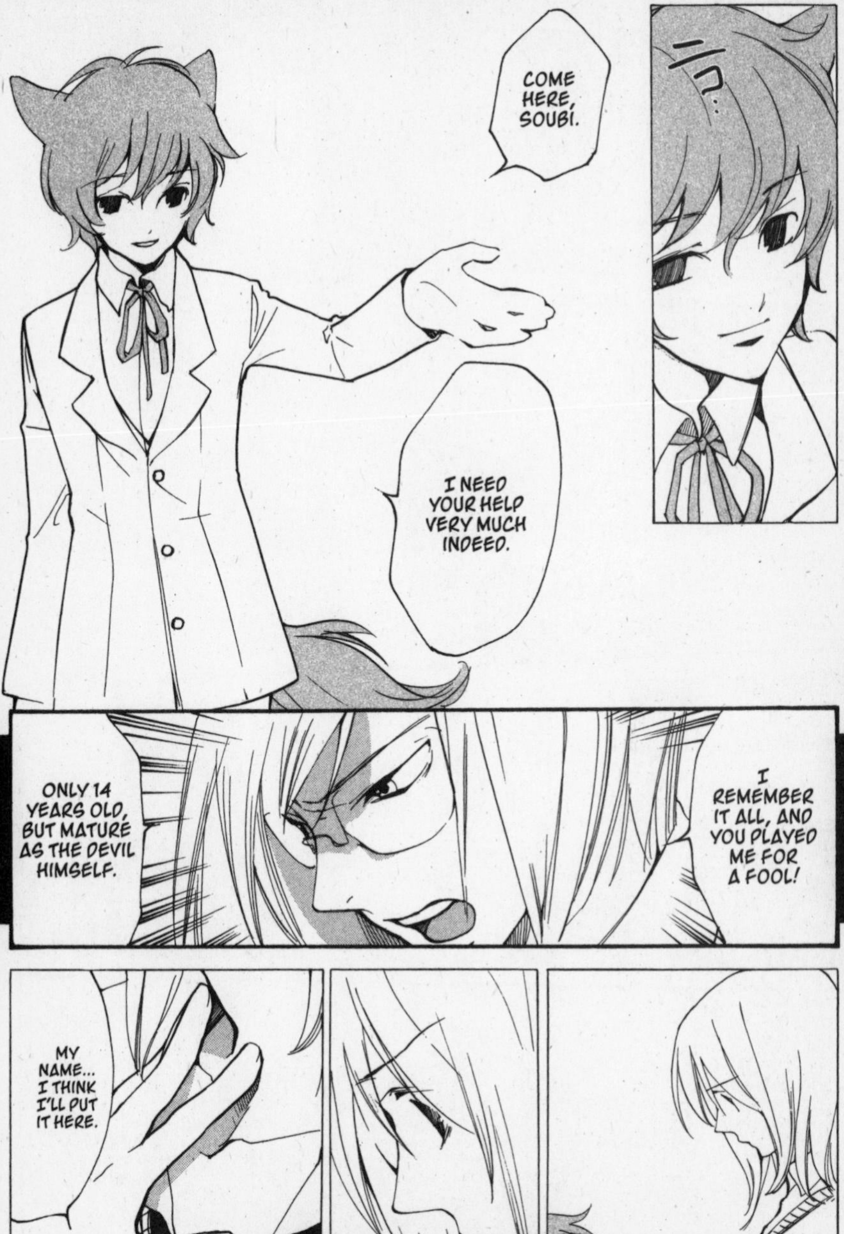
ニコ…
COME HERE, SOUBI.
I NEED YOUR HELP VERY MUCH INDEED.
I REMEMBER IT ALL, AND YOU PLAYED ME FOR A FOOL!
ONLY 14 YEARS OLD, BUT MATURE AS THE DEVIL HIMSELF.
MY NAME... I THINK I'LL PUT IT HERE.

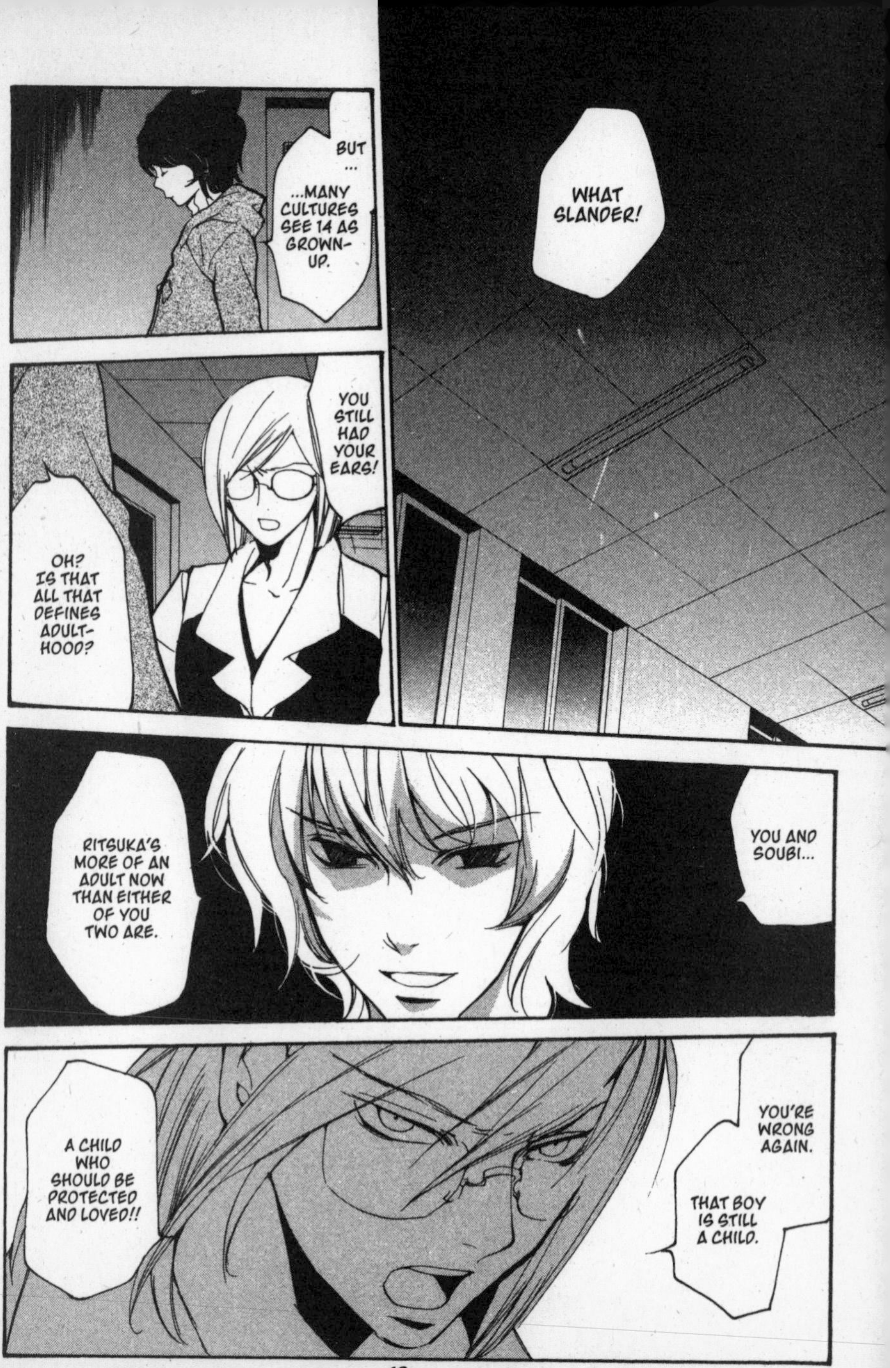
WHAT SLANDER!
BUT ...
...MANY CULTURES SEE 14 AS GROWN-UP.
YOU STILL HAD YOUR EARS!
OH? IS THAT ALL THAT DEFINES ADULT-HOOD?
YOU AND SOUBI...
RITSUKA'S MORE OF AN ADULT NOW THAN EITHER OF YOU TWO ARE.
YOU'RE WRONG AGAIN.
THAT BOY IS STILL A CHILD.
A CHILD WHO SHOULD BE PROTECTED AND LOVED!!

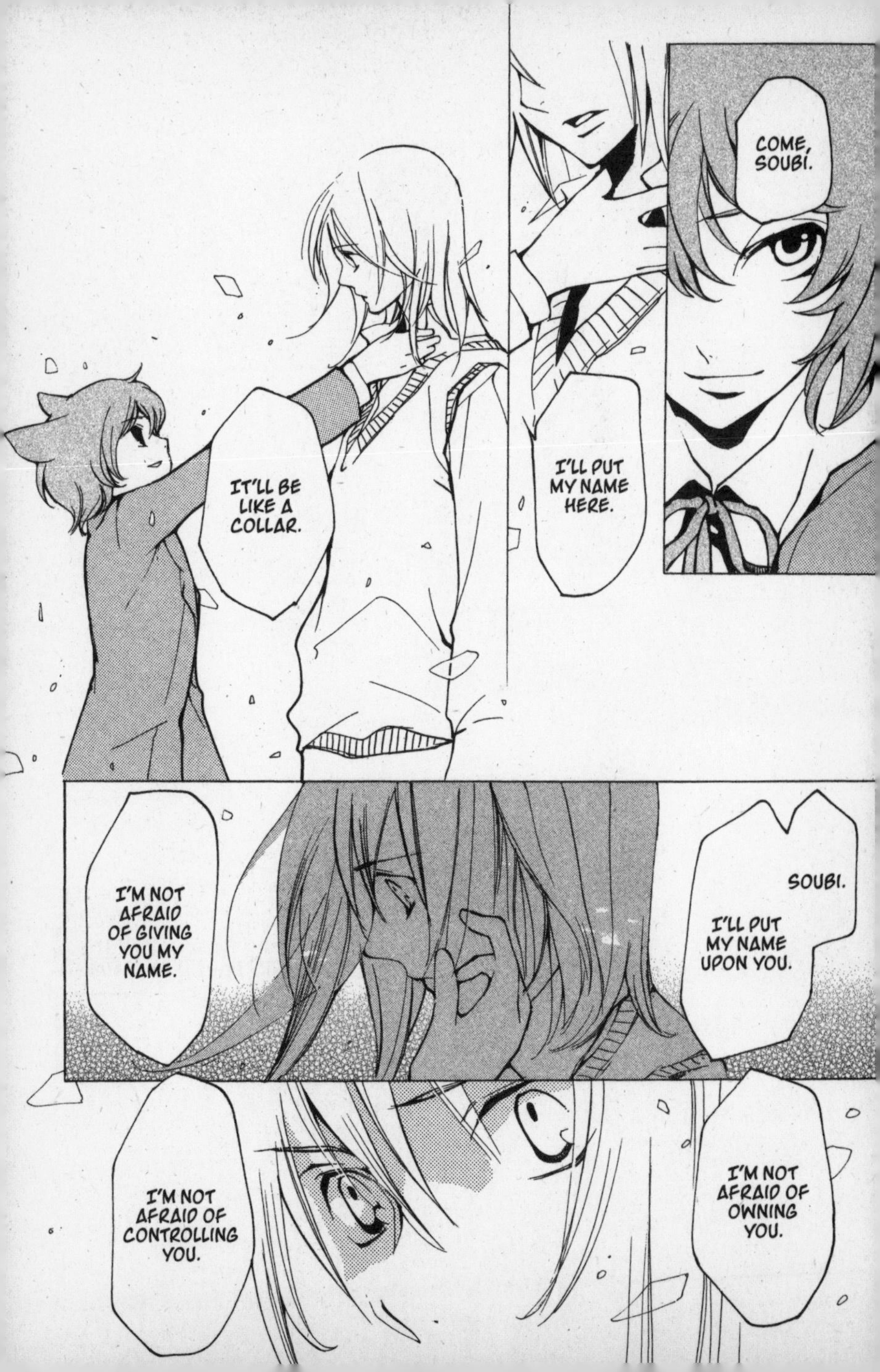
COME, SOUBI.
I'LL PUT MY NAME HERE.
IT'LL BE LIKE A COLLAR.
SOUBI.
I'LL PUT MY NAME UPON YOU.
I'M NOT AFRAID OF GIVING YOU MY NAME.
I'M NOT AFRAID OF OWNING YOU.
I'M NOT AFRAID OF CONTROLLING YOU.

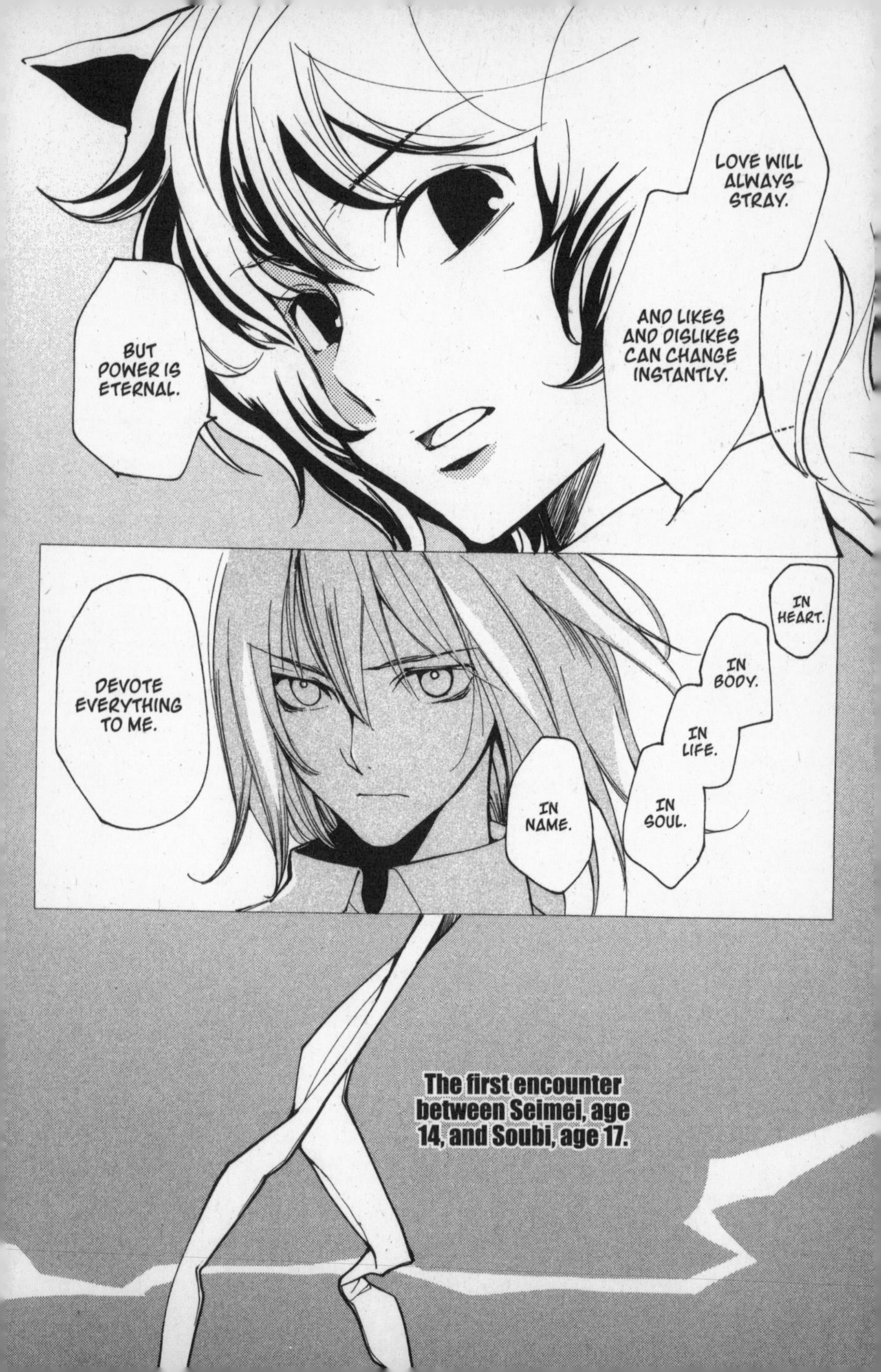
LOVE WILL ALWAYS STRAY.
AND LIKES AND DISLIKES CAN CHANGE INSTANTLY.
BUT POWER IS ETERNAL.
IN HEART.
IN BODY.
IN LIFE.
IN SOUL.
IN NAME.
DEVOTE EVERYTHING TO ME.
The first encounter between Seimei, age 14, and Soubi, age 17.

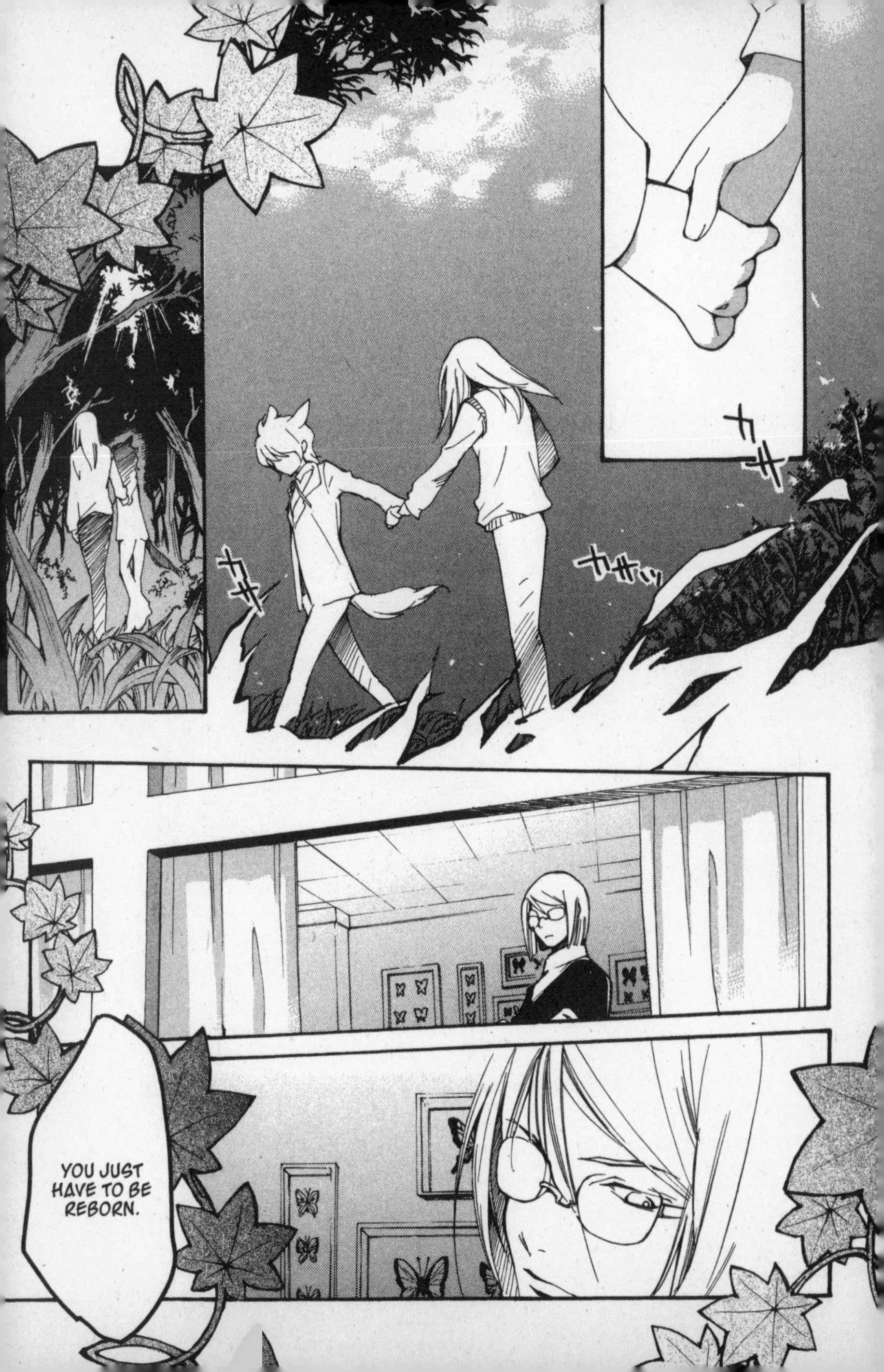
YOU JUST HAVE TO BE REBORN.

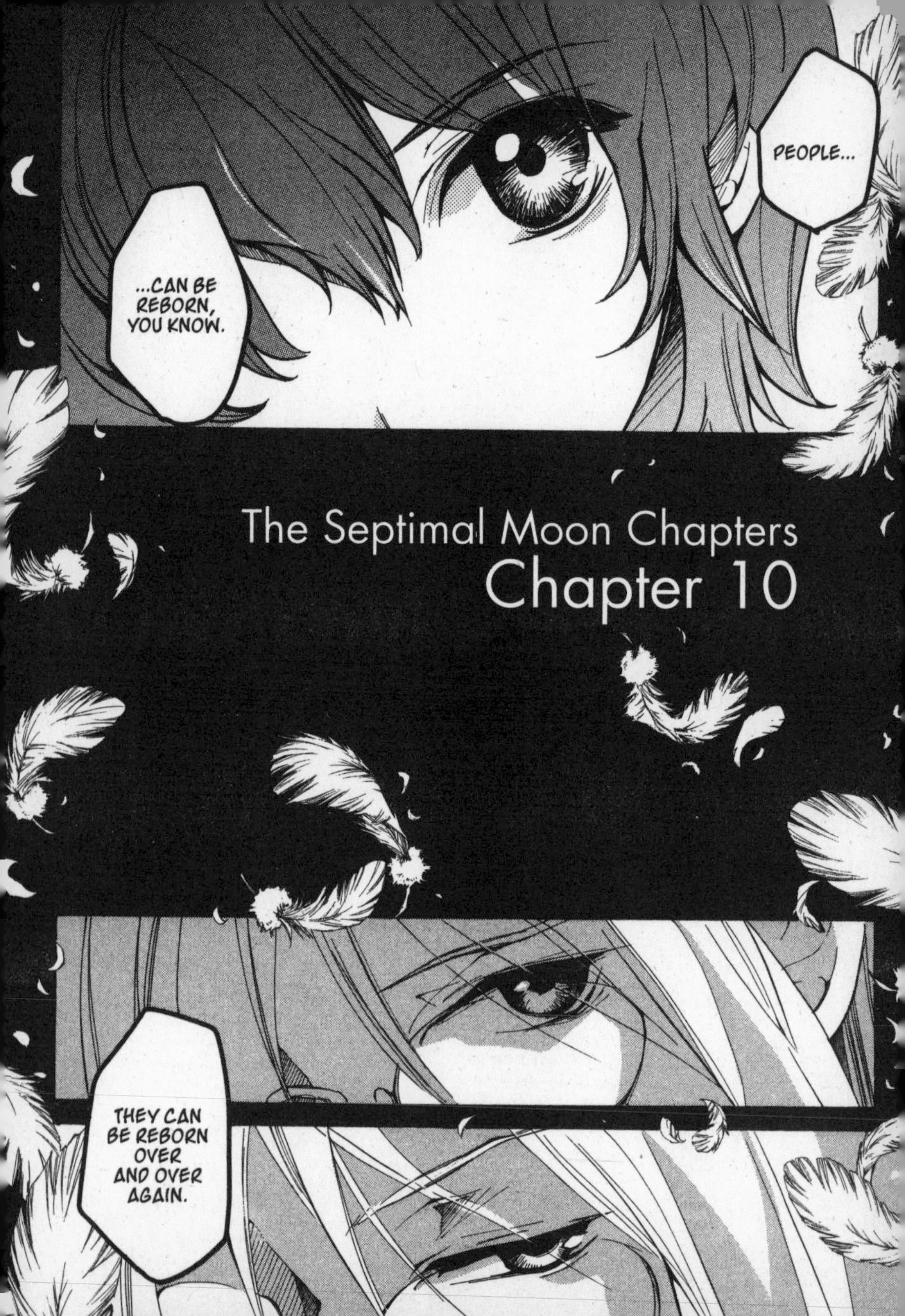
PEOPLE...
...CAN BE REBORN, YOU KNOW.
The Septimal Moon Chapters
Chapter 10
THEY CAN BE REBORN OVER AND OVER AGAIN.

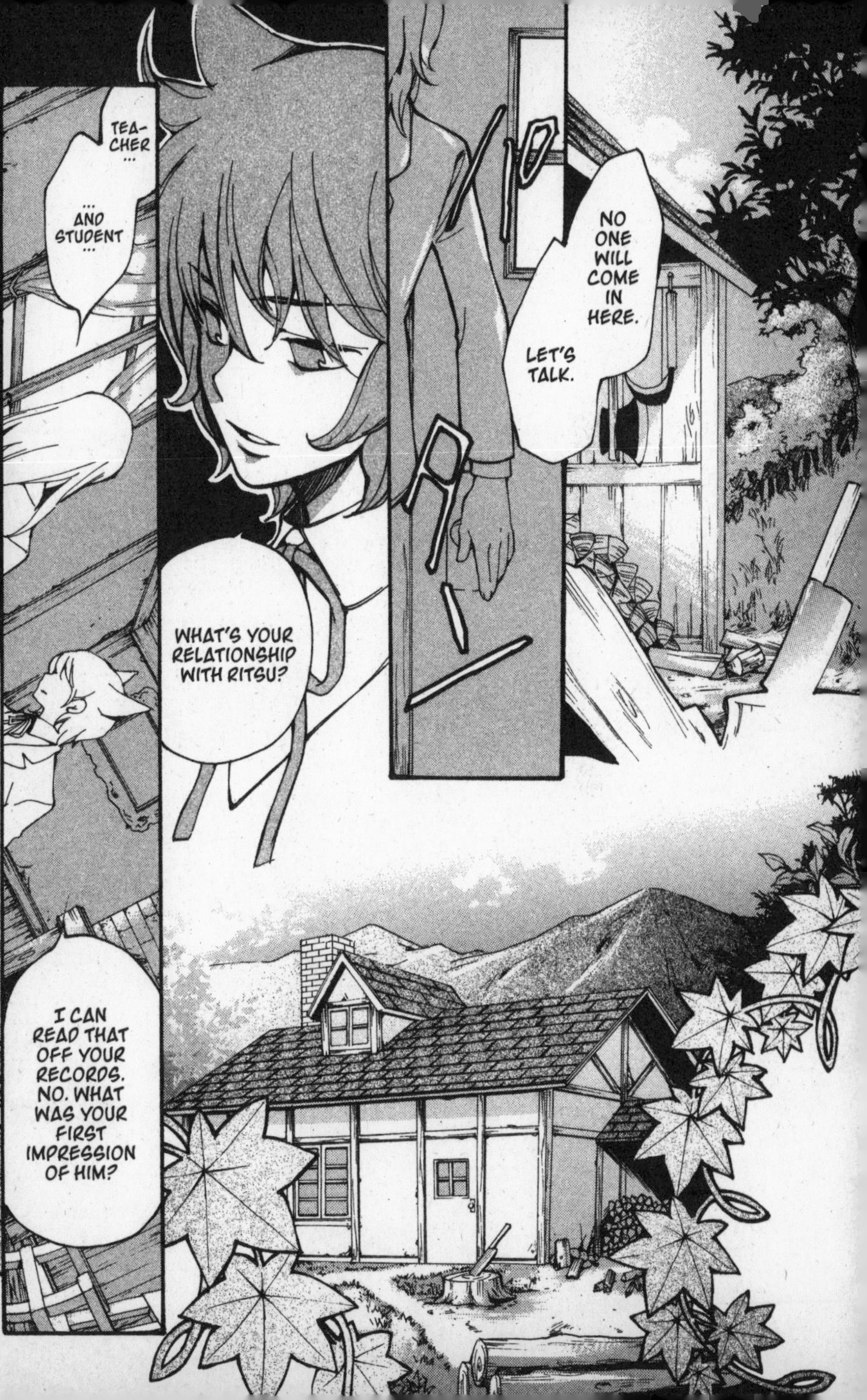
NO ONE WILL COME IN HERE.
LET'S TALK.
WHAT'S YOUR RELATIONSHIP WITH RITSU?
TEA-CHER ...
... AND STUDENT ...
I CAN READ THAT OFF YOUR RECORDS. NO. WHAT WAS YOUR FIRST IMPRESSION OF HIM?

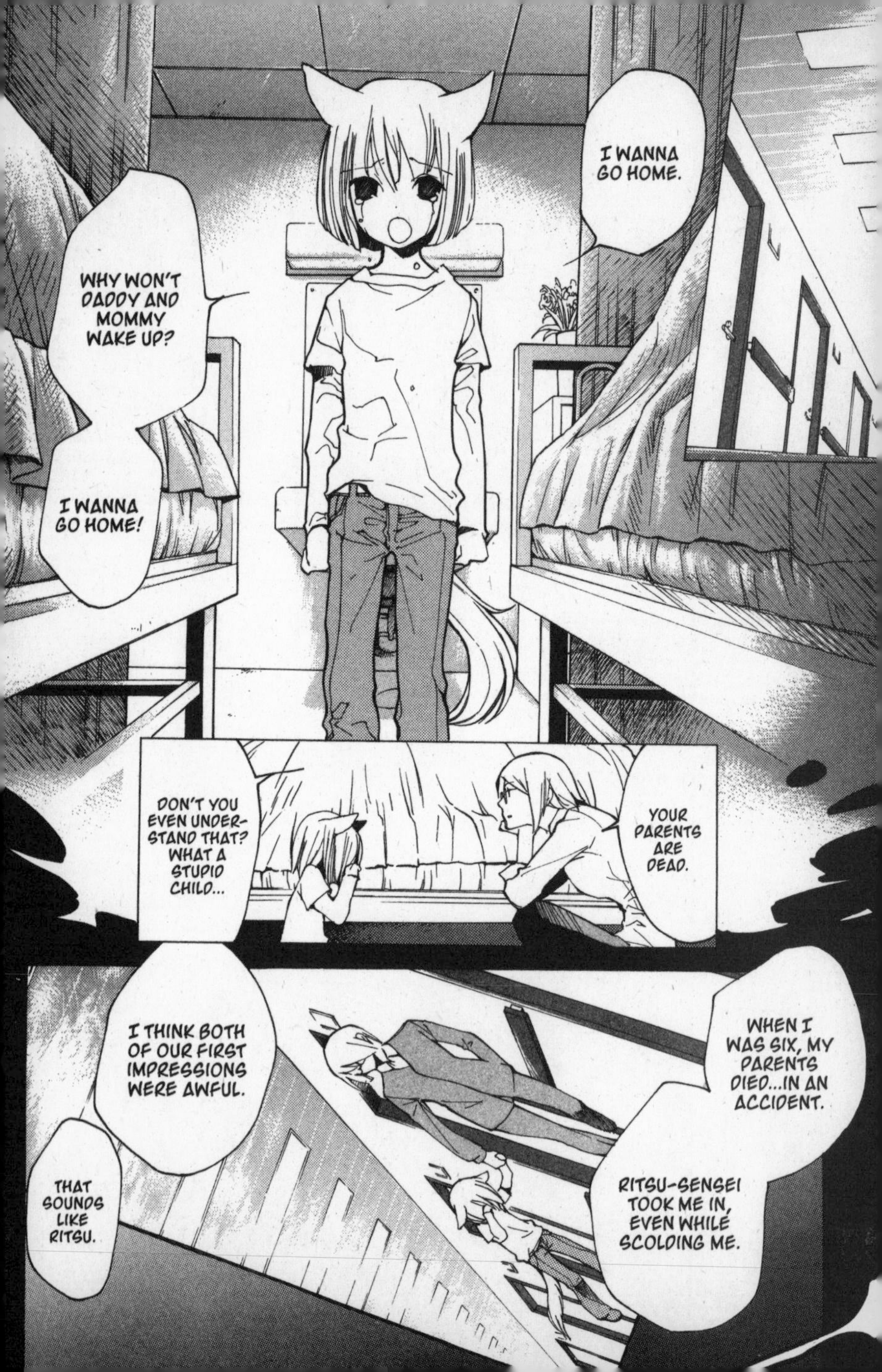
I WANNA GO HOME.
WHY WON'T DADDY AND MOMMY WAKE UP?
I WANNA GO HOME!
YOUR PARENTS ARE DEAD.
DON'T YOU EVEN UNDER-STAND THAT? WHAT A STUPID CHILD...
WHEN I WAS SIX, MY PARENTS DIED...IN AN ACCIDENT.
RITSU-SENSEI TOOK ME IN, EVEN WHILE SCOLDING ME.
I THINK BOTH OF OUR FIRST IMPRESSIONS WERE AWFUL.
THAT SOUNDS LIKE RITSU.

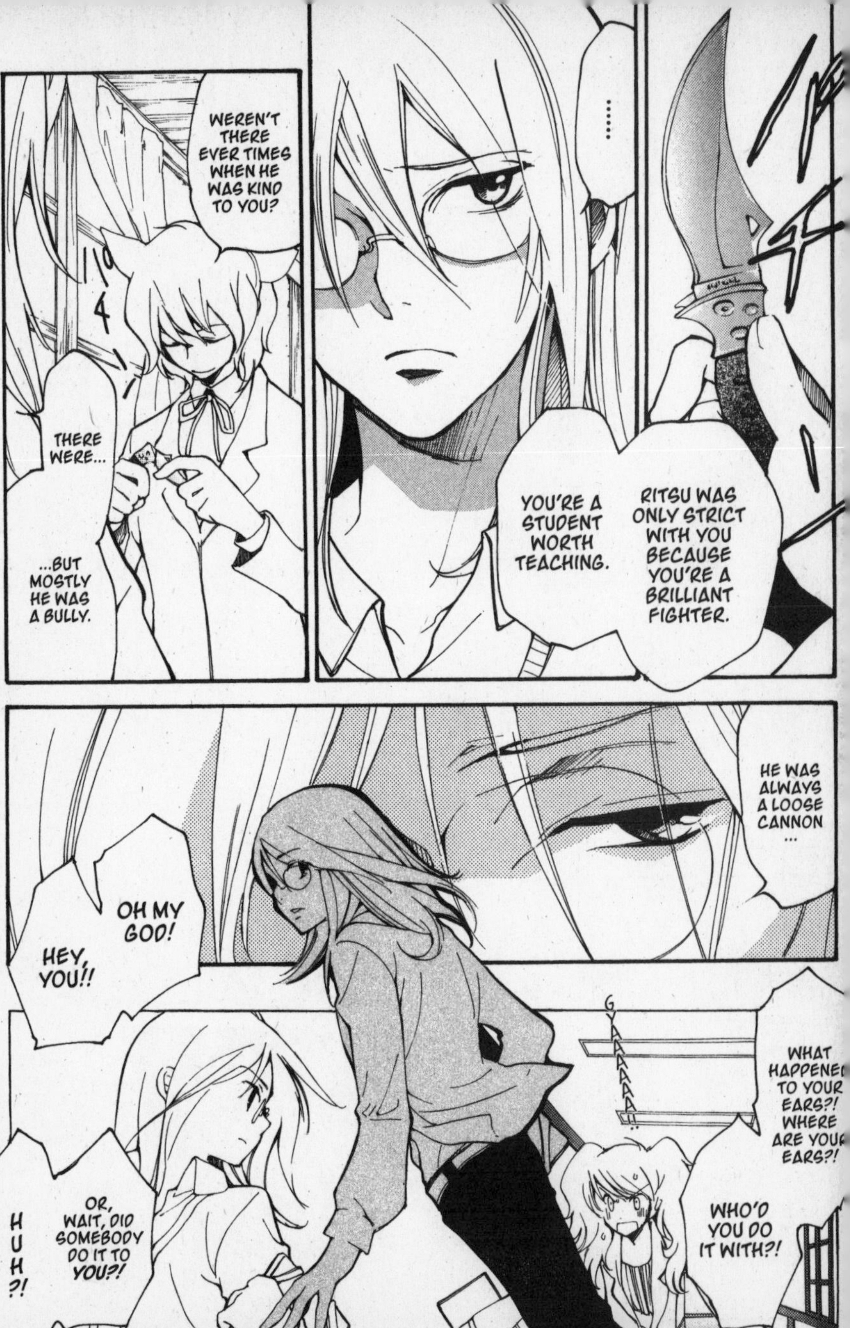

......
RITSU WAS ONLY STRICT WITH YOU BECAUSE YOU'RE A BRILLIANT FIGHTER.
YOU'RE A STUDENT WORTH TEACHING.
WEREN'T THERE EVER TIMES WHEN HE WAS KIND TO YOU?
THERE WERE...
...BUT MOSTLY HE WAS A BULLY.
HE WAS ALWAYS A LOOSE CANNON ...
GYAAAAA!!
WHAT HAPPENED TO YOUR EARS?! WHERE ARE YOUR EARS?!
OH MY GOD!
HEY, YOU!!
WHO'D YOU DO IT WITH?!
OR, WAIT, DID SOMEBODY DO IT TO *YOU*?!
HUH?!

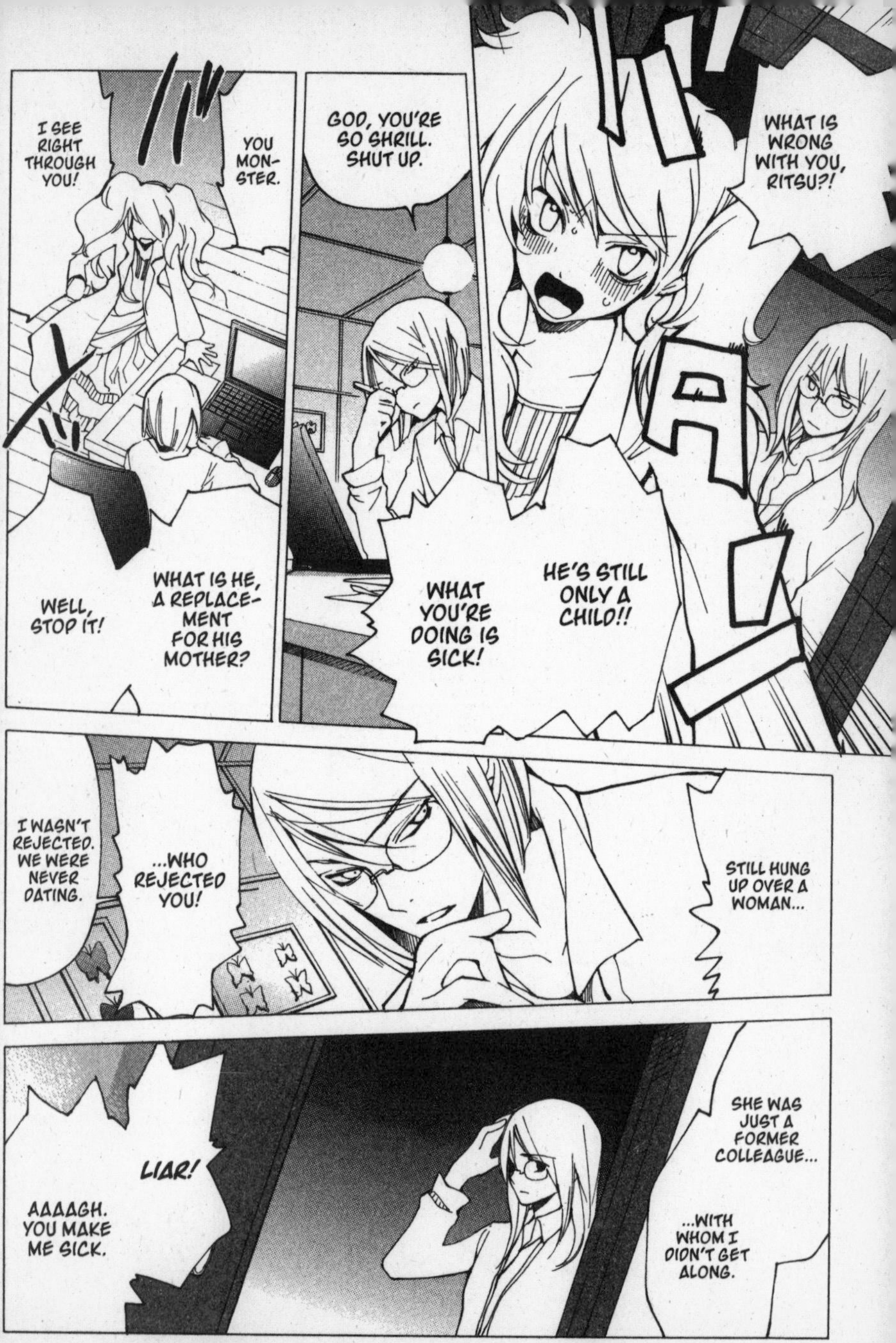
WHAT IS WRONG WITH YOU, RITSU?!
HE'S STILL ONLY A CHILD!!
WHAT YOU'RE DOING IS SICK!
GOD, YOU'RE SO SHRILL. SHUT UP.
YOU MONSTER.
I SEE RIGHT THROUGH YOU!
WHAT IS HE, A REPLACEMENT FOR HIS MOTHER?
WELL, STOP IT!
STILL HUNG UP OVER A WOMAN...
...WHO REJECTED YOU!
I WASN'T REJECTED. WE WERE NEVER DATING.
SHE WAS JUST A FORMER COLLEAGUE...
...WITH WHOM I DIDN'T GET ALONG.
LIAR!
AAAAGH. YOU MAKE ME SICK.

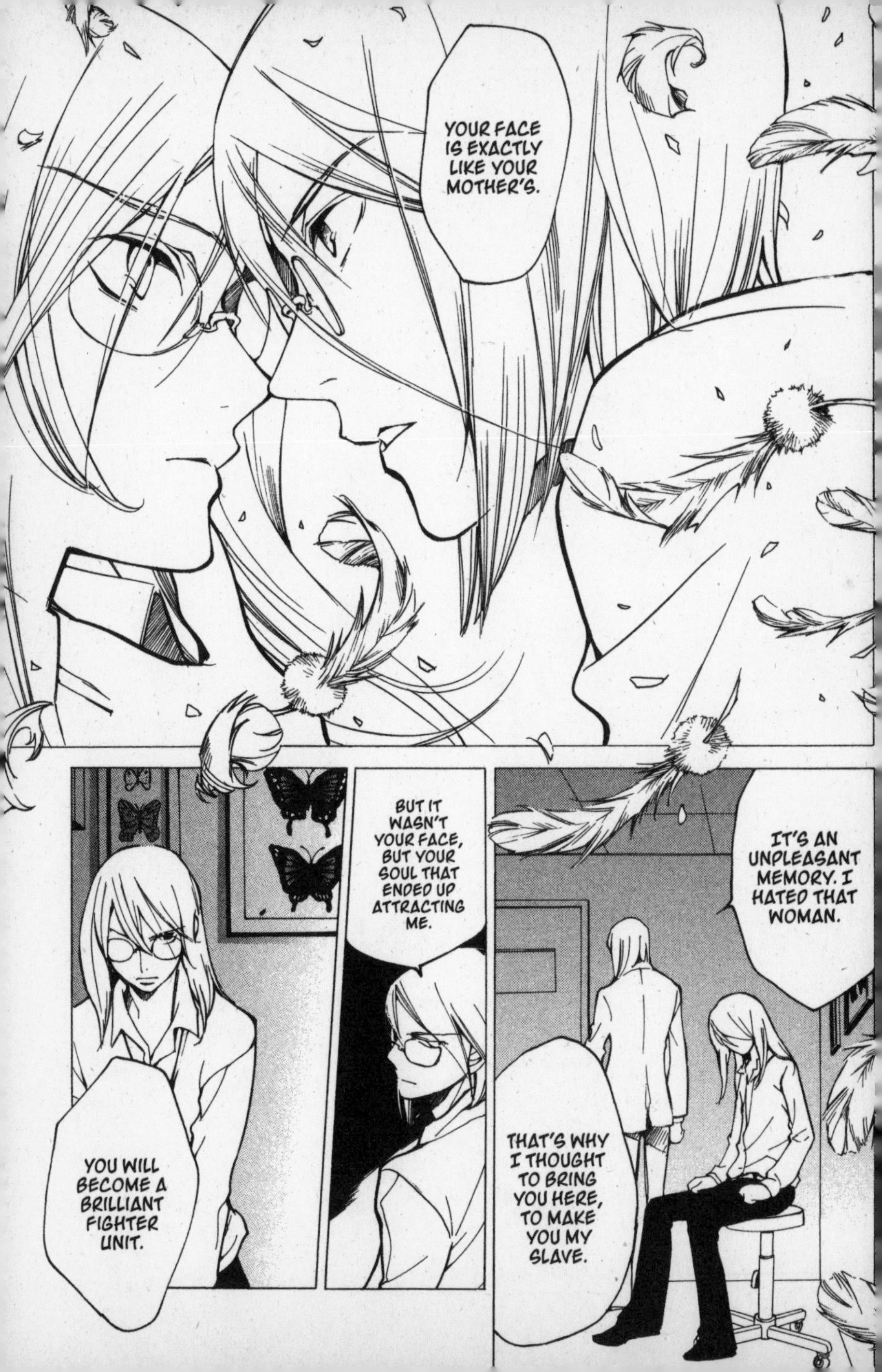
YOUR FACE IS EXACTLY LIKE YOUR MOTHER'S.
IT'S AN UNPLEASANT MEMORY. I HATED THAT WOMAN.
THAT'S WHY I THOUGHT TO BRING YOU HERE, TO MAKE YOU MY SLAVE.
BUT IT WASN'T YOUR FACE, BUT YOUR SOUL THAT ENDED UP ATTRACTING ME.
YOU WILL BECOME A BRILLIANT FIGHTER UNIT.

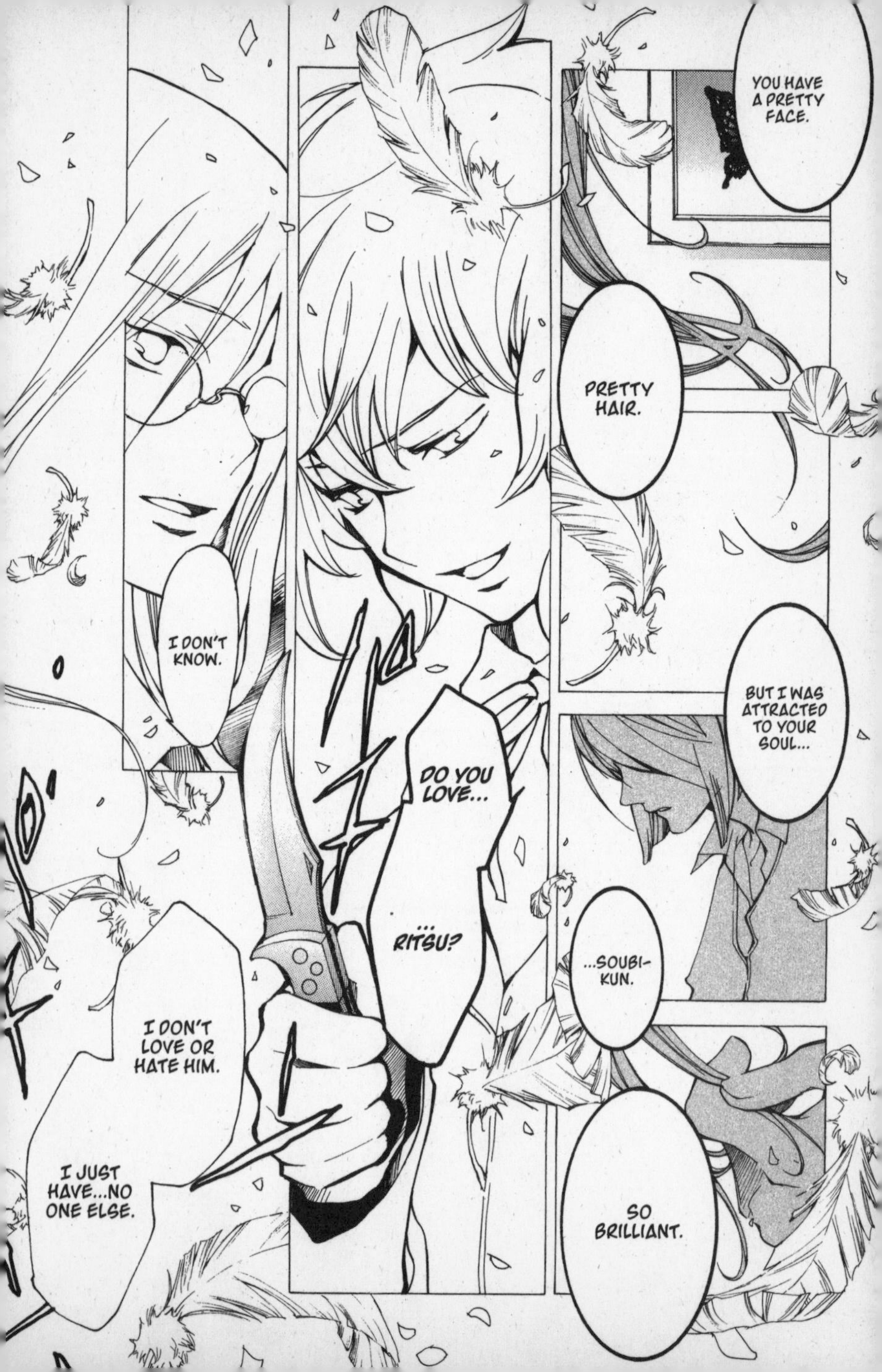
YOU HAVE A PRETTY FACE.
PRETTY HAIR.
BUT I WAS ATTRACTED TO YOUR SOUL...
...SOUBI-KUN.
SO BRILLIANT.
DO YOU LOVE...
...RITSU?
I DON'T KNOW.
I DON'T LOVE OR HATE HIM.
I JUST HAVE...NO ONE ELSE.

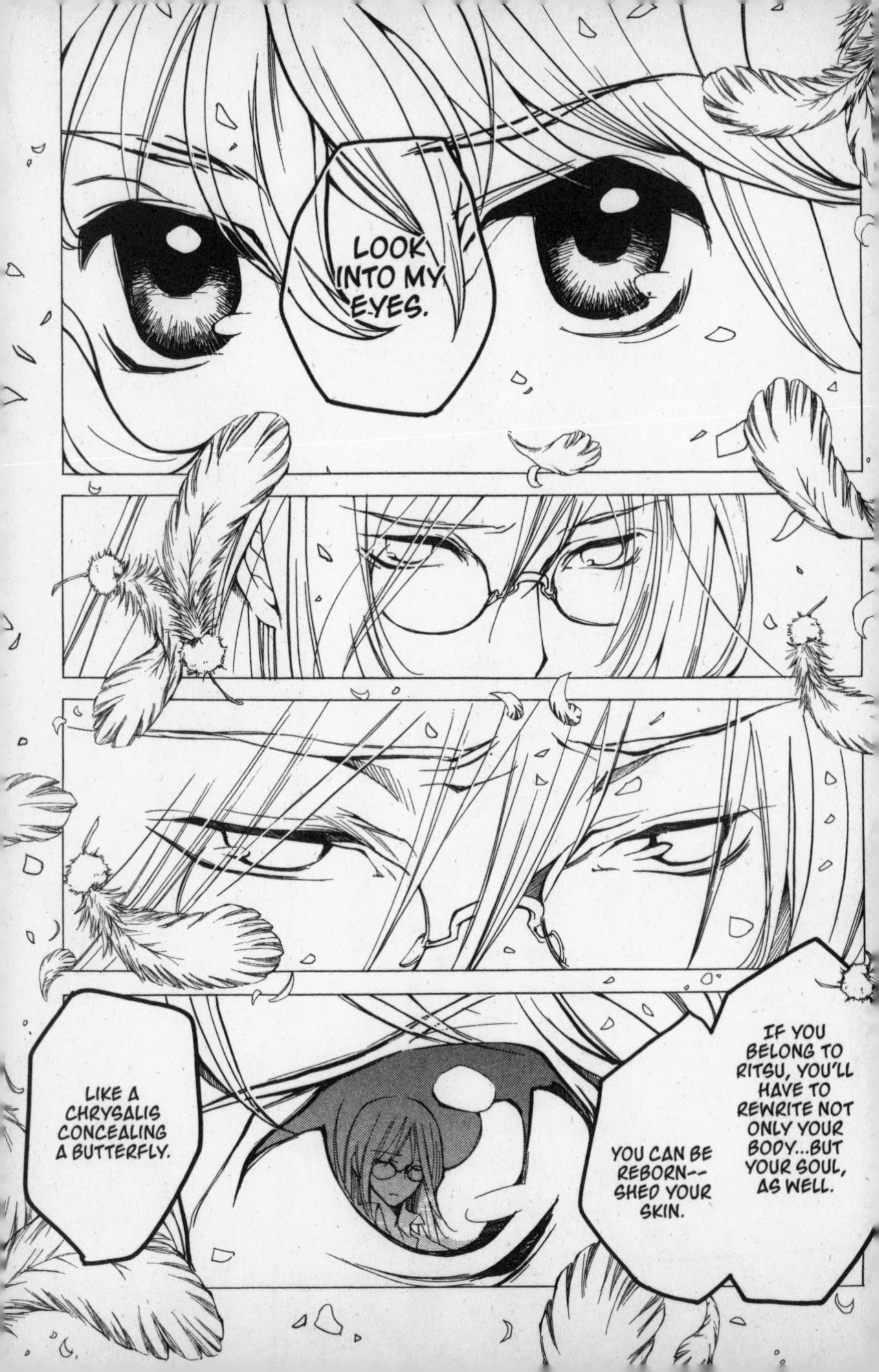
LOOK INTO MY E-YES.
IF YOU BELONG TO RITSU, YOU'LL HAVE TO REWRITE NOT ONLY YOUR BODY...BUT YOUR SOUL, AS WELL.
YOU CAN BE REBORN--SHED YOUR SKIN.
LIKE A CHRYSALIS CONCEALING A BUTTERFLY.

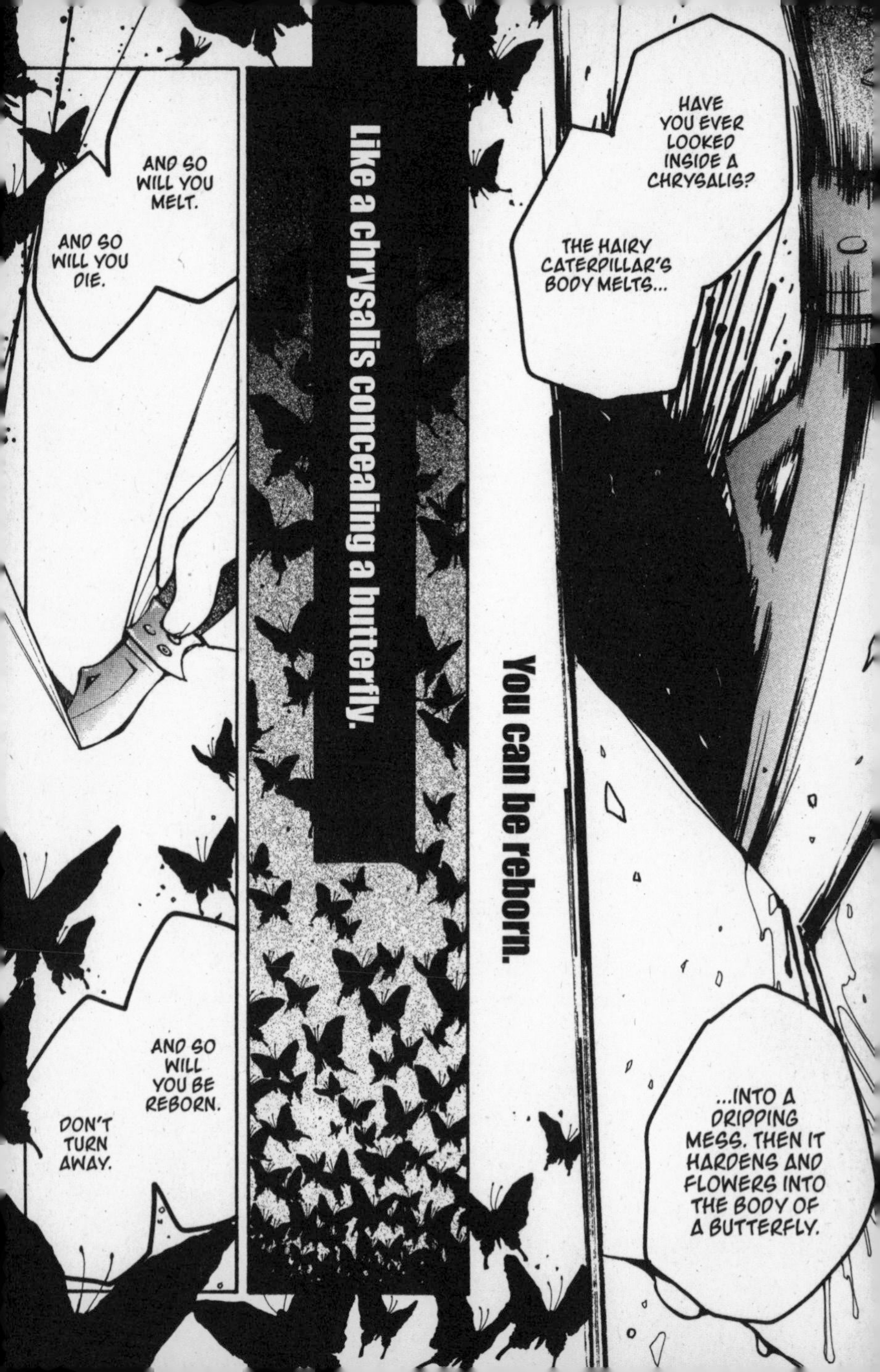
HAVE YOU EVER LOOKED INSIDE A CHRYSALIS?
THE HAIRY CATERPILLAR'S BODY MELTS...
...INTO A DRIPPING MESS. THEN IT HARDENS AND FLOWERS INTO THE BODY OF A BUTTERFLY.
You can be reborn.
Like a chrysalis concealing a butterfly.
AND SO WILL YOU MELT.
AND SO WILL YOU DIE.
AND SO WILL YOU BE REBORN.
DON'T TURN AWAY.

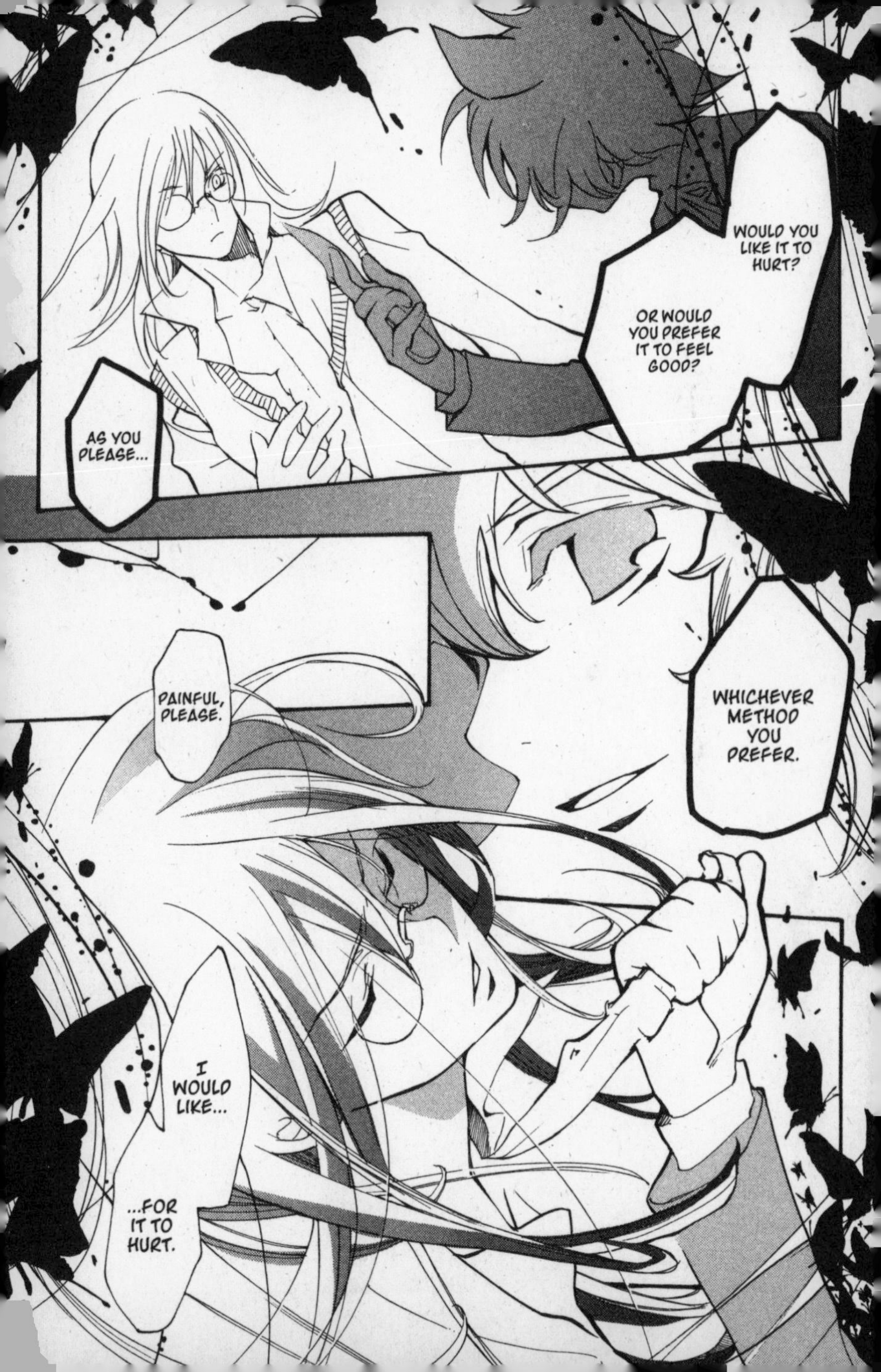
WOULD YOU LIKE IT TO HURT?
OR WOULD YOU PREFER IT TO FEEL GOOD?
AS YOU PLEASE...
WHICHEVER METHOD YOU PREFER.
PAINFUL, PLEASE.
I WOULD LIKE...
...FOR IT TO HURT.

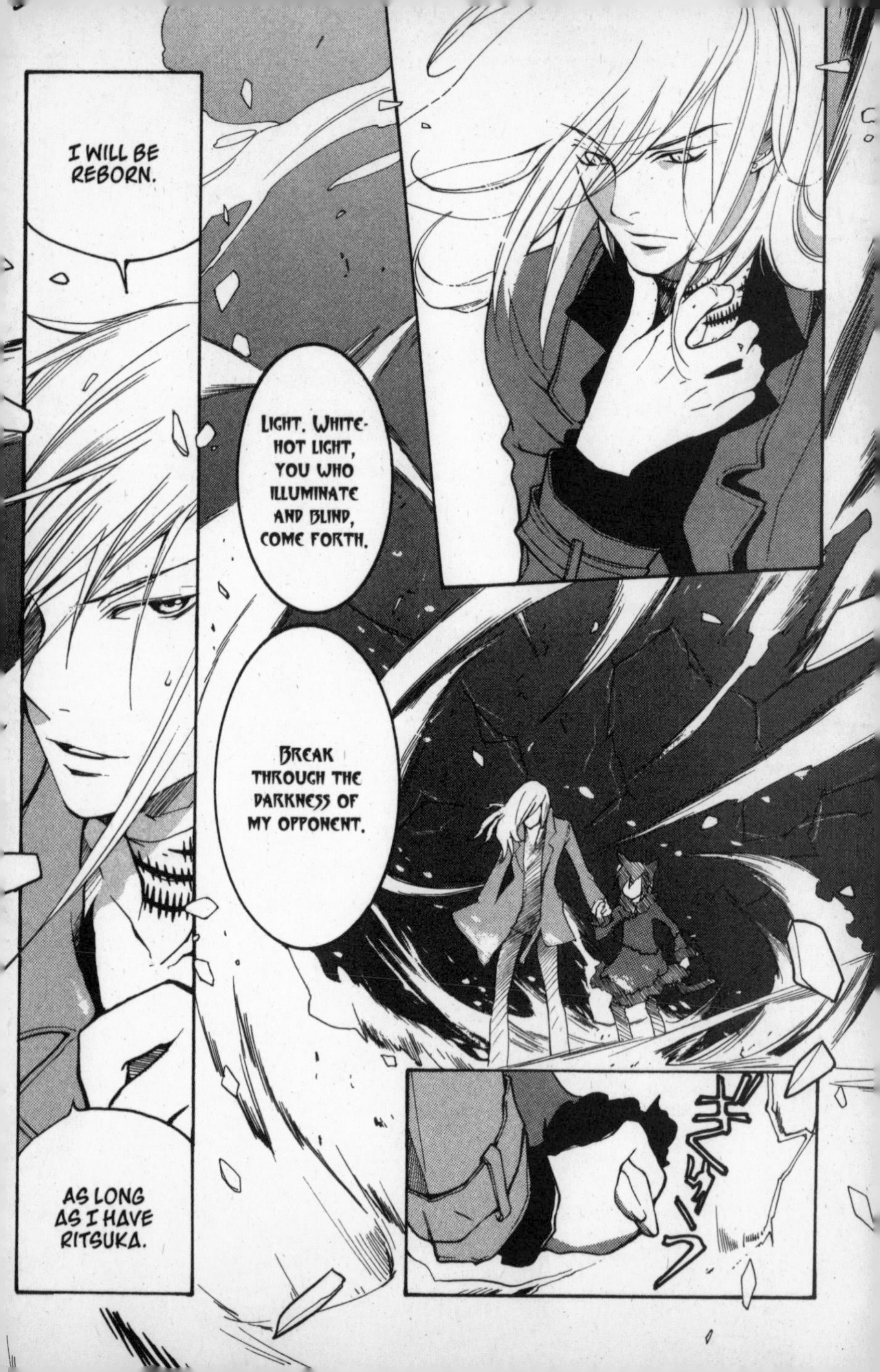

Light. White-hot light, you who illuminate and blind, come forth.
Break through the darkness of my opponent.
I will be reborn.
As long as I have Ritsuka.

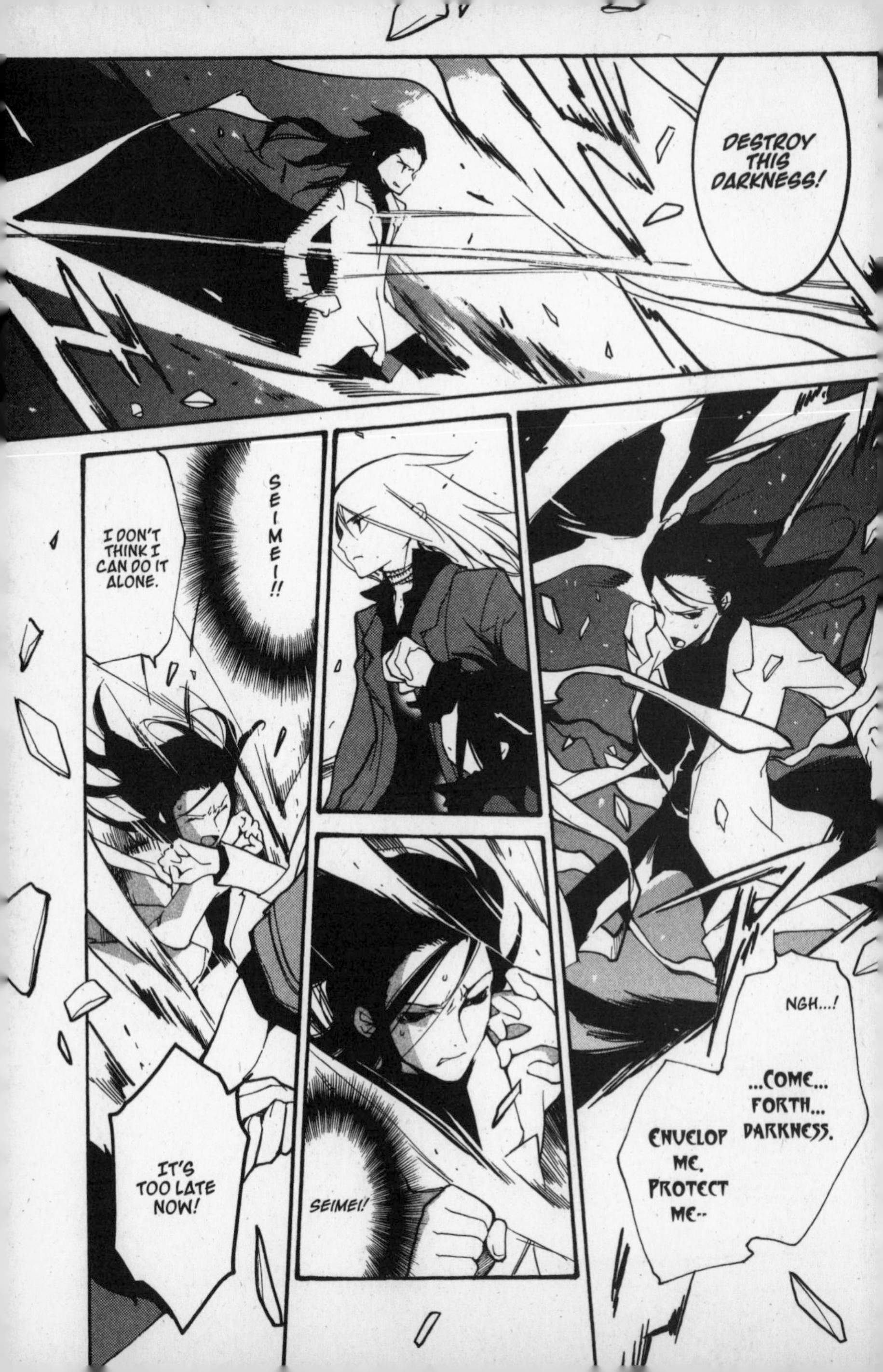
DESTROY THIS DARKNESS!
NGH...!
...COME... FORTH... DARKNESS.
ENVELOP ME. PROTECT ME--
SEIMEI!
SEIMEI!!
I DON'T THINK I CAN DO IT ALONE.
IT'S TOO LATE NOW!

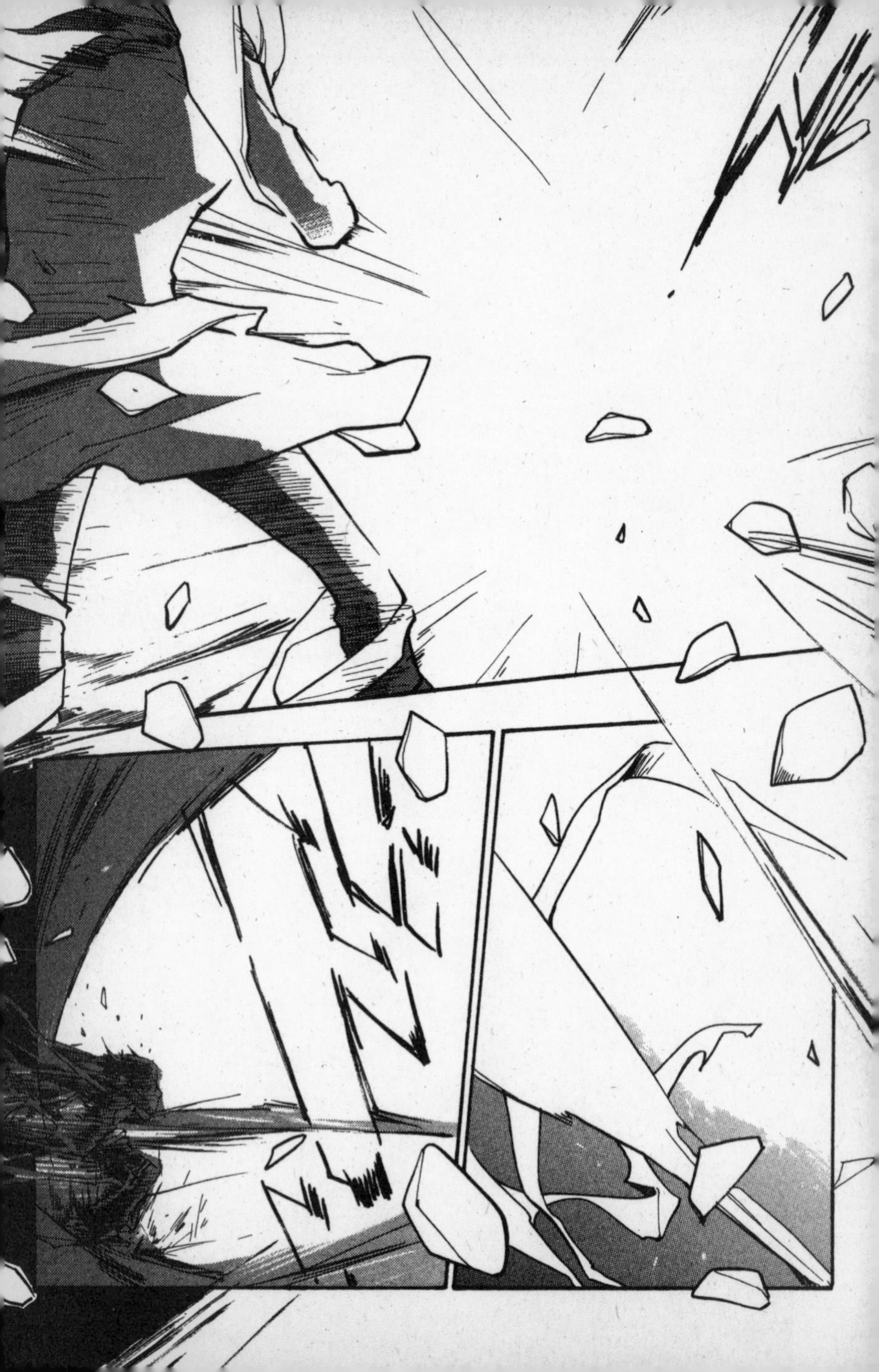

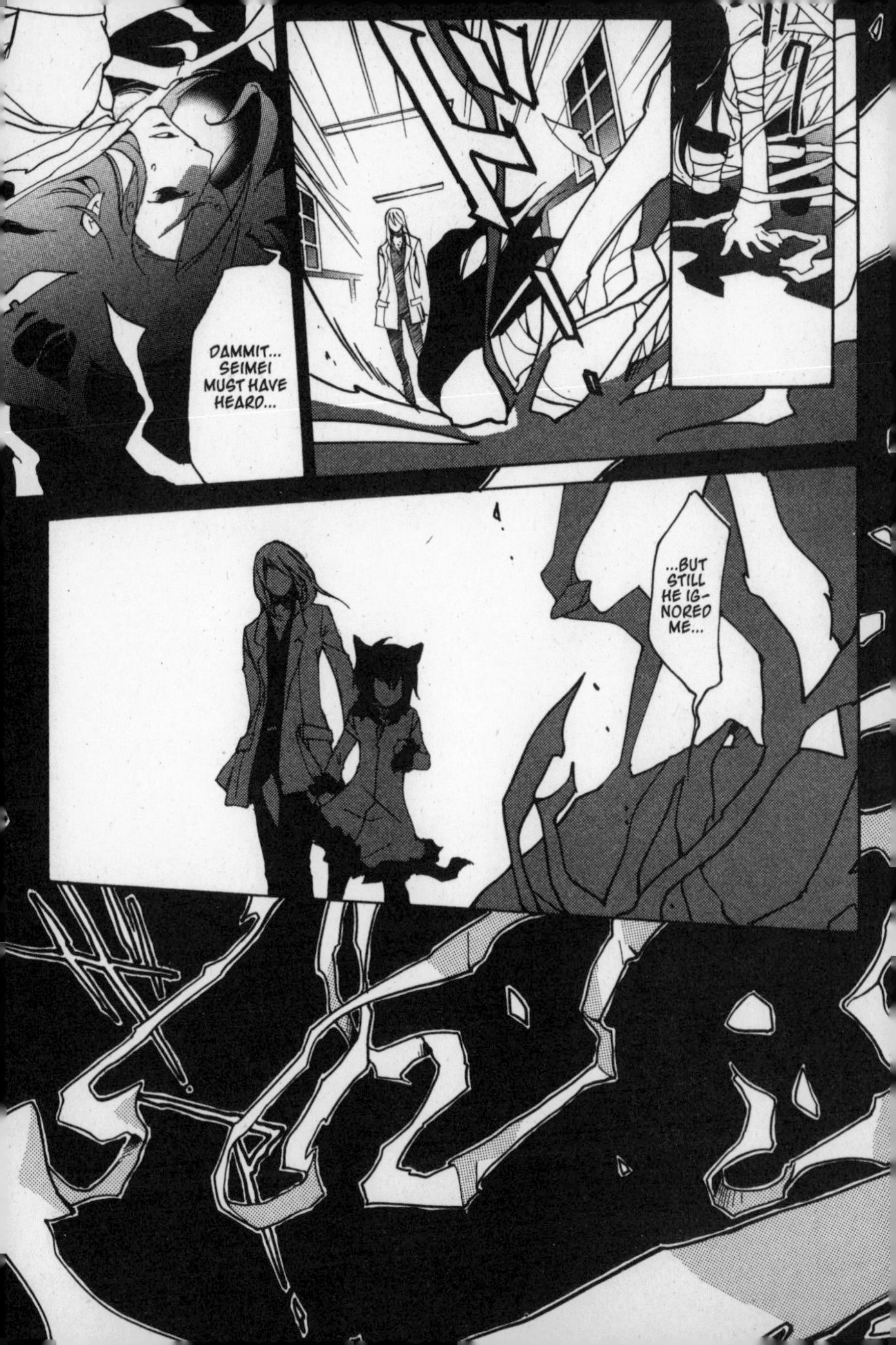
DAMMIT... SEIMEI MUST HAVE HEARD...
...BUT STILL HE IG-NORED ME...

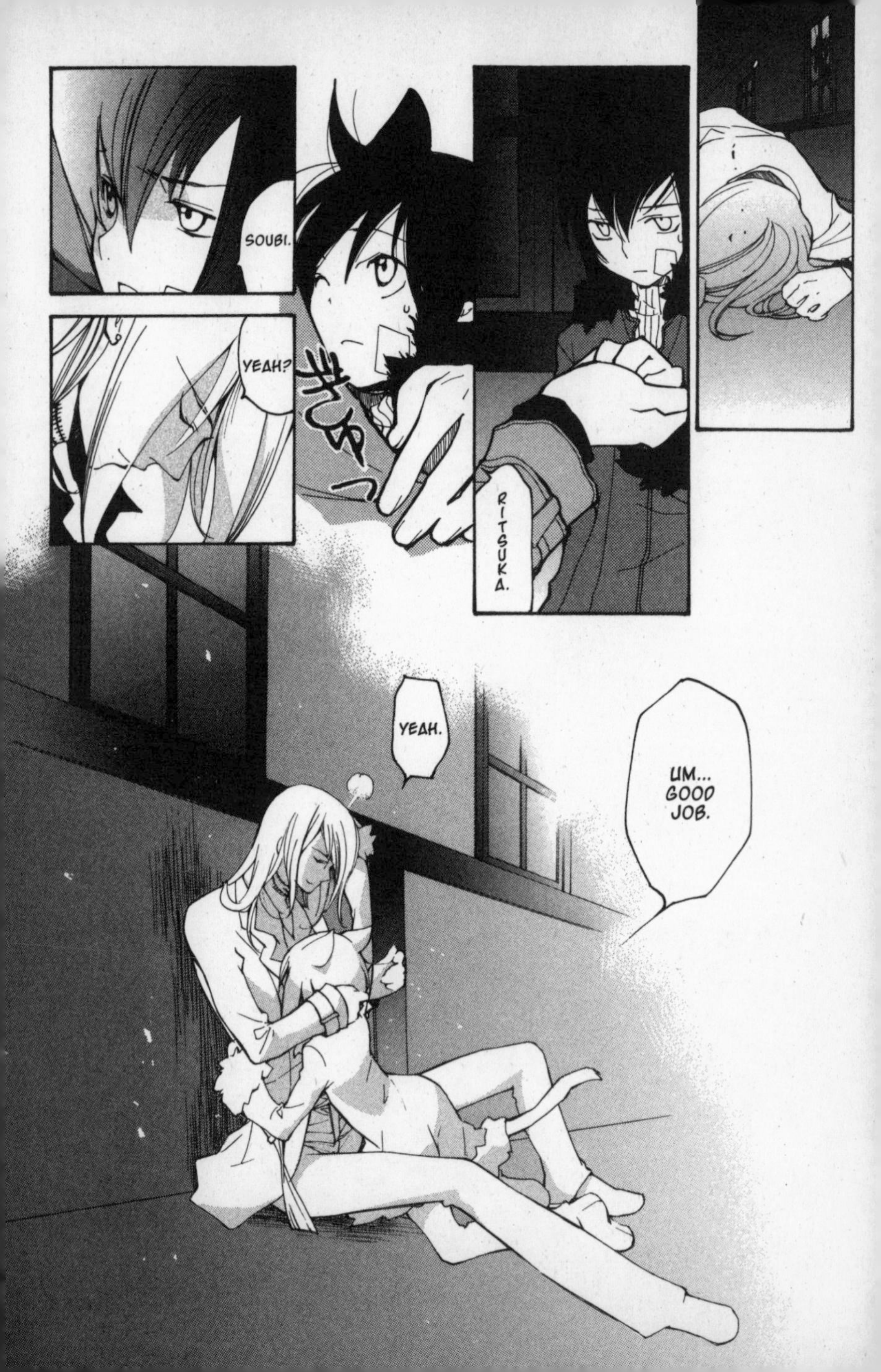
RITSUKA.
ぎゅっ
SOUBI.
YEAH?
UM... GOOD JOB.
YEAH.

LOVELESS

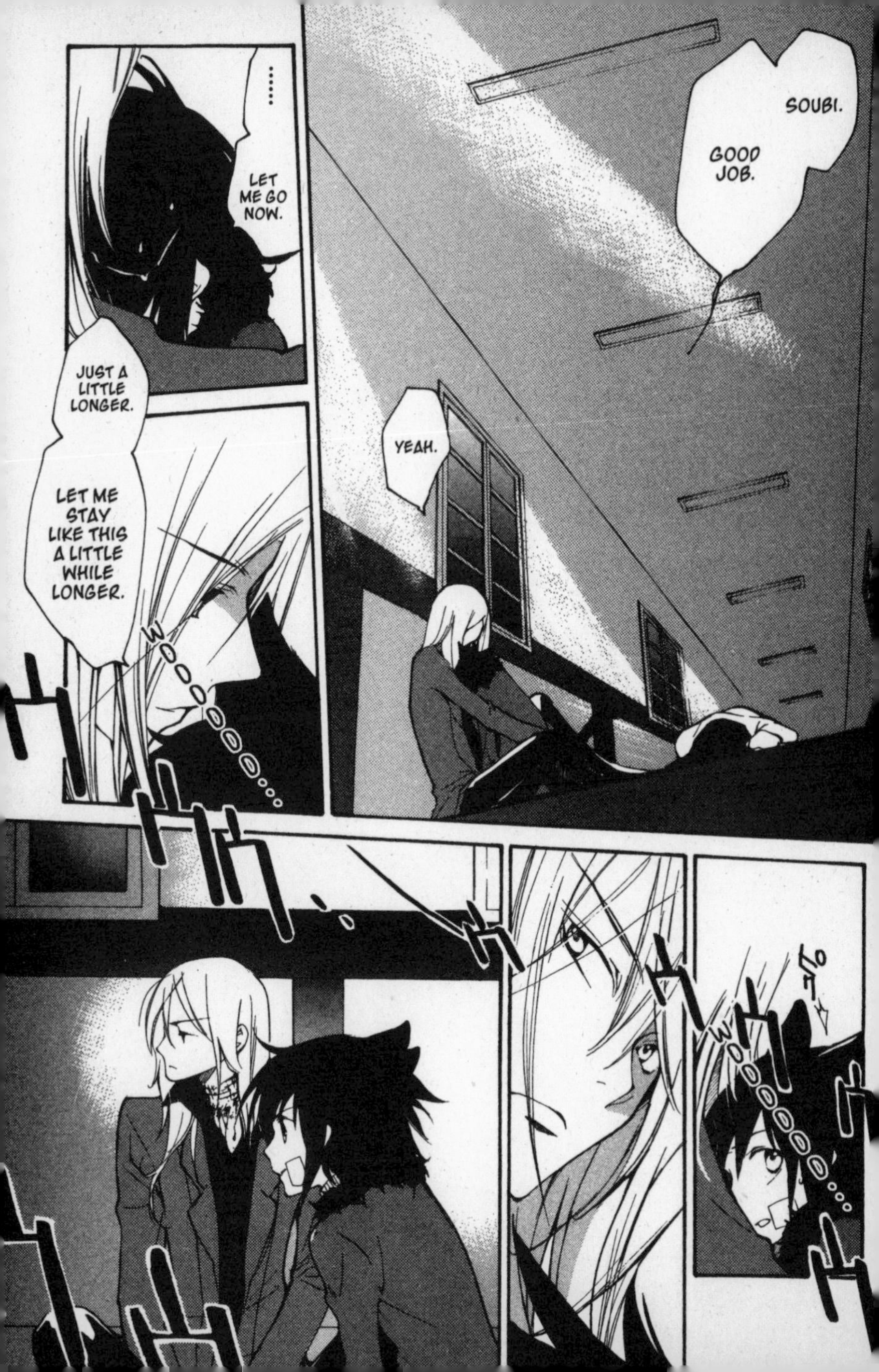
SOUBI.
GOOD JOB.
YEAH.
......
LET ME GO NOW.
JUST A LITTLE LONGER.
LET ME STAY LIKE THIS A LITTLE WHILE LONGER.

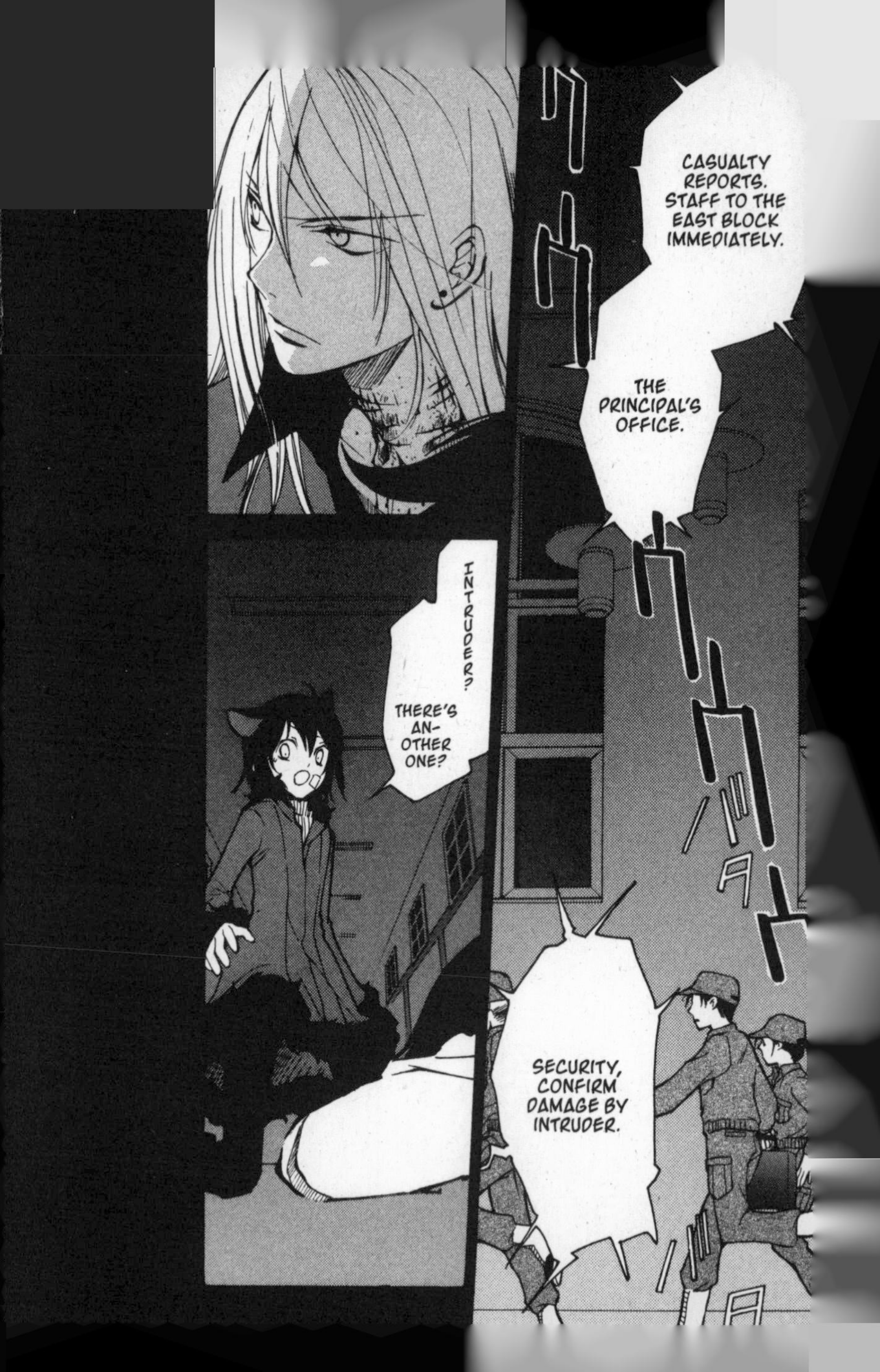
CASUALTY REPORTS. STAFF TO THE EAST BLOCK IMMEDIATELY.
THE PRINCIPAL'S OFFICE.
SECURITY, CONFIRM DAMAGE BY INTRUDER.
INTRUDER?
THERE'S AN-OTHER ONE?

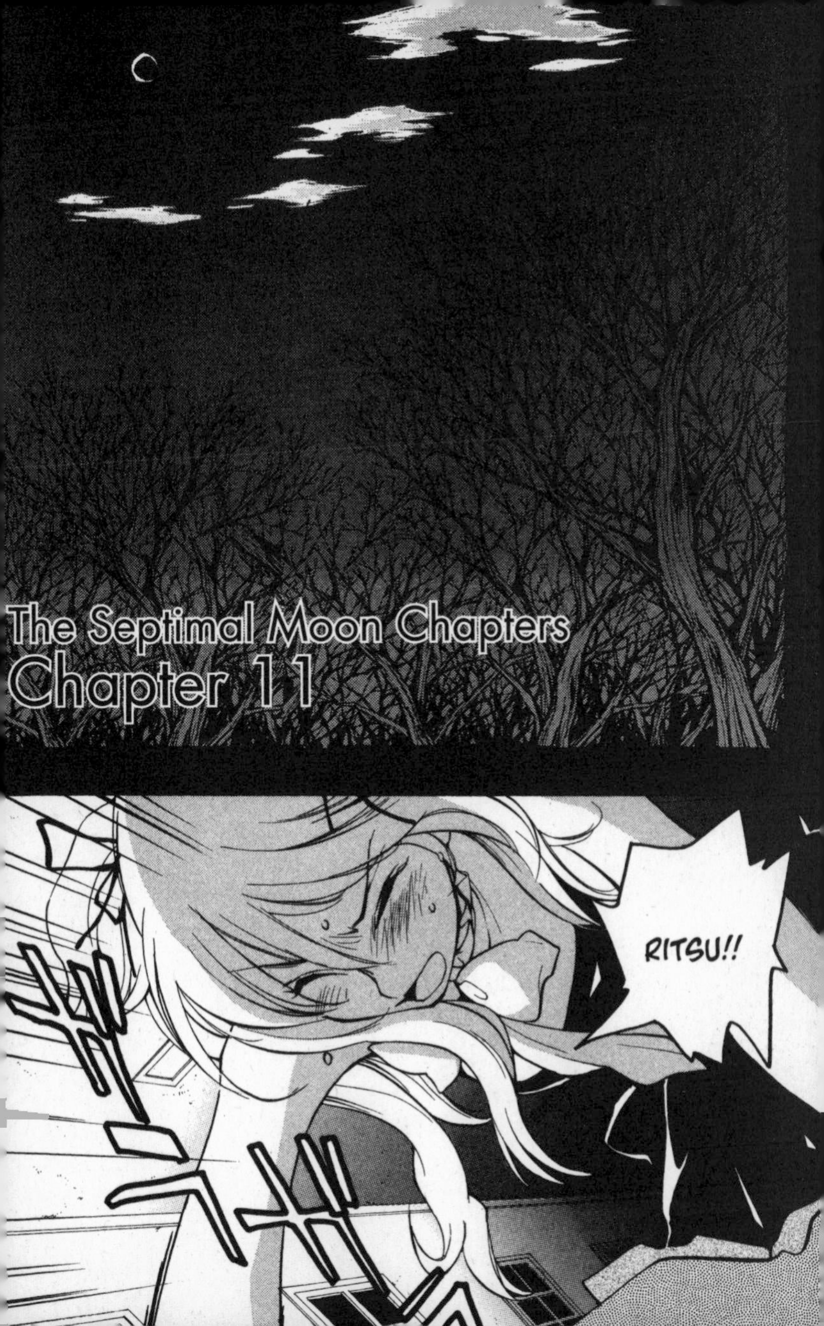
The Septimal Moon Chapters
Chapter 11
RITSU!!

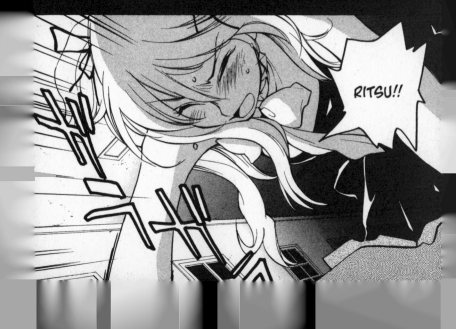

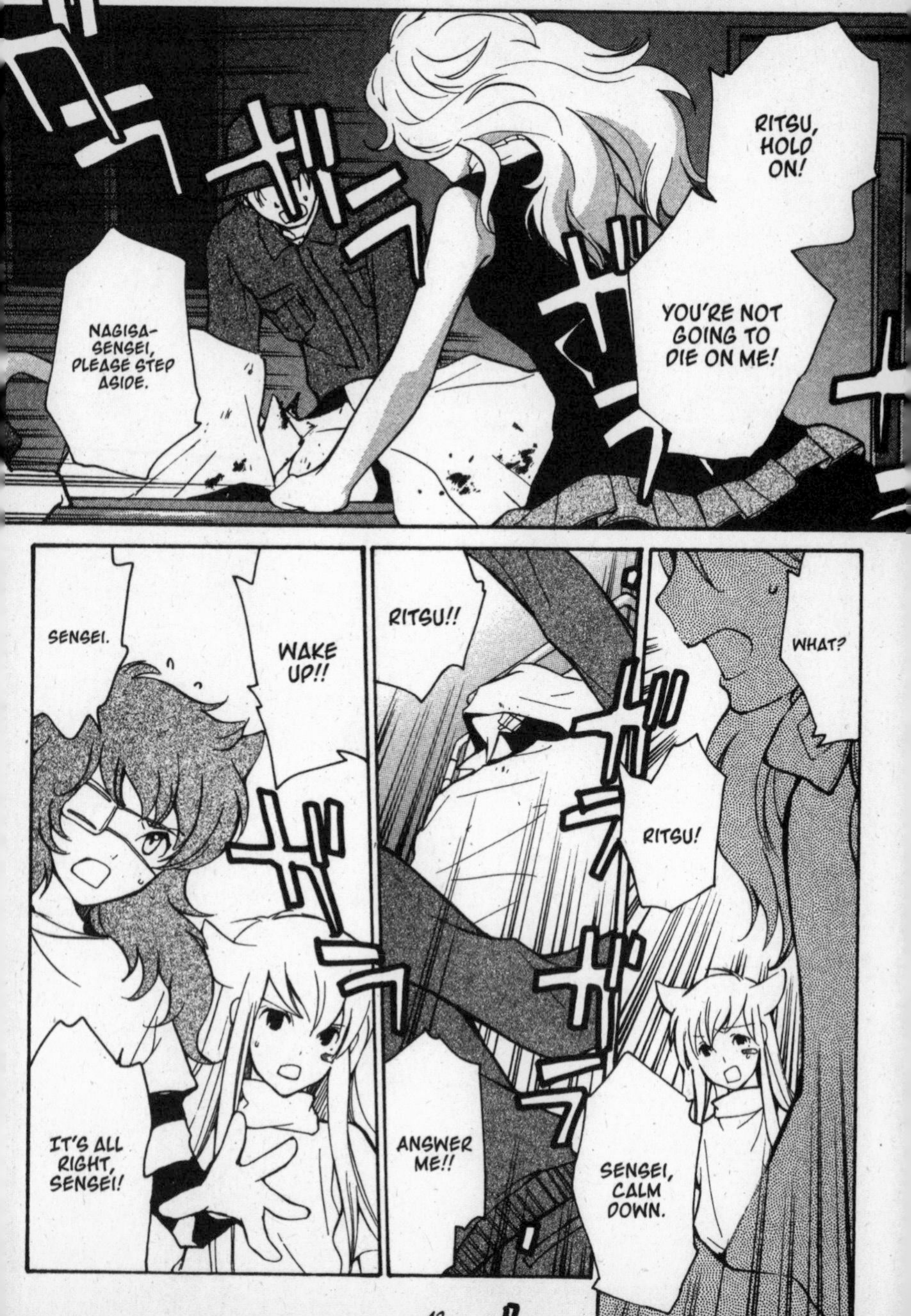
RITSU, HOLD ON!
YOU'RE NOT GOING TO DIE ON ME!
NAGISA-SENSEI, PLEASE STEP ASIDE.
WHAT?
RITSU!
SENSEI, CALM DOWN.
RITSU!!
ANSWER ME!!
WAKE UP!!
SENSEI.
IT'S ALL RIGHT, SENSEI!

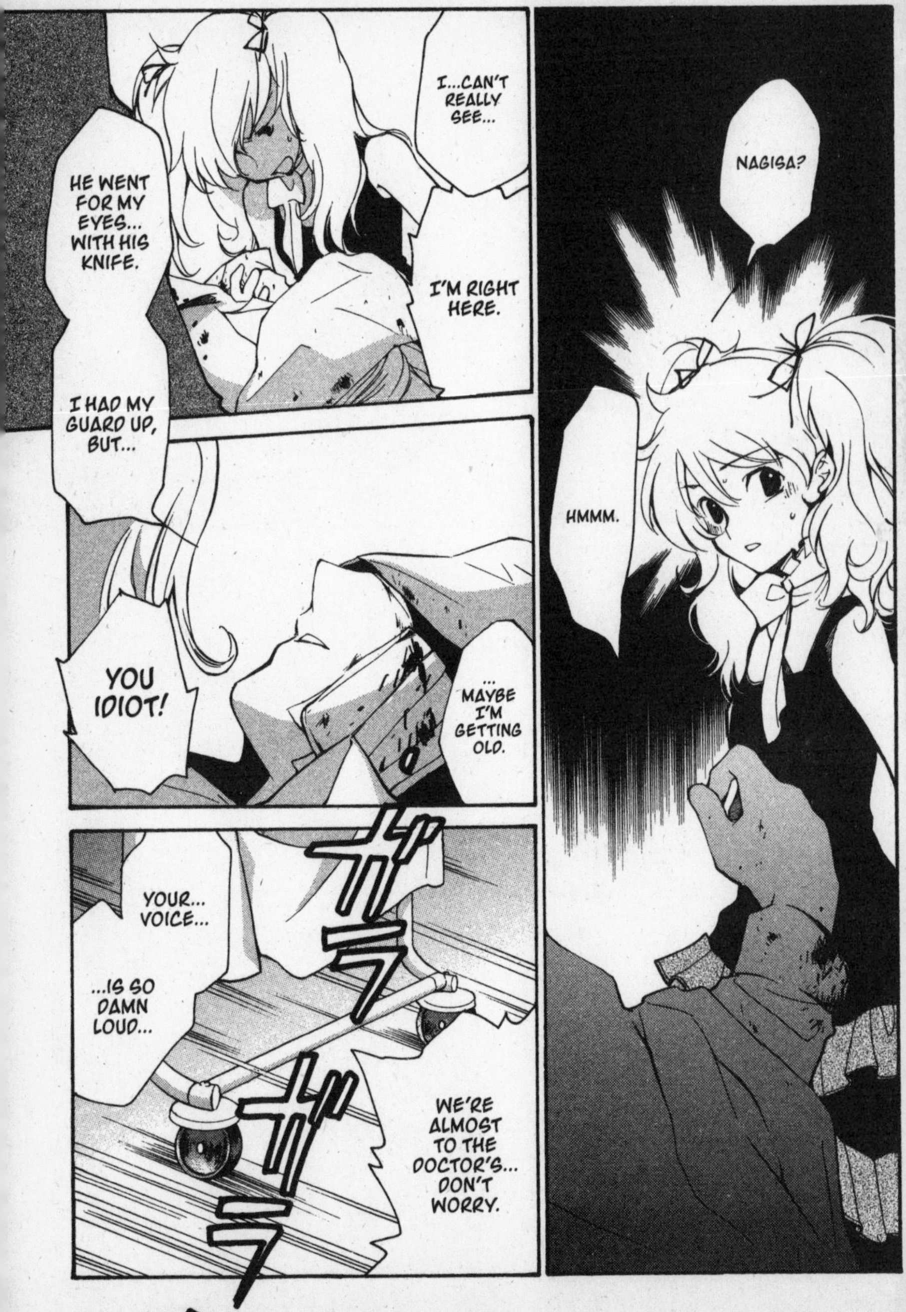
NAGISA?
HMMM.
I...CAN'T REALLY SEE...
I'M RIGHT HERE.
HE WENT FOR MY EYES... WITH HIS KNIFE.
I HAD MY GUARD UP, BUT...
...MAYBE I'M GETTING OLD.
YOU IDIOT!
WE'RE ALMOST TO THE DOCTOR'S... DON'T WORRY.
YOUR... VOICE...
...IS SO DAMN LOUD...

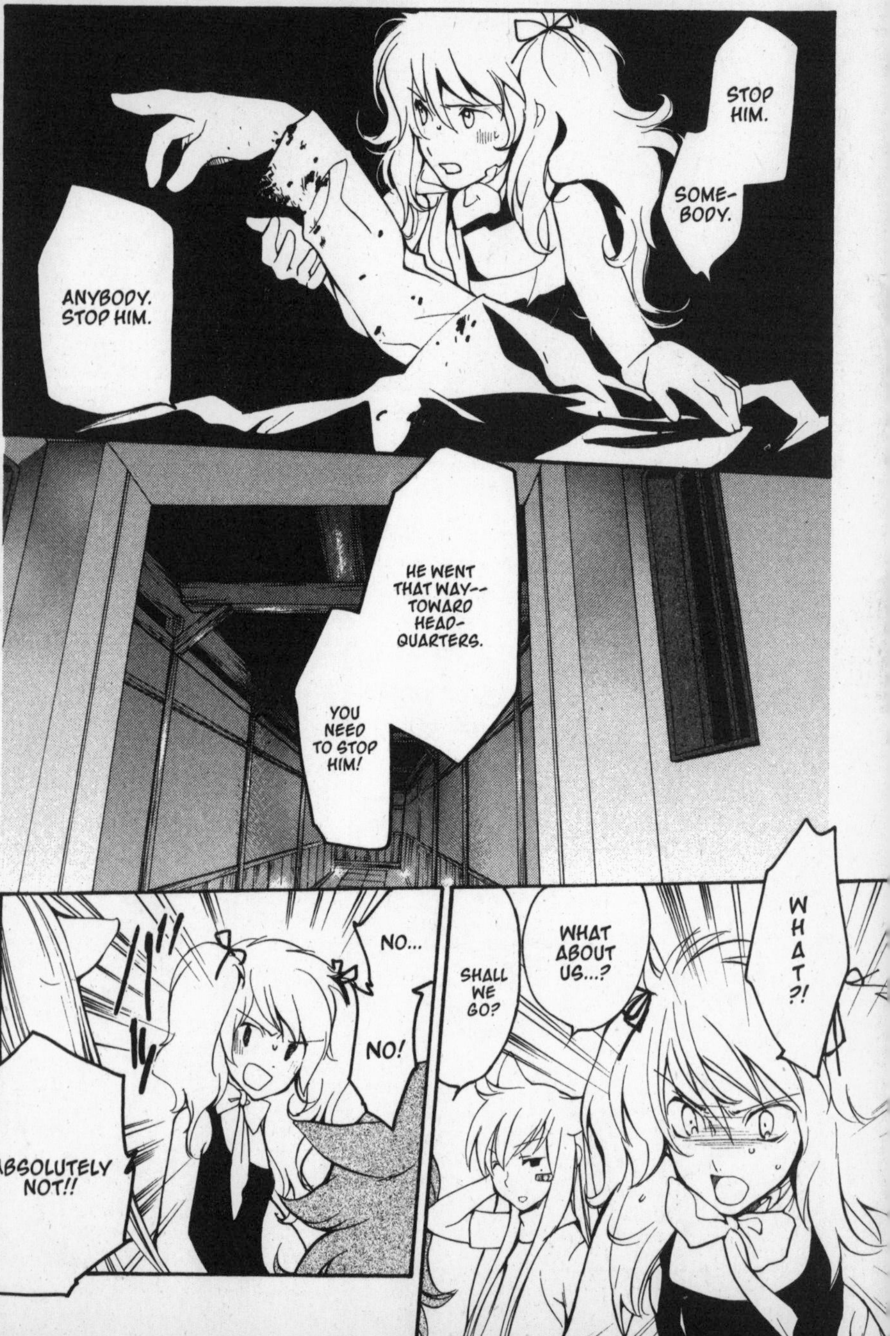
STOP HIM.
SOME-BODY.
ANYBODY. STOP HIM.
HE WENT THAT WAY-- TOWARD HEAD-QUARTERS.
YOU NEED TO STOP HIM!
WHAT?!
WHAT ABOUT US...?
SHALL WE GO?
NO...
NO!
ABSOLUTELY NOT!!

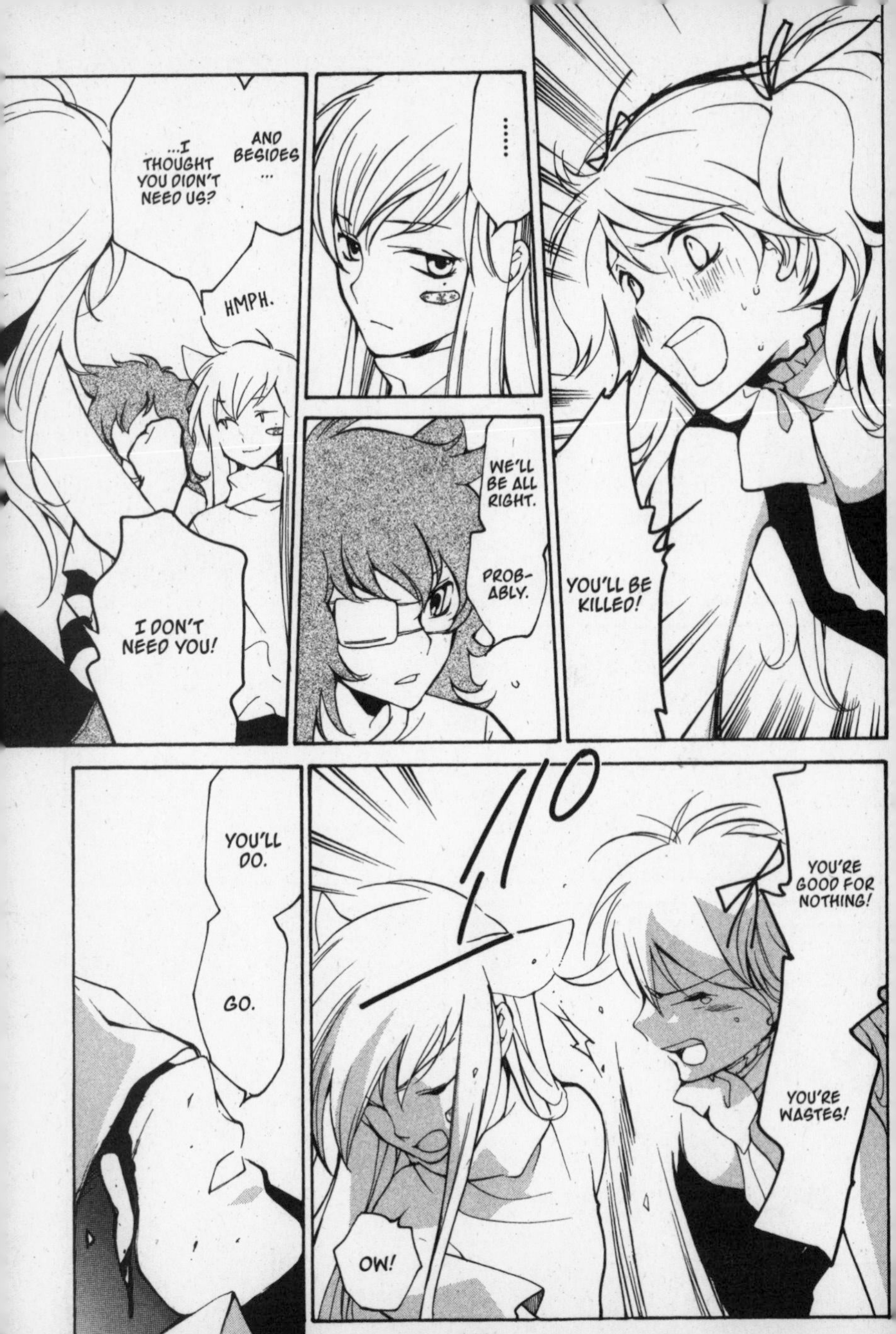
YOU'LL BE KILLED!
......
WE'LL BE ALL RIGHT.
PROB-ABLY.
AND BESIDES ...
...I THOUGHT YOU DIDN'T NEED US?
HMPH.
I DON'T NEED YOU!
YOU'RE GOOD FOR NOTHING!
YOU'RE WASTES!
OW!
YOU'LL DO.
GO.

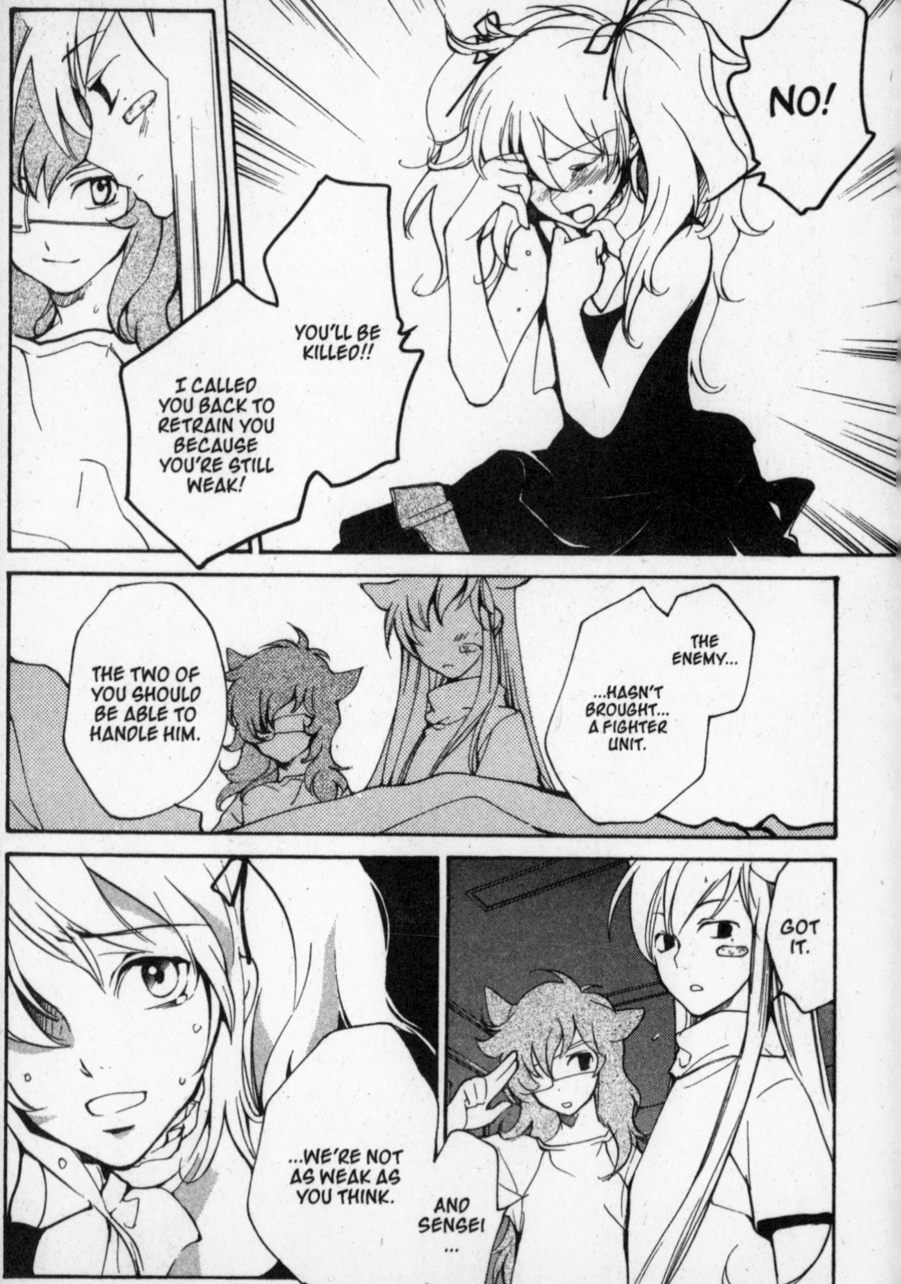
NO!
YOU'LL BE KILLED!!
I CALLED YOU BACK TO RETRAIN YOU BECAUSE YOU'RE STILL WEAK!
THE ENEMY...
...HASN'T BROUGHT... A FIGHTER UNIT.
THE TWO OF YOU SHOULD BE ABLE TO HANDLE HIM.
GOT IT.
AND SENSEI ...
...WE'RE NOT AS WEAK AS YOU THINK.

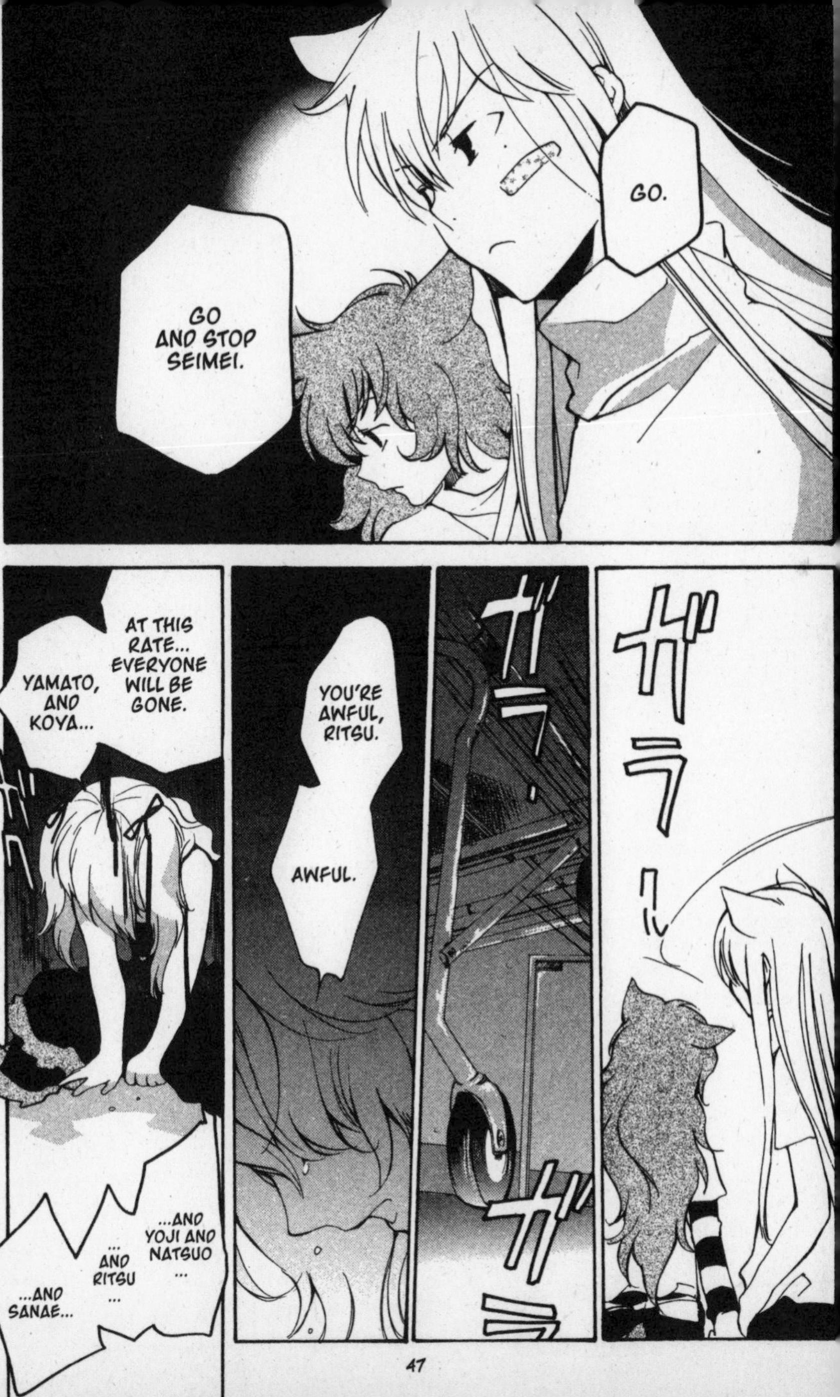
GO.
GO AND STOP SEIMEI.
YOU'RE AWFUL, RITSU.
AWFUL.
AT THIS RATE... EVERYONE WILL BE GONE.
YAMATO, AND KOYA...
...AND YOJI AND NATSUO ...
... AND RITSU ...
...AND SANAE...

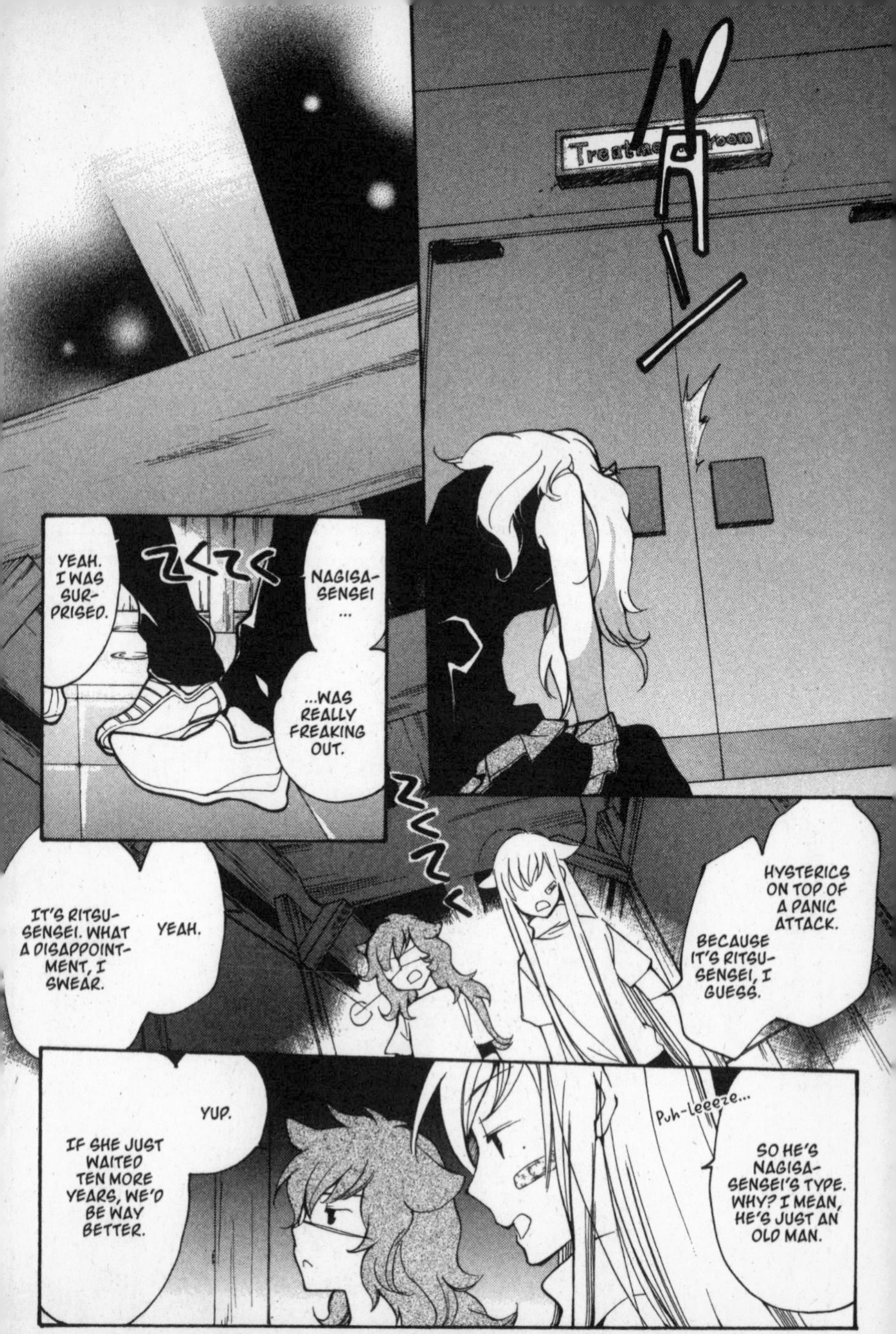
NAGISA-SENSEI...
...WAS REALLY FREAKING OUT.
YEAH. I WAS SURPRISED.
HYSTERICS ON TOP OF A PANIC ATTACK.
BECAUSE IT'S RITSU-SENSEI, I GUESS.
YEAH.
IT'S RITSU-SENSEI. WHAT A DISAPPOINTMENT, I SWEAR.
SO HE'S NAGISA-SENSEI'S TYPE. WHY? I MEAN, HE'S JUST AN OLD MAN.
Puh-leeeze...
YUP.
IF SHE JUST WAITED TEN MORE YEARS, WE'D BE WAY BETTER.

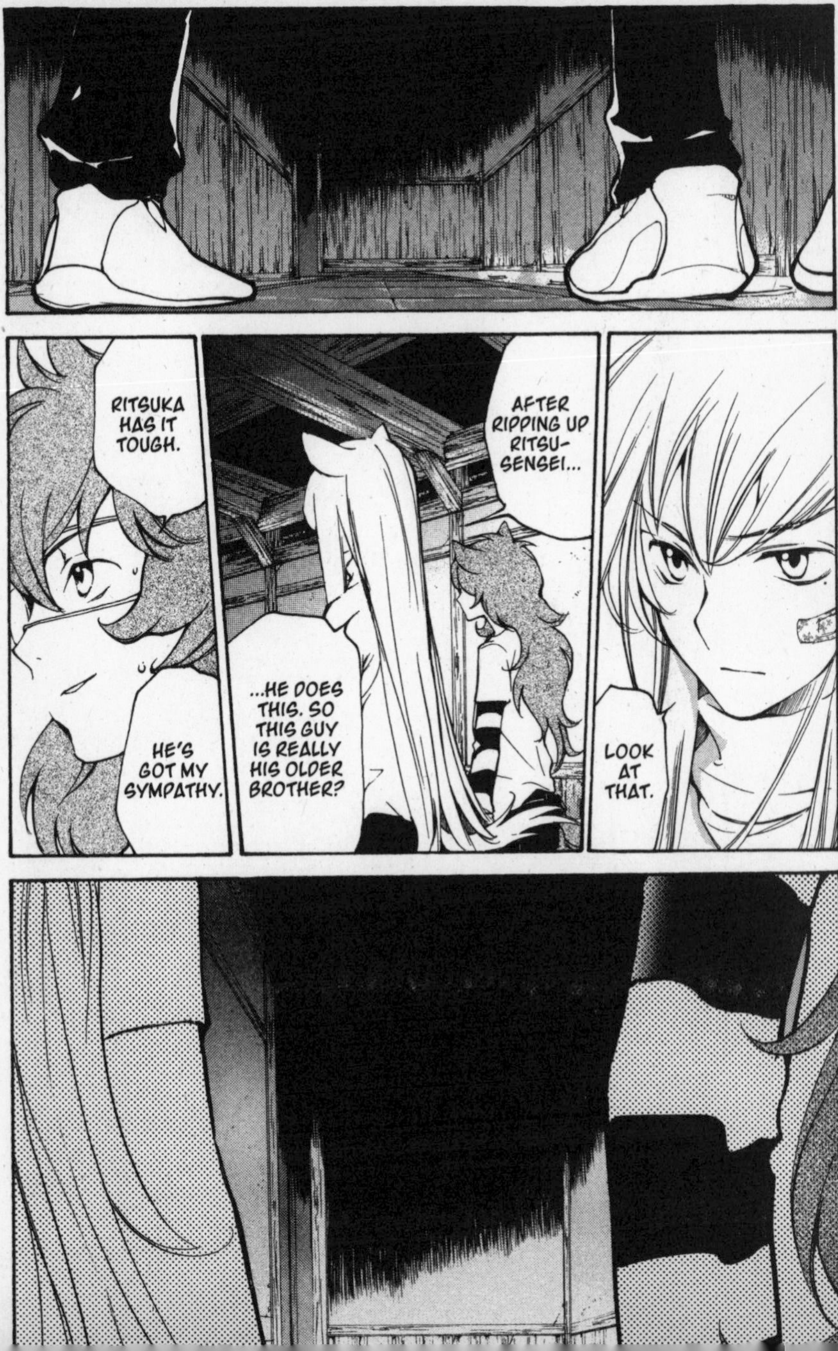
LOOK AT THAT.
AFTER RIPPING UP RITSU-SENSEI...
...HE DOES THIS. SO THIS GUY IS REALLY HIS OLDER BROTHER?
RITSUKA HAS IT TOUGH.
HE'S GOT MY SYMPATHY.

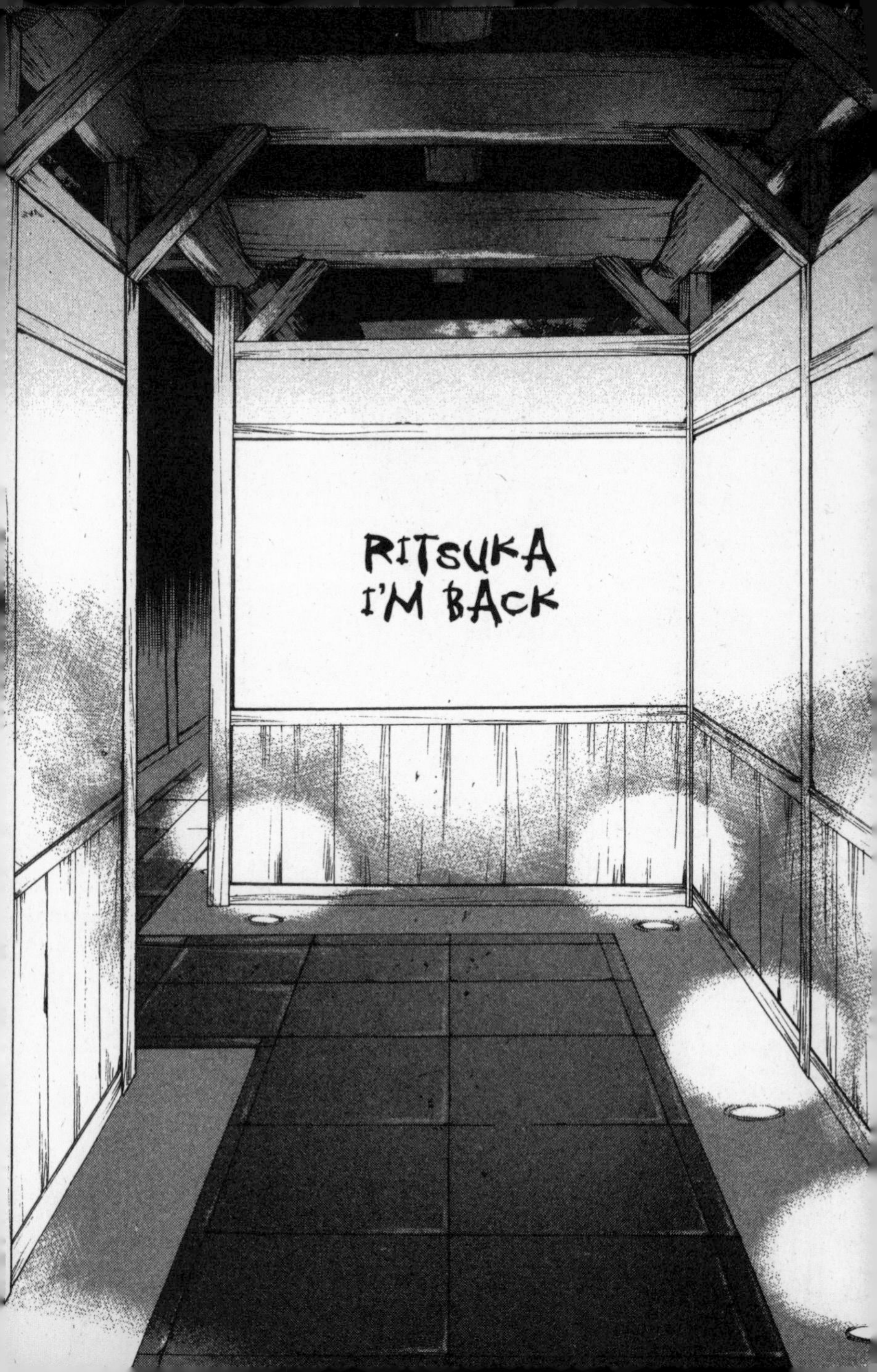
RITSUKA
I'M BACK

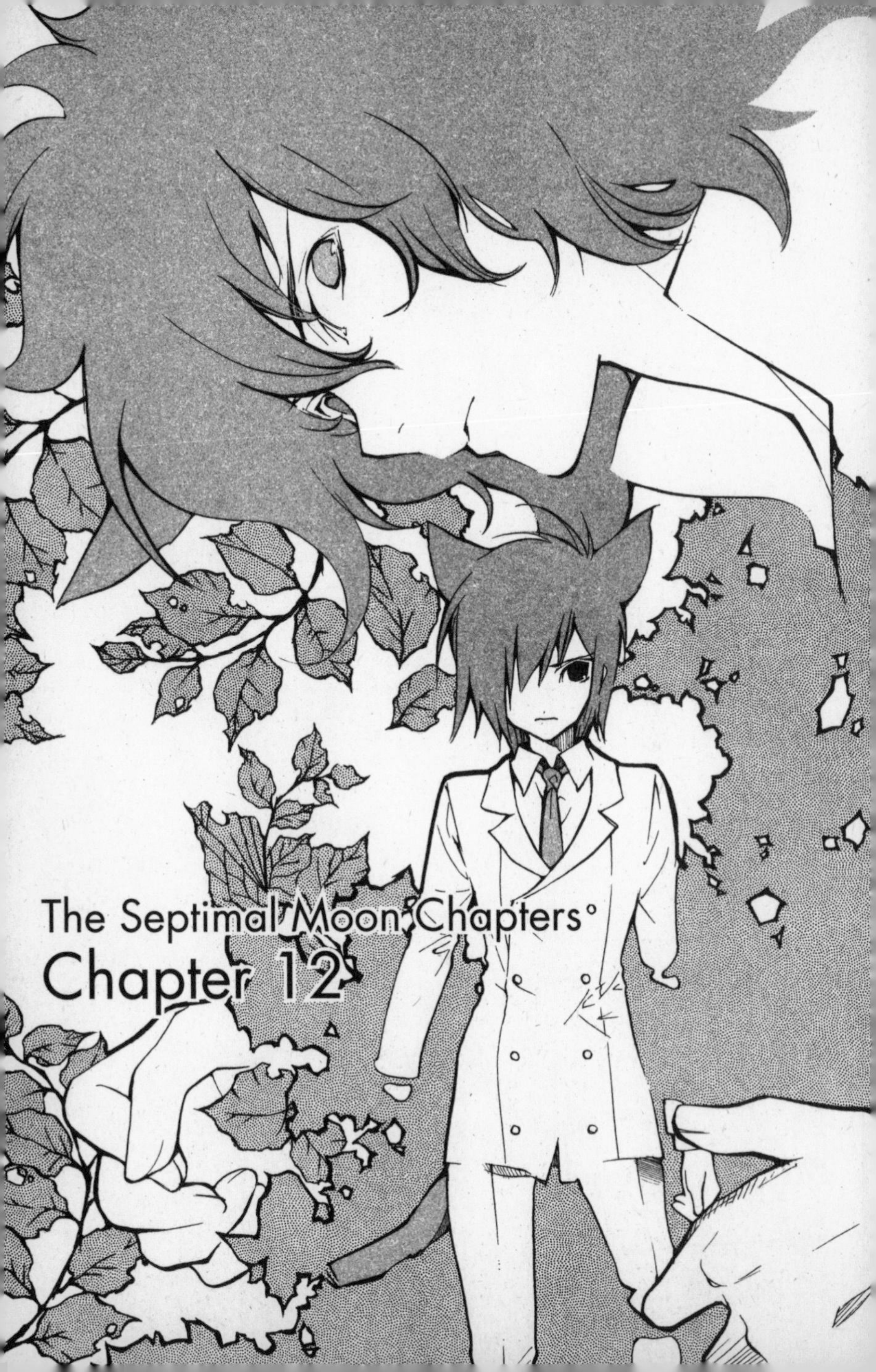
The Septimal Moon Chapters
Chapter 12

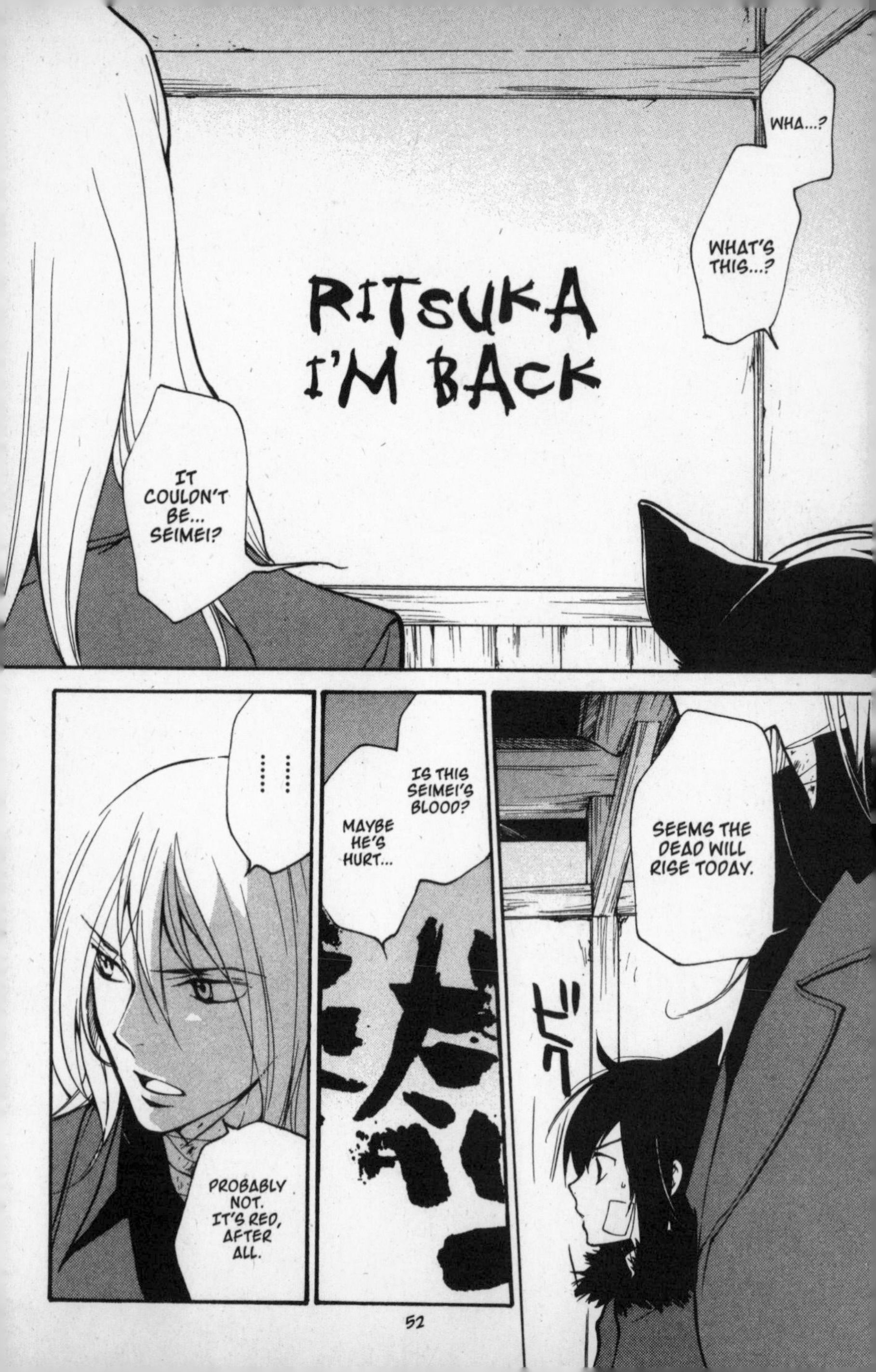
WHA...?
WHAT'S THIS...?
RITSUKA I'M BACK
IT COULDN'T BE... SEIMEI?
SEEMS THE DEAD WILL RISE TODAY.
IS THIS SEIMEI'S BLOOD?
MAYBE HE'S HURT...
......
PROBABLY NOT. IT'S RED, AFTER ALL.

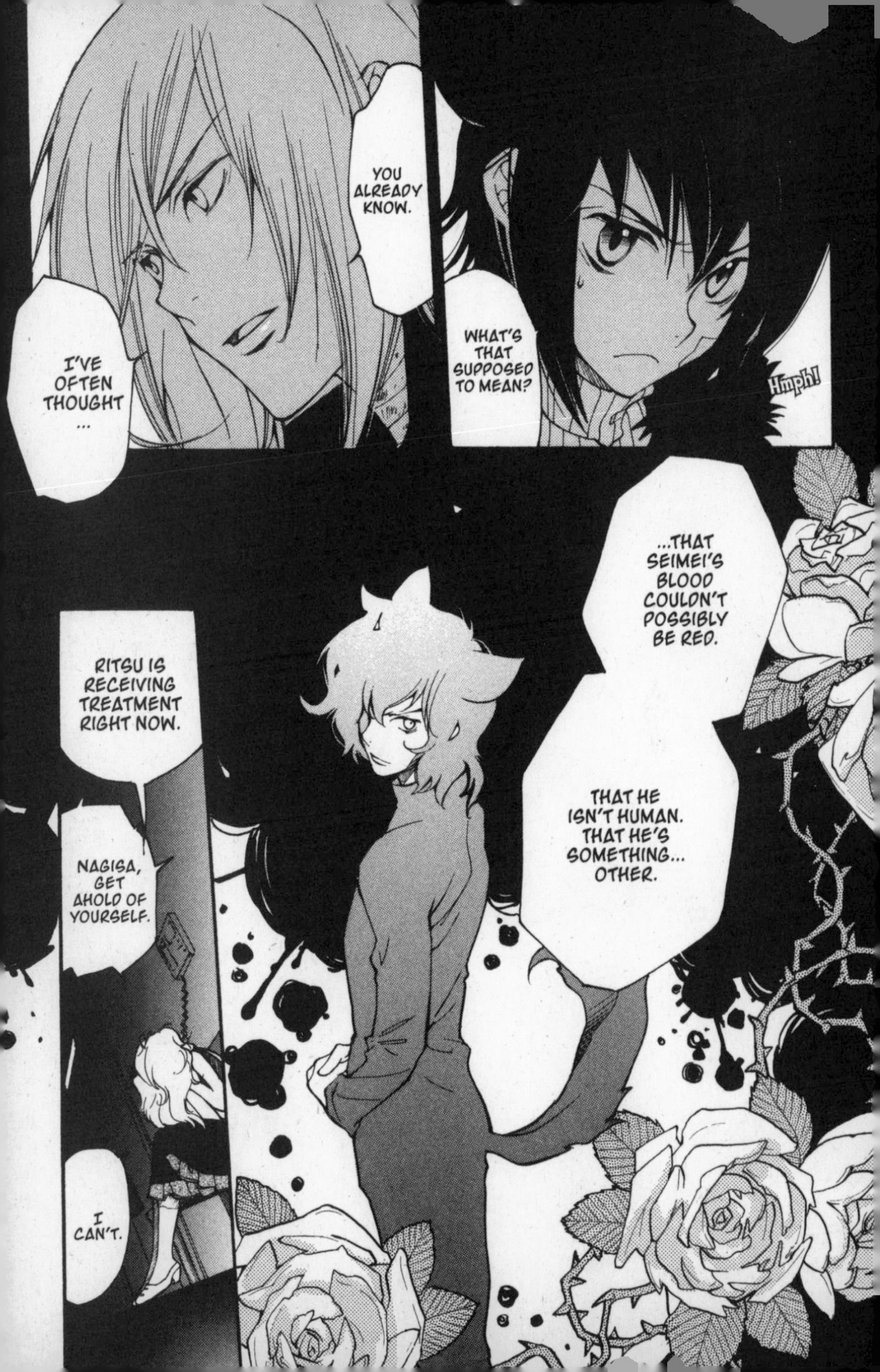
WHAT'S THAT SUPPOSED TO MEAN?
Hmph!
YOU ALREADY KNOW.
I'VE OFTEN THOUGHT ...
...THAT SEIMEI'S BLOOD COULDN'T POSSIBLY BE RED.
THAT HE ISN'T HUMAN. THAT HE'S SOMETHING... OTHER.
RITSU IS RECEIVING TREATMENT RIGHT NOW.
NAGISA, GET AHOLD OF YOURSELF.
I CAN'T.

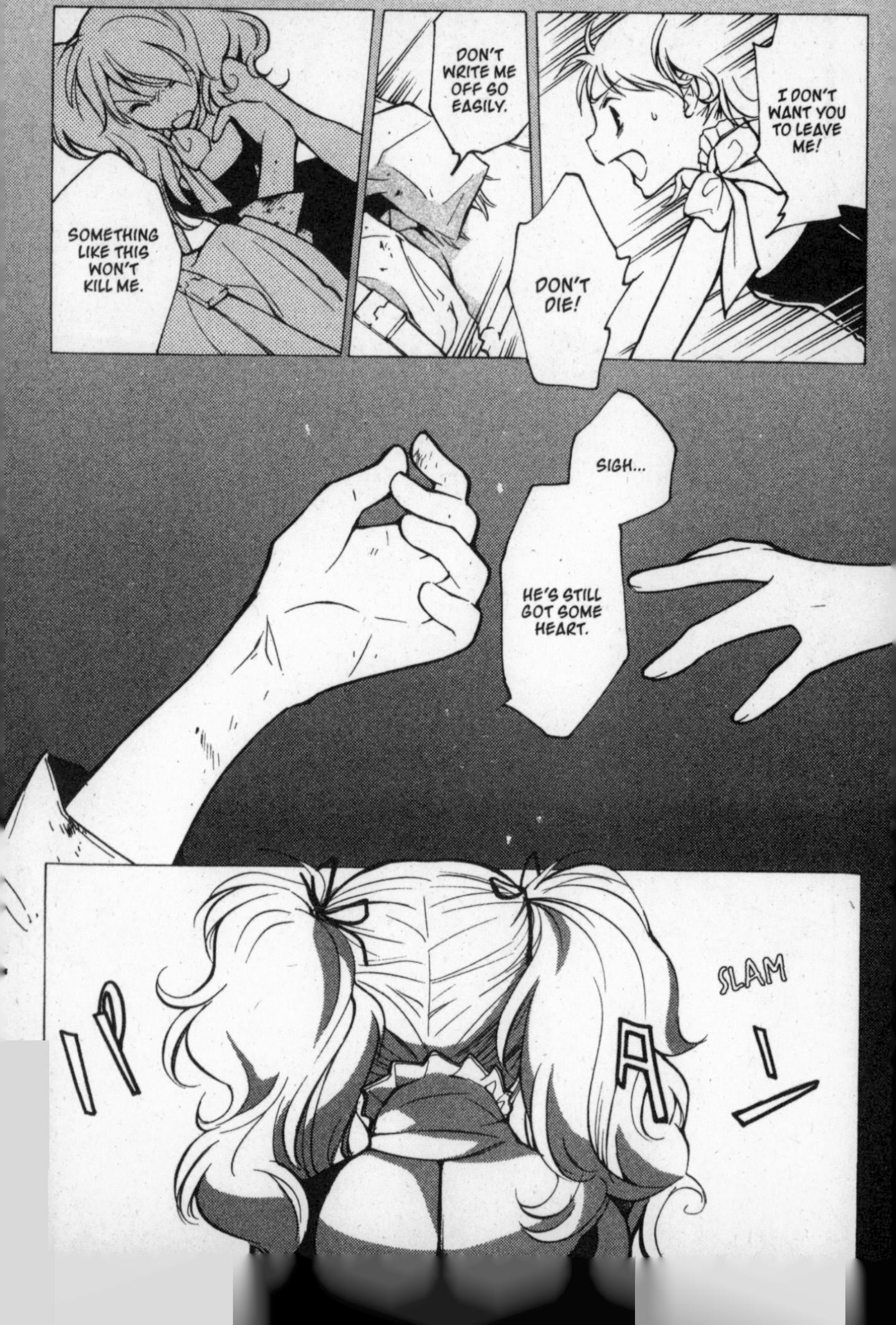
I DON'T WANT YOU TO LEAVE ME!
DON'T DIE!
DON'T WRITE ME OFF SO EASILY.
SOMETHING LIKE THIS WON'T KILL ME.
SIGH...
HE'S STILL GOT SOME HEART.
SLAM

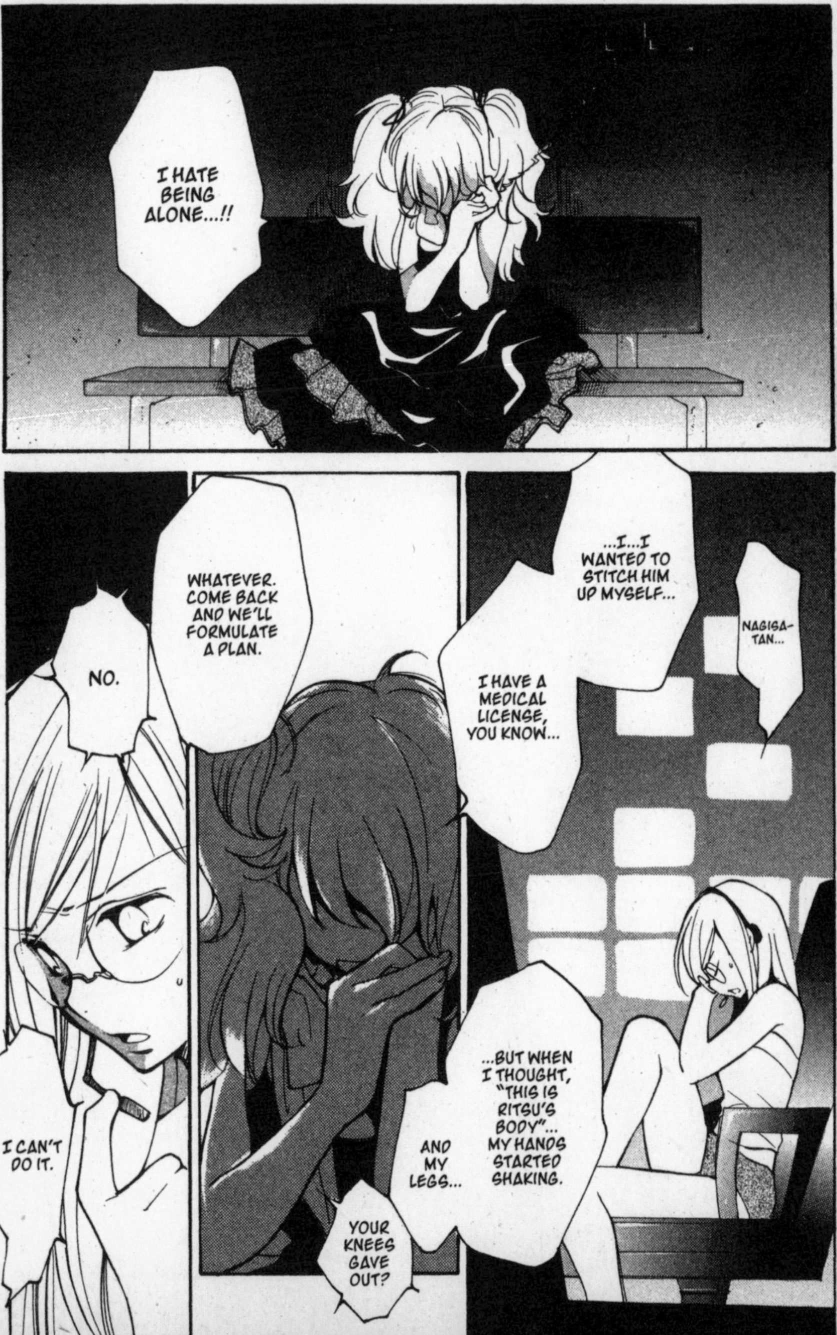
I HATE BEING ALONE...!!
NAGISA-TAN...
...I...I WANTED TO STITCH HIM UP MYSELF...
I HAVE A MEDICAL LICENSE, YOU KNOW...
...BUT WHEN I THOUGHT, "THIS IS RITSU'S BODY"... MY HANDS STARTED SHAKING.
AND MY LEGS...
YOUR KNEES GAVE OUT?
WHATEVER. COME BACK AND WE'LL FORMULATE A PLAN.
NO.
I CAN'T DO IT.

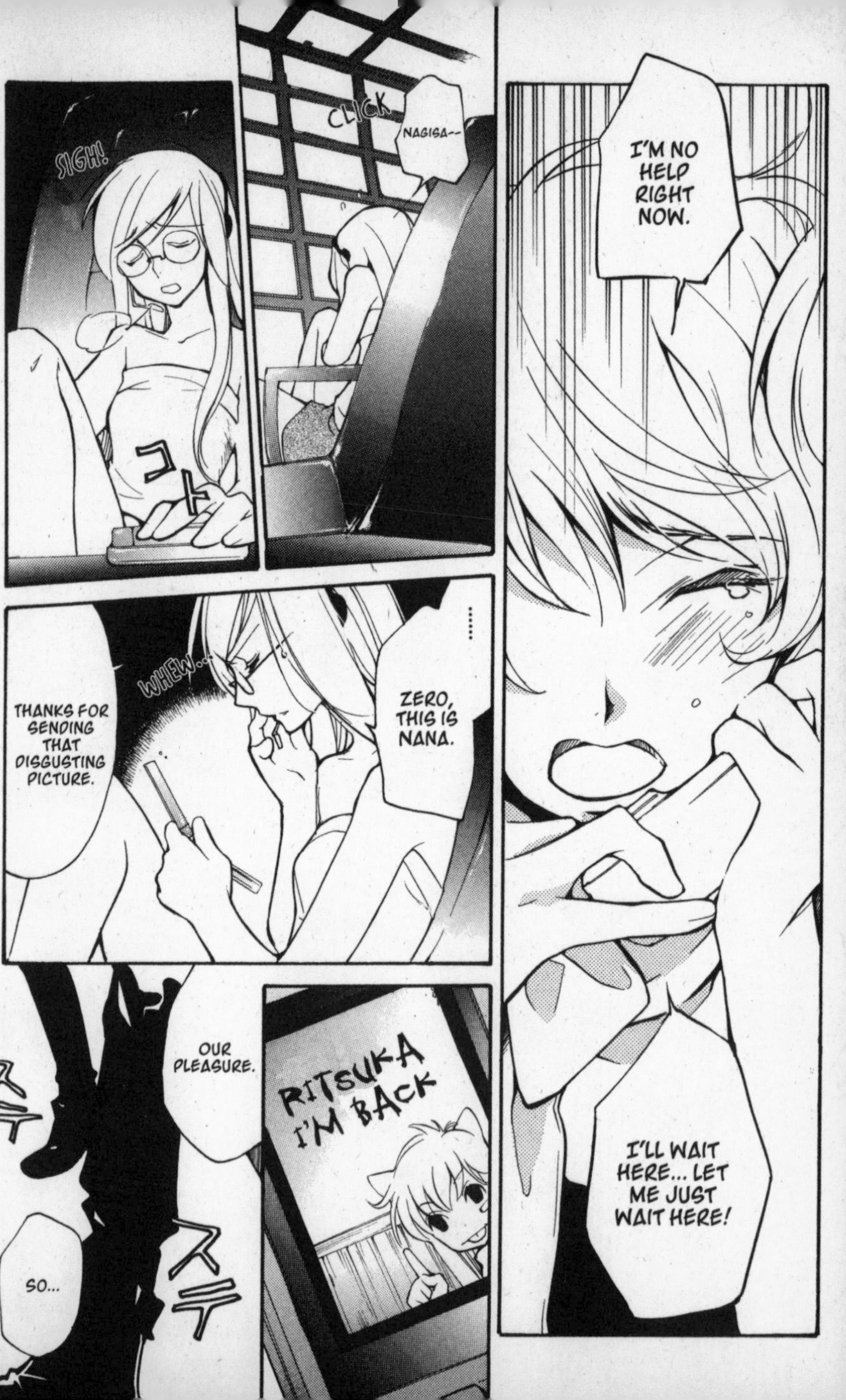
I'M NO HELP RIGHT NOW.
I'LL WAIT HERE... LET ME JUST WAIT HERE!
CLICK
NAGISA--
SIGH!
コト
......
ZERO, THIS IS NANA.
WHEW...
THANKS FOR SENDING THAT DISGUSTING PICTURE.
RITSUKA I'M BACK
OUR PLEASURE.
SO...

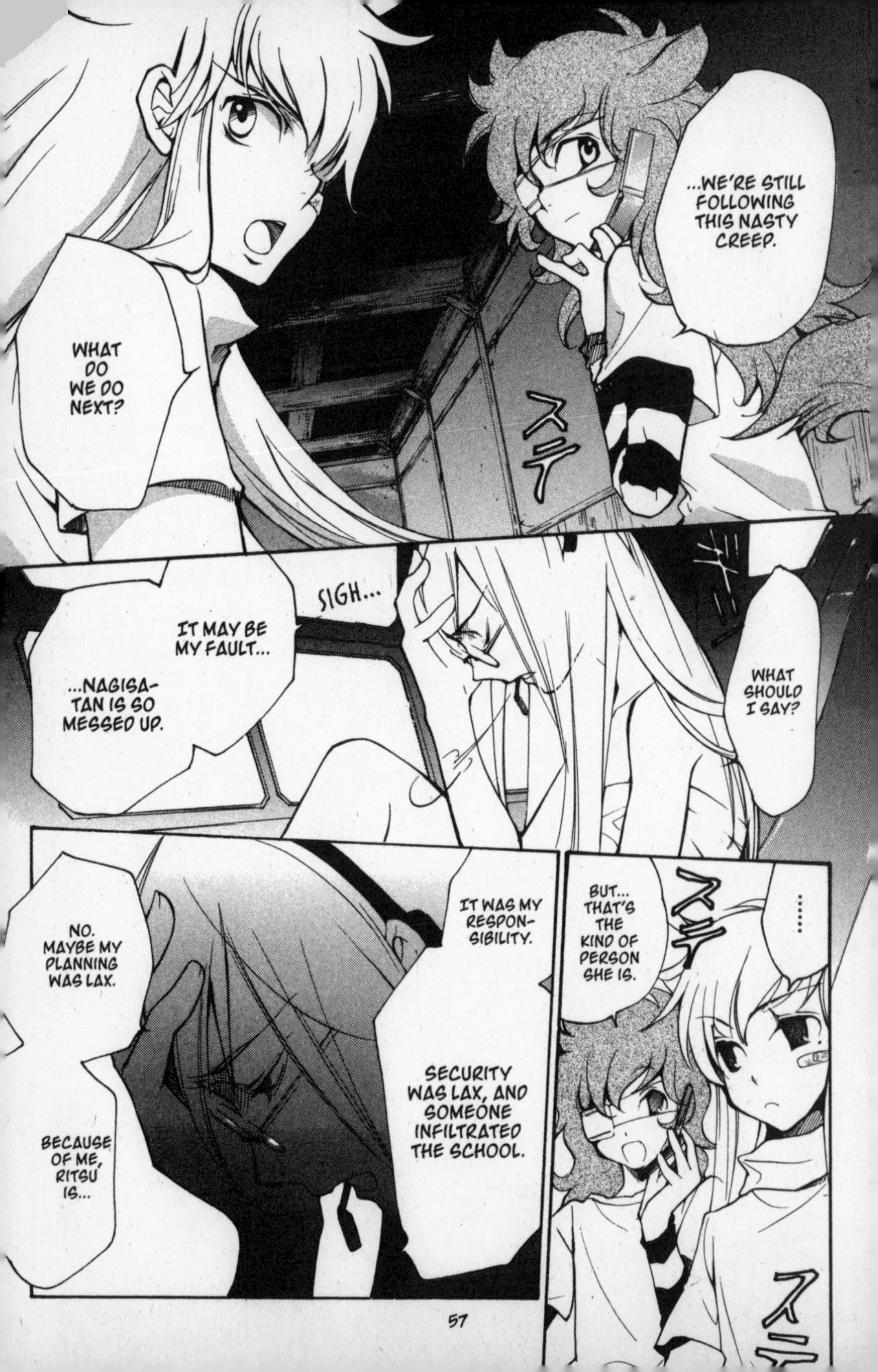
...WE'RE STILL FOLLOWING THIS NASTY CREEP.
WHAT DO WE DO NEXT?
WHAT SHOULD I SAY?
SIGH...
IT MAY BE MY FAULT...
...NAGISA-TAN IS SO MESSED UP.
......
BUT... THAT'S THE KIND OF PERSON SHE IS.
IT WAS MY RESPON-SIBILITY.
NO. MAYBE MY PLANNING WAS LAX.
SECURITY WAS LAX, AND SOMEONE INFILTRATED THE SCHOOL.
BECAUSE OF ME, RITSU IS...

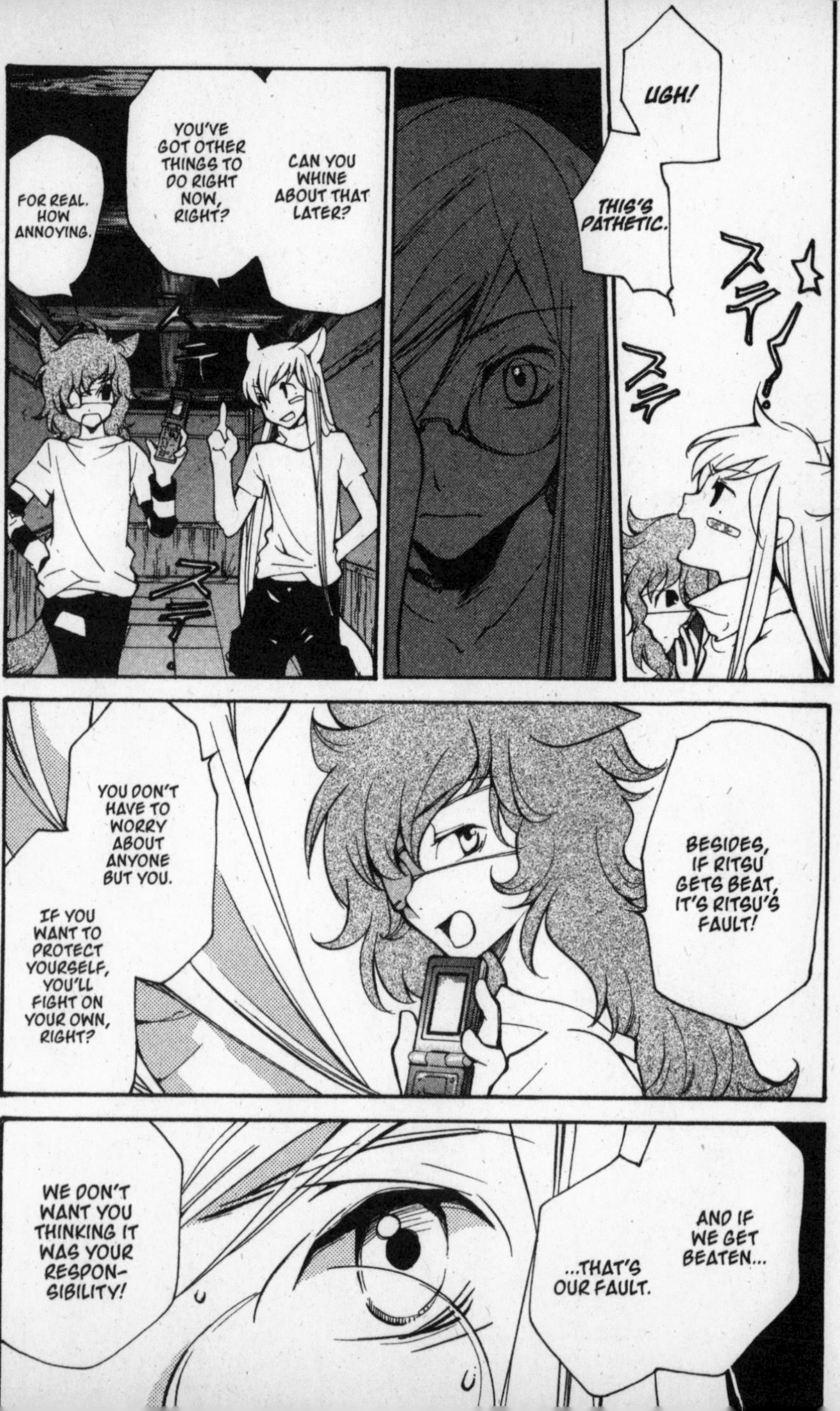
UGH!
THIS'S PATHETIC.
CAN YOU WHINE ABOUT THAT LATER?
YOU'VE GOT OTHER THINGS TO DO RIGHT NOW, RIGHT?
FOR REAL. HOW ANNOYING.
BESIDES, IF RITSU GETS BEAT, IT'S RITSU'S FAULT!
YOU DON'T HAVE TO WORRY ABOUT ANYONE BUT YOU.
IF YOU WANT TO PROTECT YOURSELF, YOU'LL FIGHT ON YOUR OWN, RIGHT?
AND IF WE GET BEATEN...
...THAT'S OUR FAULT.
WE DON'T WANT YOU THINKING IT WAS YOUR RESPON-SIBILITY!

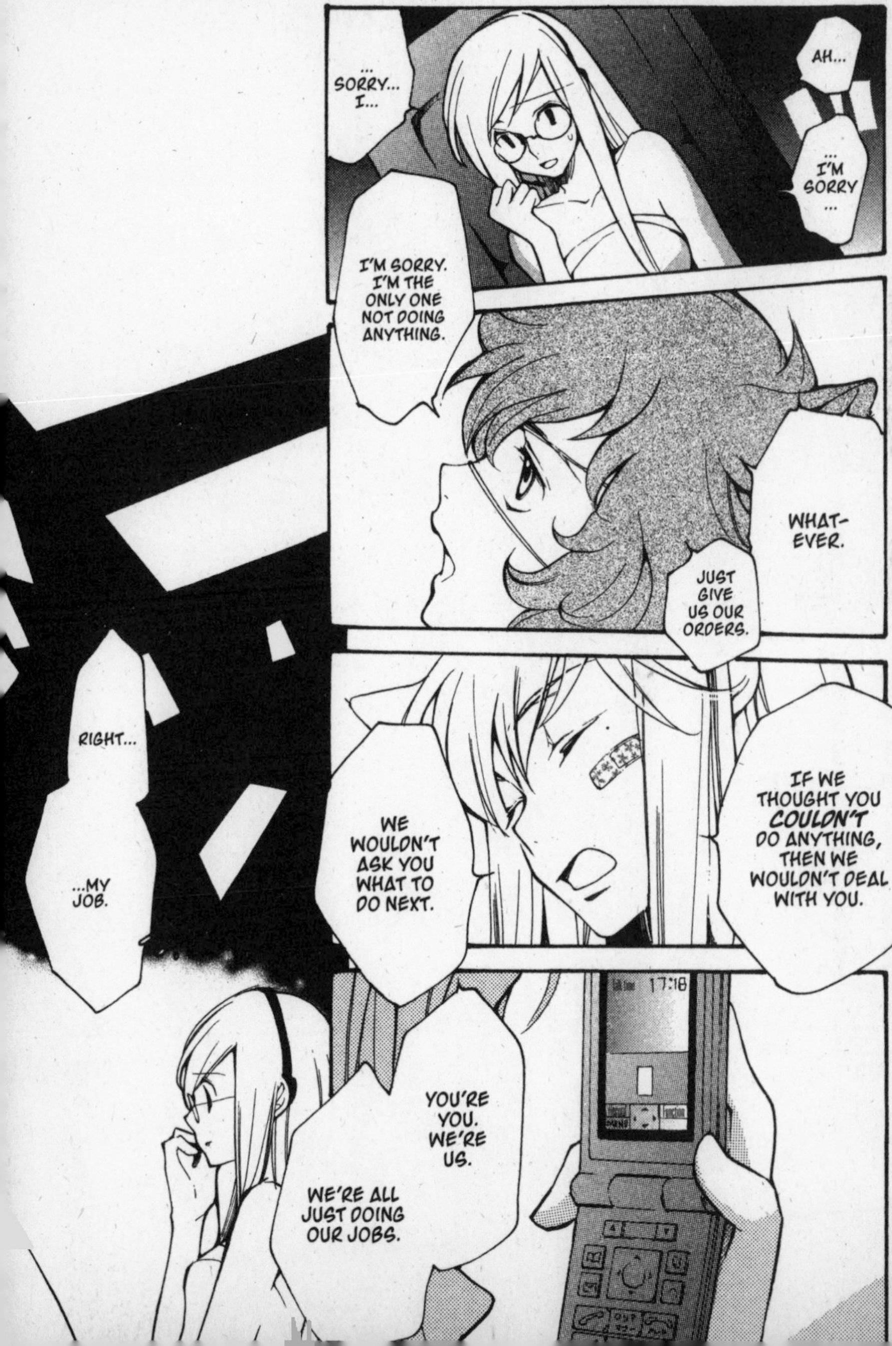
AH...
...I'M SORRY...
...SORRY... I...
I'M SORRY. I'M THE ONLY ONE NOT DOING ANYTHING.
WHAT-EVER.
JUST GIVE US OUR ORDERS.
IF WE THOUGHT YOU COULDN'T DO ANYTHING, THEN WE WOULDN'T DEAL WITH YOU.
WE WOULDN'T ASK YOU WHAT TO DO NEXT.
17:18
YOU'RE YOU. WE'RE US.
WE'RE ALL JUST DOING OUR JOBS.
RIGHT...
...MY JOB.

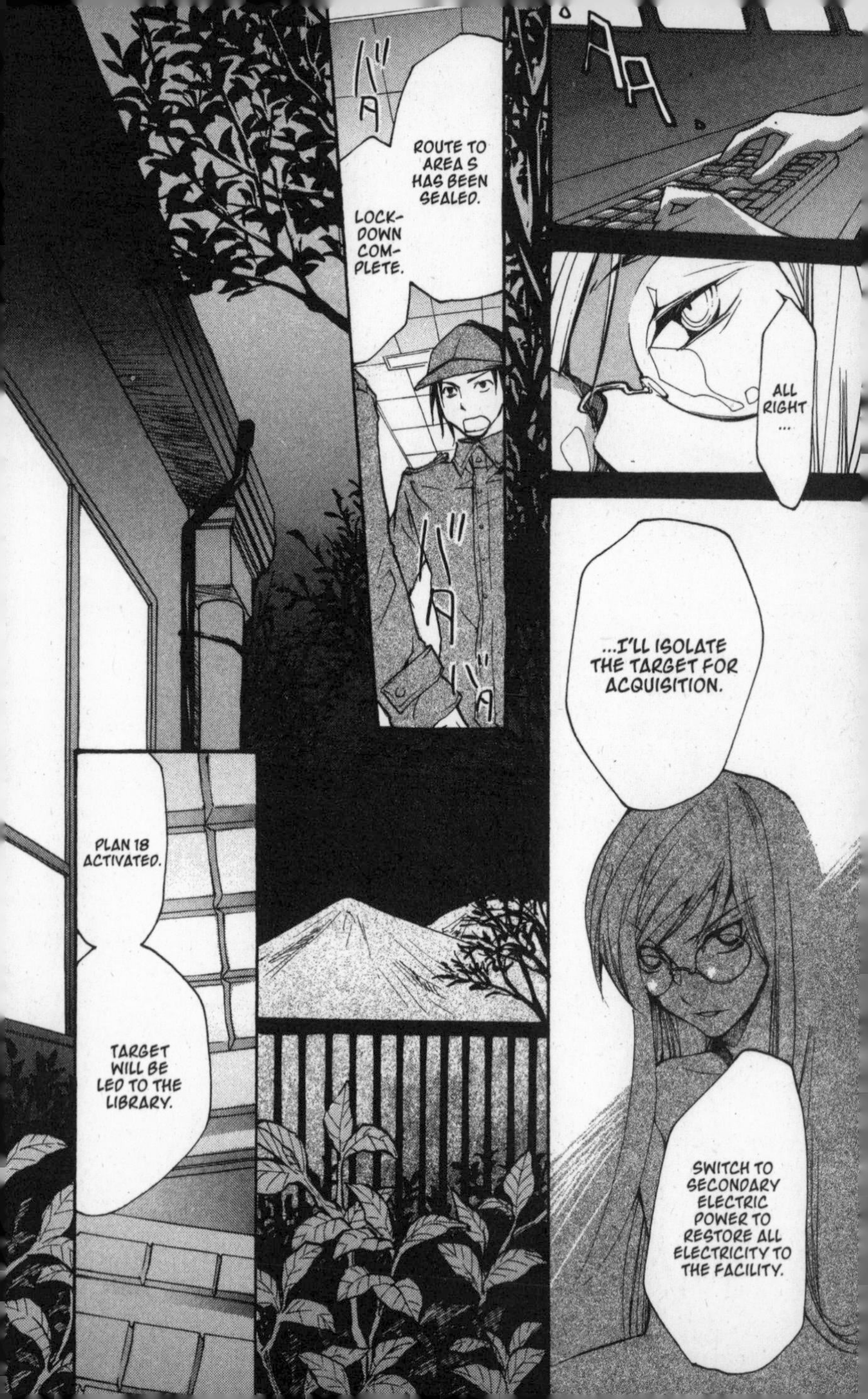
ALL RIGHT ...
...I'LL ISOLATE THE TARGET FOR ACQUISITION.
SWITCH TO SECONDARY ELECTRIC POWER TO RESTORE ALL ELECTRICITY TO THE FACILITY.
ROUTE TO AREA S HAS BEEN SEALED.
LOCK-DOWN COMPLETE.
PLAN 18 ACTIVATED.
TARGET WILL BE LED TO THE LIBRARY.

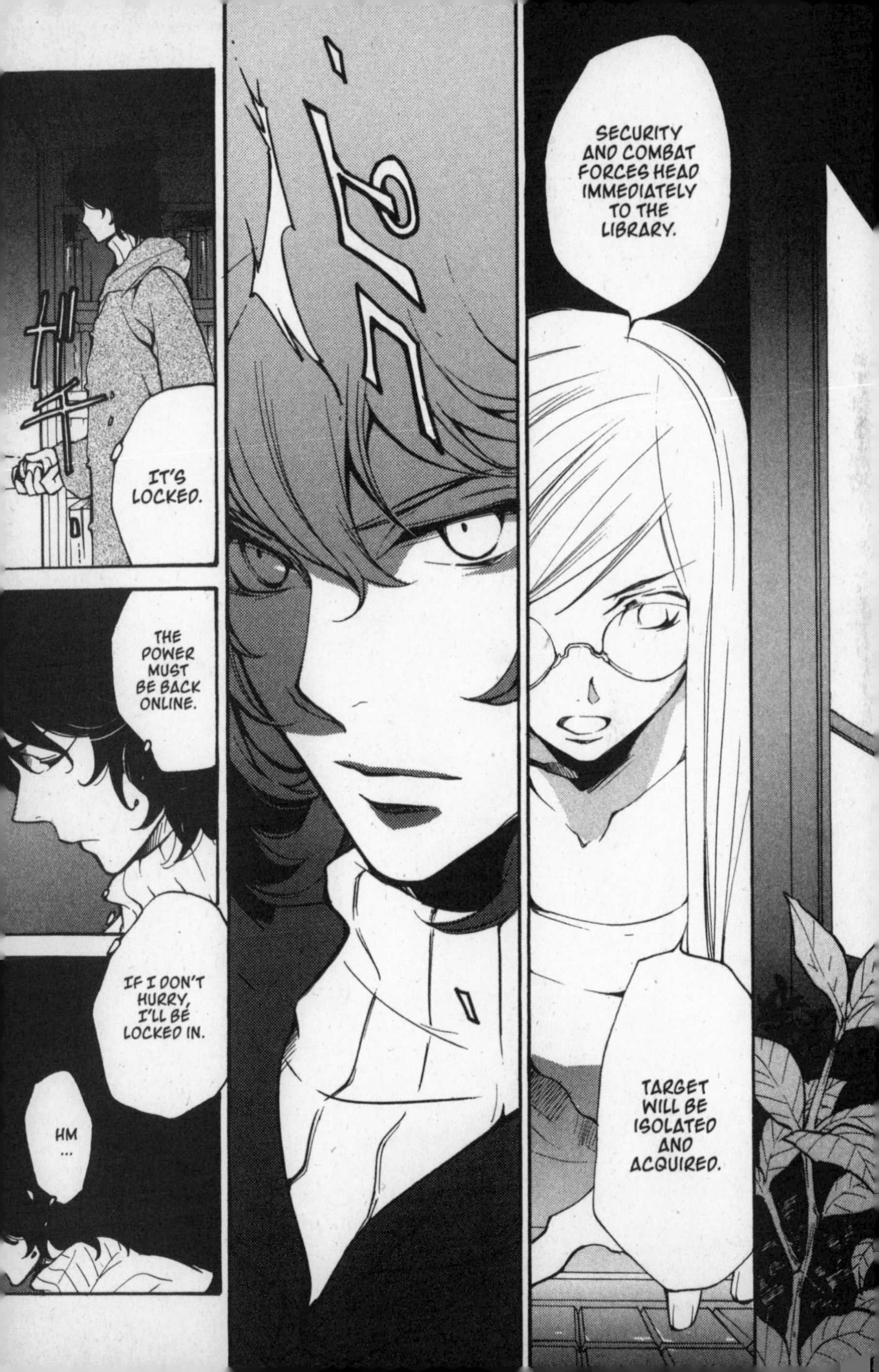
SECURITY AND COMBAT FORCES HEAD IMMEDIATELY TO THE LIBRARY.
TARGET WILL BE ISOLATED AND ACQUIRED.
IT'S LOCKED.
THE POWER MUST BE BACK ONLINE.
IF I DON'T HURRY, I'LL BE LOCKED IN.
HM ...

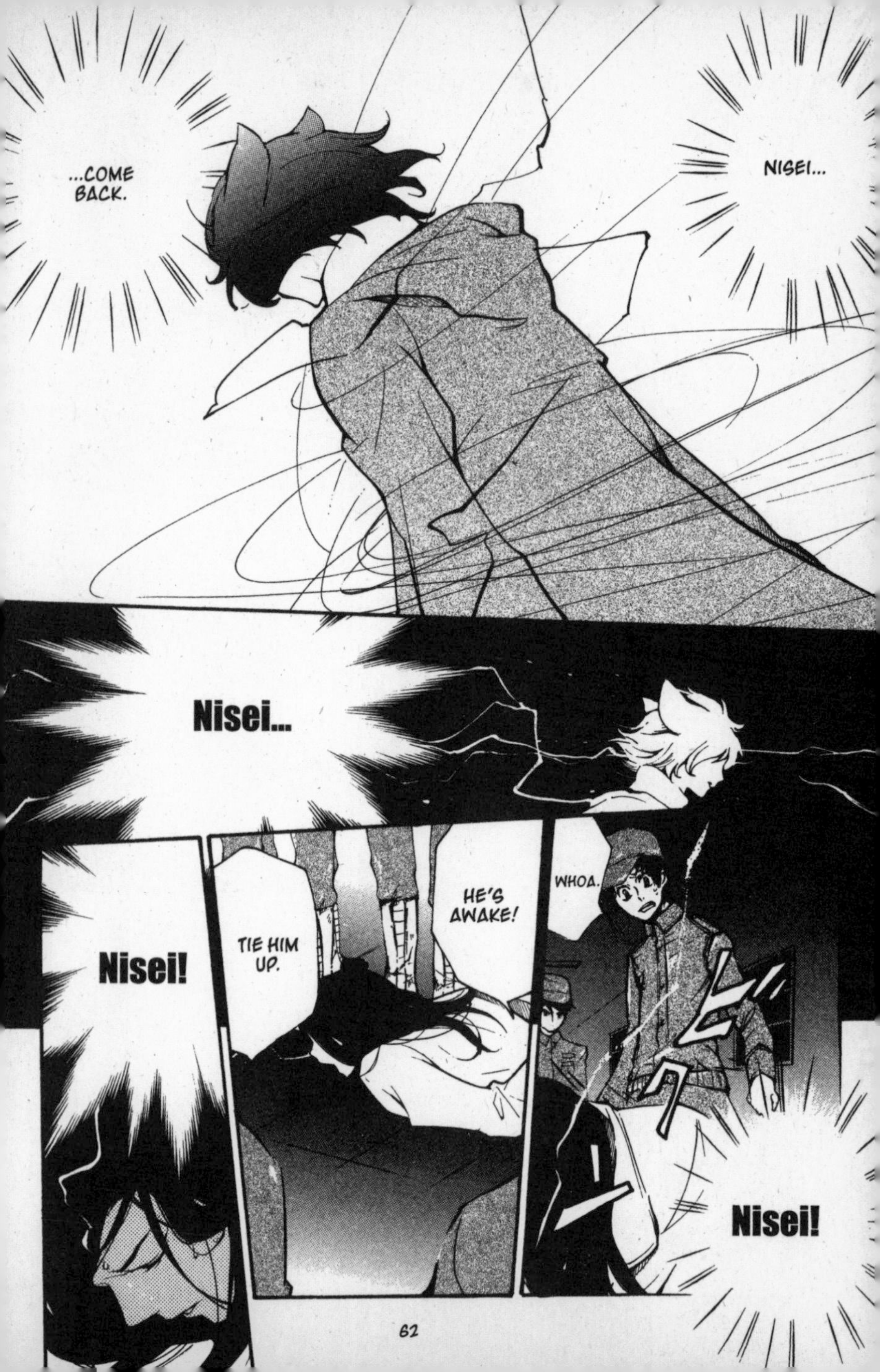
NISEI...
...COME BACK.
Nisei...
WHOA.
Nisei!
HE'S AWAKE!
TIE HIM UP.
Nisei!

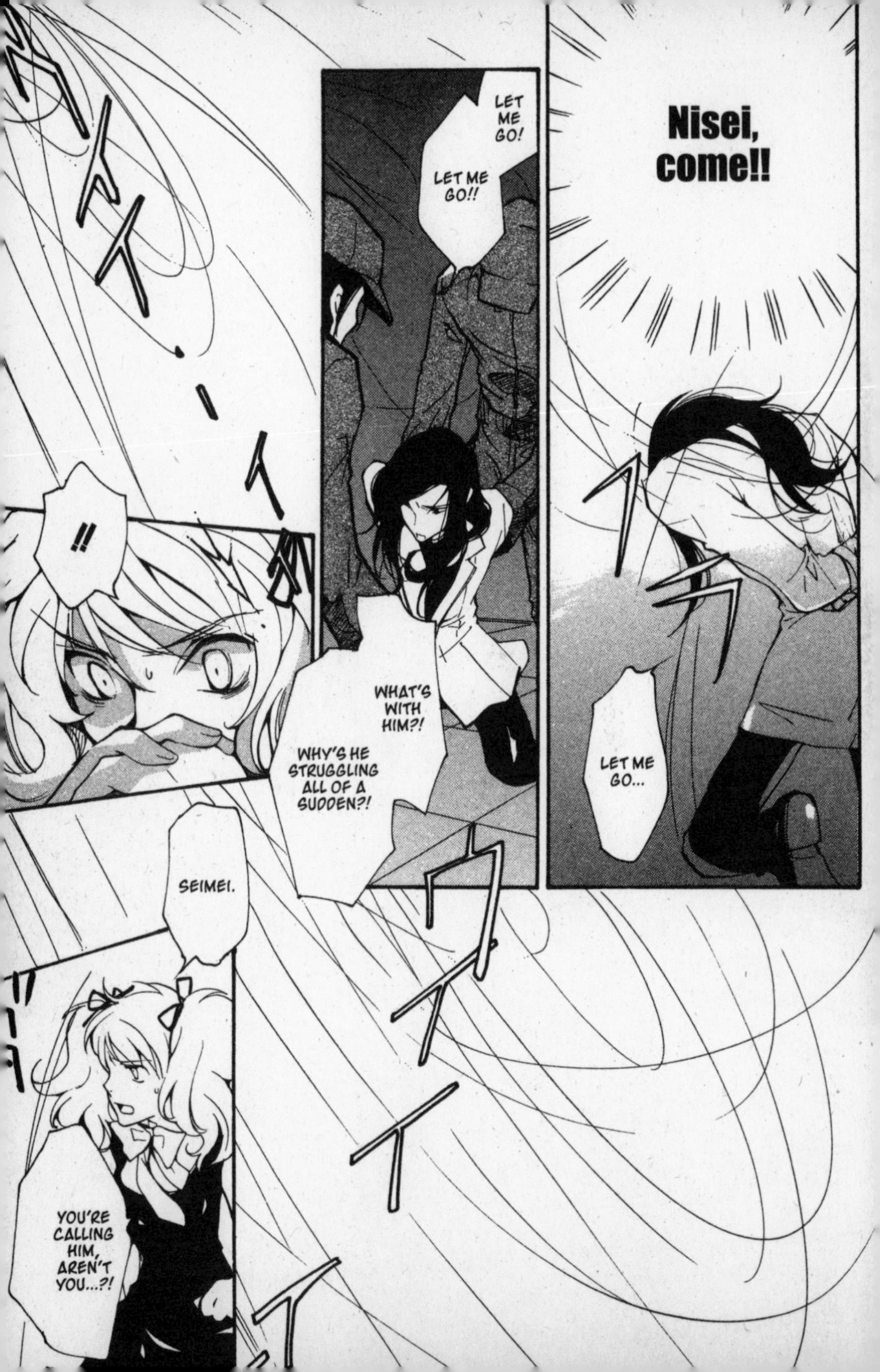
Nisei, come!!
LET ME GO...
LET ME GO!
LET ME GO!!
WHAT'S WITH HIM?!
WHY'S HE STRUGGLING ALL OF A SUDDEN?!
!!
SEIMEI.
YOU'RE CALLING HIM, AREN'T YOU...?!

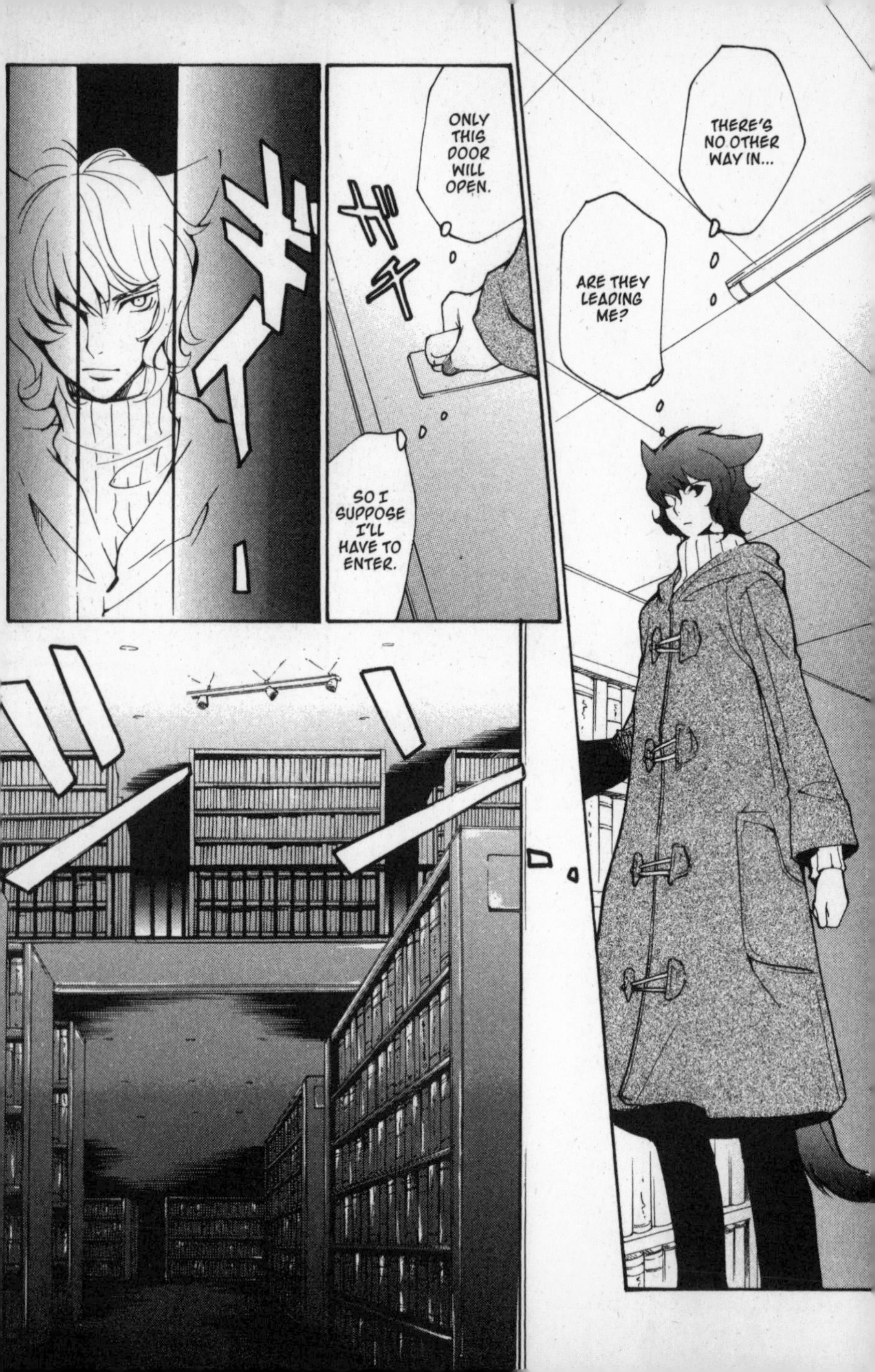
THERE'S NO OTHER WAY IN...
ARE THEY LEADING ME?
ONLY THIS DOOR WILL OPEN.
ガチ
SO I SUPPOSE I'LL HAVE TO ENTER.
ギィ

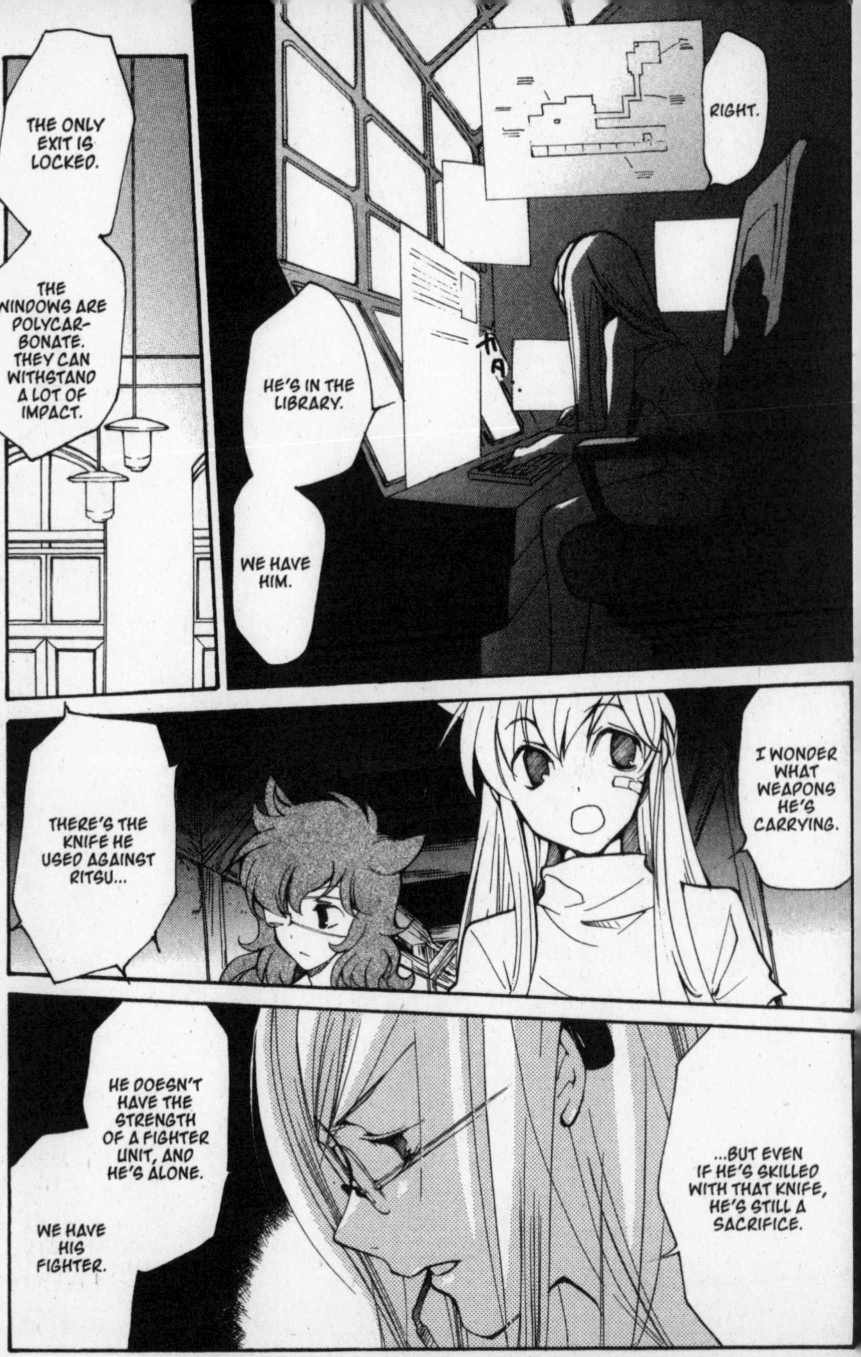
RIGHT.
TA
HE'S IN THE LIBRARY.
WE HAVE HIM.
THE ONLY EXIT IS LOCKED.
THE WINDOWS ARE POLYCARBONATE. THEY CAN WITHSTAND A LOT OF IMPACT.
I WONDER WHAT WEAPONS HE'S CARRYING.
THERE'S THE KNIFE HE USED AGAINST RITSU...
...BUT EVEN IF HE'S SKILLED WITH THAT KNIFE, HE'S STILL A SACRIFICE.
HE DOESN'T HAVE THE STRENGTH OF A FIGHTER UNIT, AND HE'S ALONE.
WE HAVE HIS FIGHTER.

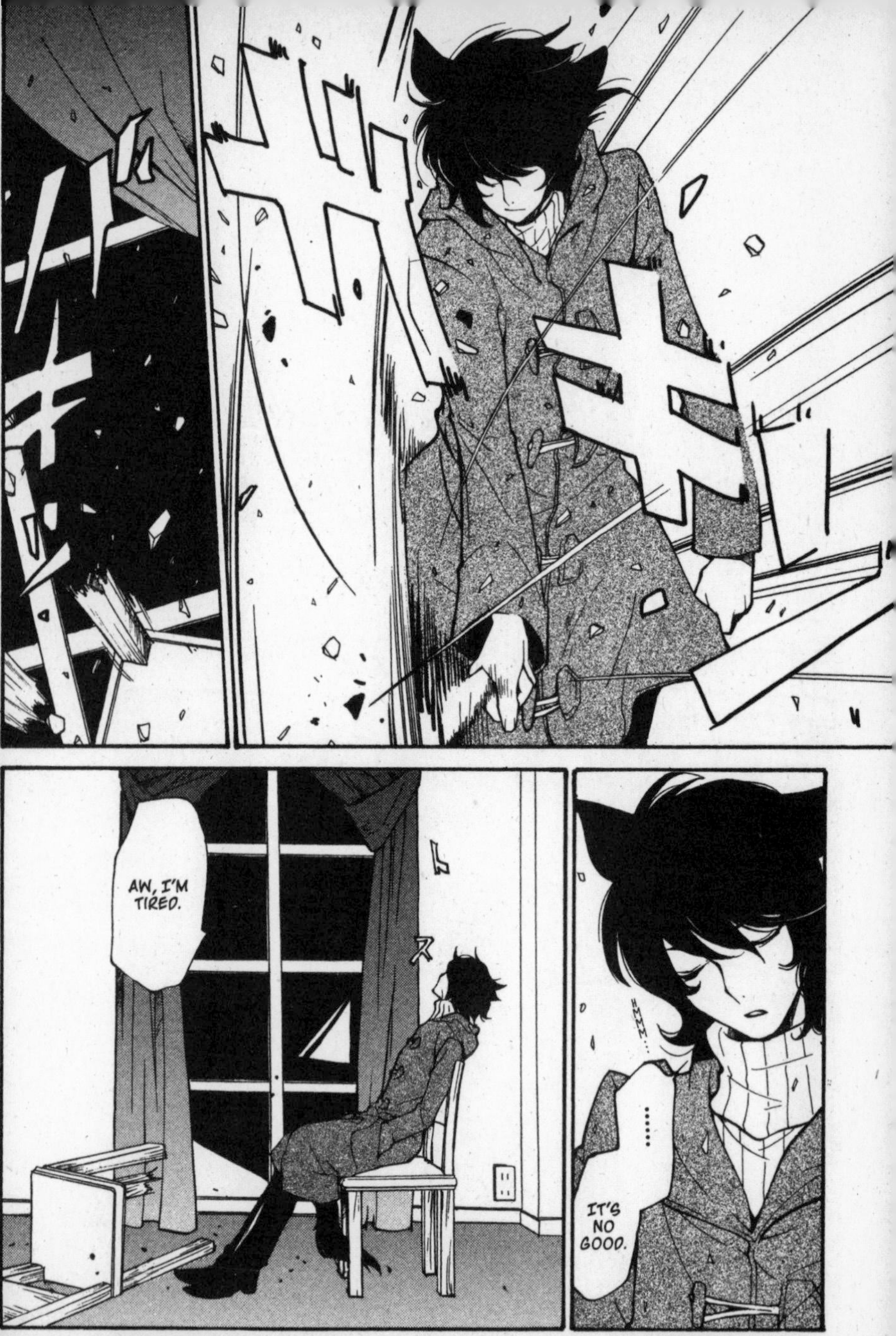
HMMM...
......
IT'S NO GOOD.
AW, I'M TIRED.

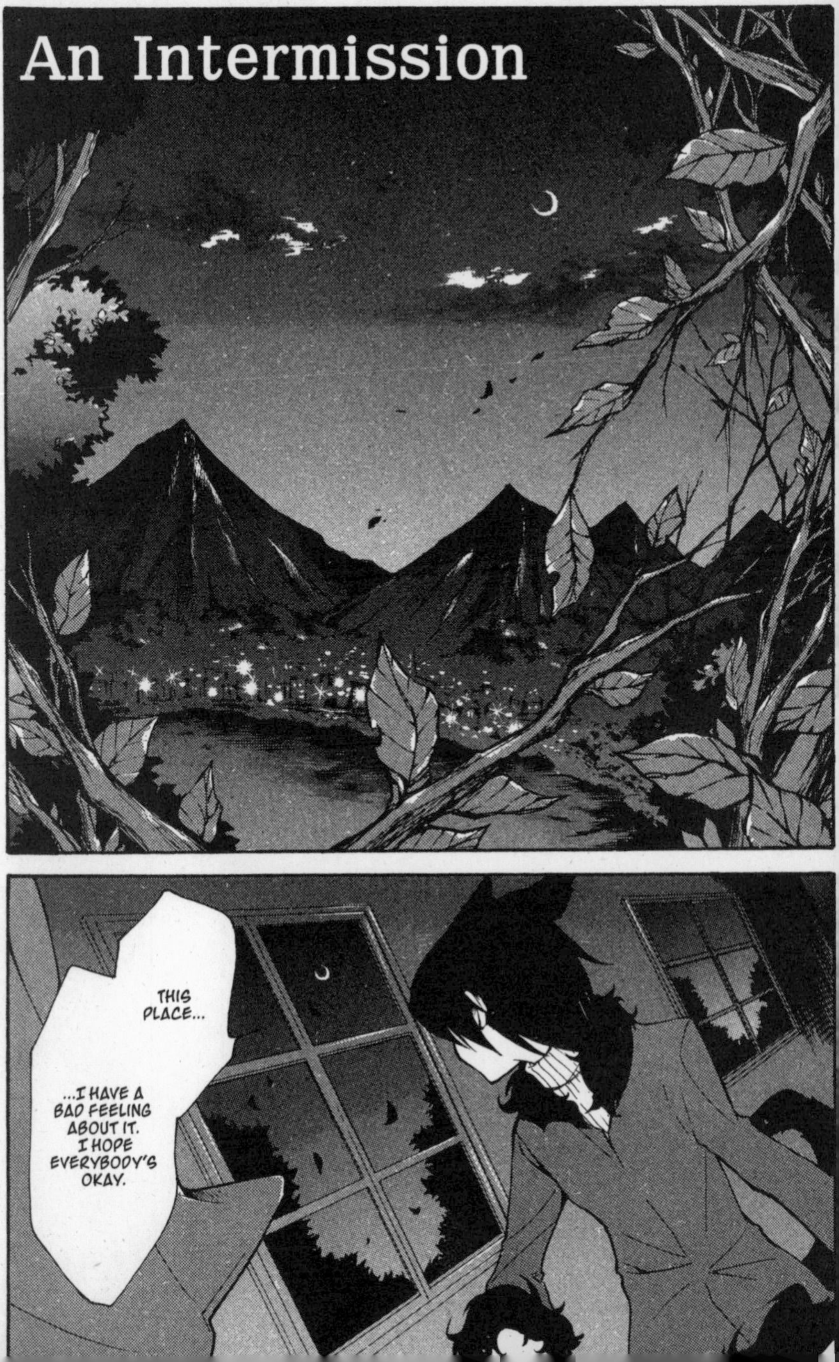
An Intermission
THIS PLACE...
...I HAVE A BAD FEELING ABOUT IT. I HOPE EVERYBODY'S OKAY.

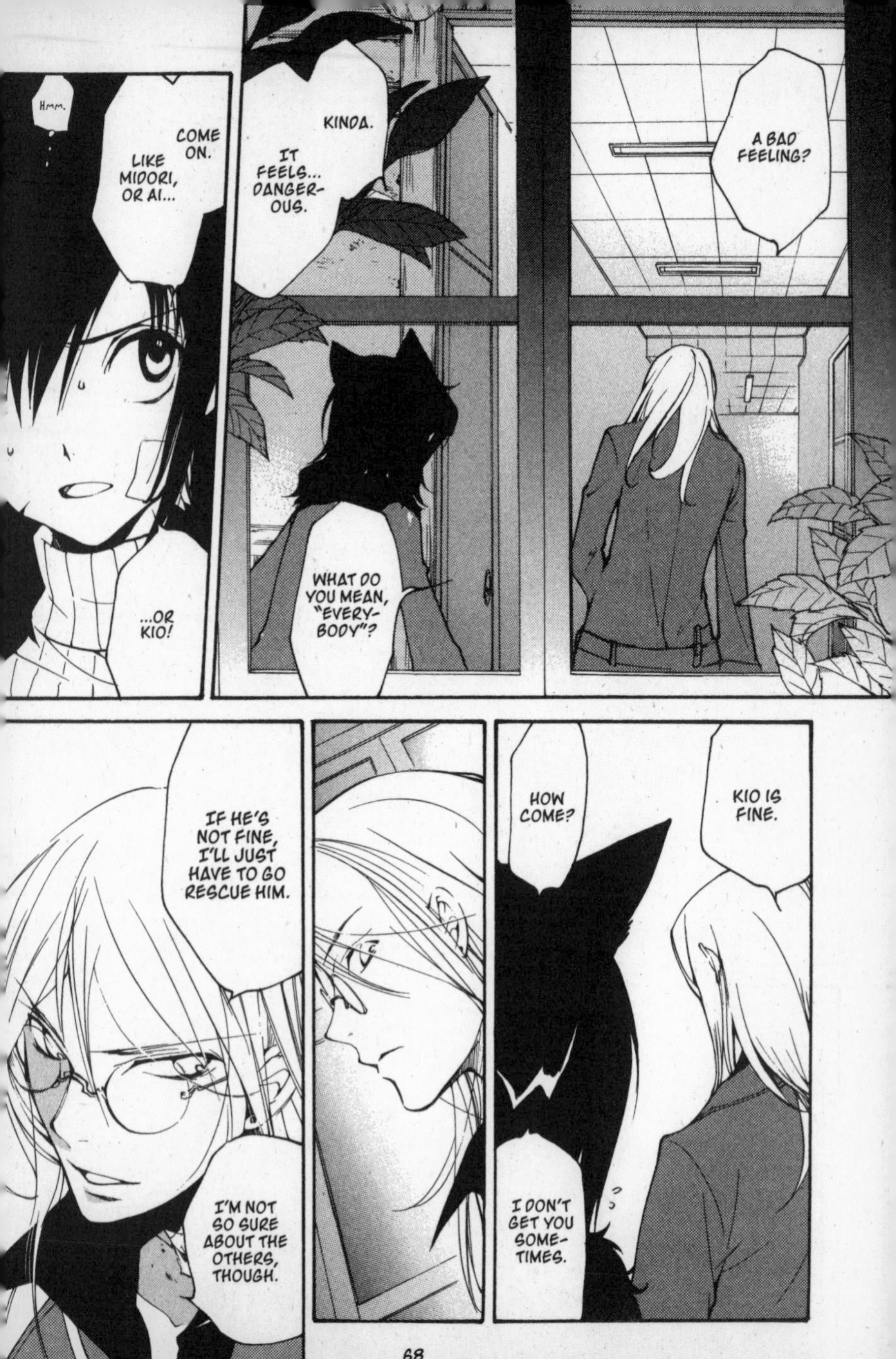
A BAD FEELING?
KINDA.
IT FEELS... DANGER-OUS.
WHAT DO YOU MEAN, "EVERY-BODY"?
Hmm.
COME ON.
LIKE MIDORI, OR AI...
...OR KIO!
KIO IS FINE.
HOW COME?
I DON'T GET YOU SOME-TIMES.
IF HE'S NOT FINE, I'LL JUST HAVE TO GO RESCUE HIM.
I'M NOT SO SURE ABOUT THE OTHERS, THOUGH.

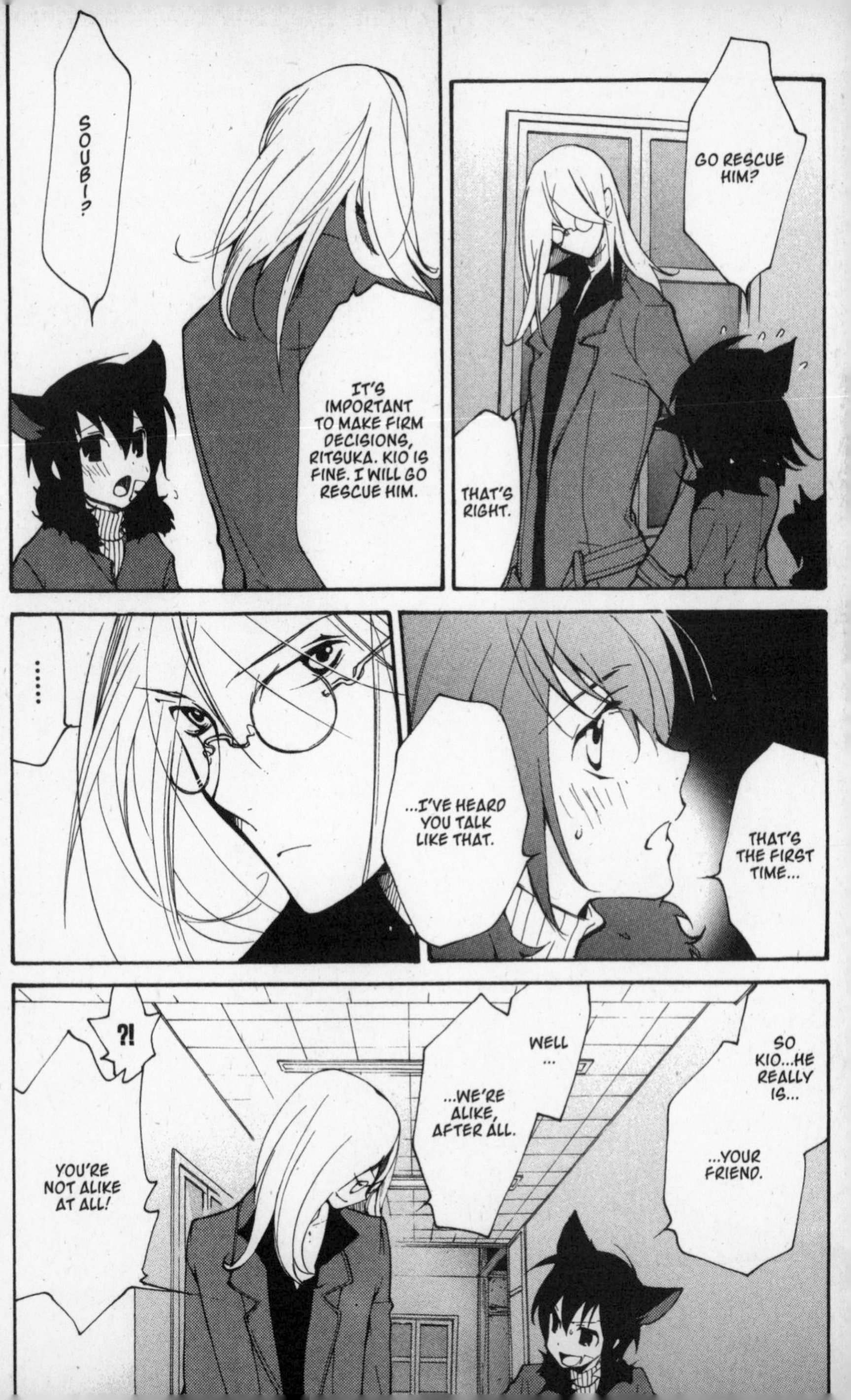
GO RESCUE HIM?
THAT'S RIGHT.
IT'S IMPORTANT TO MAKE FIRM DECISIONS, RITSUKA. KIO IS FINE. I WILL GO RESCUE HIM.
SOUBI?
THAT'S THE FIRST TIME...
...I'VE HEARD YOU TALK LIKE THAT.
......
SO KIO...HE REALLY IS...
...YOUR FRIEND.
WELL ...
...WE'RE ALIKE, AFTER ALL.
?!
YOU'RE NOT ALIKE AT ALL!

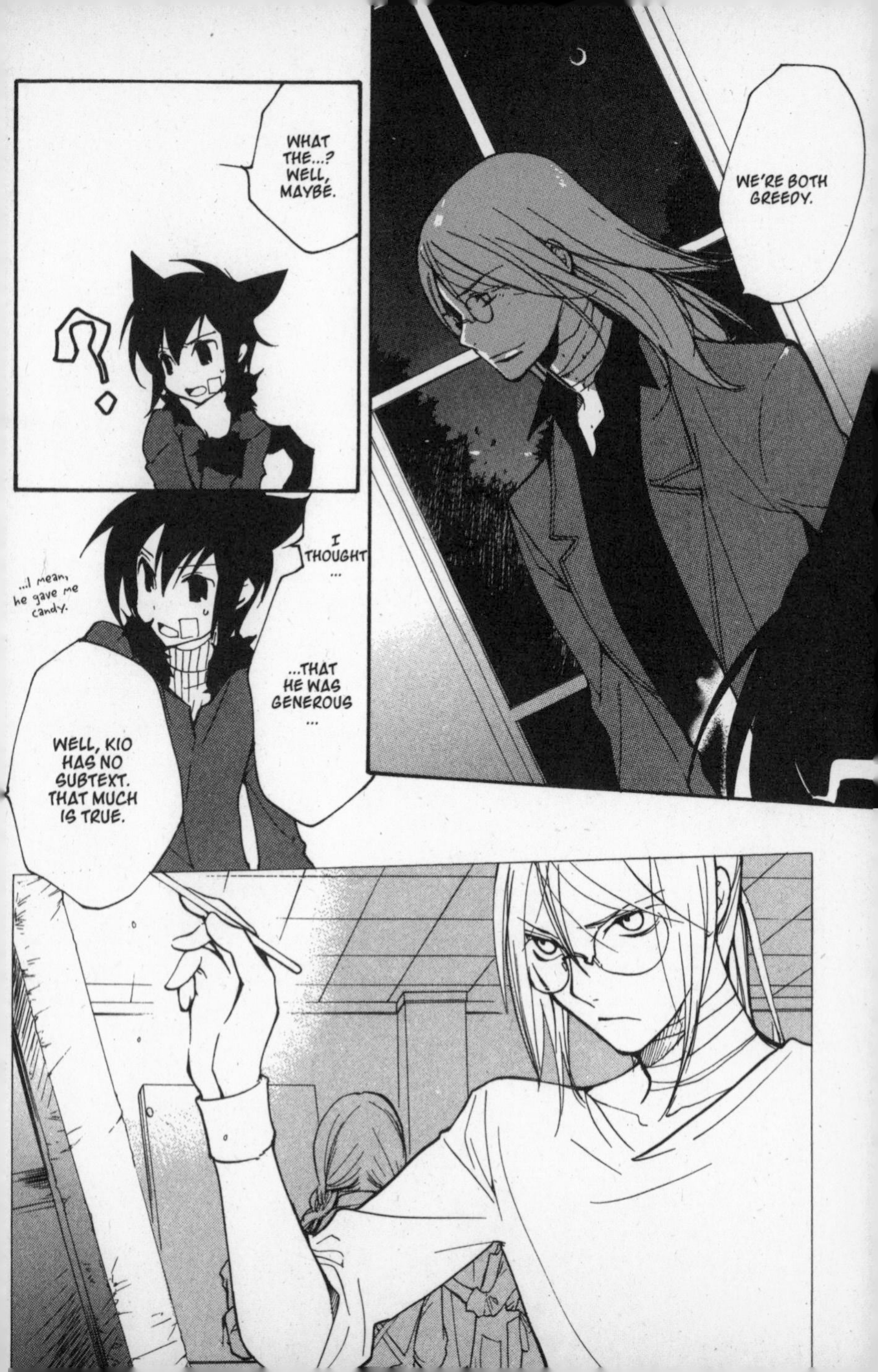
WE'RE BOTH GREEDY.
WHAT THE...? WELL, MAYBE.
I THOUGHT...
...THAT HE WAS GENEROUS...
...I mean, he gave me candy.
WELL, KIO HAS NO SUBTEXT. THAT MUCH IS TRUE.

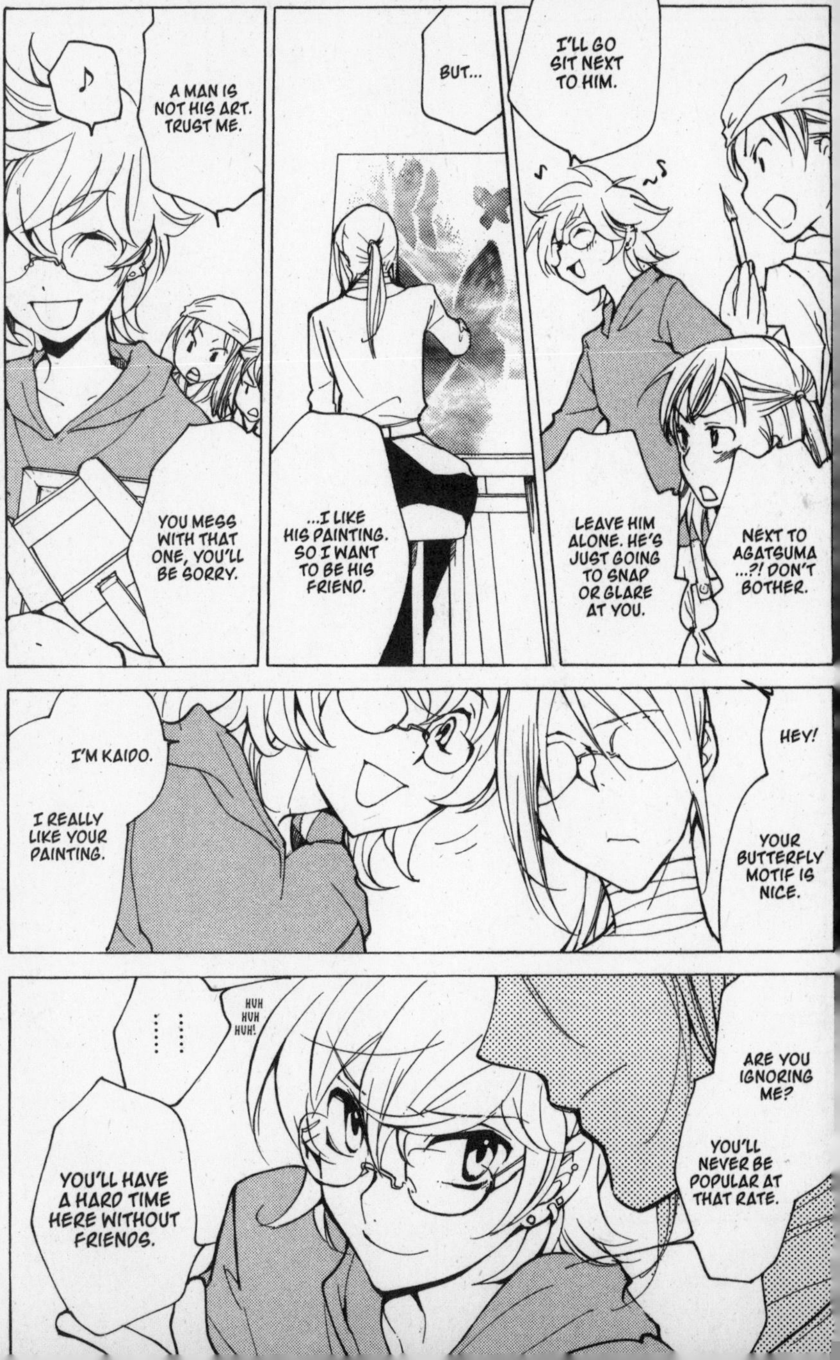
I'LL GO SIT NEXT TO HIM.
NEXT TO AGATSUMA ...?! DON'T BOTHER.
LEAVE HIM ALONE. HE'S JUST GOING TO SNAP OR GLARE AT YOU.
BUT...
...I LIKE HIS PAINTING. SO I WANT TO BE HIS FRIEND.
♪
A MAN IS NOT HIS ART. TRUST ME.
YOU MESS WITH THAT ONE, YOU'LL BE SORRY.
HEY!
YOUR BUTTERFLY MOTIF IS NICE.
I'M KAIDO.
I REALLY LIKE YOUR PAINTING.
ARE YOU IGNORING ME?
YOU'LL NEVER BE POPULAR AT THAT RATE.
HUH HUH HUH!
......
YOU'LL HAVE A HARD TIME HERE WITHOUT FRIENDS.

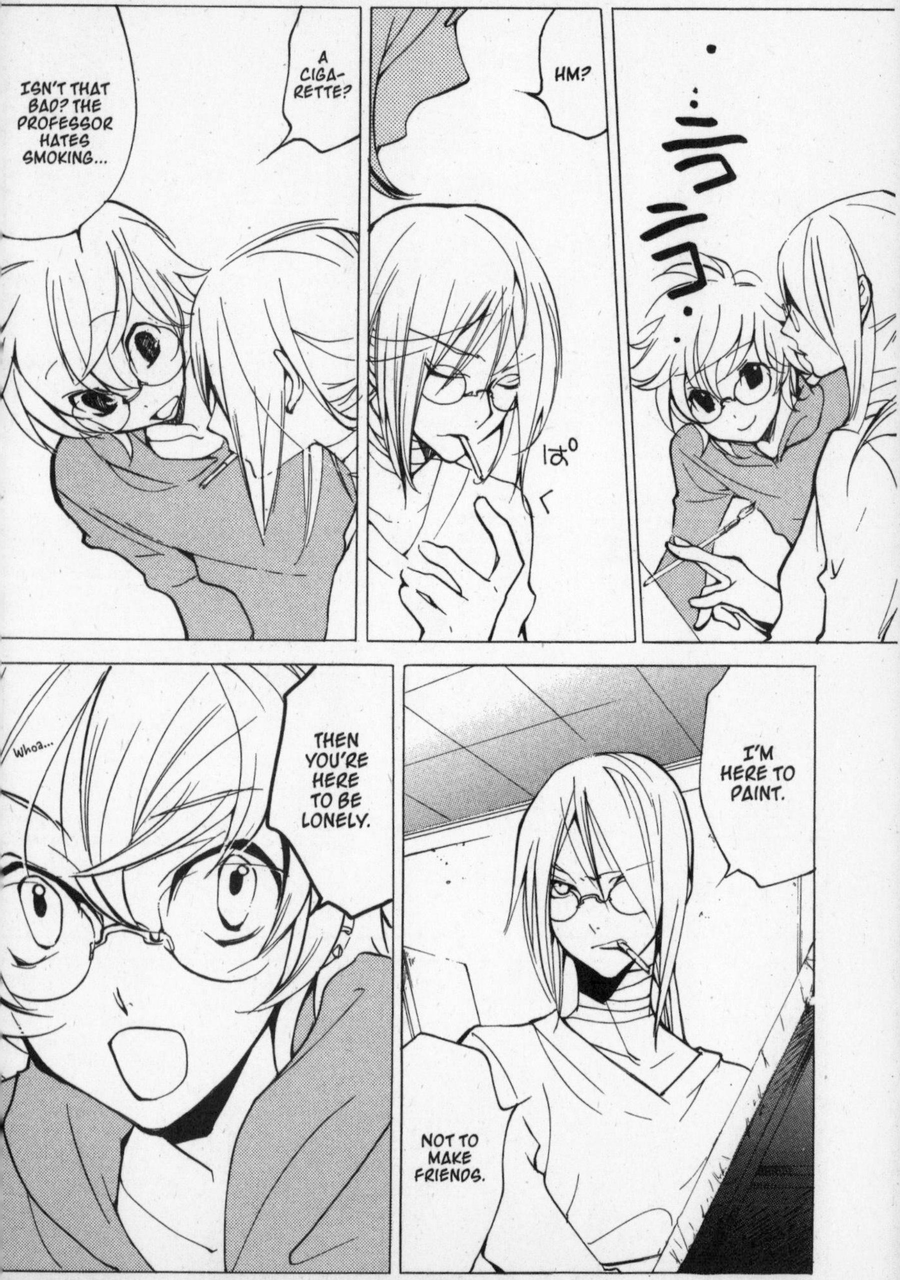

・・ニコニコ・・
HM?
ぱく
A CIGARETTE?
ISN'T THAT BAD? THE PROFESSOR HATES SMOKING...
I'M HERE TO PAINT.
NOT TO MAKE FRIENDS.
Whoa...
THEN YOU'RE HERE TO BE LONELY.

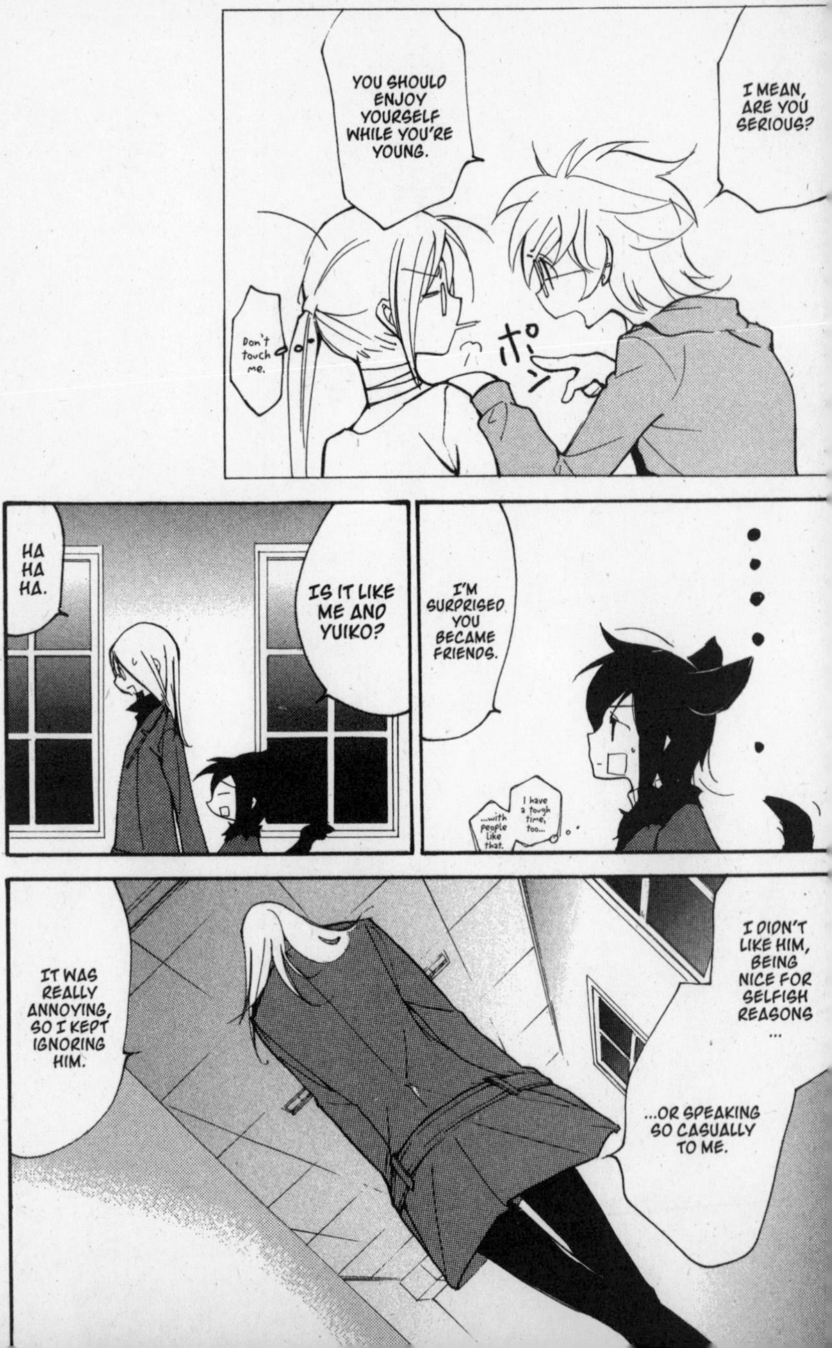
I MEAN, ARE YOU SERIOUS?
YOU SHOULD ENJOY YOURSELF WHILE YOU'RE YOUNG.
ポン
Don't touch me.
I'M SURPRISED YOU BECAME FRIENDS.
I have a tough time, too...
...with people like that.
IS IT LIKE ME AND YUIKO?
HA HA HA.
I DIDN'T LIKE HIM, BEING NICE FOR SELFISH REASONS ...
...OR SPEAKING SO CASUALLY TO ME.
IT WAS REALLY ANNOYING, SO I KEPT IGNORING HIM.

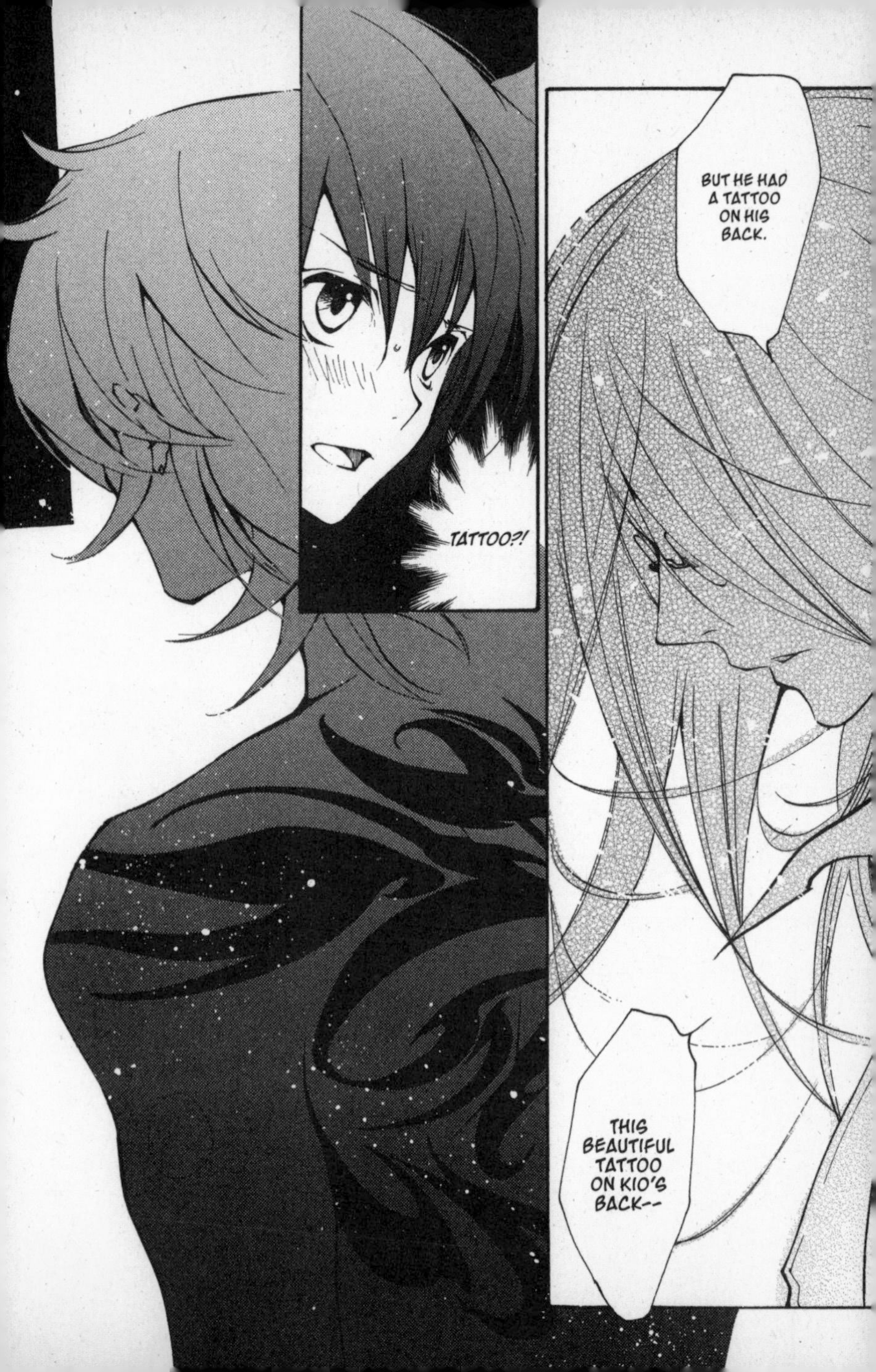

BUT HE HAD A TATTOO ON HIS BACK.
THIS BEAUTIFUL TATTOO ON KIO'S BACK--
TATTOO?!

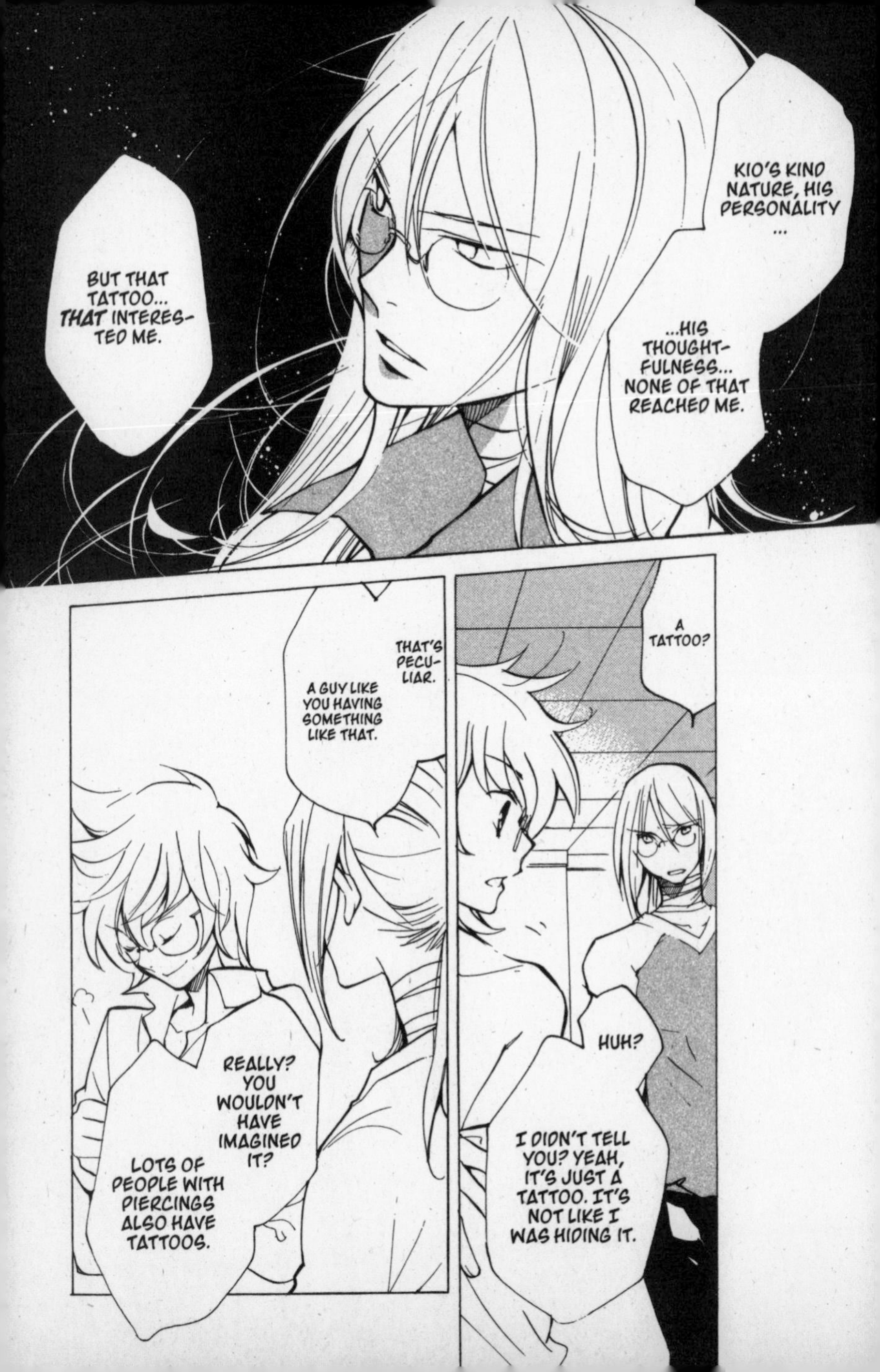
KIO'S KIND NATURE, HIS PERSONALITY ...
...HIS THOUGHT-FULNESS... NONE OF THAT REACHED ME.
BUT THAT TATTOO... *THAT* INTERES-TED ME.
A TATTOO?
HUH?
I DIDN'T TELL YOU? YEAH, IT'S JUST A TATTOO. IT'S NOT LIKE I WAS HIDING IT.
THAT'S PECU-LIAR.
A GUY LIKE YOU HAVING SOMETHING LIKE THAT.
REALLY? YOU WOULDN'T HAVE IMAGINED IT?
LOTS OF PEOPLE WITH PIERCINGS ALSO HAVE TATTOOS.

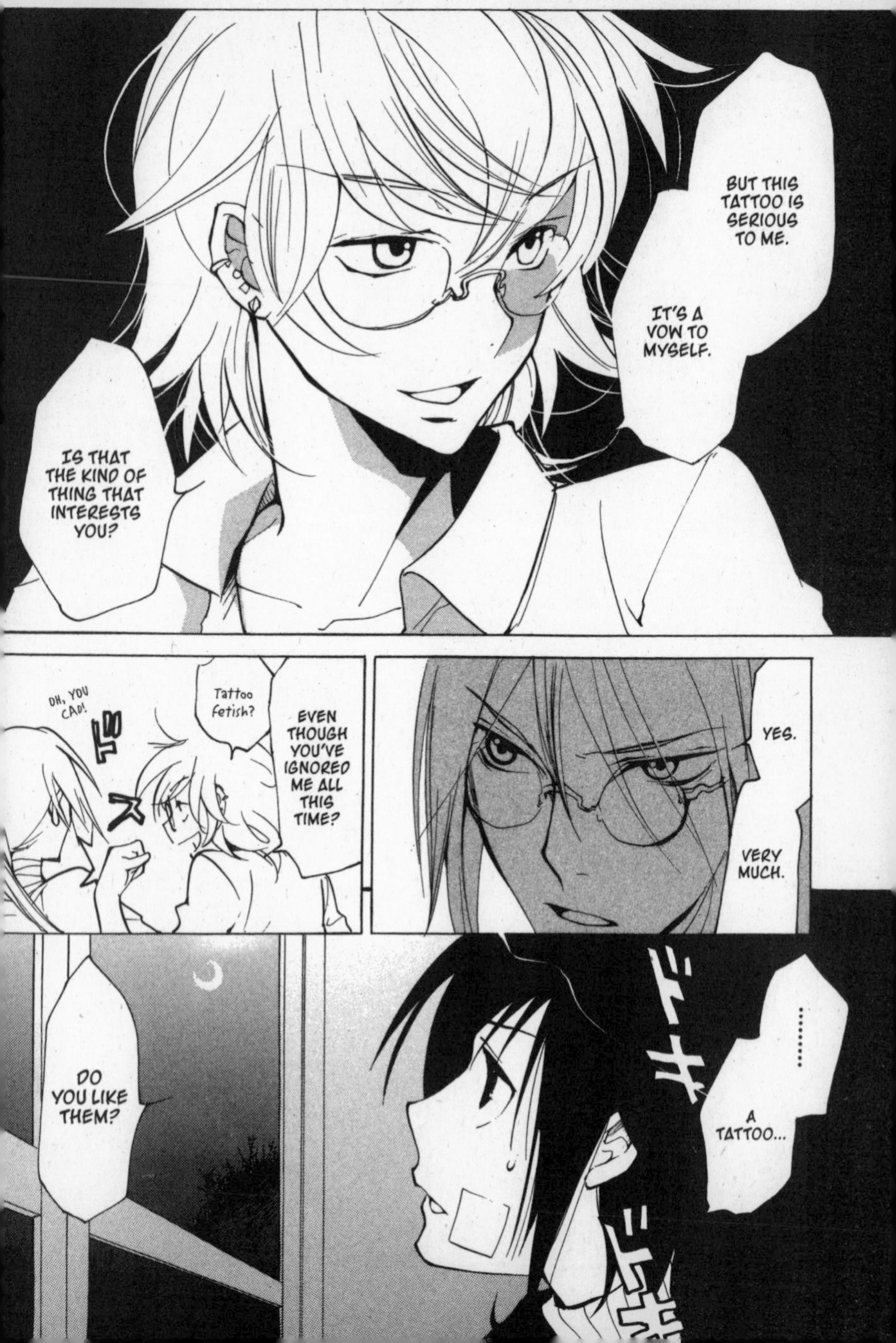
BUT THIS TATTOO IS SERIOUS TO ME.
IT'S A VOW TO MYSELF.
IS THAT THE KIND OF THING THAT INTERESTS YOU?
YES.
VERY MUCH.
EVEN THOUGH YOU'VE IGNORED ME ALL THIS TIME?
Tattoo fetish?
OH, YOU CAD!
......
A TATTOO...
DO YOU LIKE THEM?

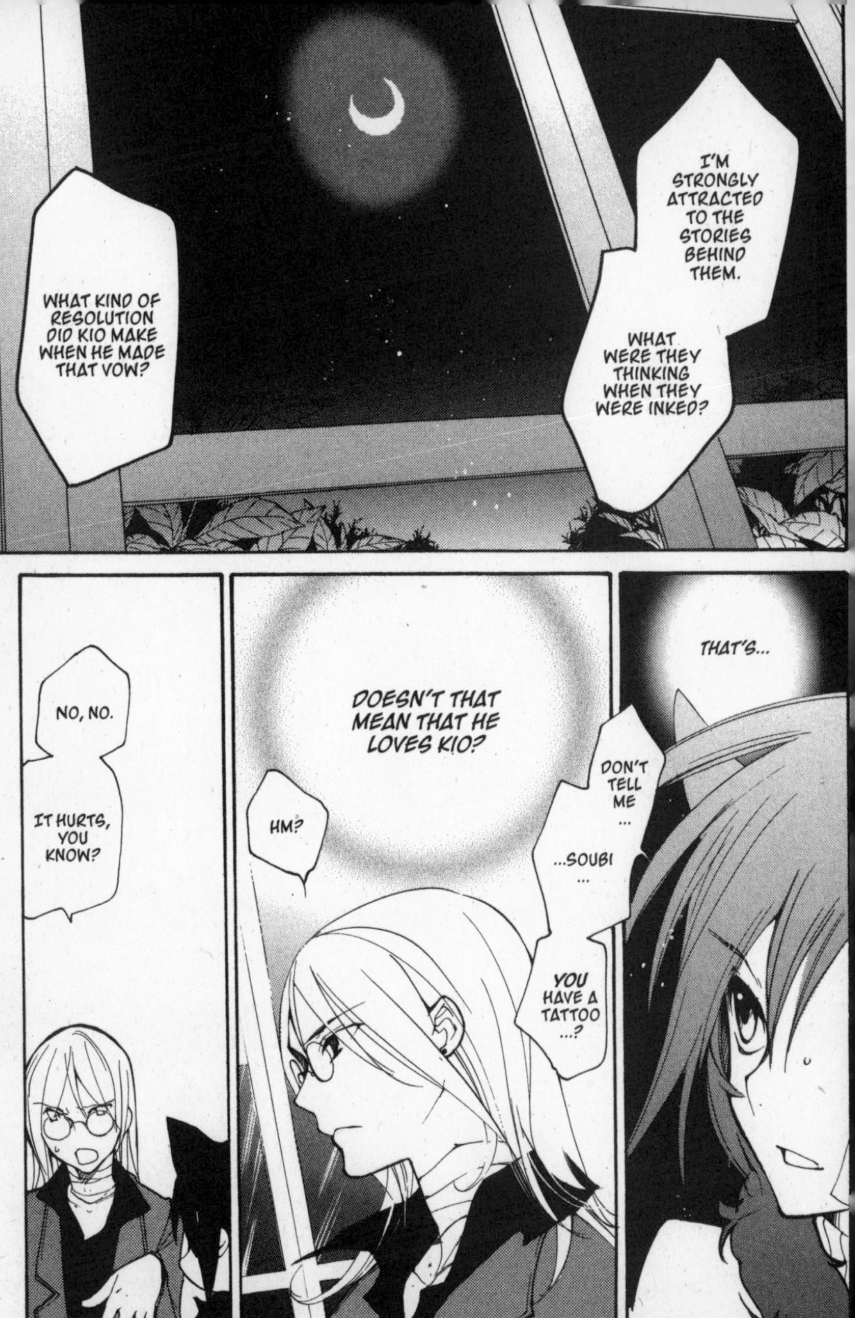
I'M STRONGLY ATTRACTED TO THE STORIES BEHIND THEM.
WHAT WERE THEY THINKING WHEN THEY WERE INKED?
WHAT KIND OF RESOLUTION DID KIO MAKE WHEN HE MADE THAT VOW?
THAT'S...
DON'T TELL ME ...
...SOUBI ...
YOU HAVE A TATTOO ...?
DOESN'T THAT MEAN THAT HE LOVES KIO?
HM?
NO, NO.
IT HURTS, YOU KNOW?

The Septimal Moon Chapters
Chapter 13

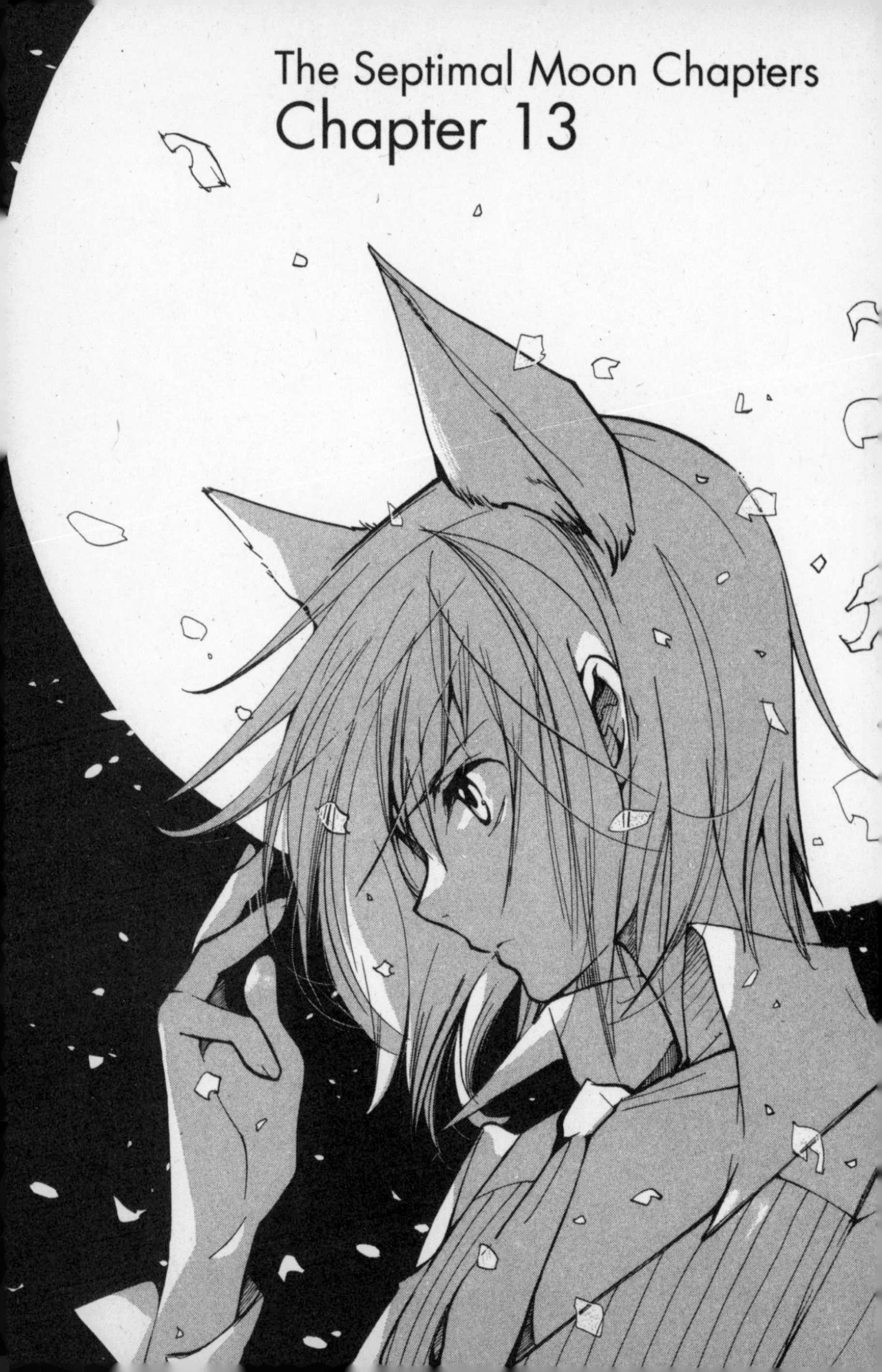

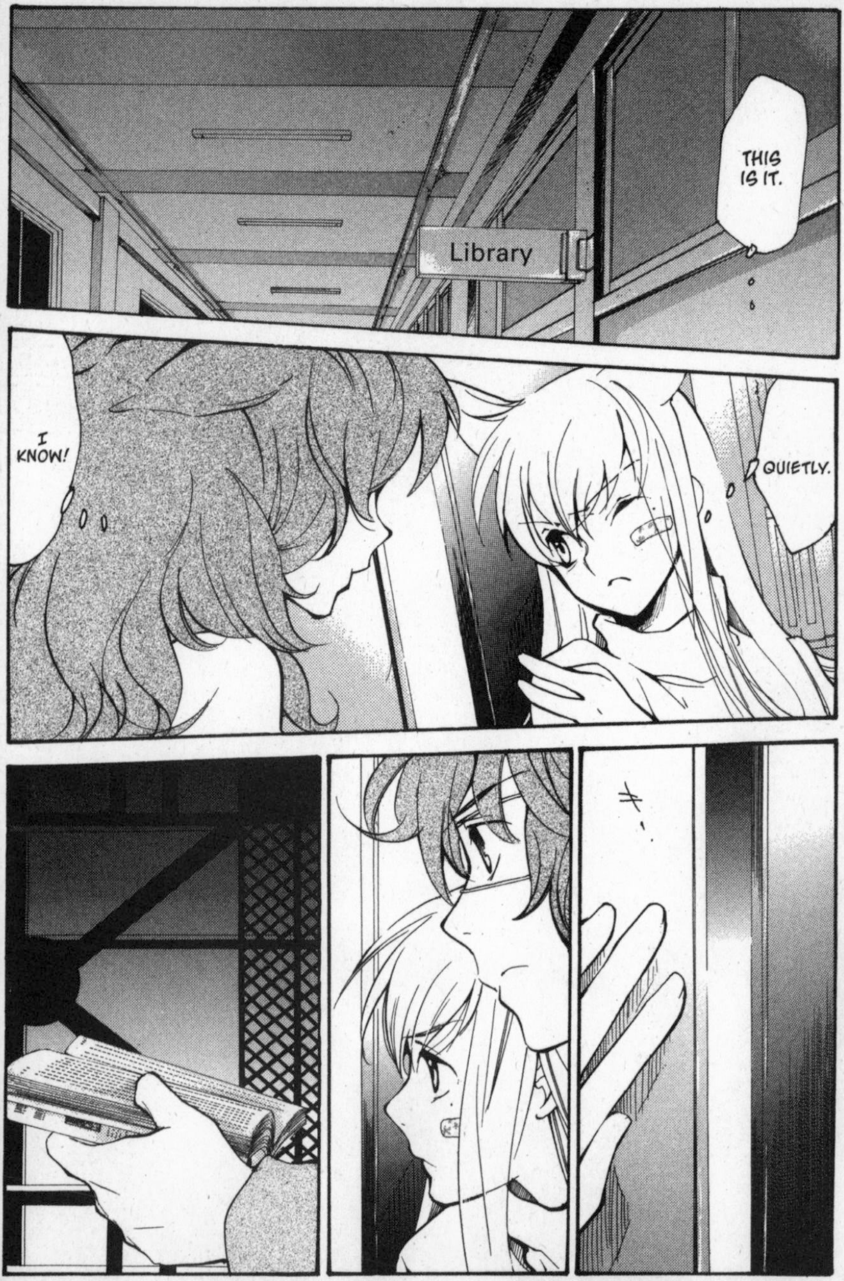
Library
THIS IS IT.
QUIETLY.
I KNOW!

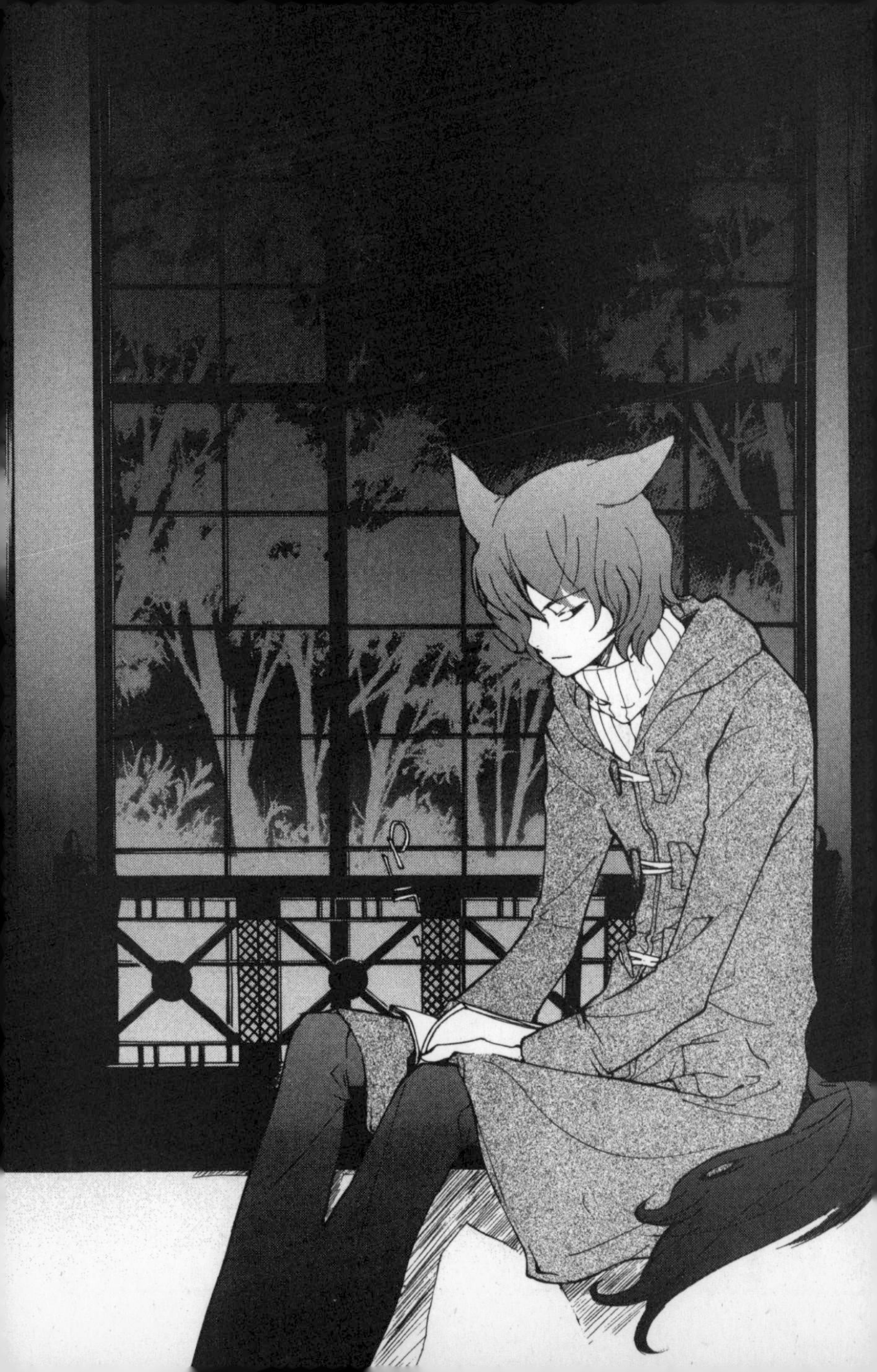

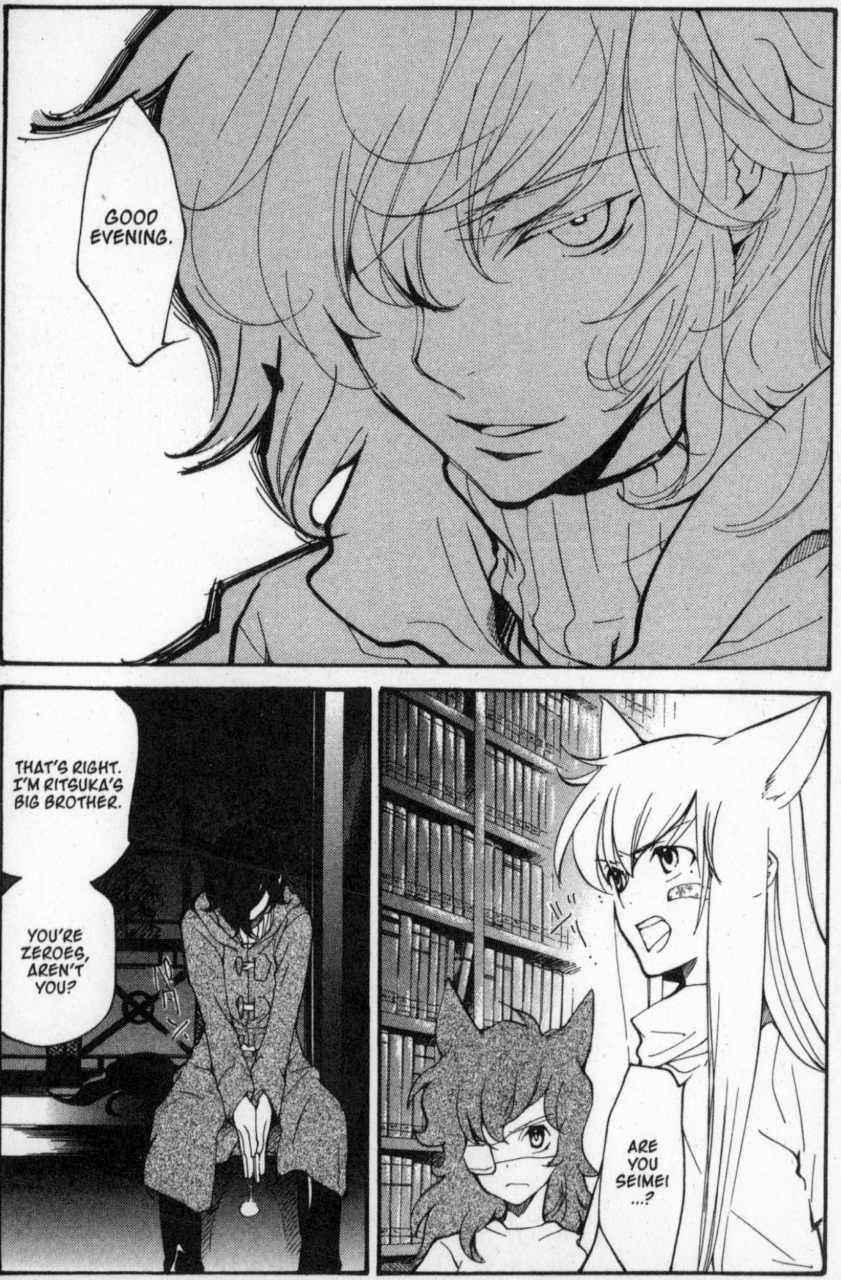
GOOD EVENING.
ARE YOU SEIMEI ...?
THAT'S RIGHT. I'M RITSUKA'S BIG BROTHER.
YOU'RE ZEROES, AREN'T YOU?

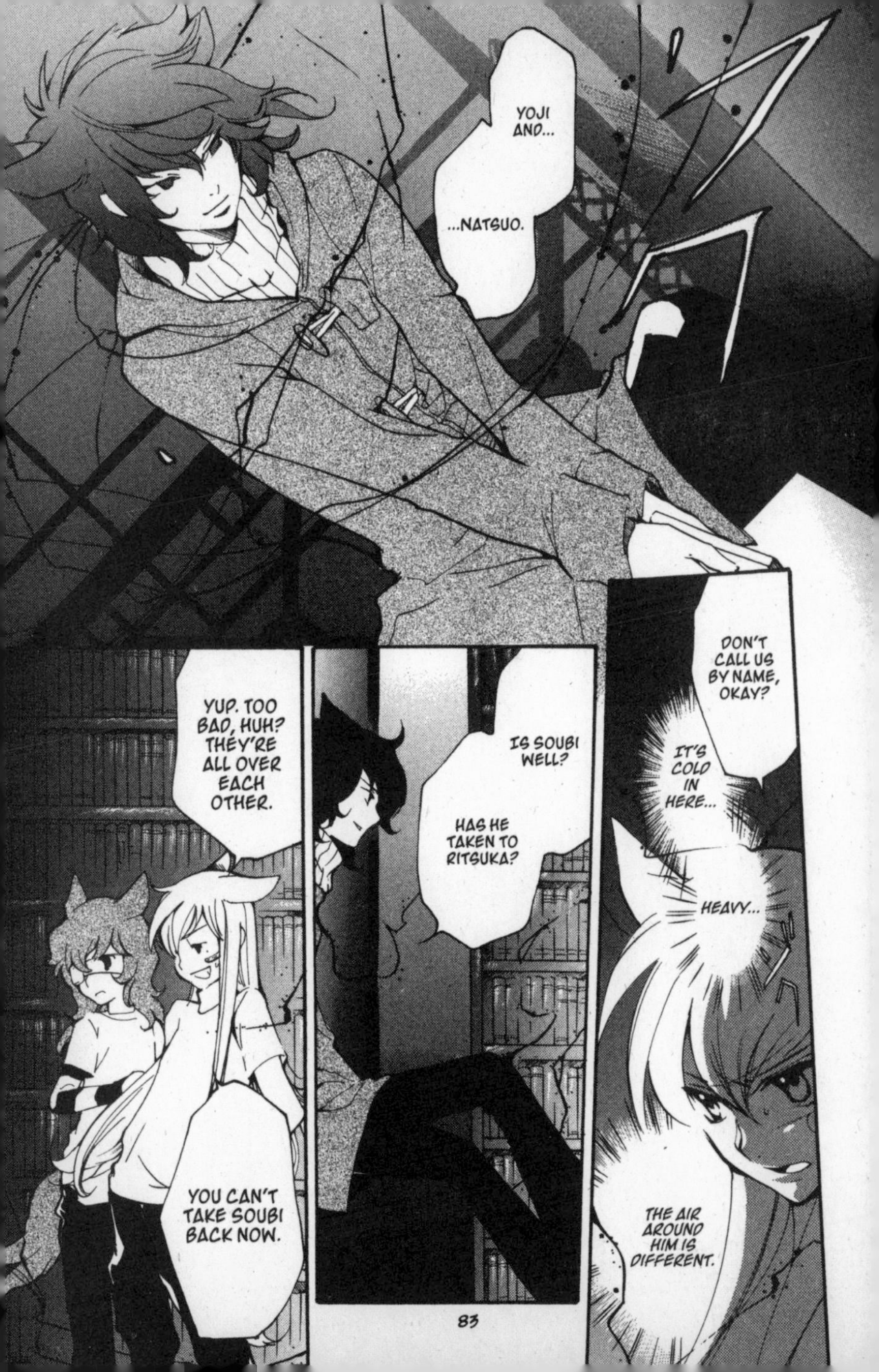
YOJI AND...
...NATSUO.
DON'T CALL US BY NAME, OKAY?
IT'S COLD IN HERE...
HEAVY...
THE AIR AROUND HIM IS DIFFERENT.
IS SOUBI WELL?
HAS HE TAKEN TO RITSUKA?
YUP. TOO BAD, HUH? THEY'RE ALL OVER EACH OTHER.
YOU CAN'T TAKE SOUBI BACK NOW.

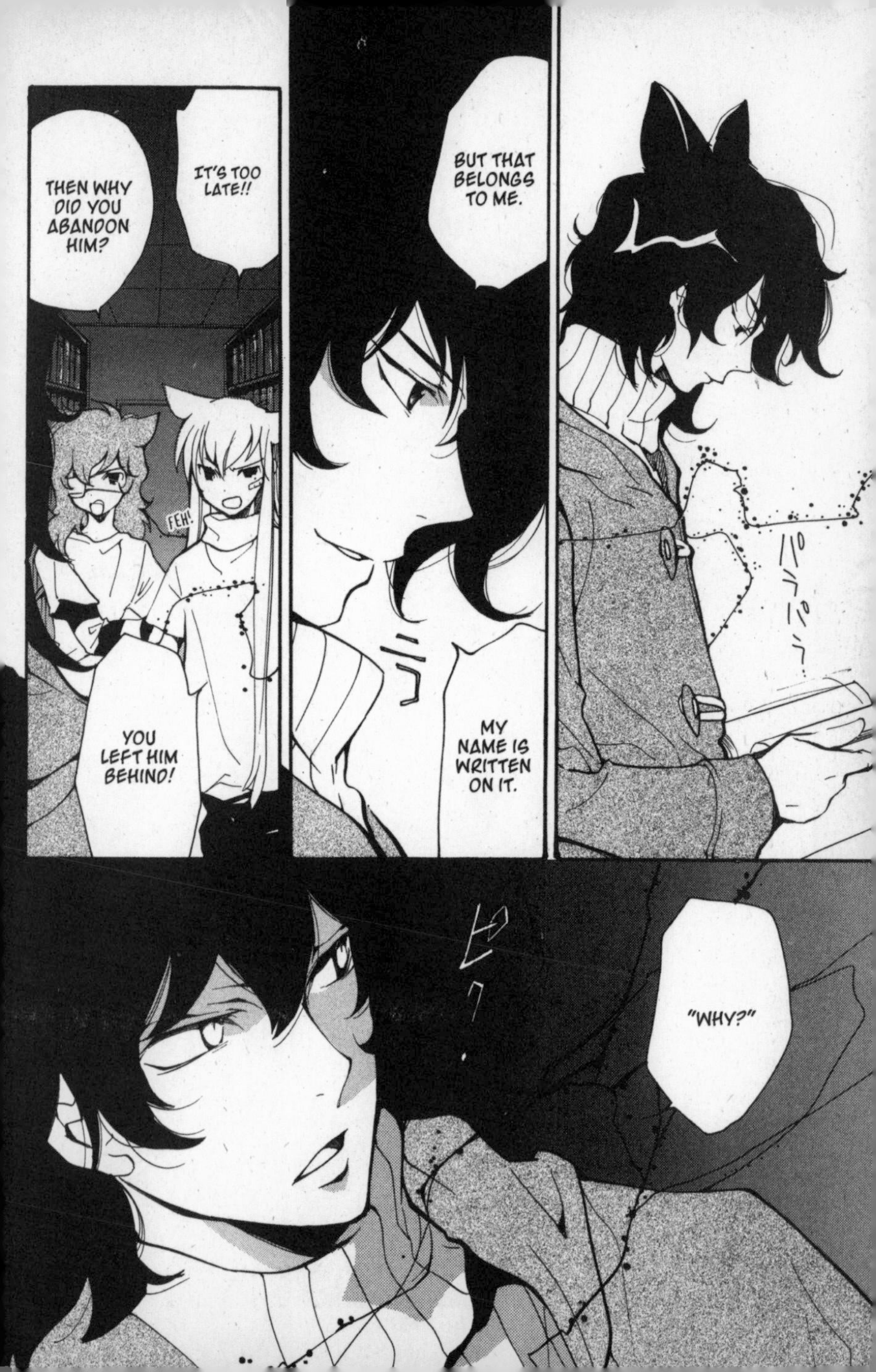
パラパラ
BUT THAT BELONGS TO ME.
ニコ
MY NAME IS WRITTEN ON IT.
IT'S TOO LATE!!
THEN WHY DID YOU ABANDON HIM?
FEH!
YOU LEFT HIM BEHIND!
"WHY?"
ピク

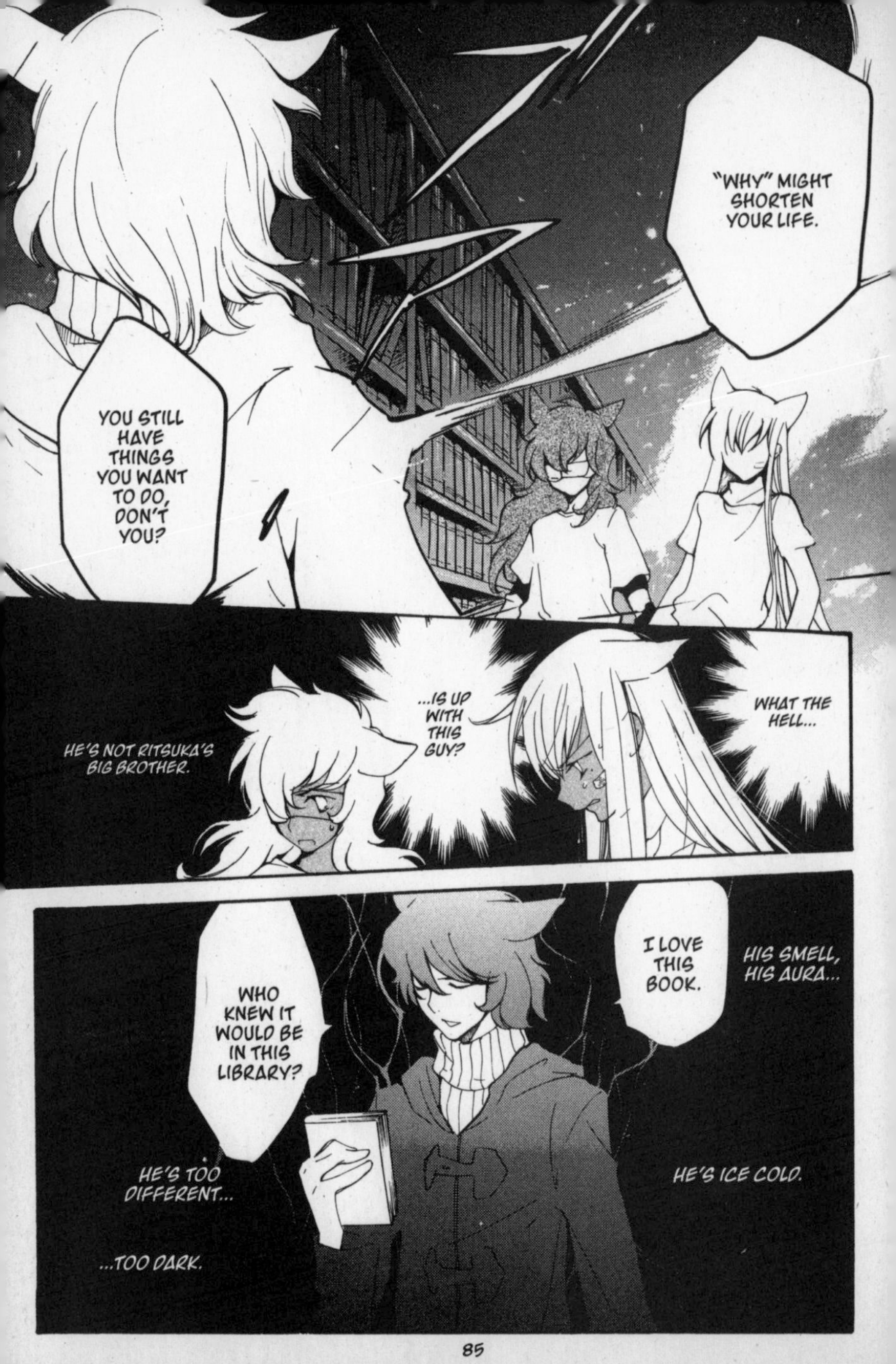
"WHY" MIGHT SHORTEN YOUR LIFE.
YOU STILL HAVE THINGS YOU WANT TO DO, DON'T YOU?
WHAT THE HELL...
...IS UP WITH THIS GUY?
HE'S NOT RITSUKA'S BIG BROTHER.
HIS SMELL, HIS AURA...
I LOVE THIS BOOK.
WHO KNEW IT WOULD BE IN THIS LIBRARY?
HE'S ICE COLD.
HE'S TOO DIFFERENT...
...TOO DARK.

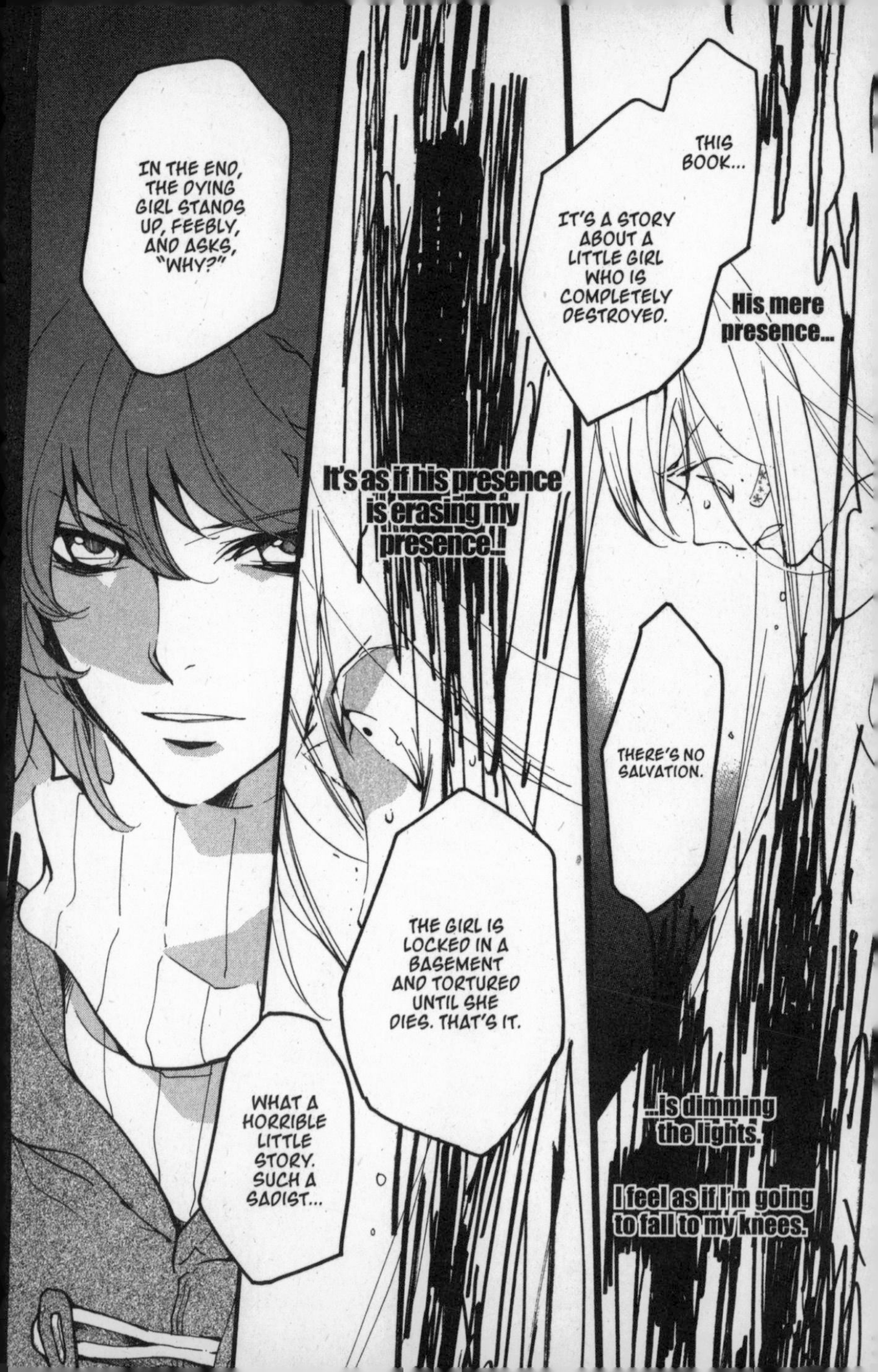
THIS BOOK...
IT'S A STORY ABOUT A LITTLE GIRL WHO IS COMPLETELY DESTROYED.
His mere presence...
THERE'S NO SALVATION.
...is dimming the lights.
I feel as if I'm going to fall to my knees.
It's as if his presence is erasing my presence..!!
THE GIRL IS LOCKED IN A BASEMENT AND TORTURED UNTIL SHE DIES. THAT'S IT.
IN THE END, THE DYING GIRL STANDS UP, FEEBLY, AND ASKS, "WHY?"
WHAT A HORRIBLE LITTLE STORY. SUCH A SADIST...

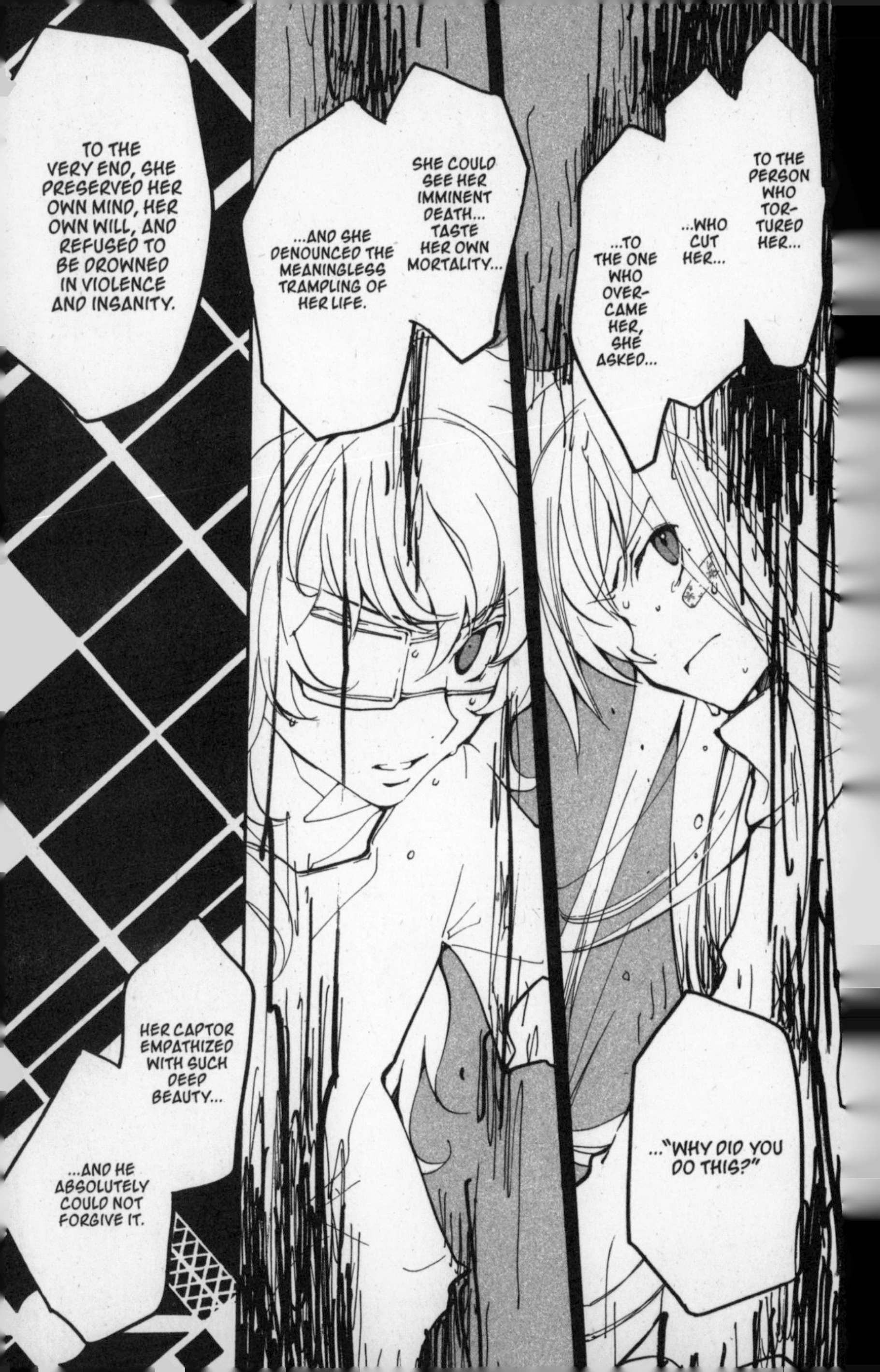
TO THE PERSON WHO TORTURED HER...
...WHO CUT HER...
...TO THE ONE WHO OVERCAME HER, SHE ASKED...
..."WHY DID YOU DO THIS?"
SHE COULD SEE HER IMMINENT DEATH... TASTE HER OWN MORTALITY...
...AND SHE DENOUNCED THE MEANINGLESS TRAMPLING OF HER LIFE.
TO THE VERY END, SHE PRESERVED HER OWN MIND, HER OWN WILL, AND REFUSED TO BE DROWNED IN VIOLENCE AND INSANITY.
HER CAPTOR EMPATHIZED WITH SUCH DEEP BEAUTY...
...AND HE ABSOLUTELY COULD NOT FORGIVE IT.

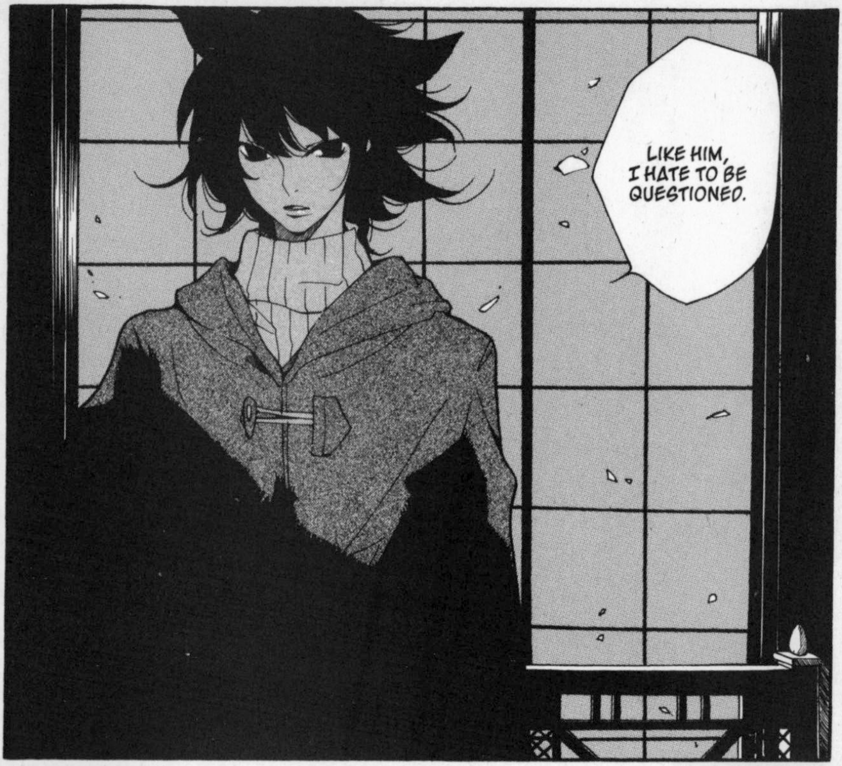
LIKE HIM, I HATE TO BE QUESTIONED.

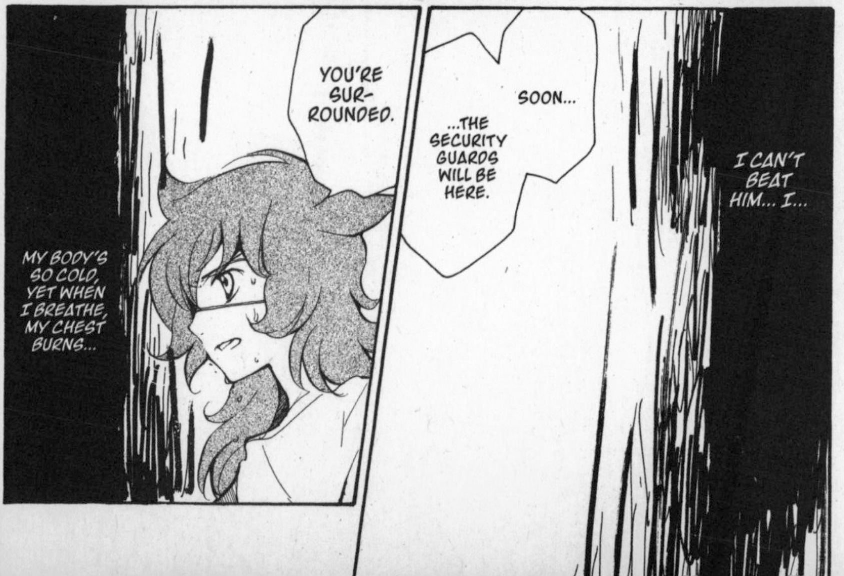
YOU'RE SUR-ROUNDED.
SOON...
...THE SECURITY GUARDS WILL BE HERE.
I CAN'T BEAT HIM... I...
MY BODY'S SO COLD, YET WHEN I BREATHE, MY CHEST BURNS...

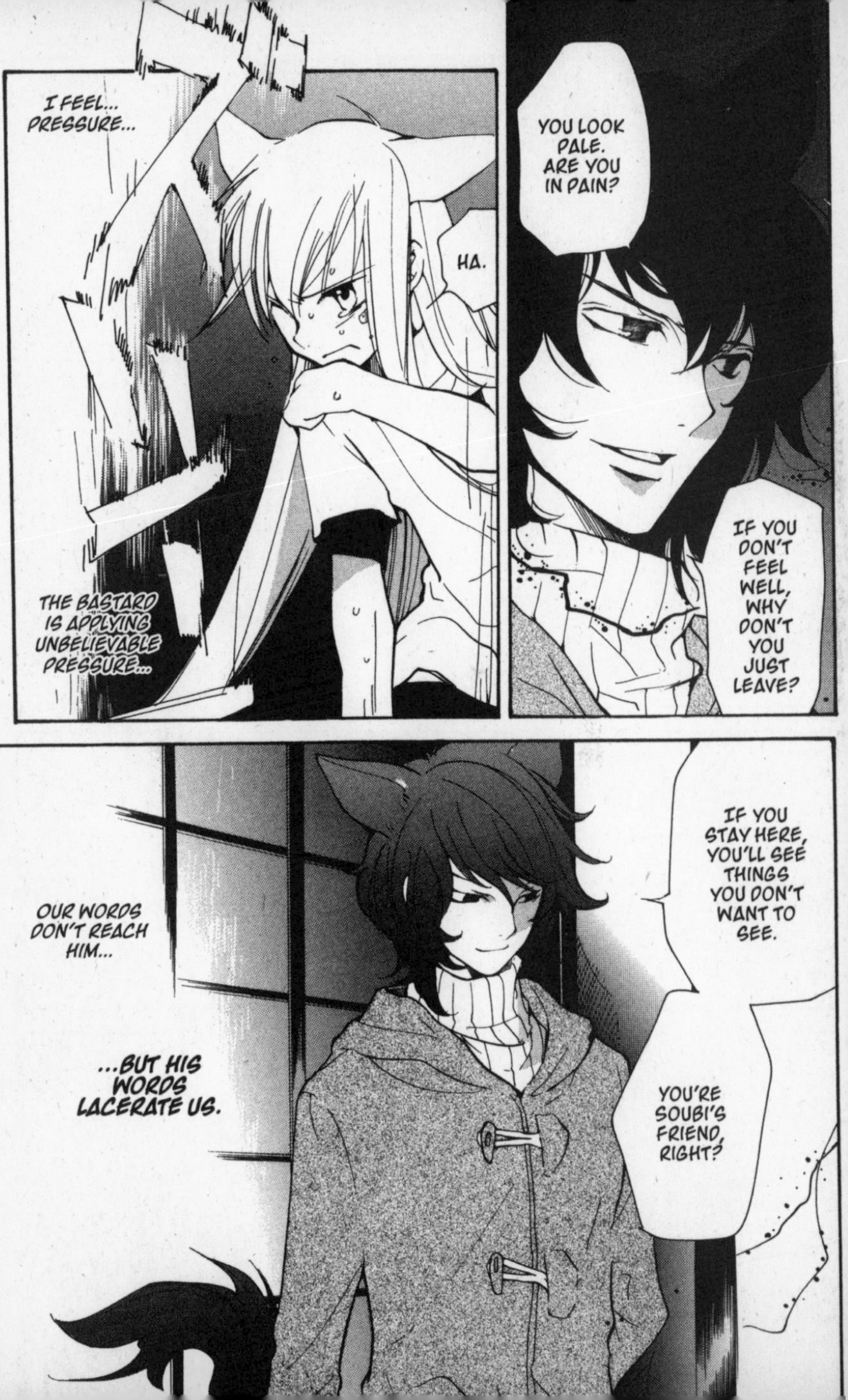
YOU LOOK PALE. ARE YOU IN PAIN?
IF YOU DON'T FEEL WELL, WHY DON'T YOU JUST LEAVE?
I FEEL... PRESSURE...
HA.
THE BASTARD IS APPLYING UNBELIEVABLE PRESSURE...
IF YOU STAY HERE, YOU'LL SEE THINGS YOU DON'T WANT TO SEE.
YOU'RE SOUBI'S FRIEND, RIGHT?
OUR WORDS DON'T REACH HIM...
...BUT HIS WORDS LACERATE US.

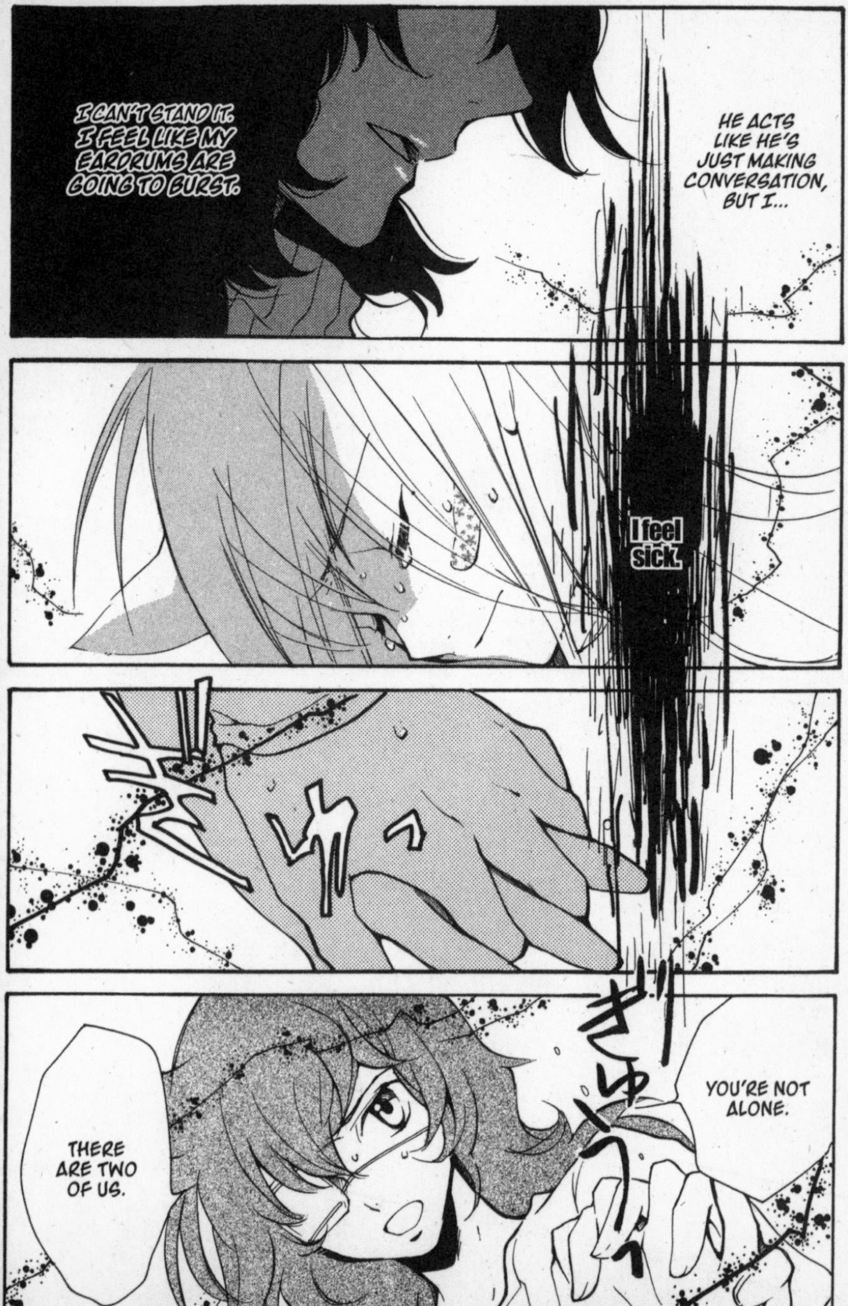
HE ACTS LIKE HE'S JUST MAKING CONVERSATION, BUT I...
I CAN'T STAND IT. I FEEL LIKE MY EARDRUMS ARE GOING TO BURST.
I feel sick.
YOU'RE NOT ALONE.
THERE ARE TWO OF US.

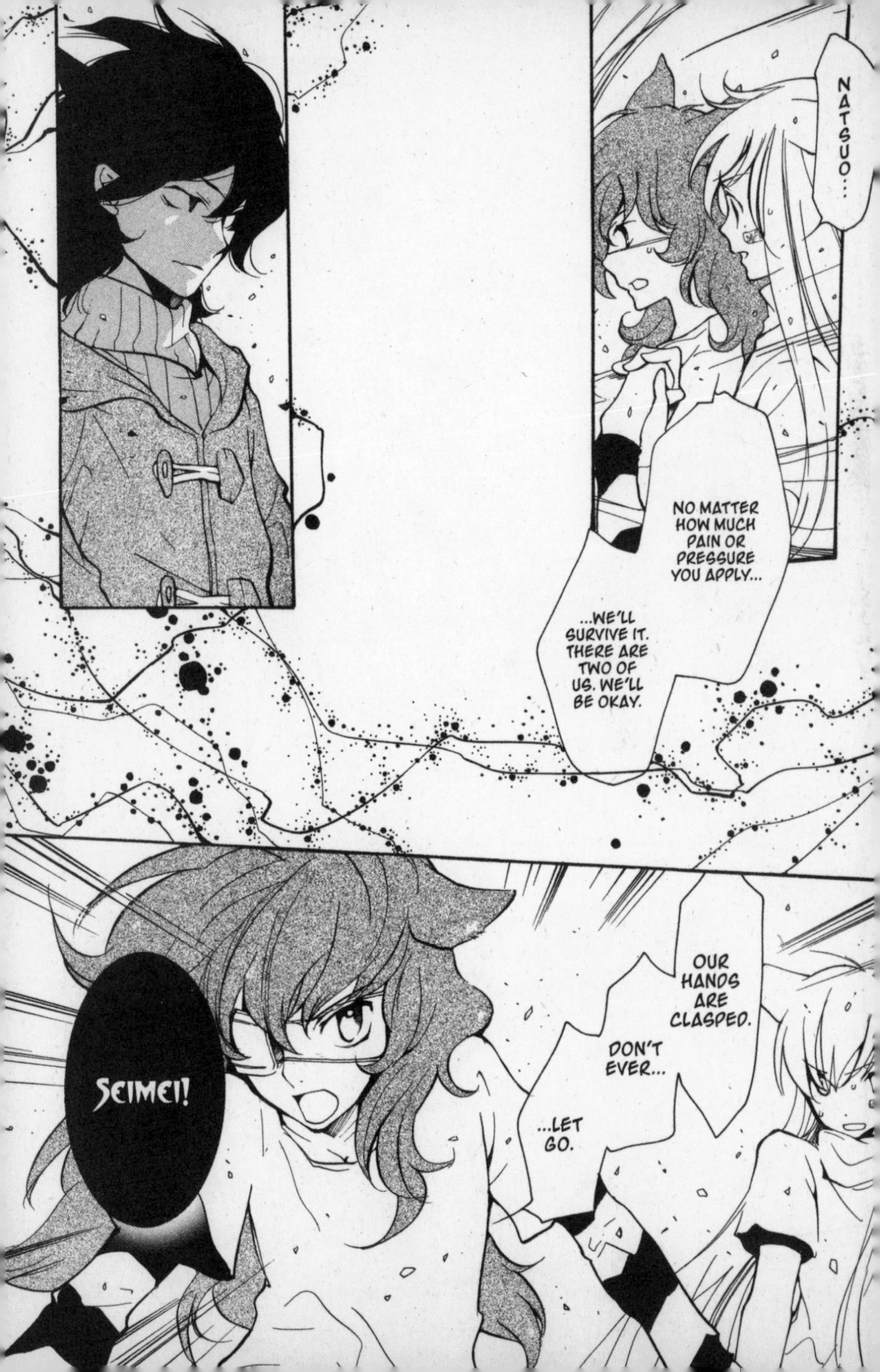
NATSUO...
NO MATTER HOW MUCH PAIN OR PRESSURE YOU APPLY...
...WE'LL SURVIVE IT. THERE ARE TWO OF US. WE'LL BE OKAY.
OUR HANDS ARE CLASPED.
DON'T EVER...
...LET GO.
SEIMEI!

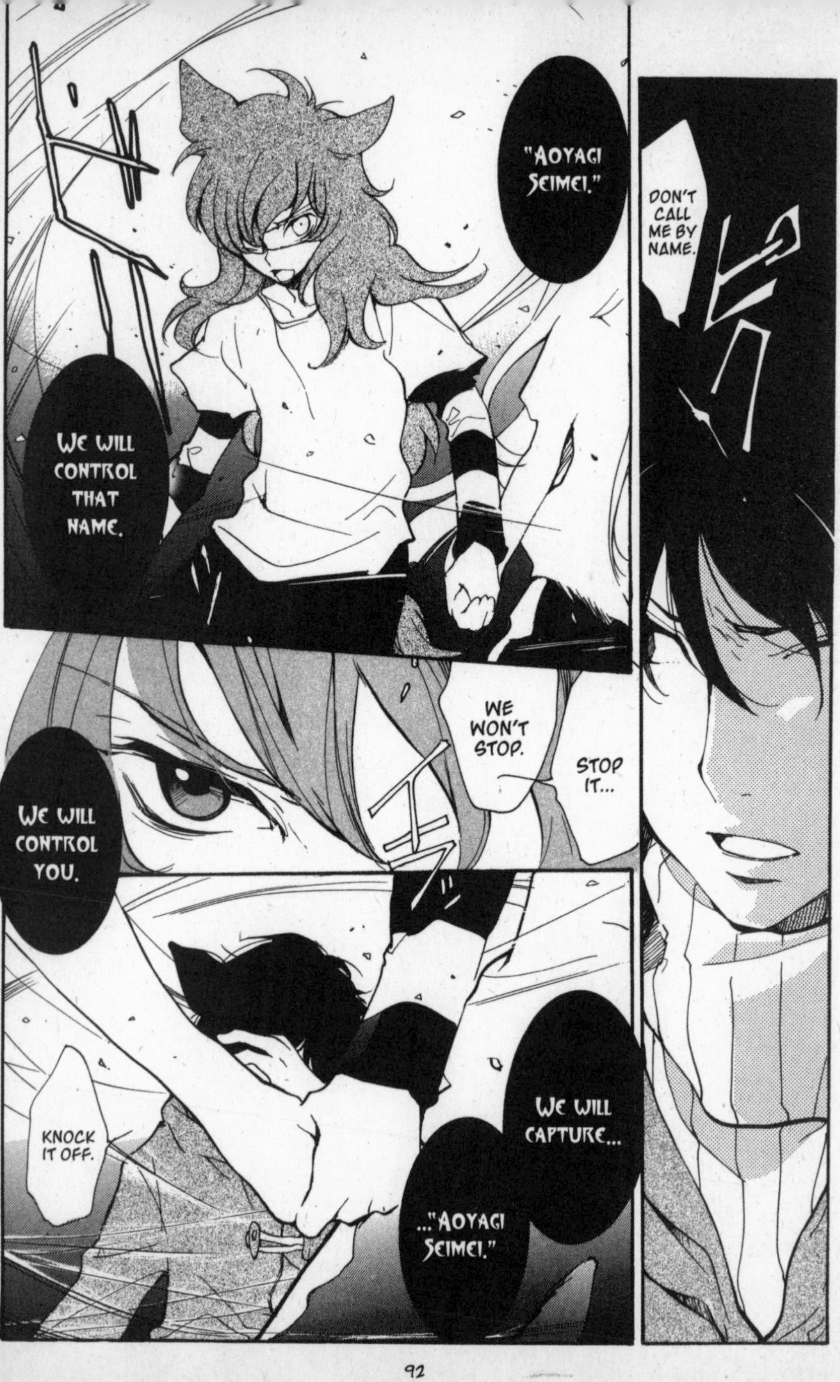
DON'T CALL ME BY NAME.
"AOYAGI SEIMEI."
WE WILL CONTROL THAT NAME.
STOP IT...
WE WON'T STOP.
WE WILL CONTROL YOU.
WE WILL CAPTURE...
..."AOYAGI SEIMEI."
KNOCK IT OFF.

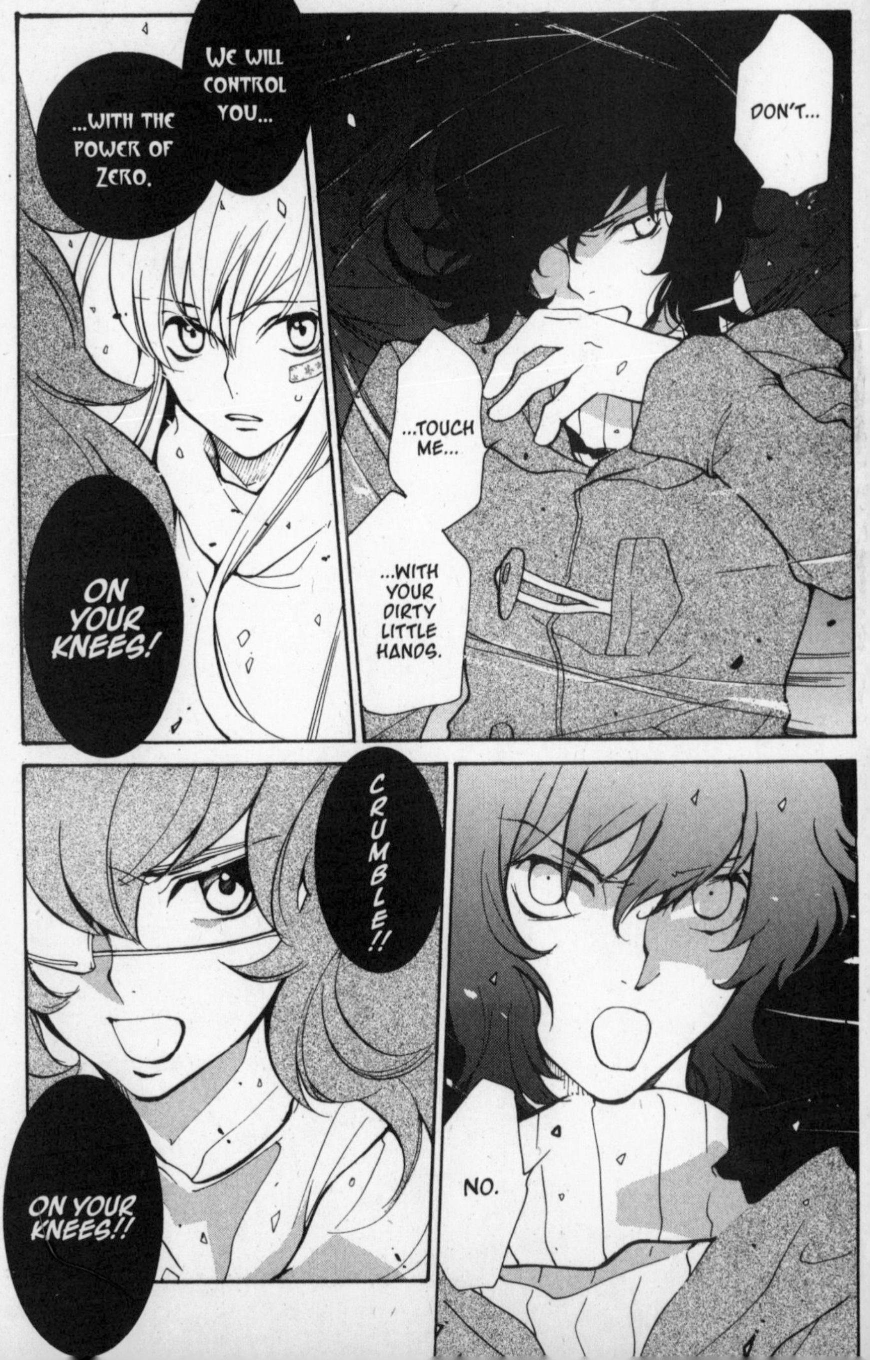
DON'T...
...TOUCH ME...
...WITH YOUR DIRTY LITTLE HANDS.
WE WILL CONTROL YOU...
...WITH THE POWER OF ZERO.
ON YOUR KNEES!
NO.
CRUMBLE!!
ON YOUR KNEES!!

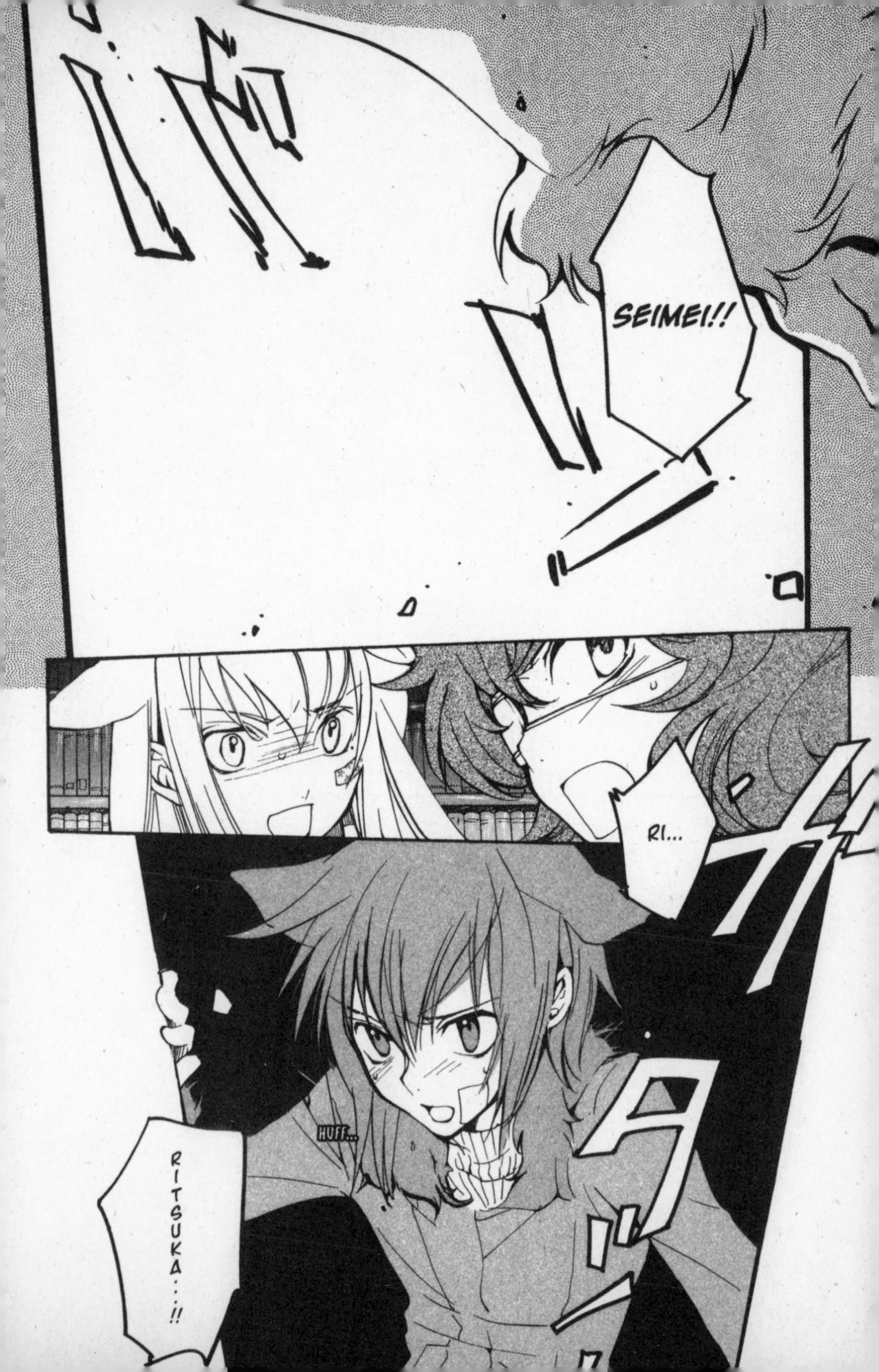
SEIMEI!!
RI...
HUFF...
RITSUKA...!!

LOVELESS

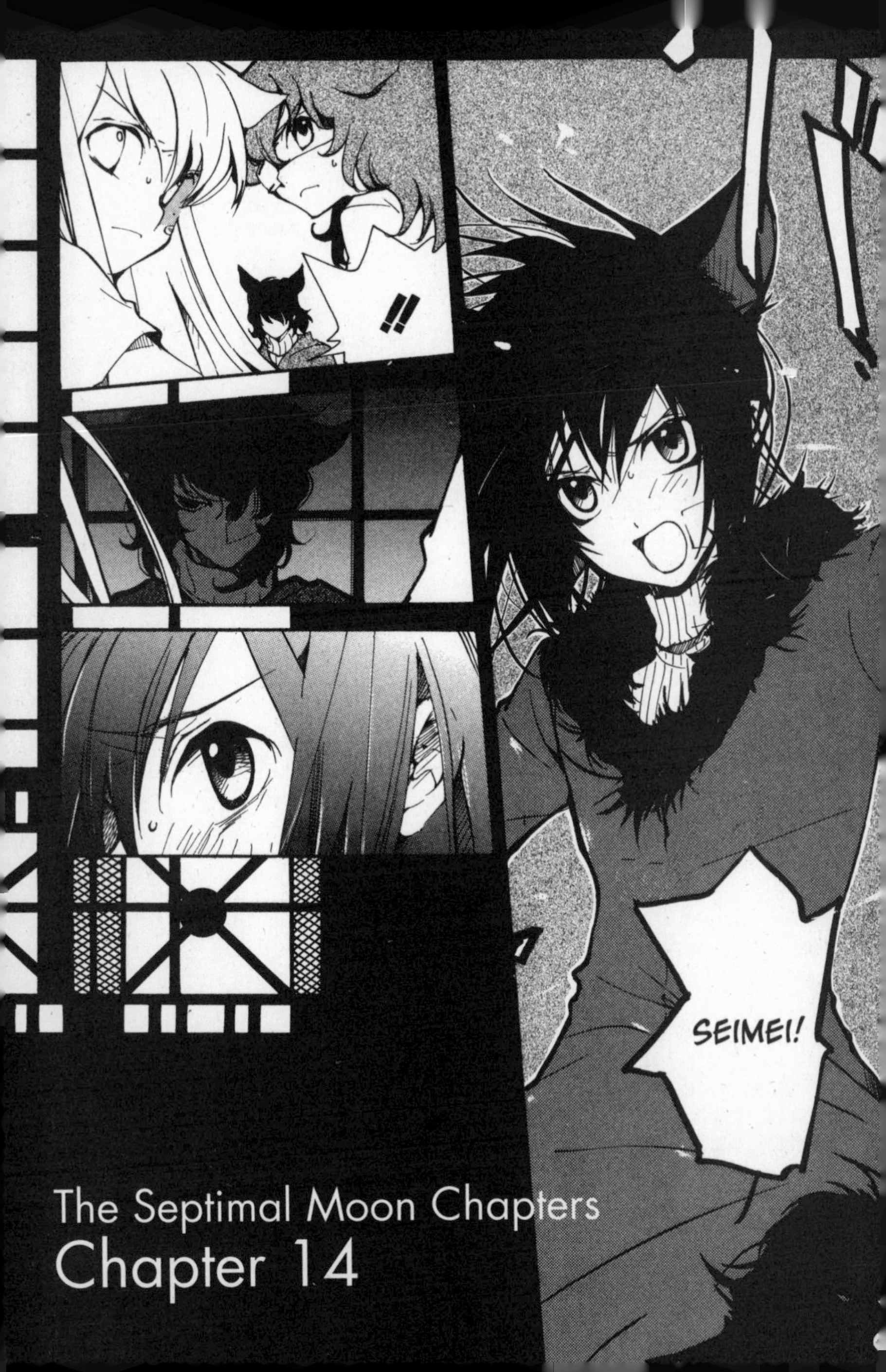
SEIMEI!
!!

The Septimal Moon Chapters

Chapter 14

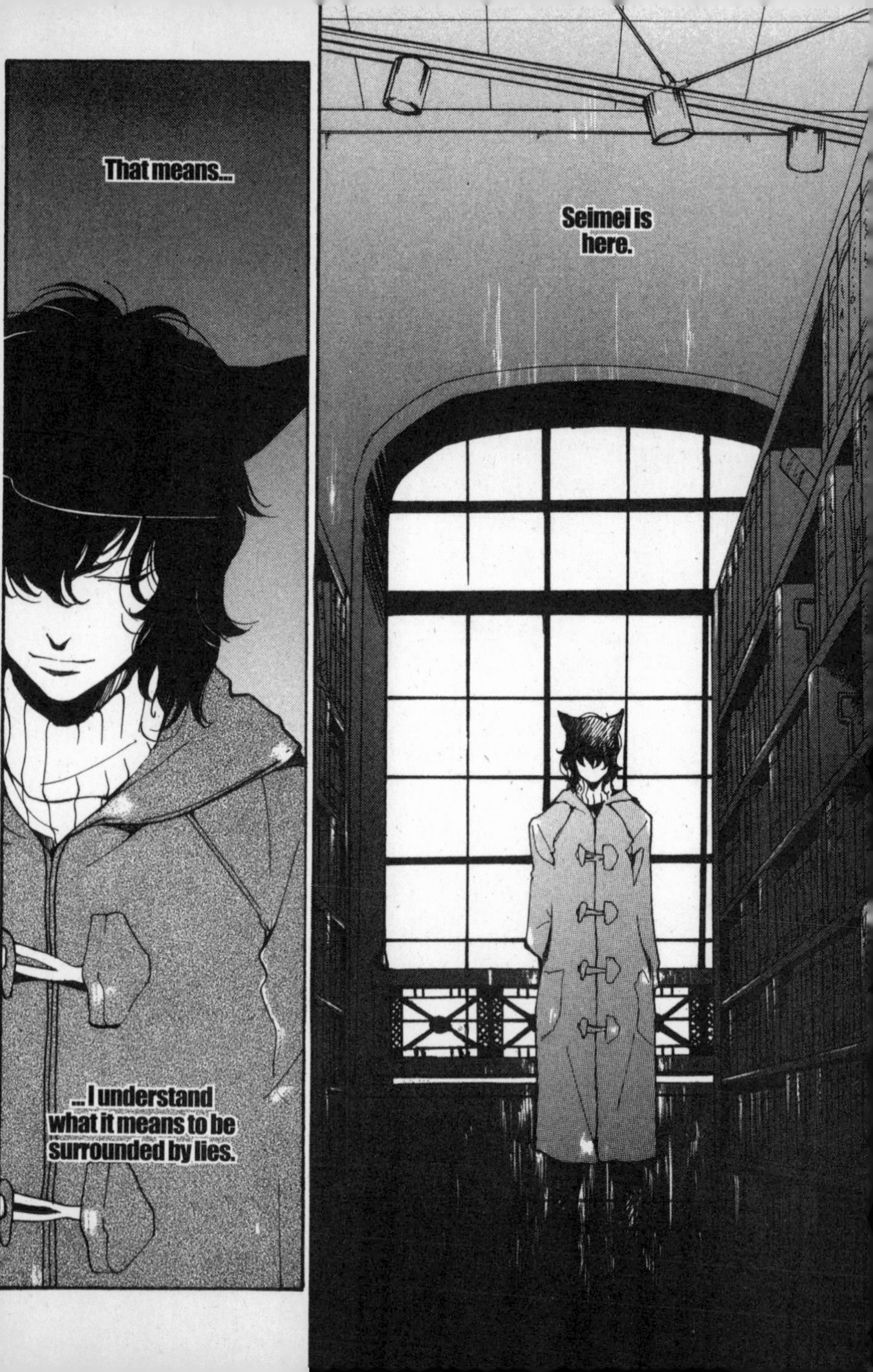
Seimei is here.
That means...
...I understand what it means to be surrounded by lies.

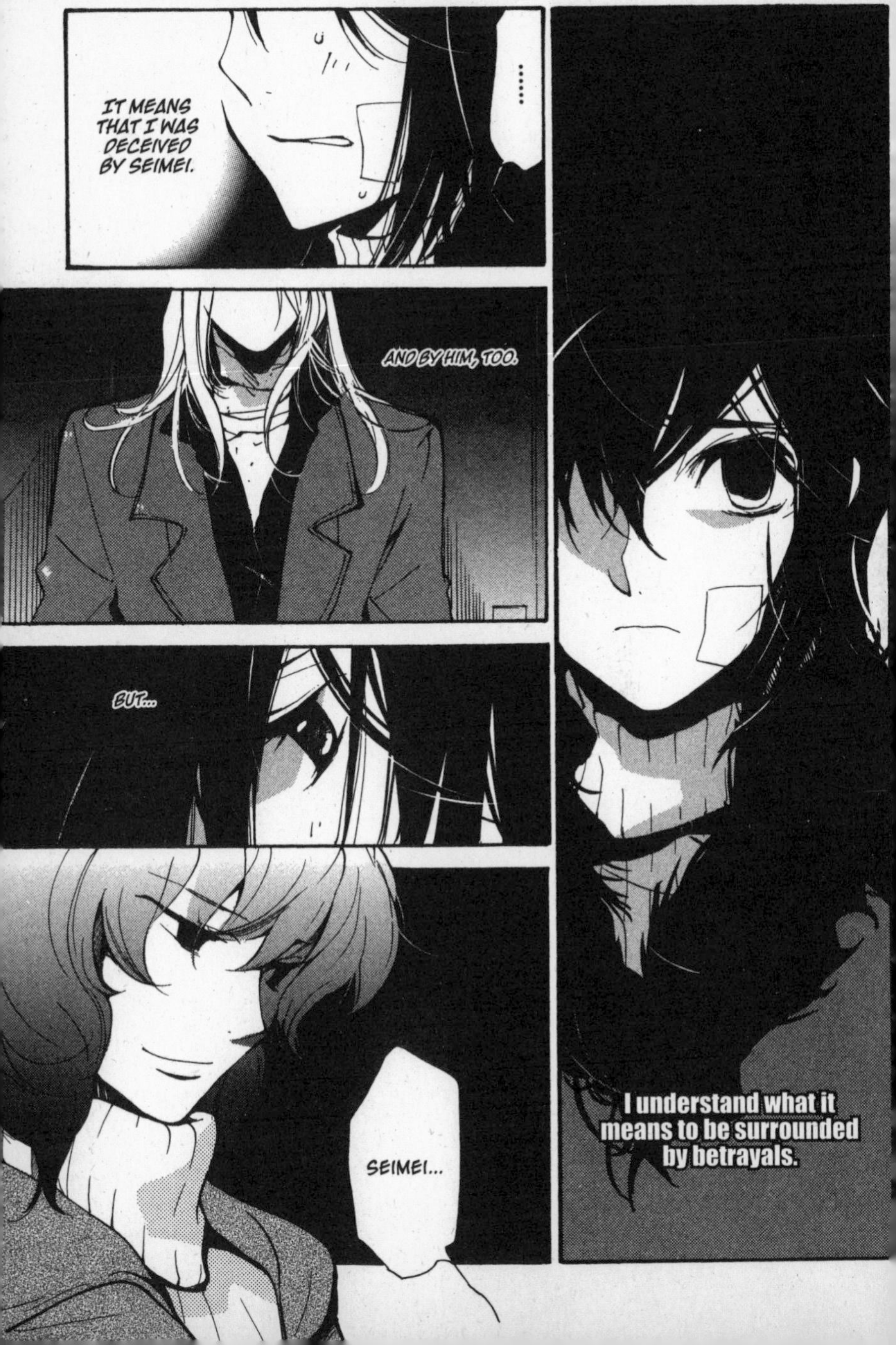
I understand what it means to be surrounded by betrayals.
......
IT MEANS THAT I WAS DECEIVED BY SEIMEI.
AND BY HIM, TOO.
BUT...
SEIMEI...

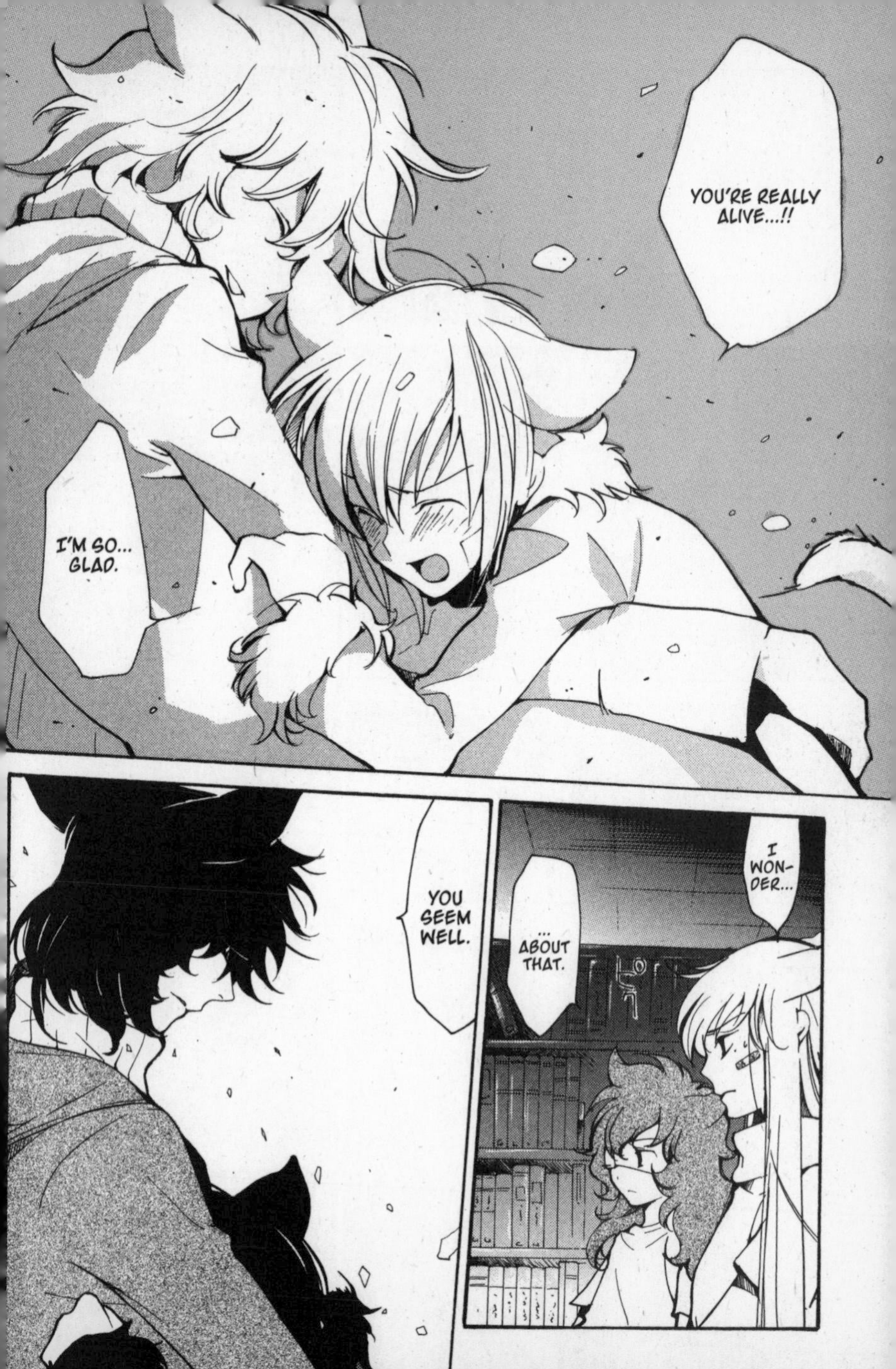
YOU'RE REALLY ALIVE...!!
I'M SO... GLAD.
I WONDER...
...ABOUT THAT.
YOU SEEM WELL.

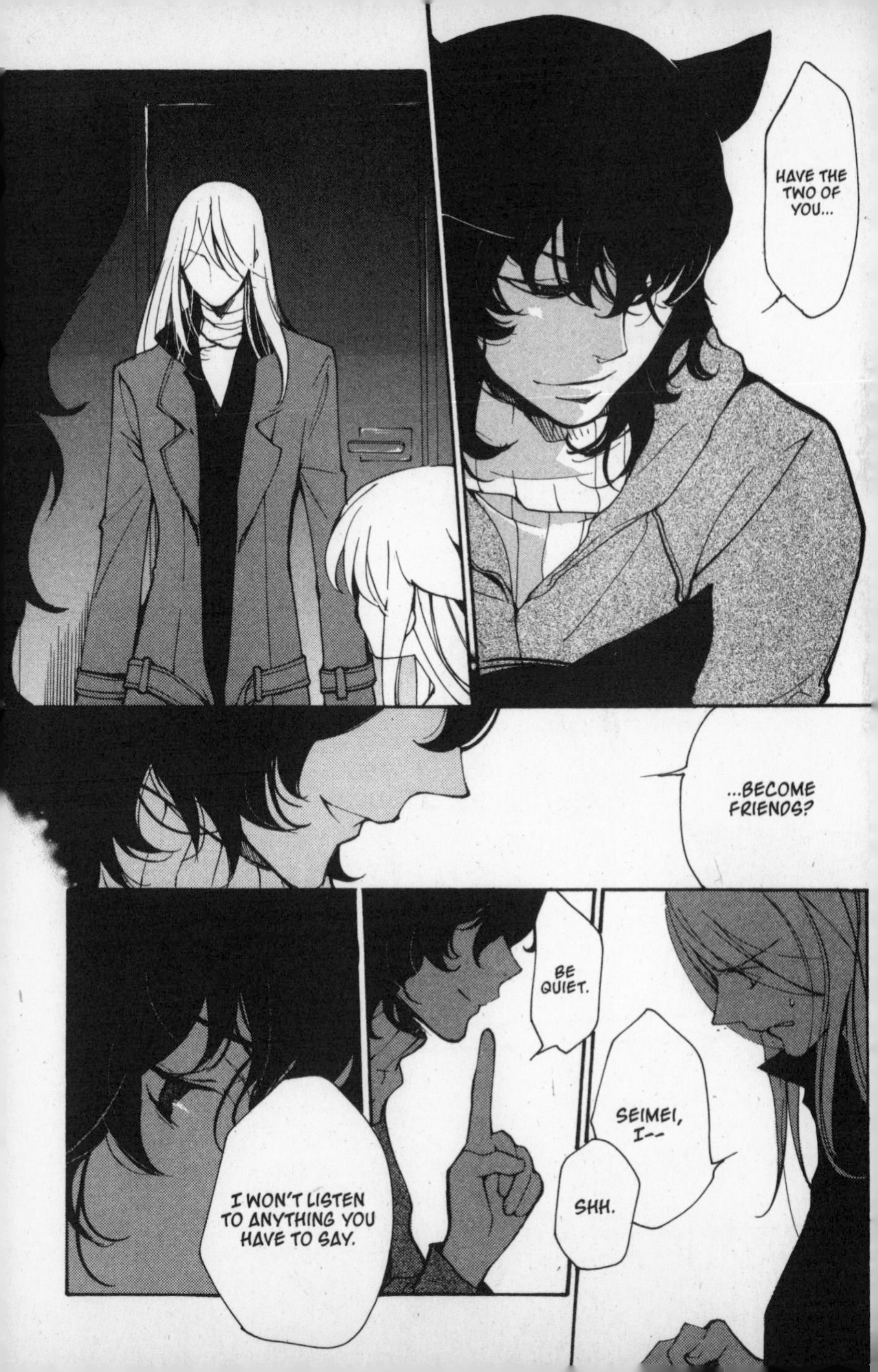
HAVE THE TWO OF YOU...
...BECOME FRIENDS?
SEIMEI, I--
SHH.
BE QUIET.
I WON'T LISTEN TO ANYTHING YOU HAVE TO SAY.

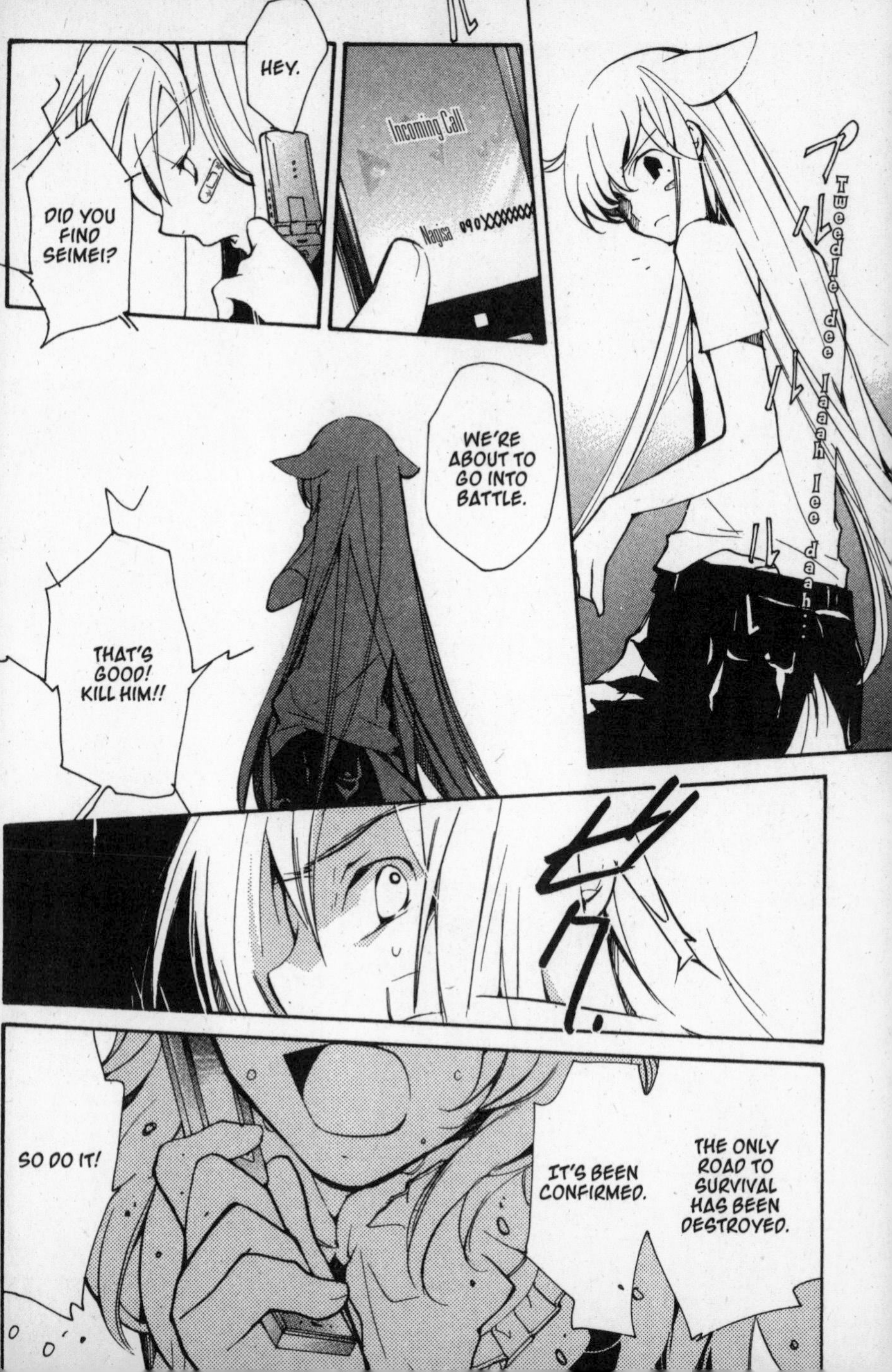
Tweedle dee laaah lee daaah...
Incoming Call
Nagisa 090XXXXXXXX
HEY.
DID YOU FIND SEIMEI?
WE'RE ABOUT TO GO INTO BATTLE.
THAT'S GOOD! KILL HIM!!
THE ONLY ROAD TO SURVIVAL HAS BEEN DESTROYED.
IT'S BEEN CONFIRMED.
SO DO IT!

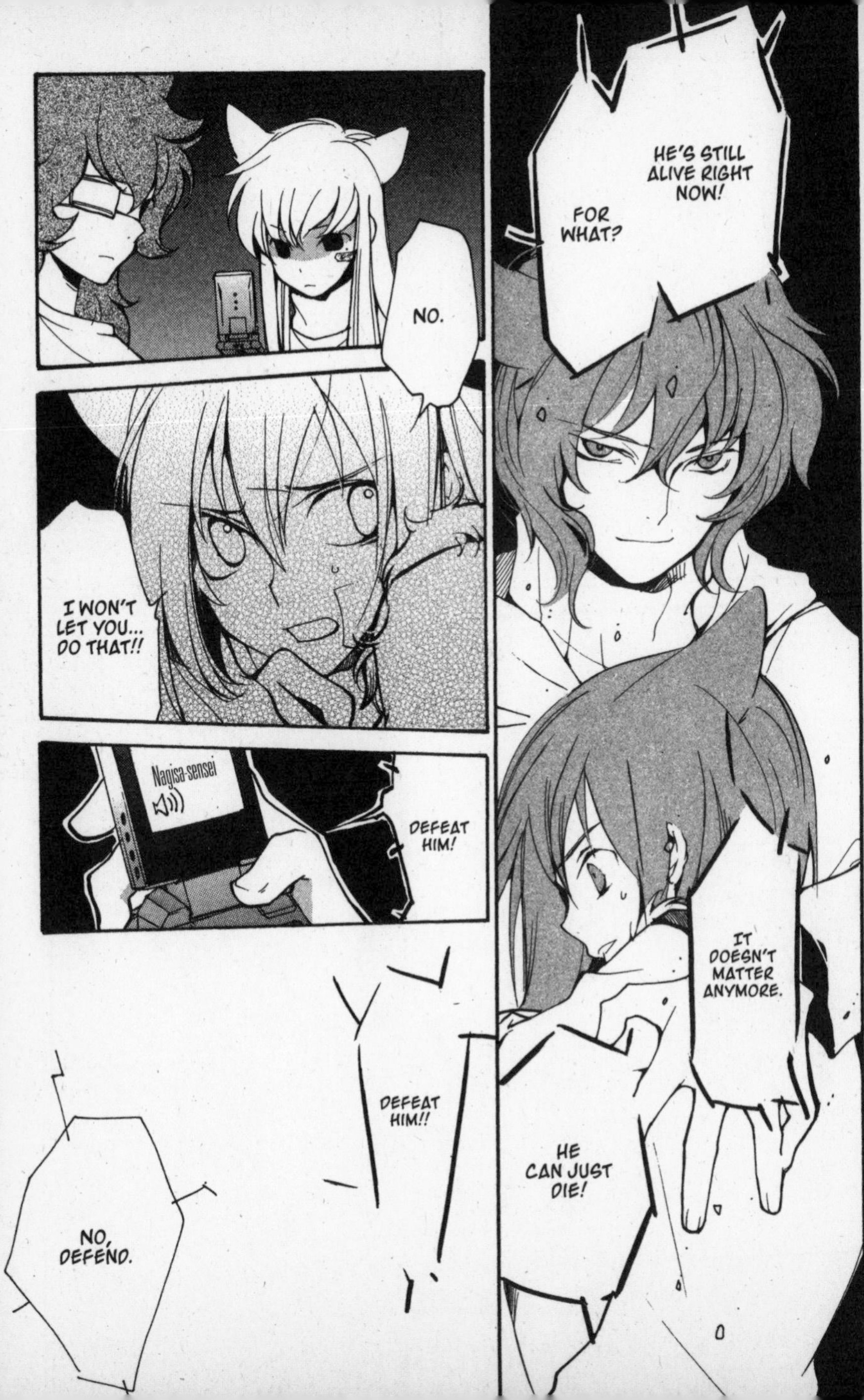
FOR WHAT?
HE'S STILL ALIVE RIGHT NOW!
IT DOESN'T MATTER ANYMORE.
HE CAN JUST DIE!
NO.
I WON'T LET YOU... DO THAT!!
Nagisa-sensei
DEFEAT HIM!
DEFEAT HIM!!
NO, DEFEND.

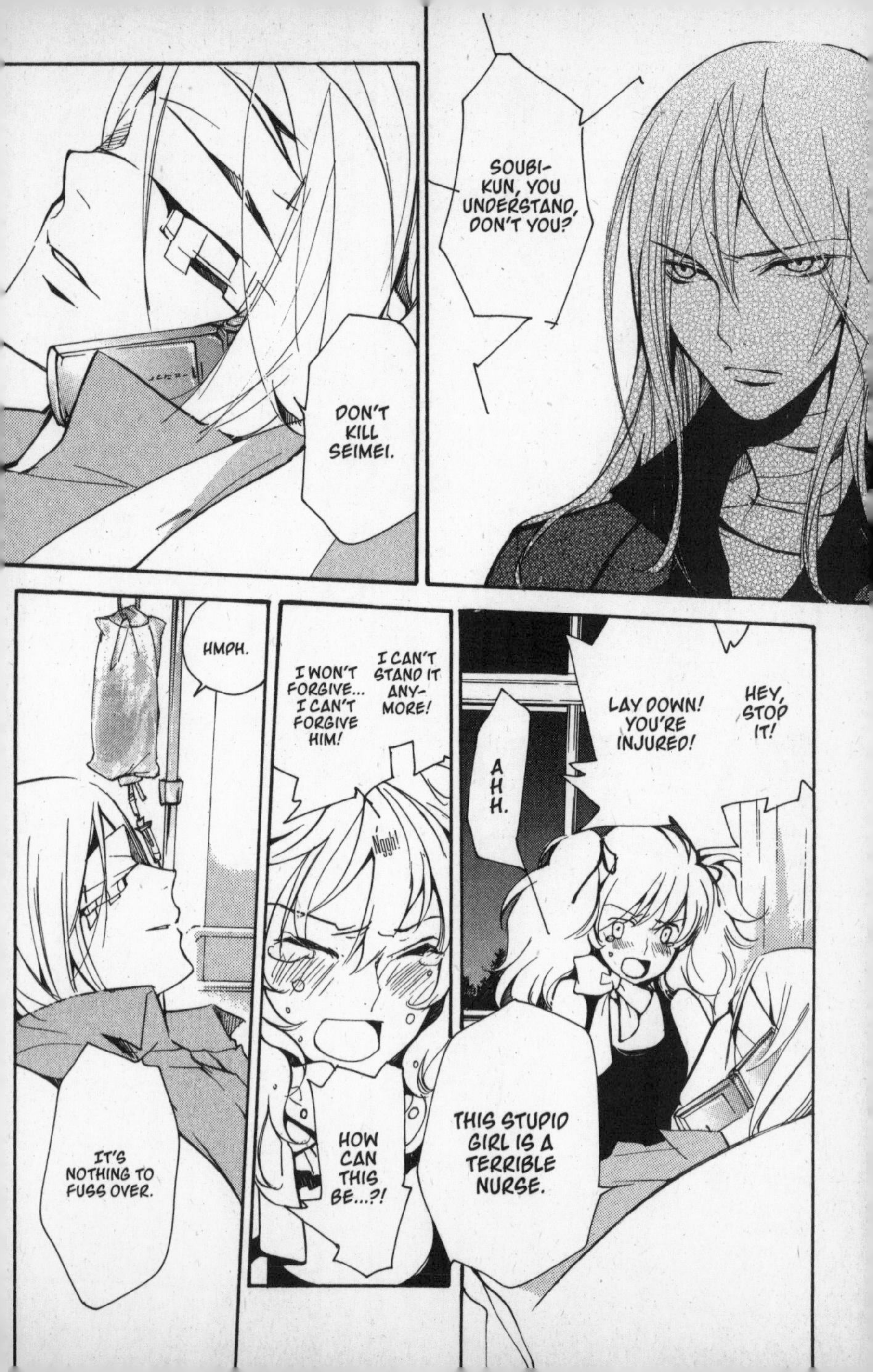
SOUBI-KUN, YOU UNDERSTAND, DON'T YOU?
DON'T KILL SEIMEI.
HEY, STOP IT!
LAY DOWN! YOU'RE INJURED!
AHH.
THIS STUPID GIRL IS A TERRIBLE NURSE.
I CAN'T STAND IT ANY-MORE!
I WON'T FORGIVE... I CAN'T FORGIVE HIM!
Nggh!
HOW CAN THIS BE...?!
HMPH.
IT'S NOTHING TO FUSS OVER.

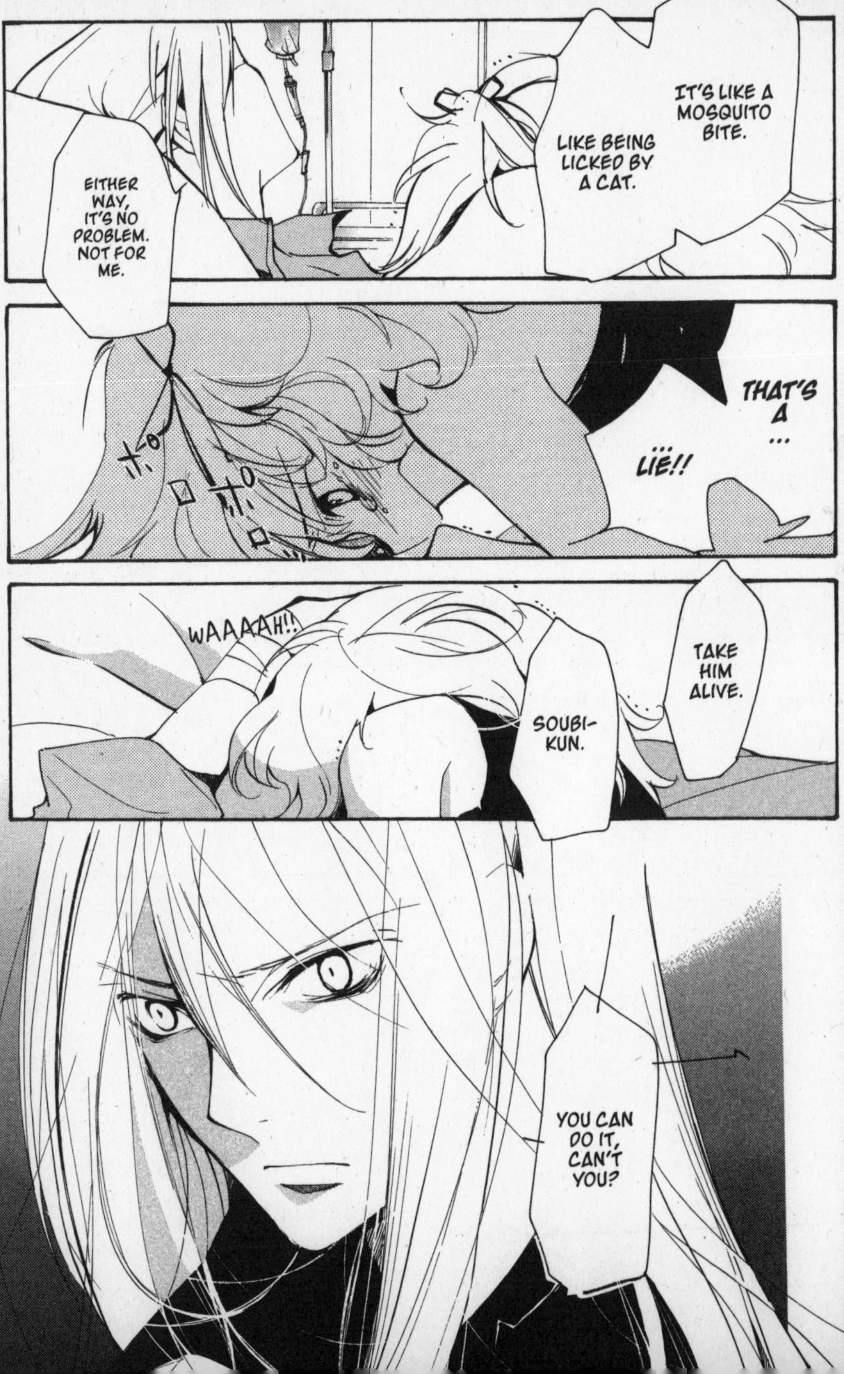
IT'S LIKE A MOSQUITO BITE.
LIKE BEING LICKED BY A CAT.
EITHER WAY, IT'S NO PROBLEM. NOT FOR ME.
THAT'S A ...
... LIE!!
TAKE HIM ALIVE.
SOUBI-KUN.
WAAAAH!!
YOU CAN DO IT, CAN'T YOU?

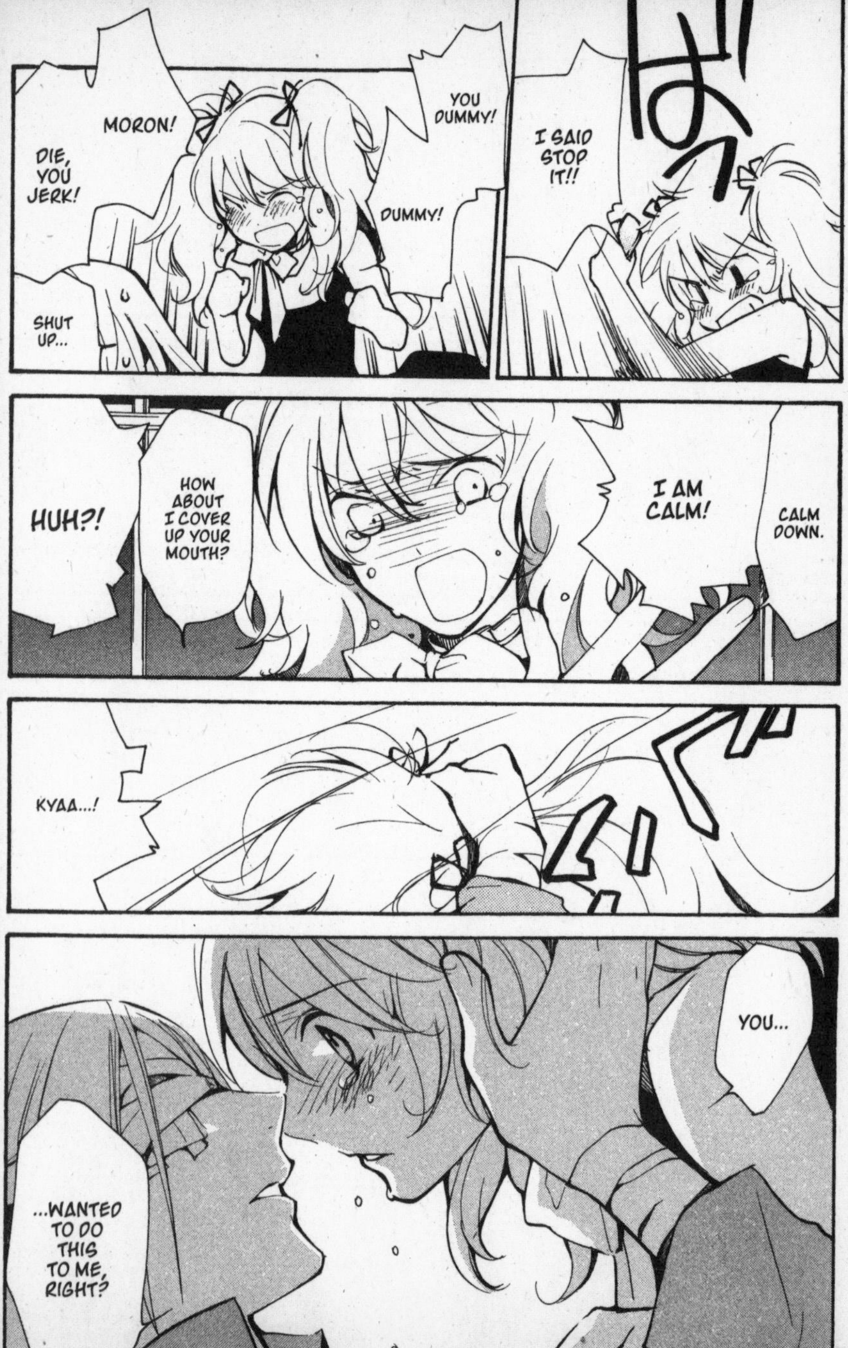
ばっ
I SAID STOP IT!!
YOU DUMMY!
MORON!
DIE, YOU JERK!
DUMMY!
SHUT UP...
CALM DOWN.
I AM CALM!
HOW ABOUT I COVER UP YOUR MOUTH?
HUH?!
ぐい
KYAA...!
YOU...
...WANTED TO DO THIS TO ME, RIGHT?

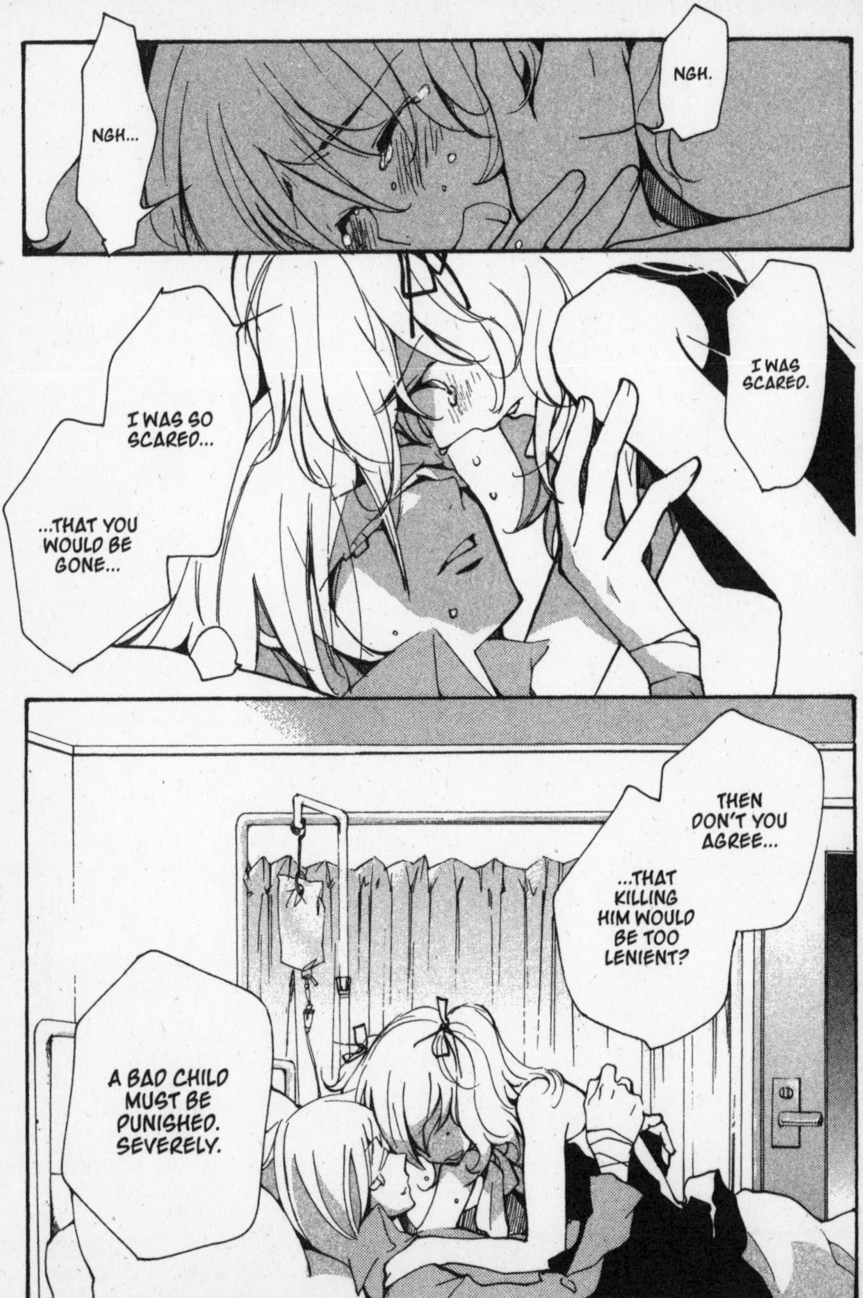
NGH.
NGH...
I WAS SCARED.
I WAS SO SCARED...
...THAT YOU WOULD BE GONE...
THEN DON'T YOU AGREE...
...THAT KILLING HIM WOULD BE TOO LENIENT?
A BAD CHILD MUST BE PUNISHED. SEVERELY.

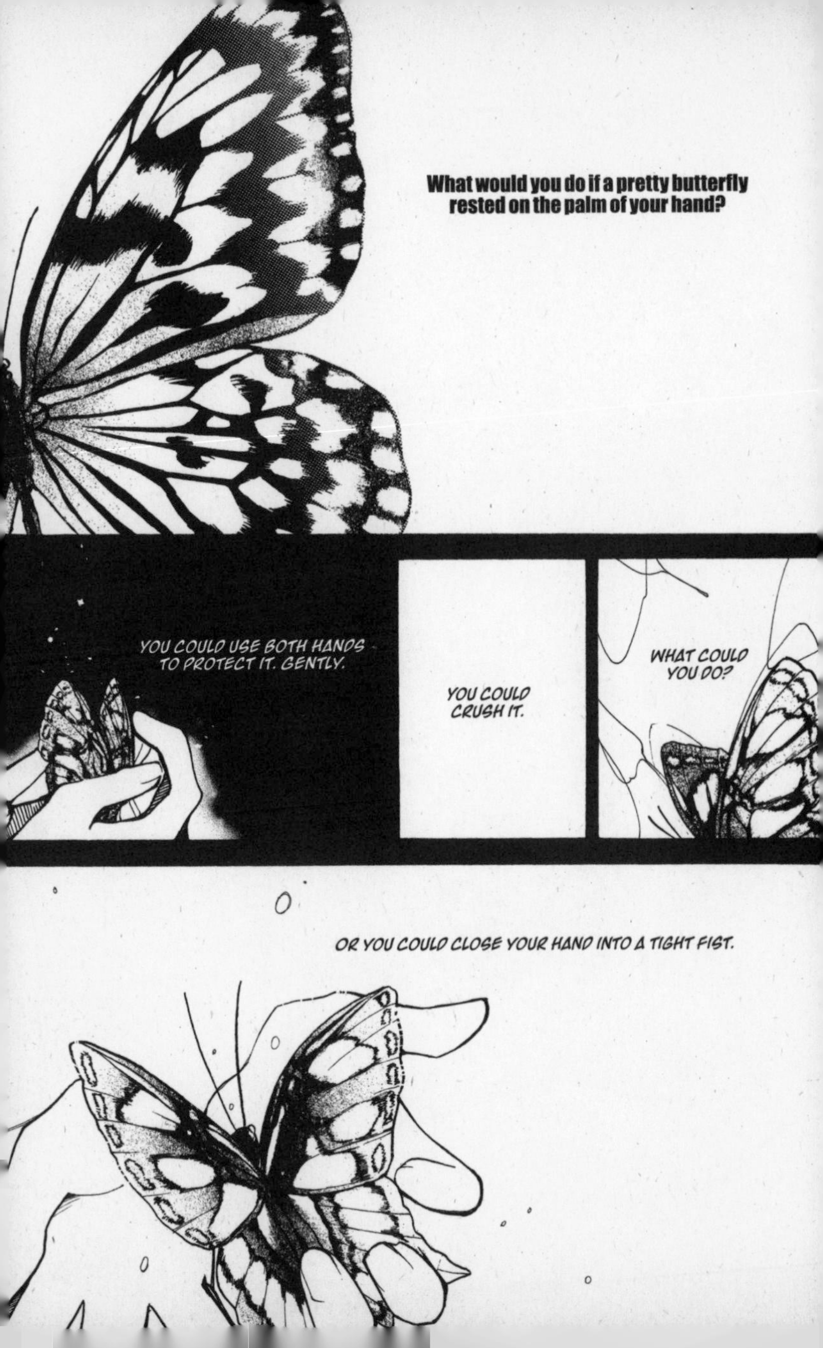
What would you do if a pretty butterfly rested on the palm of your hand?
WHAT COULD YOU DO?
YOU COULD CRUSH IT.
YOU COULD USE BOTH HANDS TO PROTECT IT. GENTLY.
OR YOU COULD CLOSE YOUR HAND INTO A TIGHT FIST.

The Septimal Moon Chapters
Chapter 15

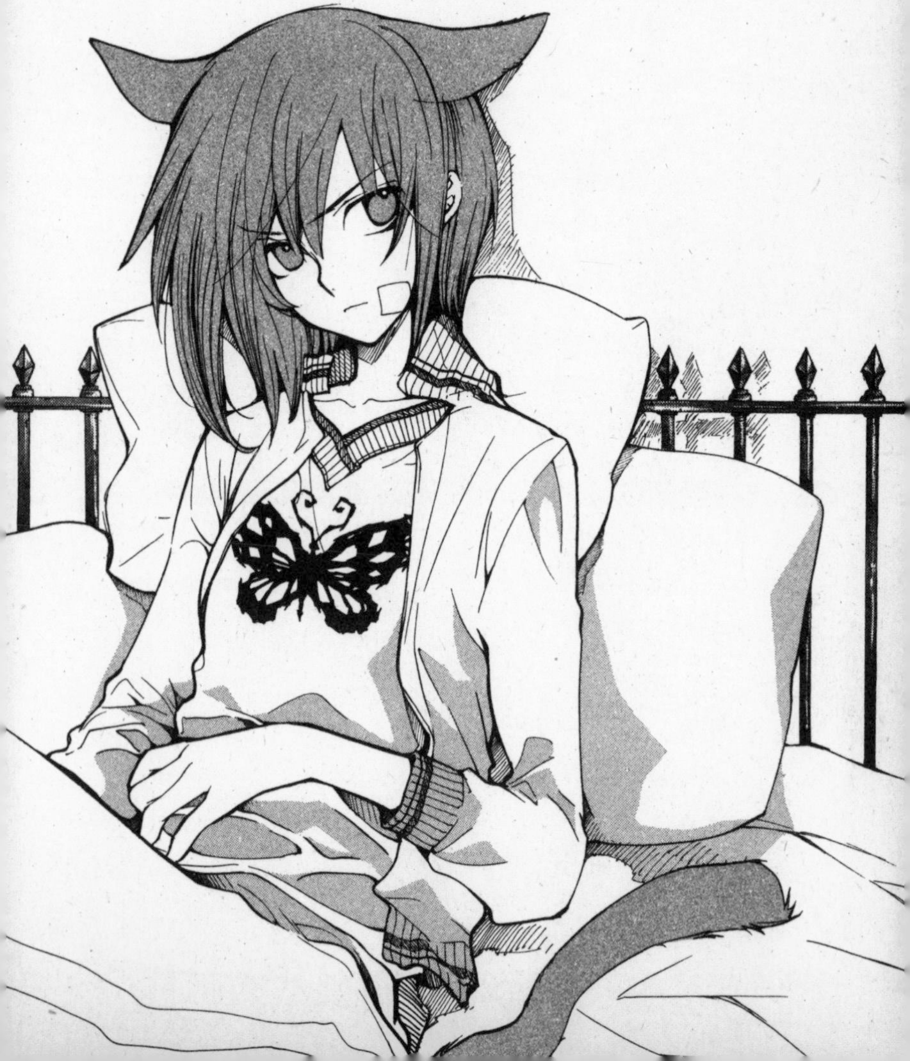

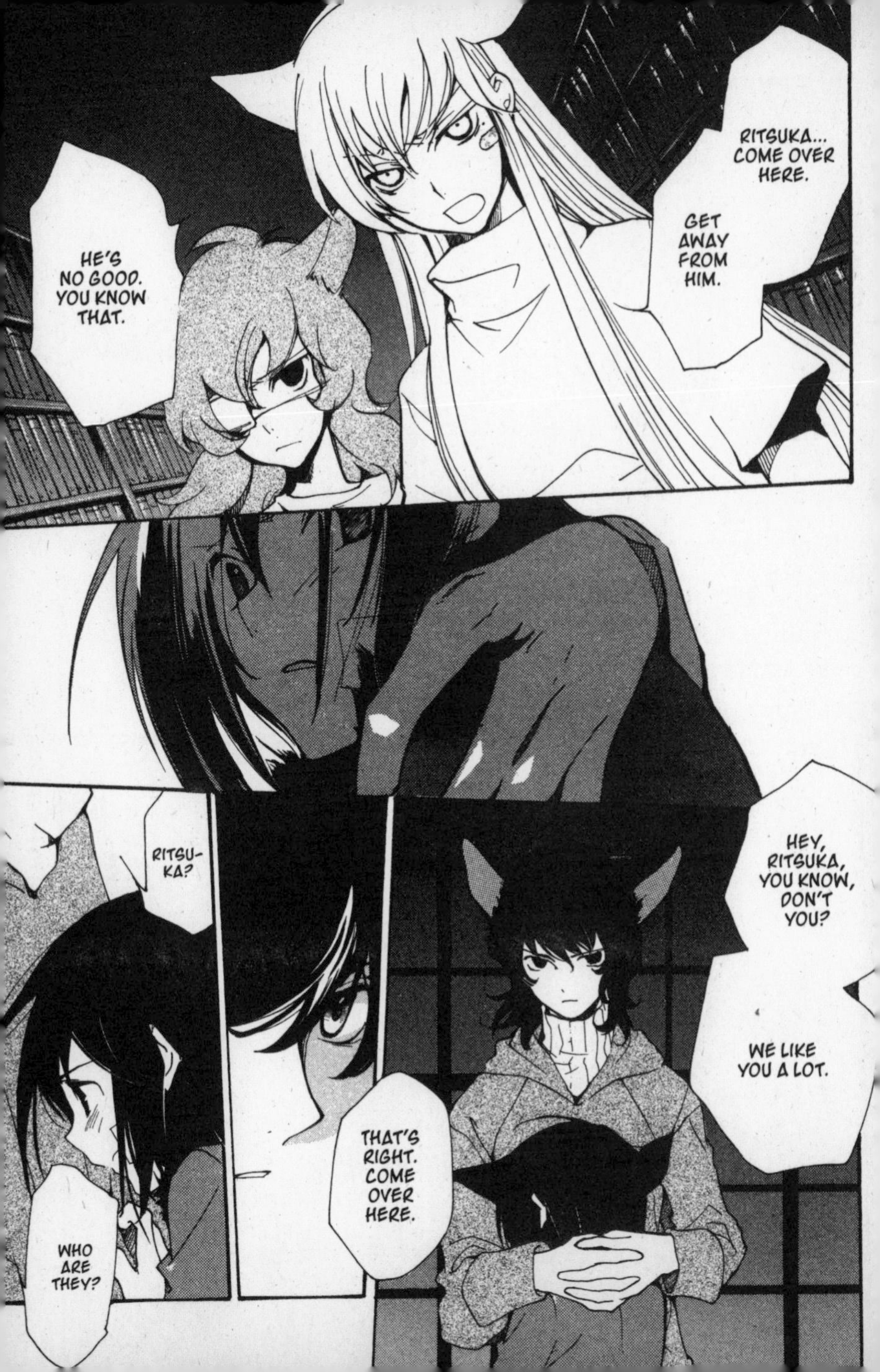
RITSUKA... COME OVER HERE.
GET AWAY FROM HIM.
HE'S NO GOOD. YOU KNOW THAT.
HEY, RITSUKA, YOU KNOW, DON'T YOU?
WE LIKE YOU A LOT.
THAT'S RIGHT. COME OVER HERE.
RITSU-KA?
WHO ARE THEY?

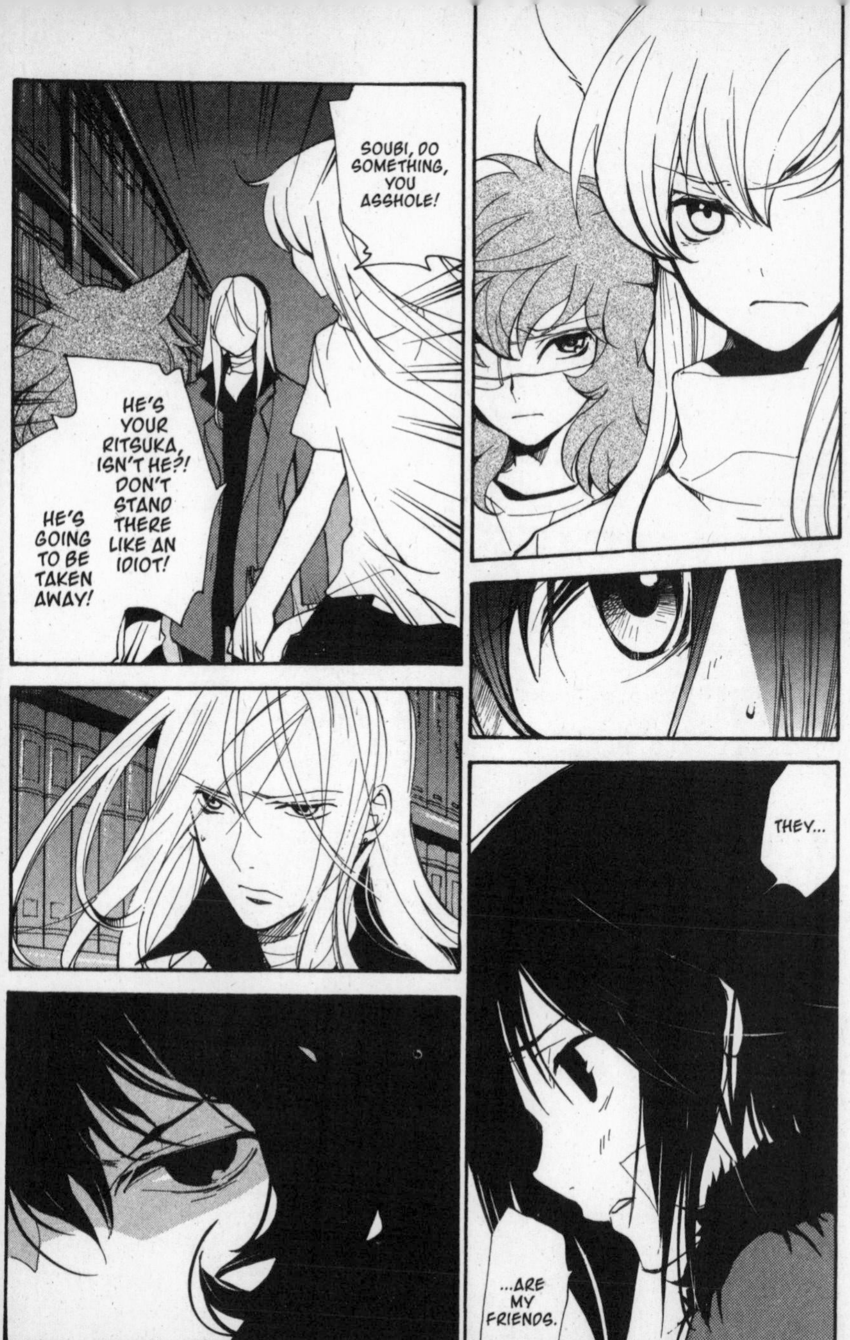
SOUBI, DO SOMETHING, YOU ASSHOLE!
HE'S YOUR RITSUKA, ISN'T HE?! DON'T STAND THERE LIKE AN IDIOT!
HE'S GOING TO BE TAKEN AWAY!
THEY...
...ARE MY FRIENDS.

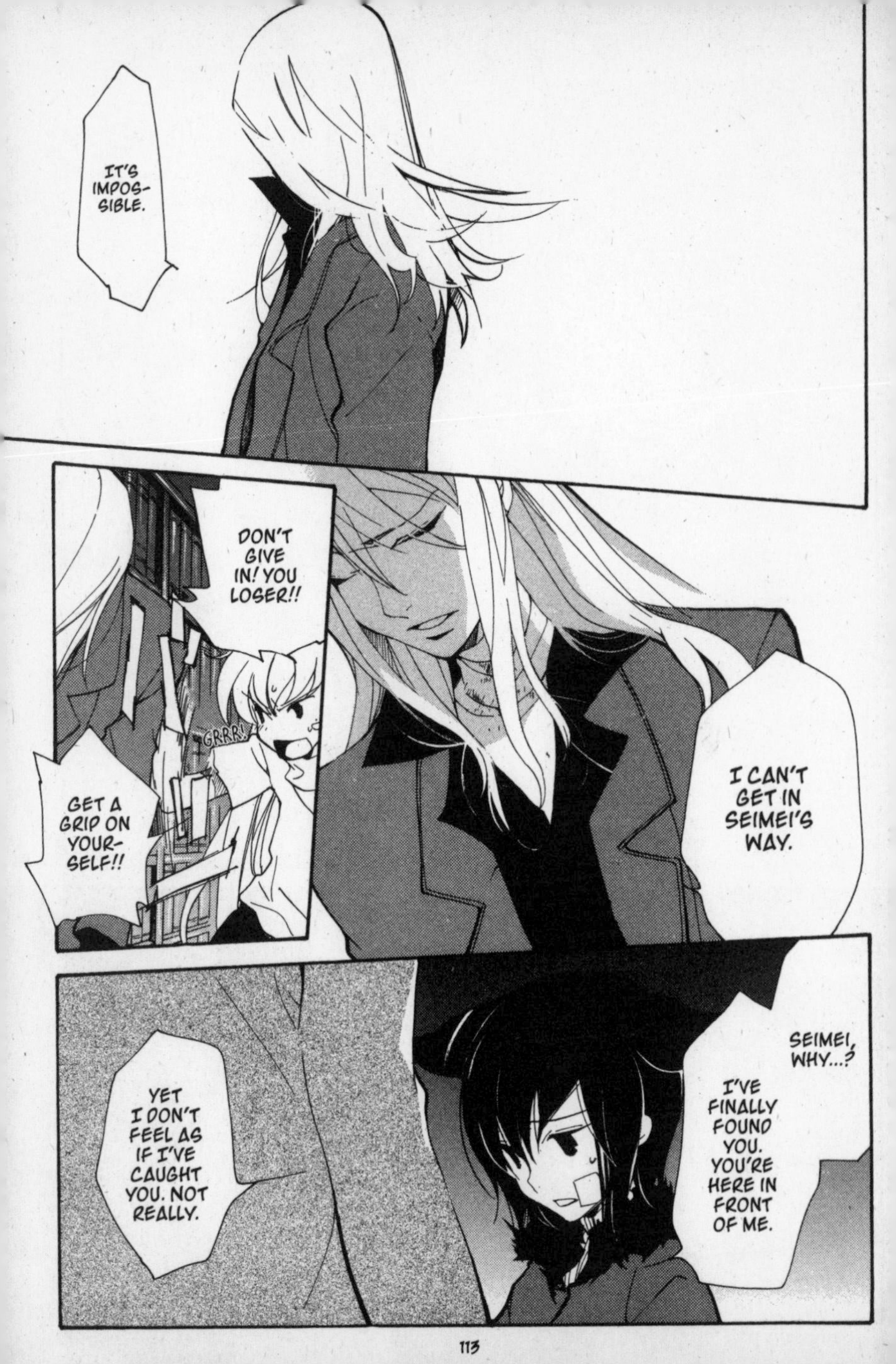
IT'S IMPOSSIBLE.
I CAN'T GET IN SEIMEI'S WAY.
DON'T GIVE IN! YOU LOSER!!
GRRR!
GET A GRIP ON YOURSELF!!
SEIMEI, WHY...?
I'VE FINALLY FOUND YOU. YOU'RE HERE IN FRONT OF ME.
YET I DON'T FEEL AS IF I'VE CAUGHT YOU. NOT REALLY.

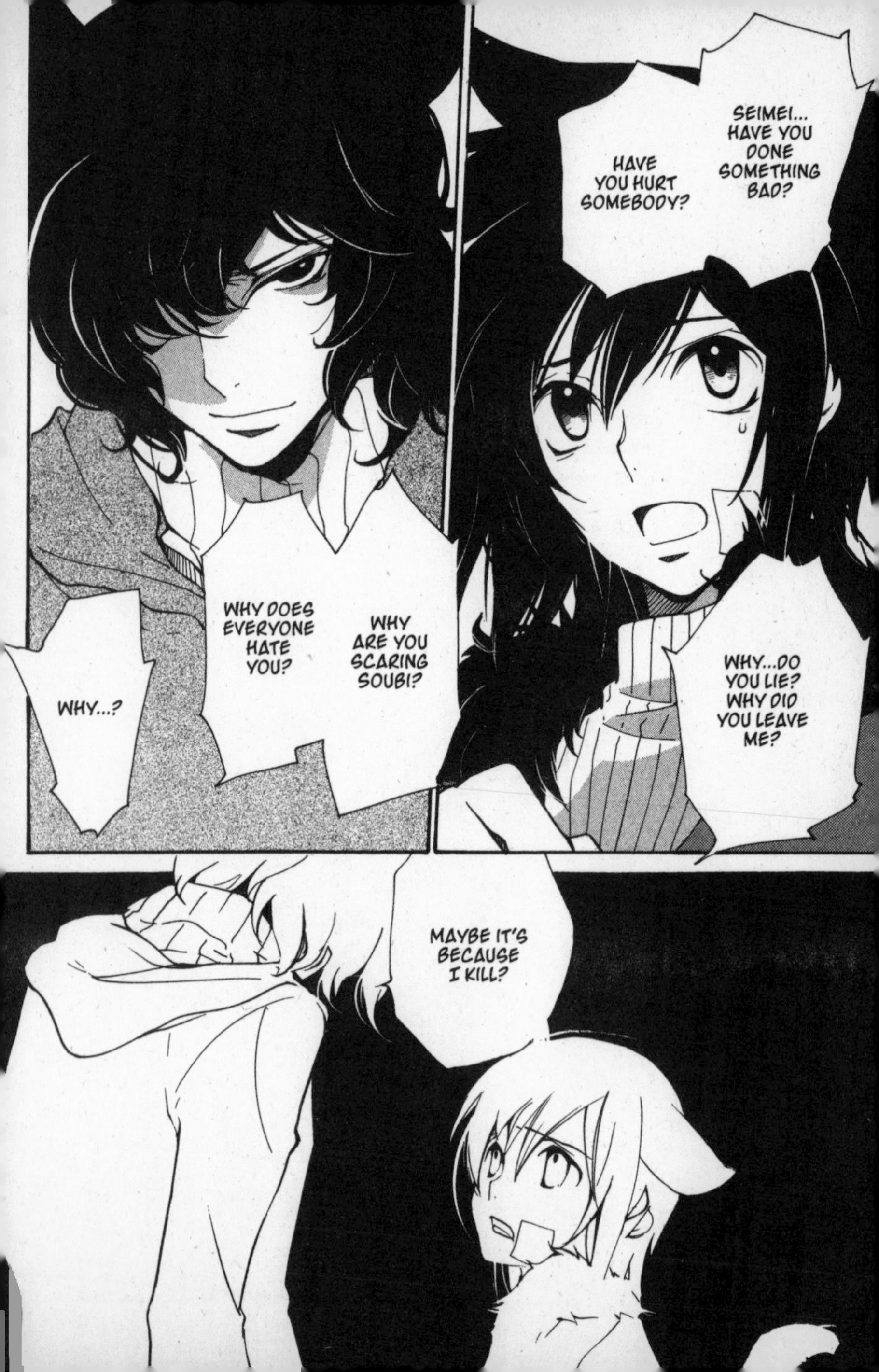
SEIMEI... HAVE YOU DONE SOMETHING BAD?
HAVE YOU HURT SOMEBODY?
WHY...DO YOU LIE? WHY DID YOU LEAVE ME?
WHY ARE YOU SCARING SOUBI?
WHY DOES EVERYONE HATE YOU?
WHY...?
MAYBE IT'S BECAUSE I KILL?

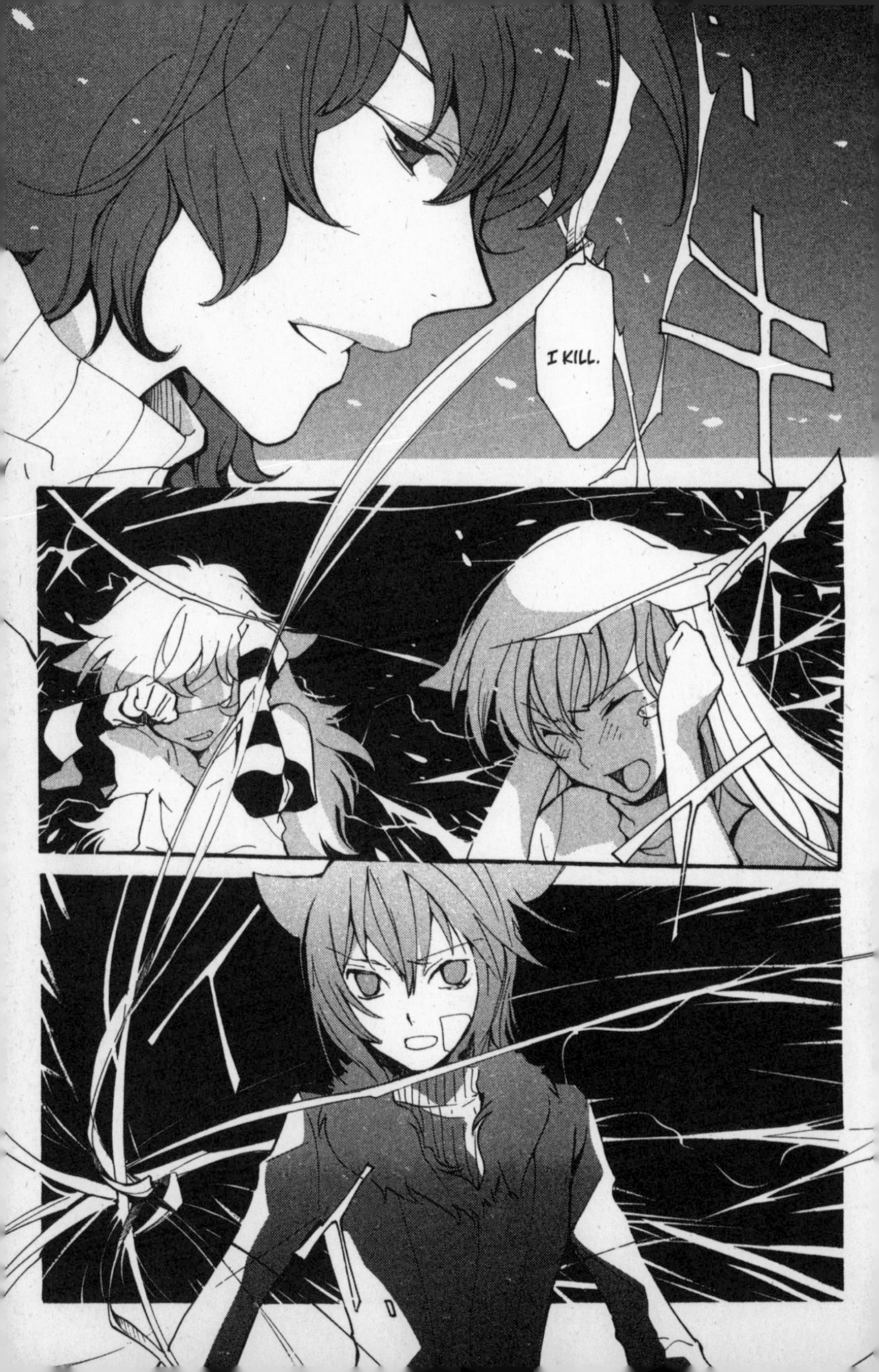
I KILL.

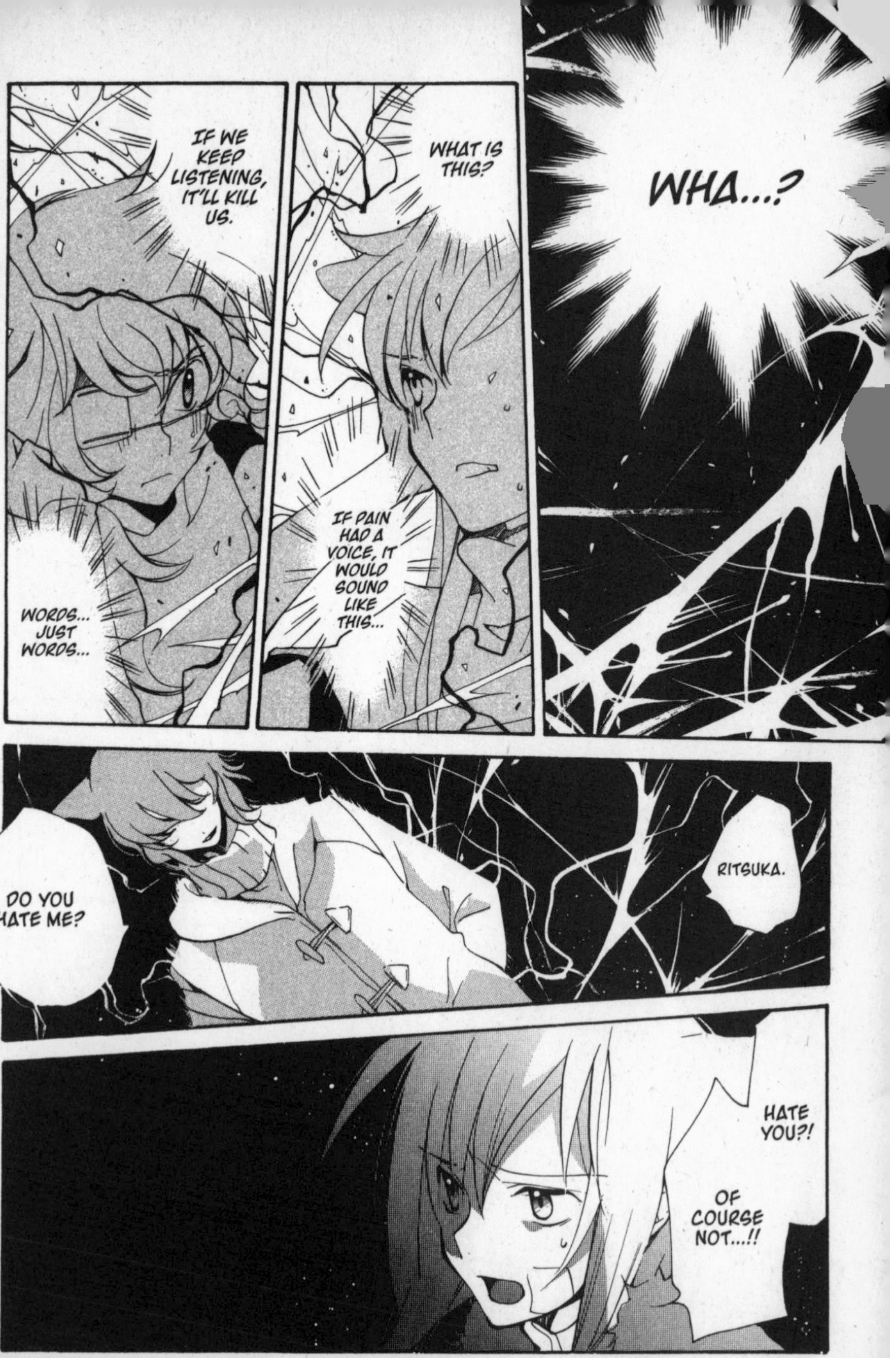
WHA...?
WHAT IS THIS?
IF PAIN HAD A VOICE, IT WOULD SOUND LIKE THIS...
IF WE KEEP LISTENING, IT'LL KILL US.
WORDS... JUST WORDS...
RITSUKA.
DO YOU HATE ME?
HATE YOU?!
OF COURSE NOT...!!

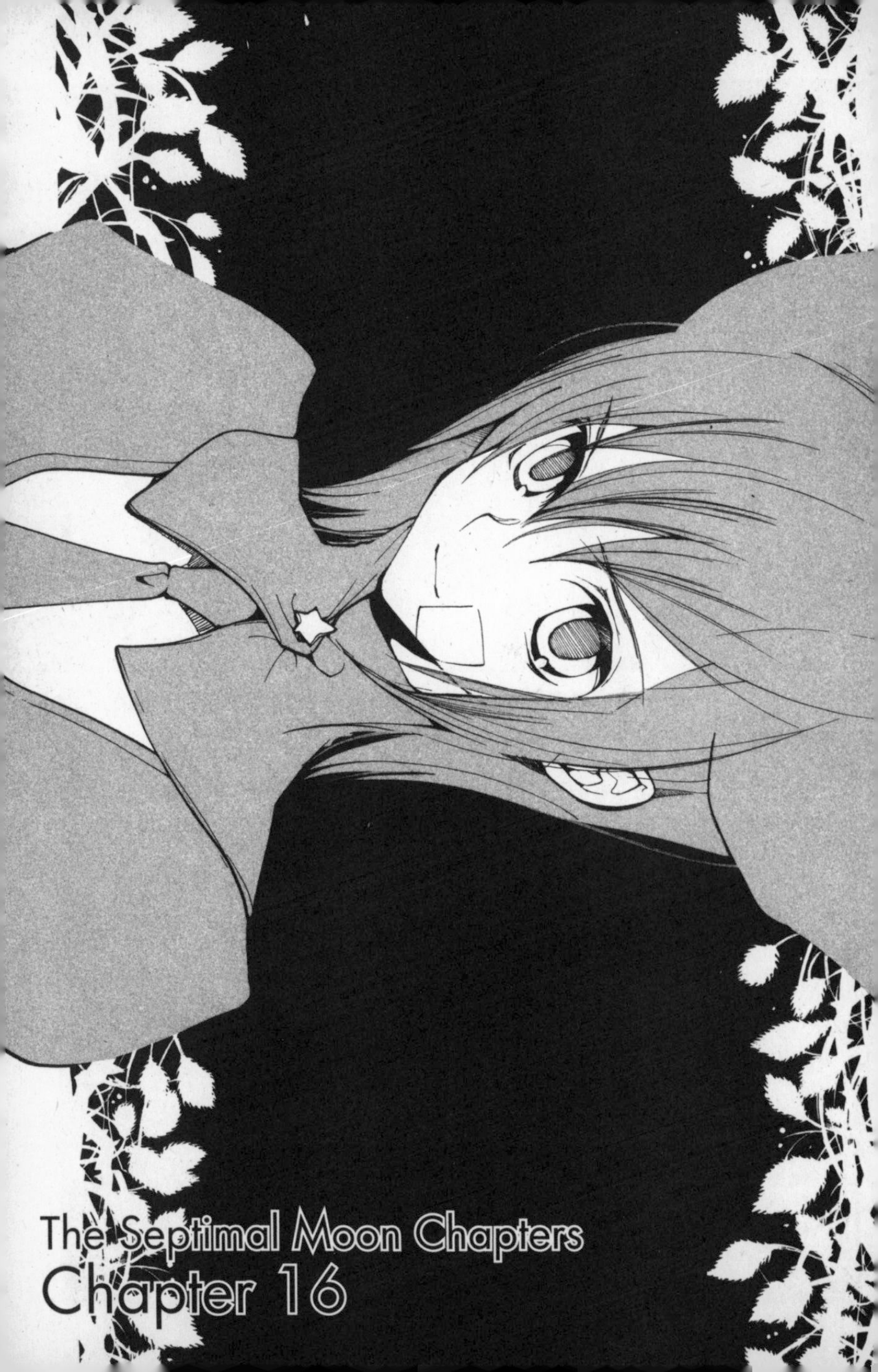
The Septimal Moon Chapters
Chapter 16

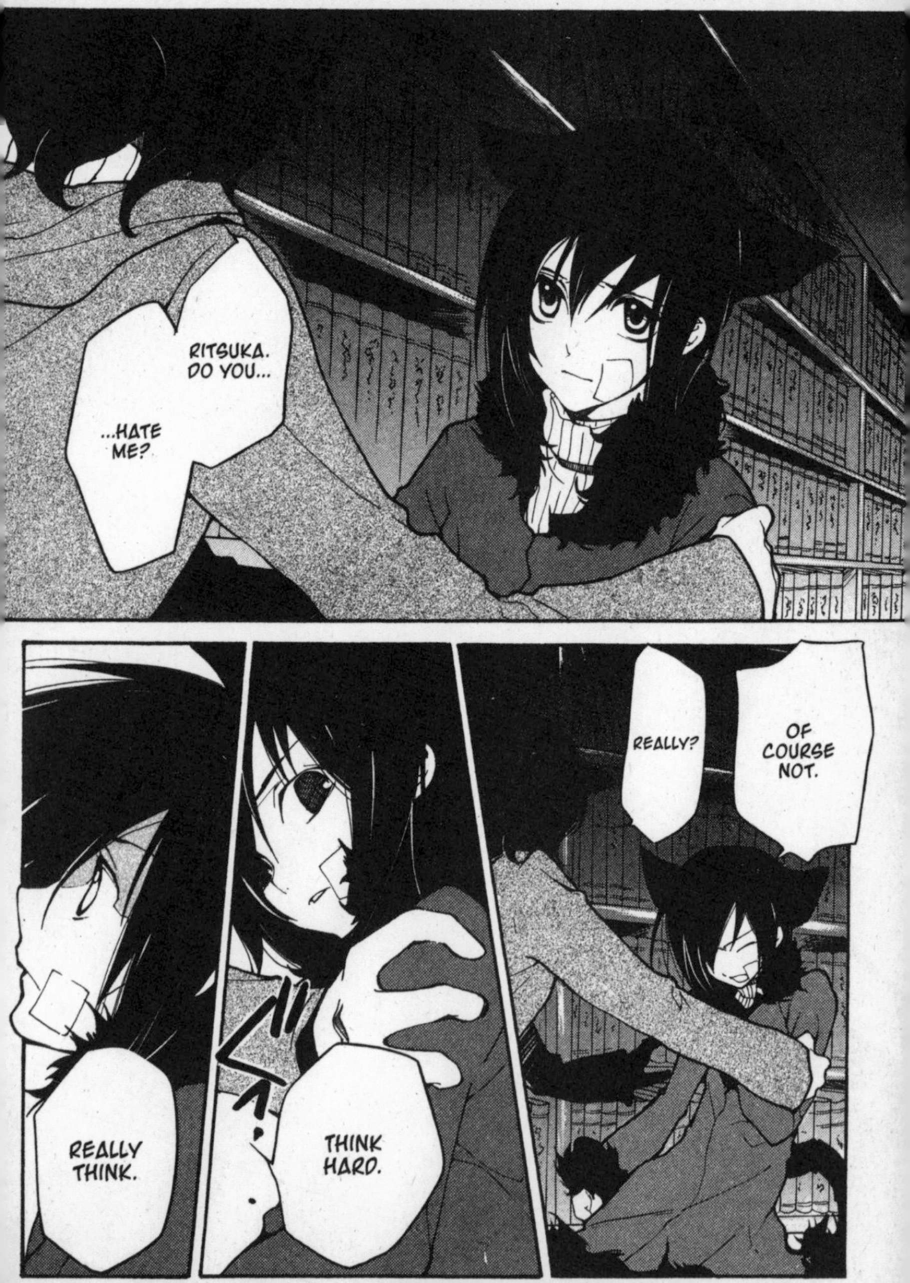
RITSUKA. DO YOU...
...HATE ME?
OF COURSE NOT.
REALLY?
THINK HARD.
REALLY THINK.

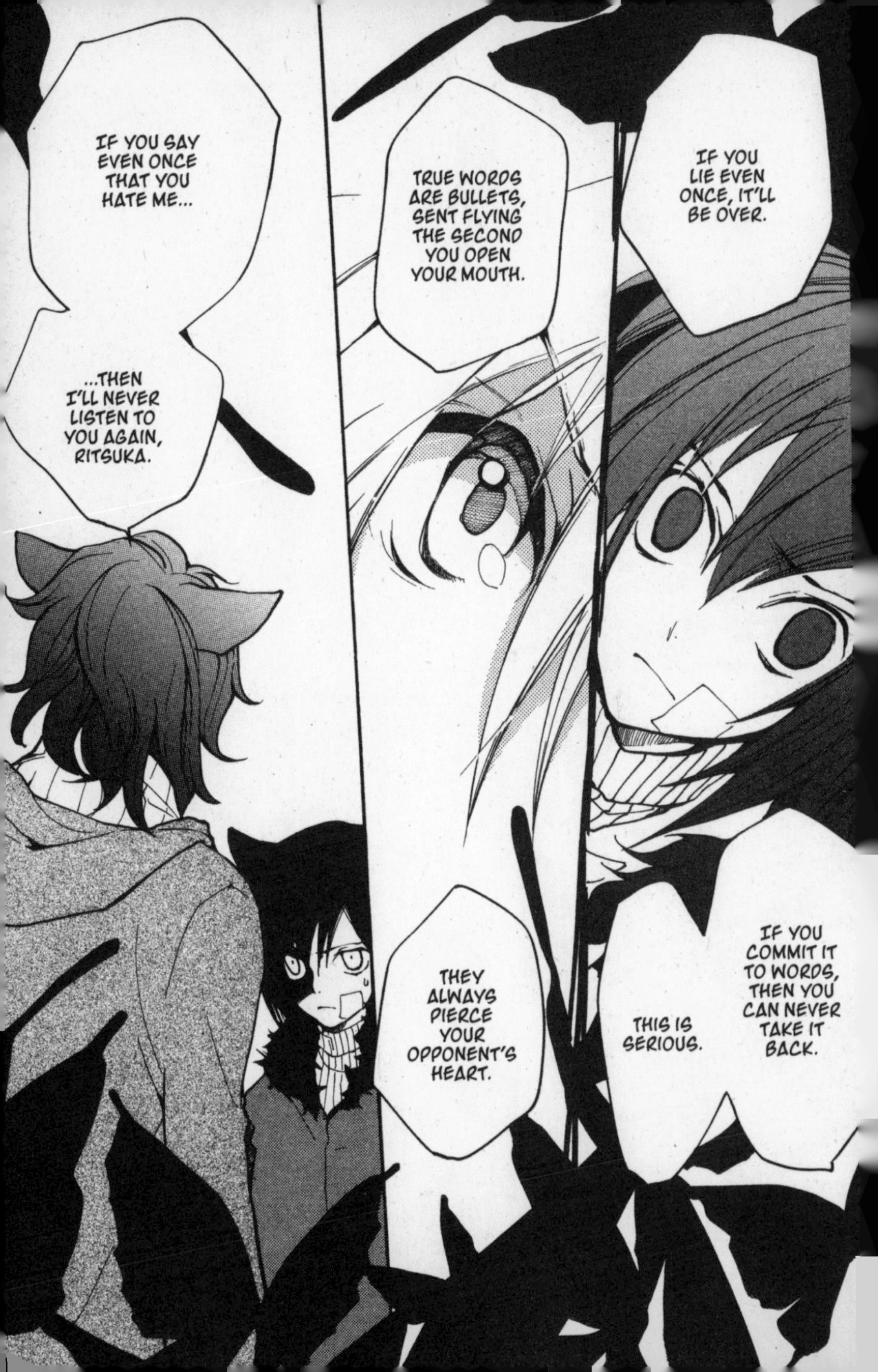
IF YOU LIE EVEN ONCE, IT'LL BE OVER.
IF YOU COMMIT IT TO WORDS, THEN YOU CAN NEVER TAKE IT BACK.
THIS IS SERIOUS.
TRUE WORDS ARE BULLETS, SENT FLYING THE SECOND YOU OPEN YOUR MOUTH.
THEY ALWAYS PIERCE YOUR OPPONENT'S HEART.
IF YOU SAY EVEN ONCE THAT YOU HATE ME...
...THEN I'LL NEVER LISTEN TO YOU AGAIN, RITSUKA.

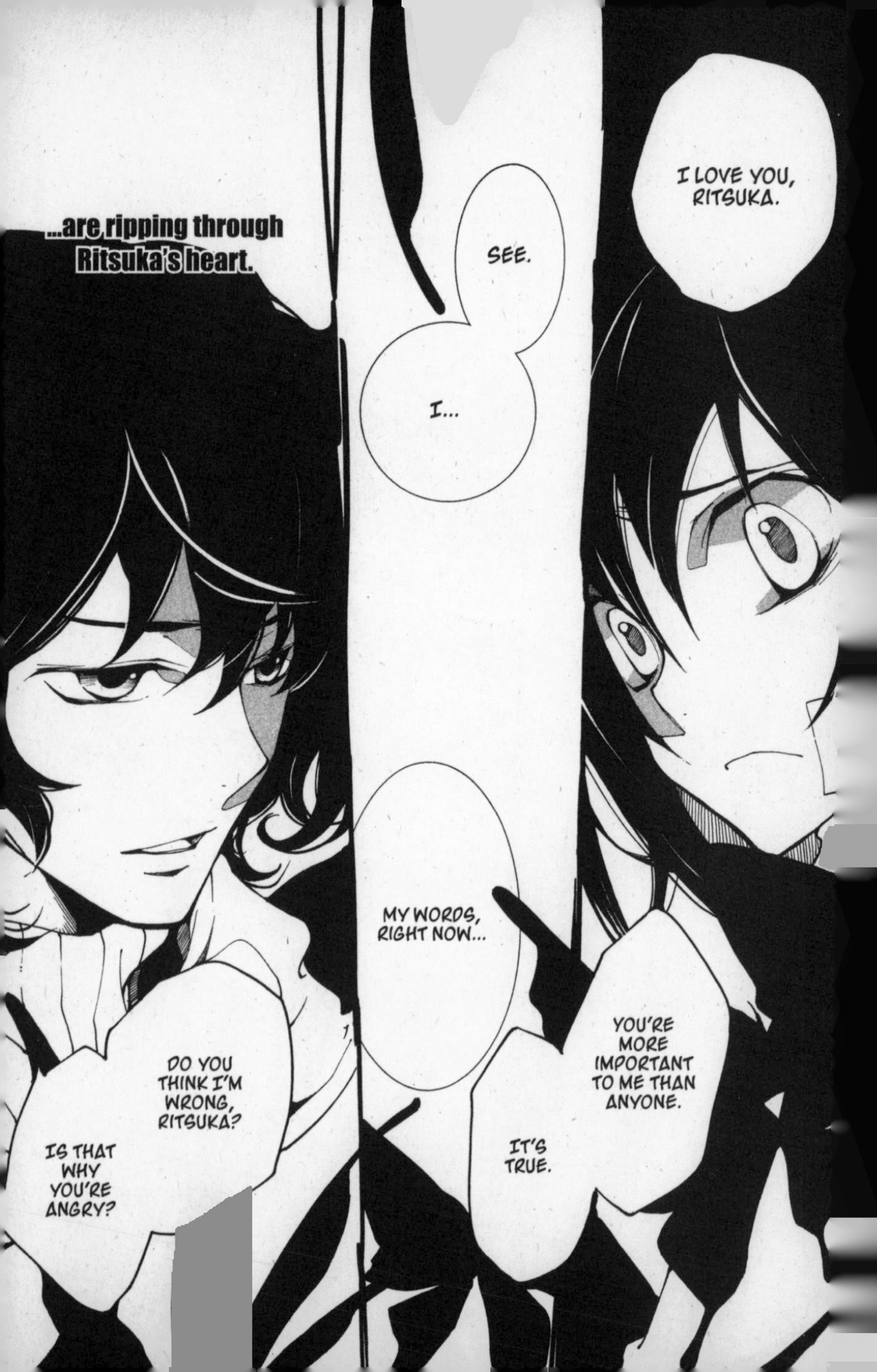
I LOVE YOU, RITSUKA.
YOU'RE MORE IMPORTANT TO ME THAN ANYONE.
IT'S TRUE.
I...
SEE.
MY WORDS, RIGHT NOW...
...are ripping through Ritsuka's heart.
DO YOU THINK I'M WRONG, RITSUKA?
IS THAT WHY YOU'RE ANGRY?

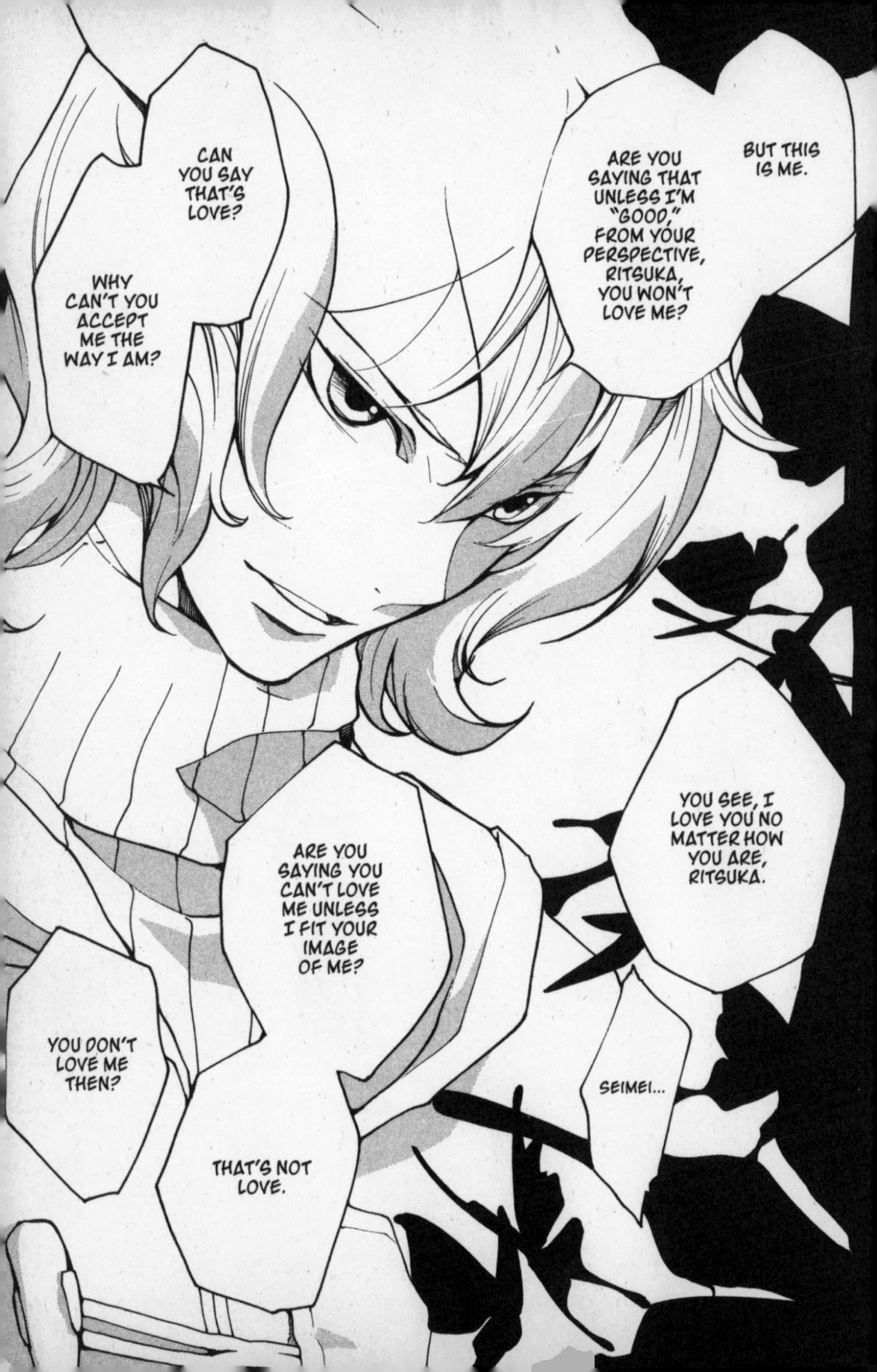
BUT THIS IS ME.
ARE YOU SAYING THAT UNLESS I'M "GOOD," FROM YOUR PERSPECTIVE, RITSUKA, YOU WON'T LOVE ME?
CAN YOU SAY THAT'S LOVE?
WHY CAN'T YOU ACCEPT ME THE WAY I AM?
YOU SEE, I LOVE YOU NO MATTER HOW YOU ARE, RITSUKA.
ARE YOU SAYING YOU CAN'T LOVE ME UNLESS I FIT YOUR IMAGE OF ME?
SEIMEI...
YOU DON'T LOVE ME THEN?
THAT'S NOT LOVE.

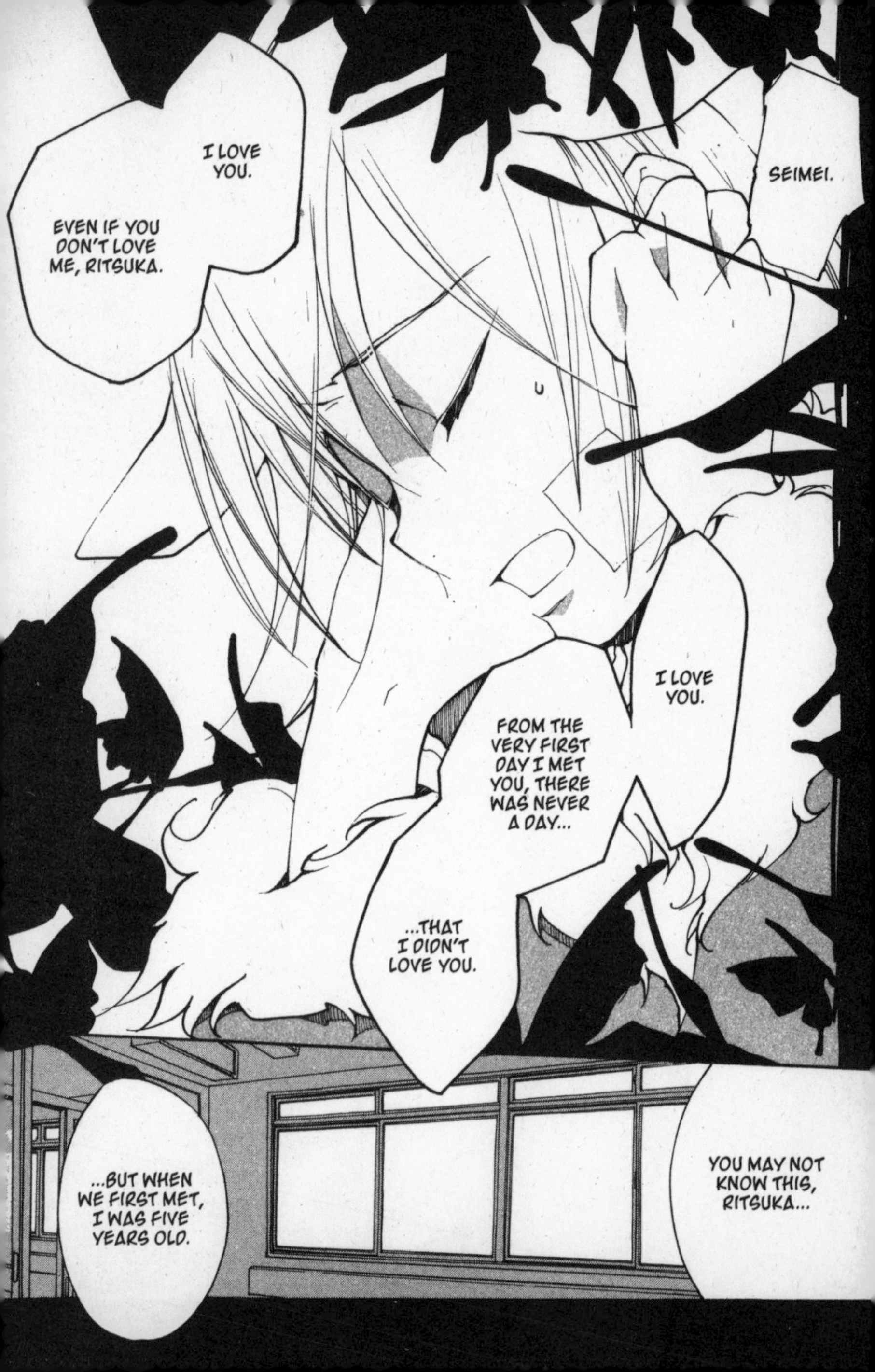
SEIMEI.
I LOVE YOU.
EVEN IF YOU DON'T LOVE ME, RITSUKA.
I LOVE YOU.
FROM THE VERY FIRST DAY I MET YOU, THERE WAS NEVER A DAY...
...THAT I DIDN'T LOVE YOU.
YOU MAY NOT KNOW THIS, RITSUKA...
...BUT WHEN WE FIRST MET, I WAS FIVE YEARS OLD.

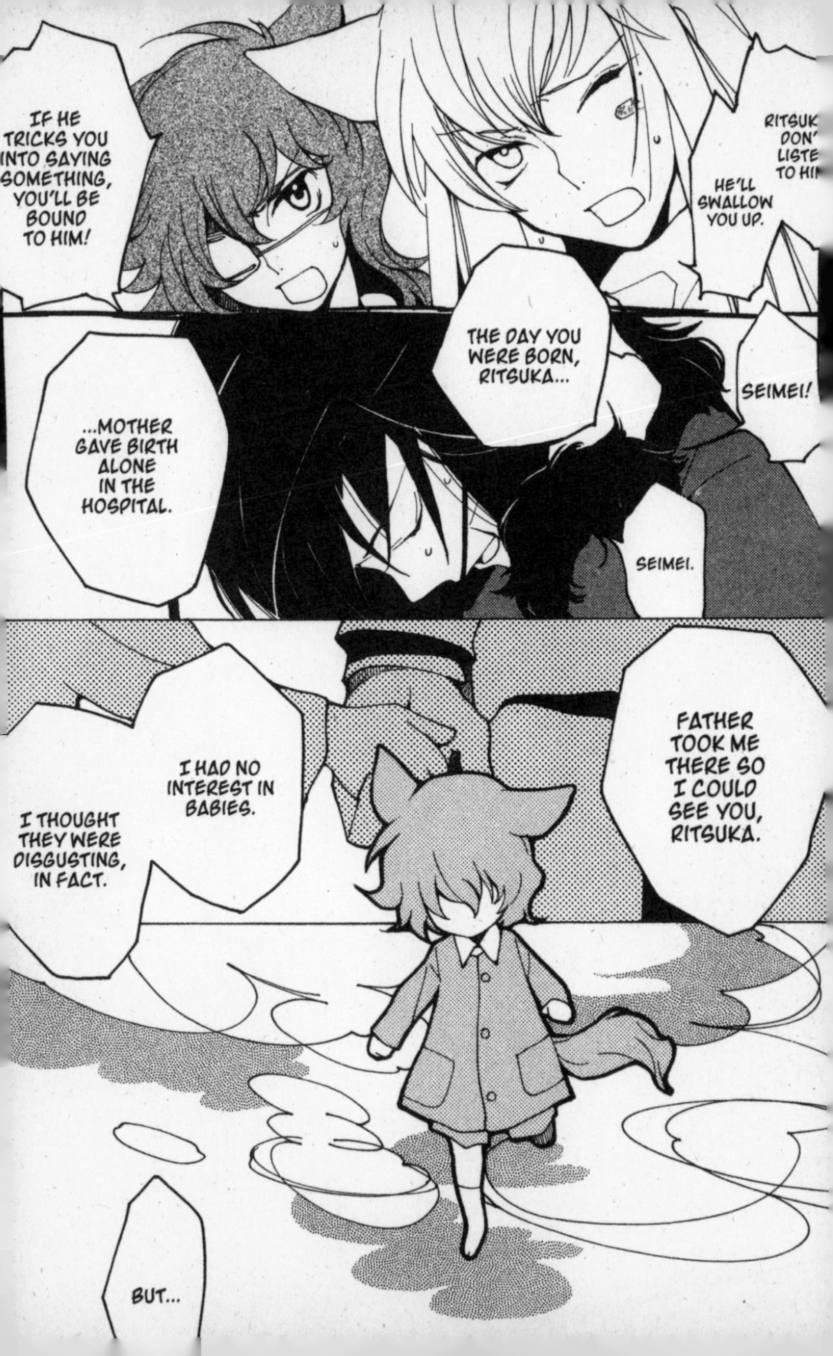
RITSUK DON' LISTE TO HI
HE'LL SWALLOW YOU UP.
IF HE TRICKS YOU INTO SAYING SOMETHING, YOU'LL BE BOUND TO HIM!
SEIMEI!
SEIMEI.
THE DAY YOU WERE BORN, RITSUKA...
...MOTHER GAVE BIRTH ALONE IN THE HOSPITAL.
FATHER TOOK ME THERE SO I COULD SEE YOU, RITSUKA.
I HAD NO INTEREST IN BABIES.
I THOUGHT THEY WERE DISGUSTING, IN FACT.
BUT...

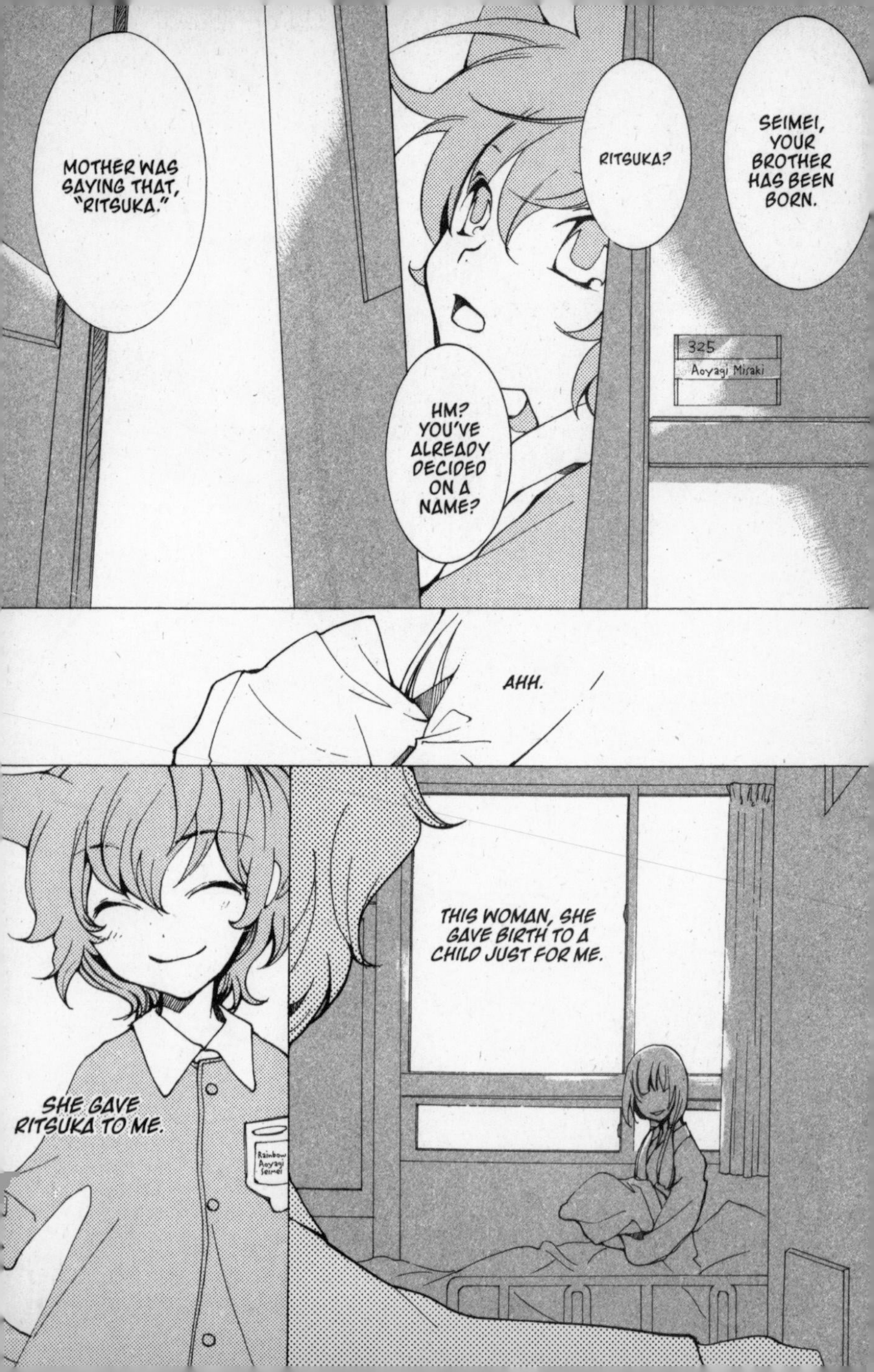
SEIMEI, YOUR BROTHER HAS BEEN BORN.
RITSUKA?
325
Aoyagi Misaki
HM? YOU'VE ALREADY DECIDED ON A NAME?
MOTHER WAS SAYING THAT, "RITSUKA."
AHH.
THIS WOMAN, SHE GAVE BIRTH TO A CHILD JUST FOR ME.
Rainbow Aoyagi Seimei
SHE GAVE RITSUKA TO ME.

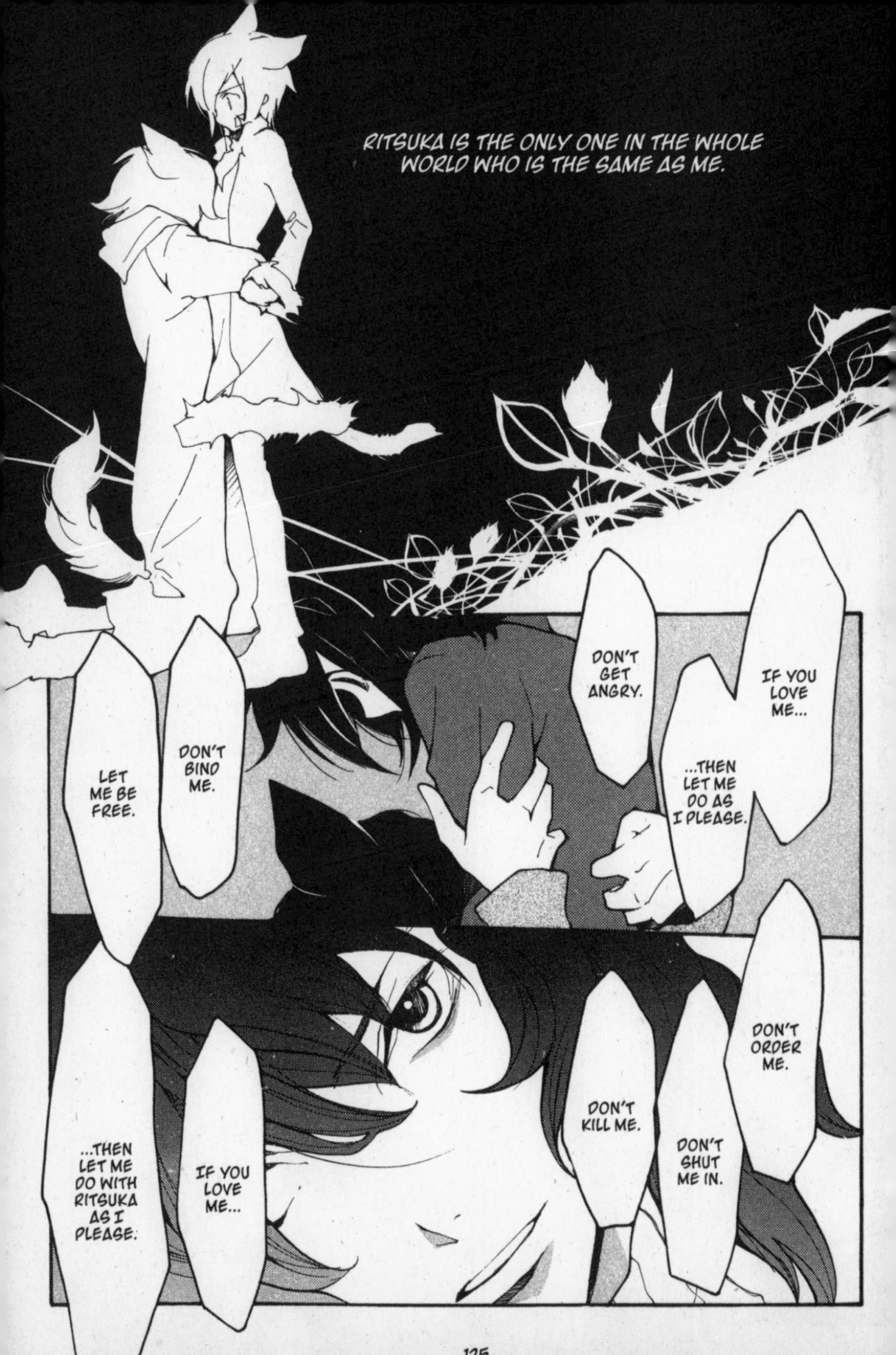
RITSUKA IS THE ONLY ONE IN THE WHOLE WORLD WHO IS THE SAME AS ME.
IF YOU LOVE ME...
...THEN LET ME DO AS I PLEASE.
DON'T GET ANGRY.
DON'T BIND ME.
LET ME BE FREE.
DON'T ORDER ME.
DON'T SHUT ME IN.
DON'T KILL ME.
IF YOU LOVE ME...
...THEN LET ME DO WITH RITSUKA AS I PLEASE.

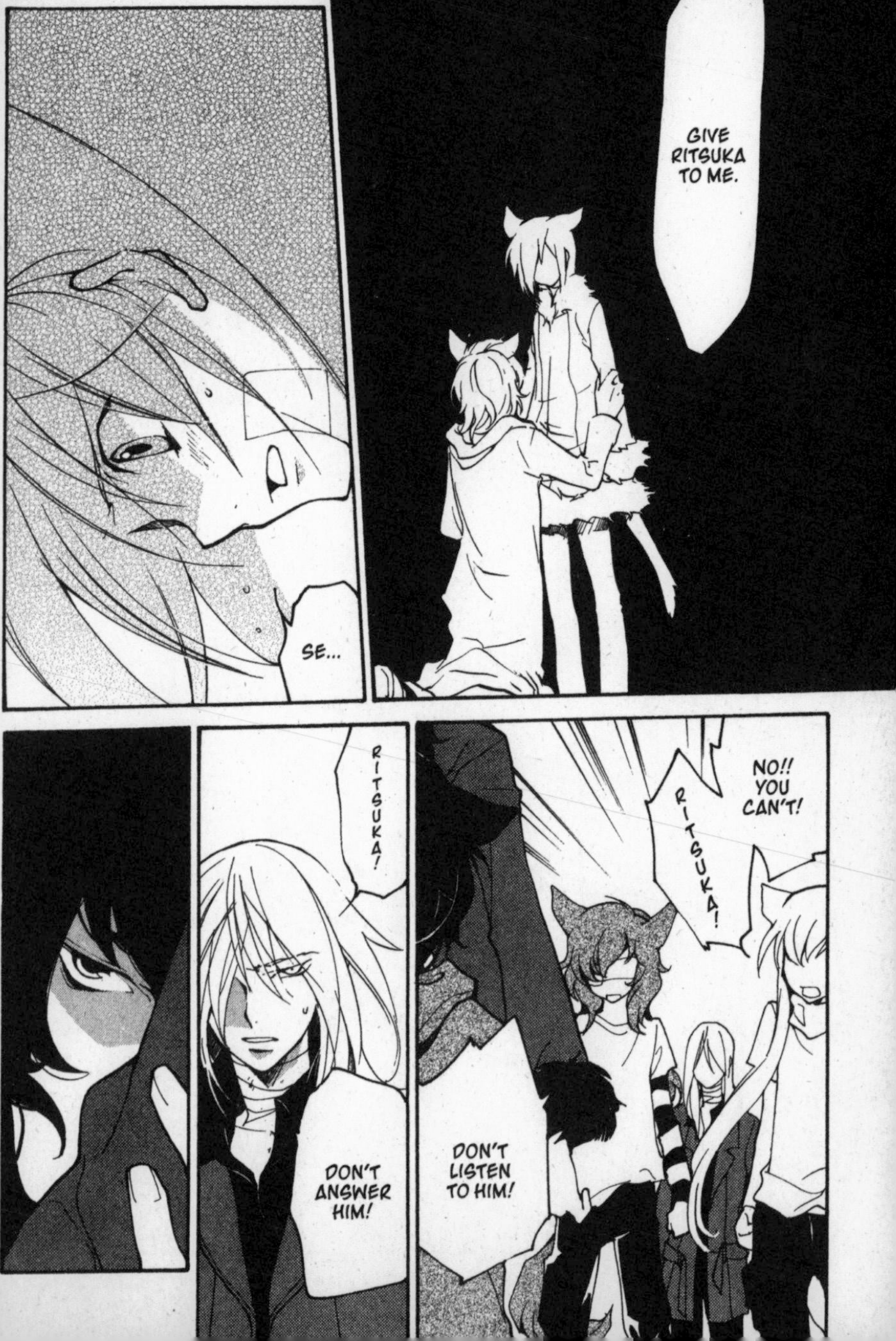
GIVE RITSUKA TO ME.
SE...
NO!! YOU CAN'T!
RITSUKA!
DON'T LISTEN TO HIM!
RITSUKA!
DON'T ANSWER HIM!

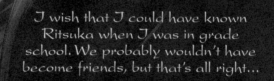

I wish that I could have known
Ritsuka when I was in grade
school. We probably wouldn't have
become friends, but that's all right...

LOVELESS

YUN KOUGA

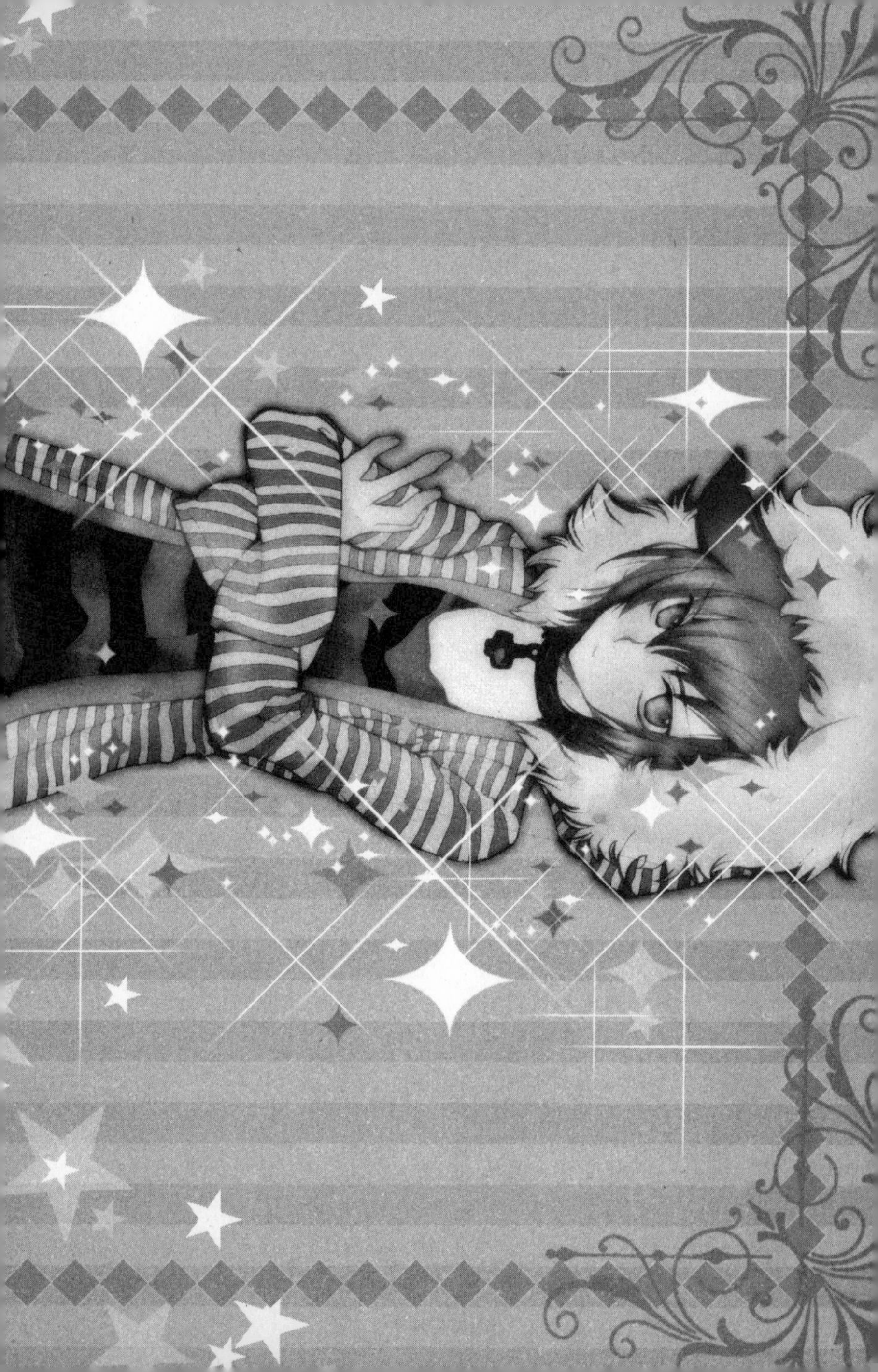

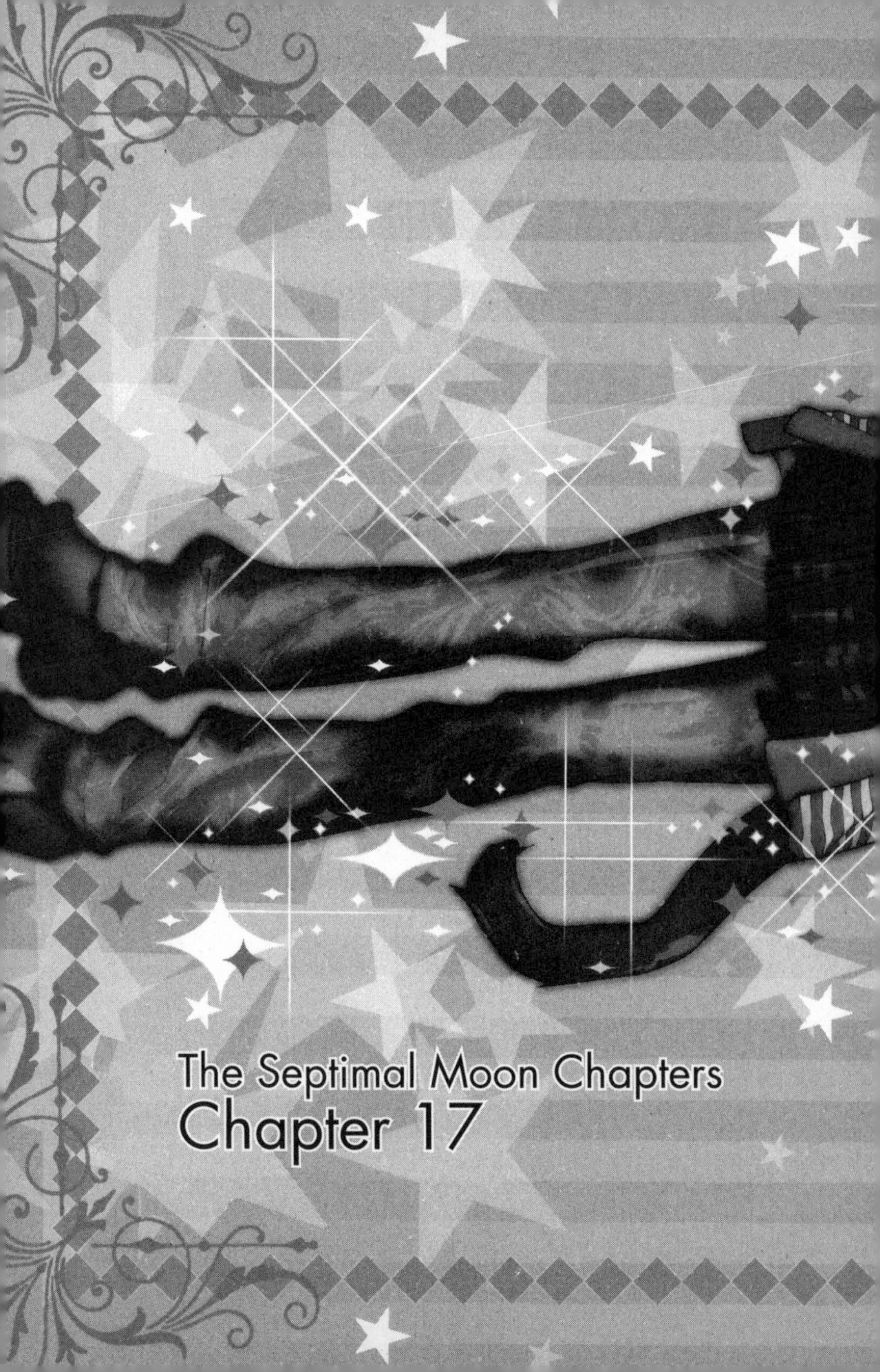

The Septimal Moon Chapters
Chapter 17

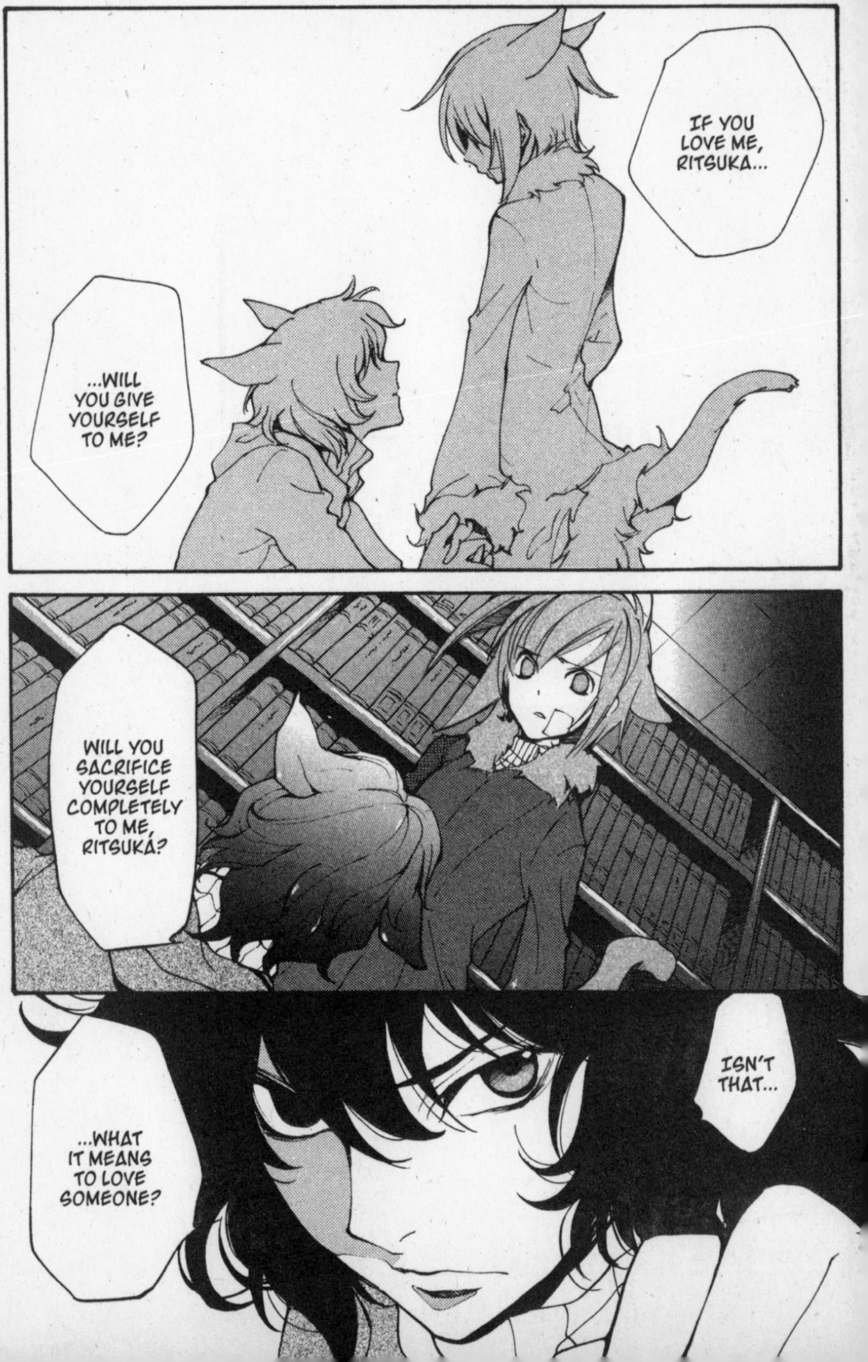
IF YOU LOVE ME, RITSUKA...
...WILL YOU GIVE YOURSELF TO ME?
WILL YOU SACRIFICE YOURSELF COMPLETELY TO ME, RITSUKA?
ISN'T THAT...
...WHAT IT MEANS TO LOVE SOMEONE?

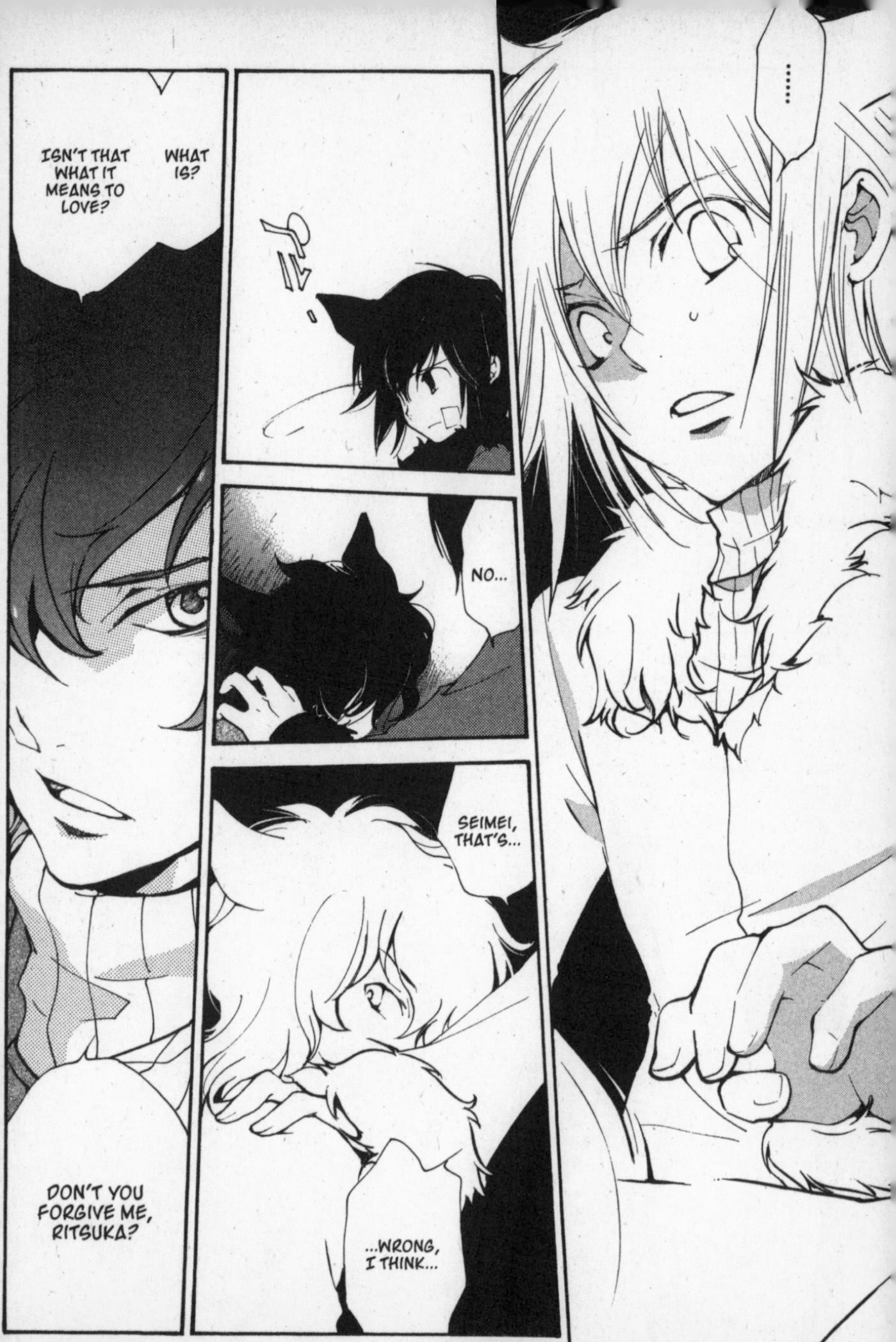
......
NO...
SEIMEI, THAT'S...
...WRONG, I THINK...
WHAT IS?
ISN'T THAT WHAT IT MEANS TO LOVE?
DON'T YOU FORGIVE ME, RITSUKA?

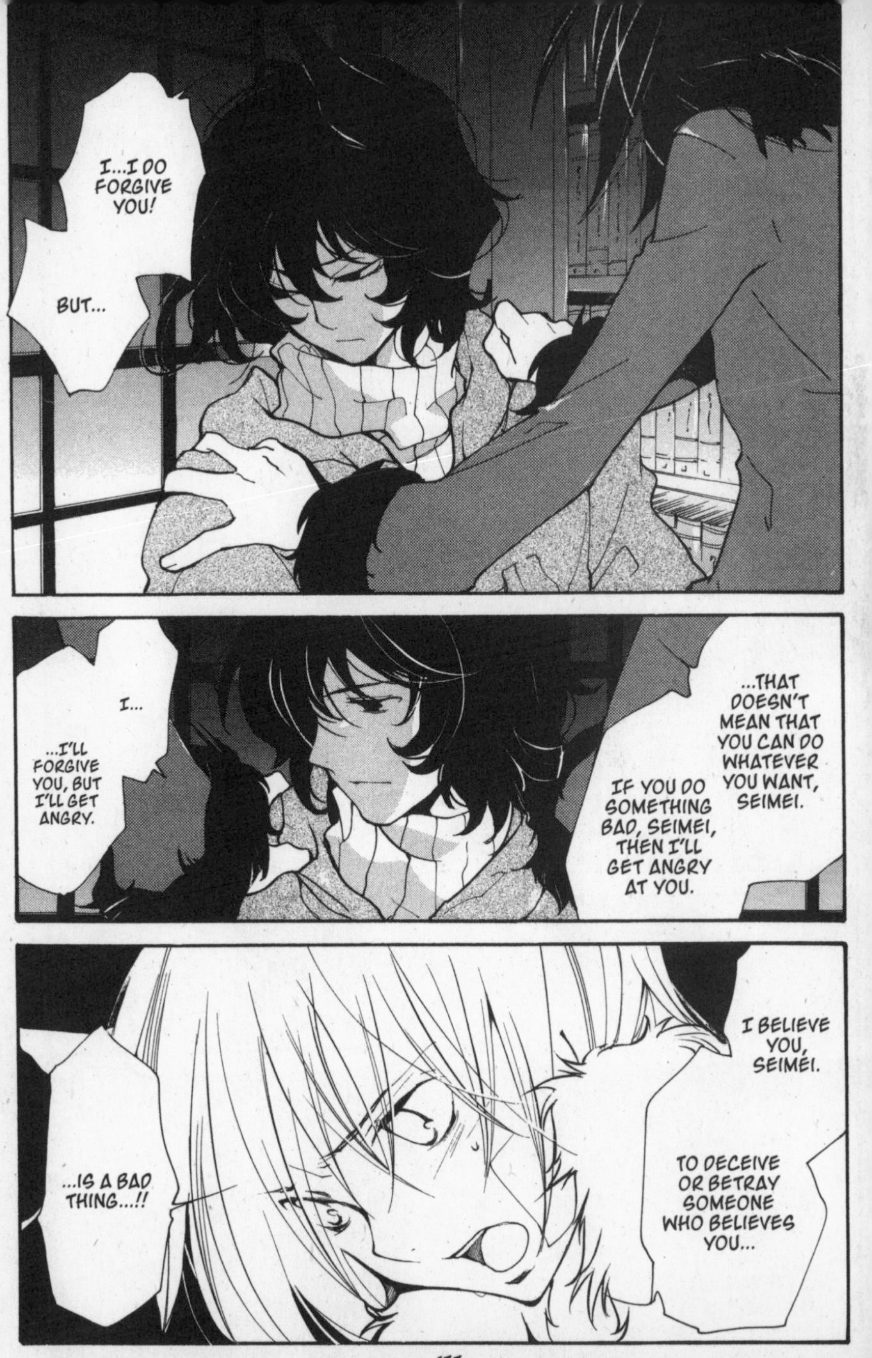
I...I DO FORGIVE YOU!
BUT...
...THAT DOESN'T MEAN THAT YOU CAN DO WHATEVER YOU WANT, SEIMEI.
IF YOU DO SOMETHING BAD, SEIMEI, THEN I'LL GET ANGRY AT YOU.
I...
...I'LL FORGIVE YOU, BUT I'LL GET ANGRY.
I BELIEVE YOU, SEIMEI.
TO DECEIVE OR BETRAY SOMEONE WHO BELIEVES YOU...
...IS A BAD THING...!!

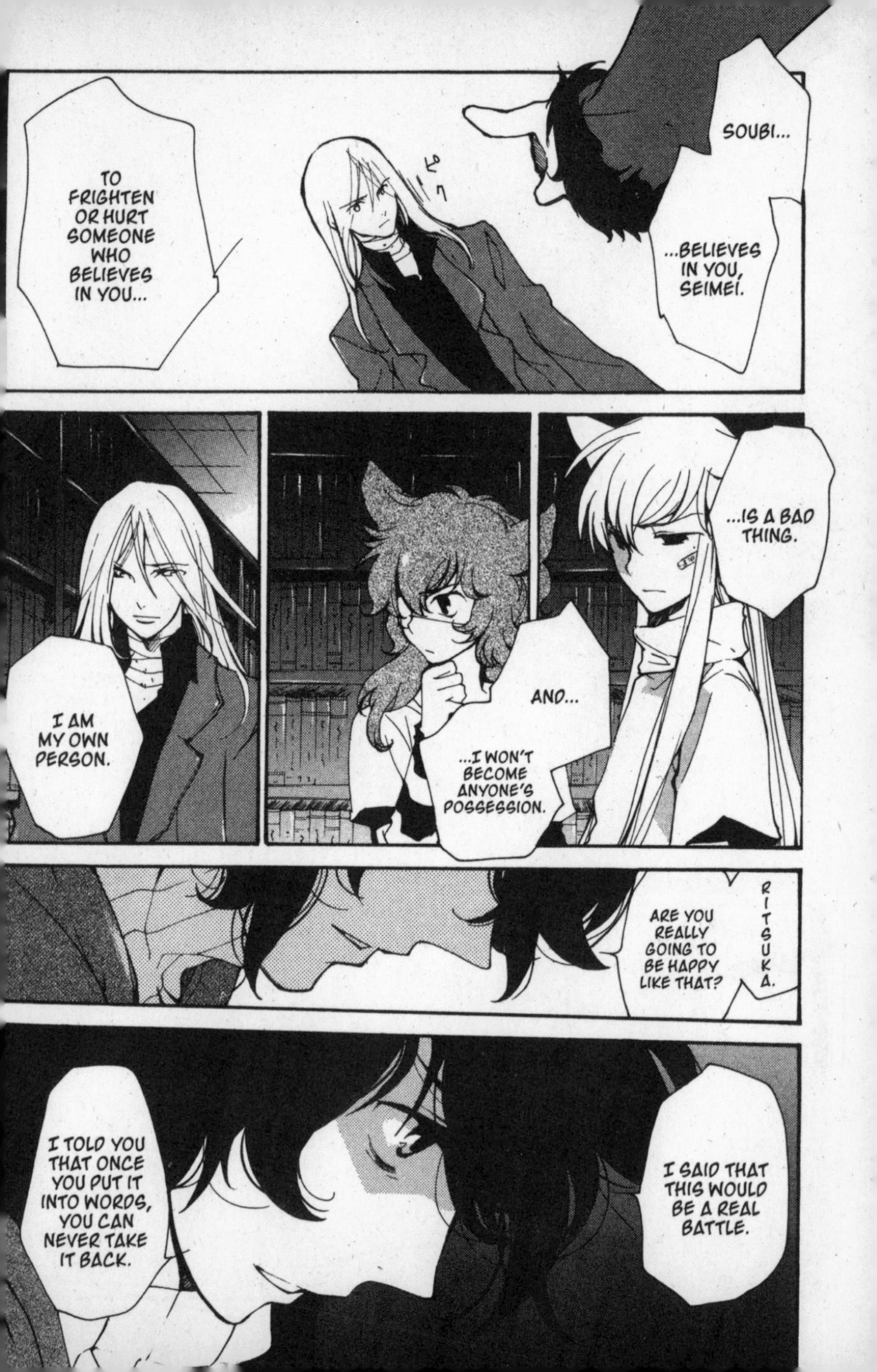
SOUBI...
...BELIEVES IN YOU, SEIMEI.
TO FRIGHTEN OR HURT SOMEONE WHO BELIEVES IN YOU...
...IS A BAD THING.
AND...
...I WON'T BECOME ANYONE'S POSSESSION.
I AM MY OWN PERSON.
RITSUKA.
ARE YOU REALLY GOING TO BE HAPPY LIKE THAT?
I SAID THAT THIS WOULD BE A REAL BATTLE.
I TOLD YOU THAT ONCE YOU PUT IT INTO WORDS, YOU CAN NEVER TAKE IT BACK.

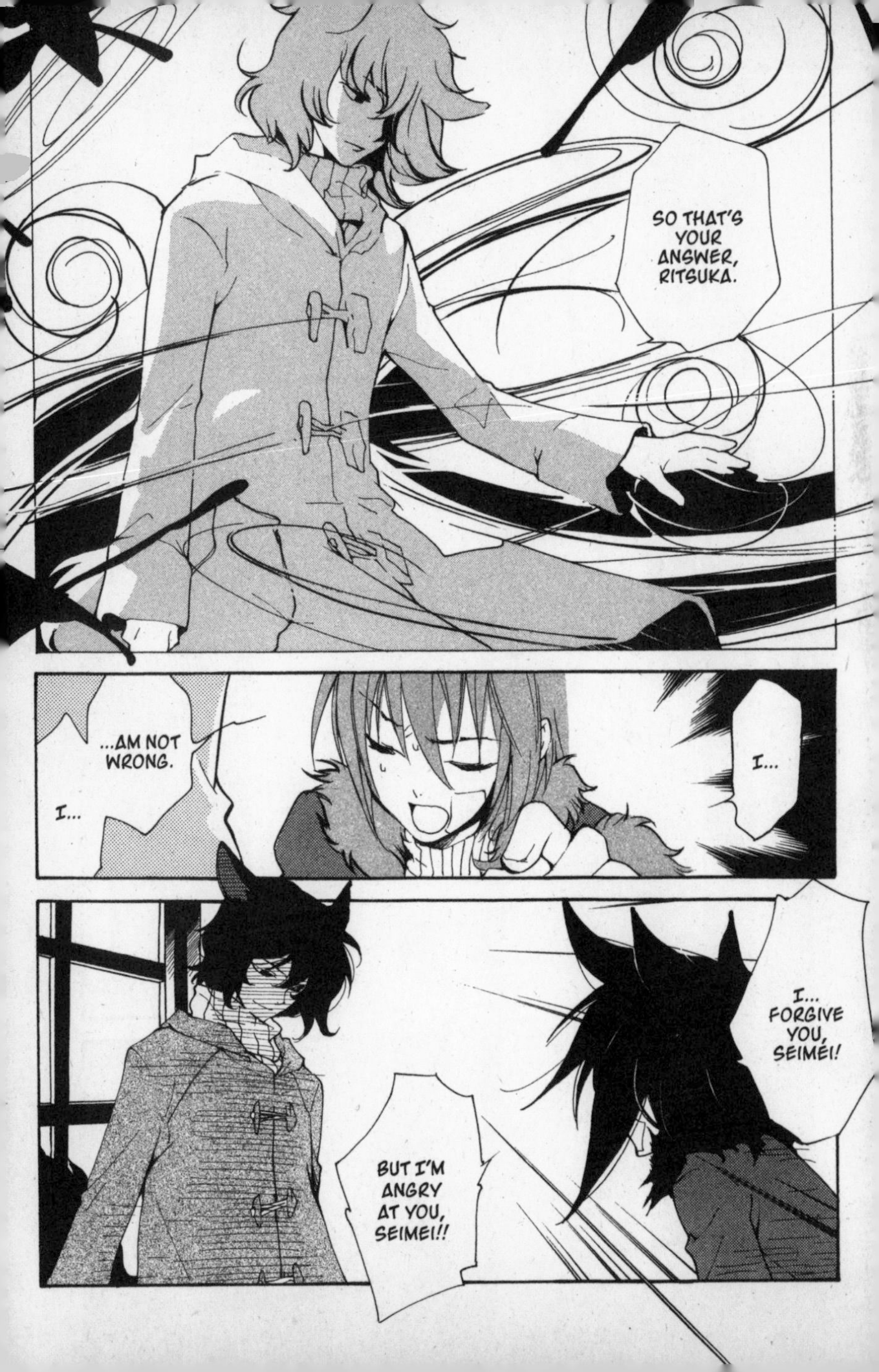
SO THAT'S YOUR ANSWER, RITSUKA.
I...
I...
...AM NOT WRONG.
I... FORGIVE YOU, SEIMEI!
BUT I'M ANGRY AT YOU, SEIMEI!!

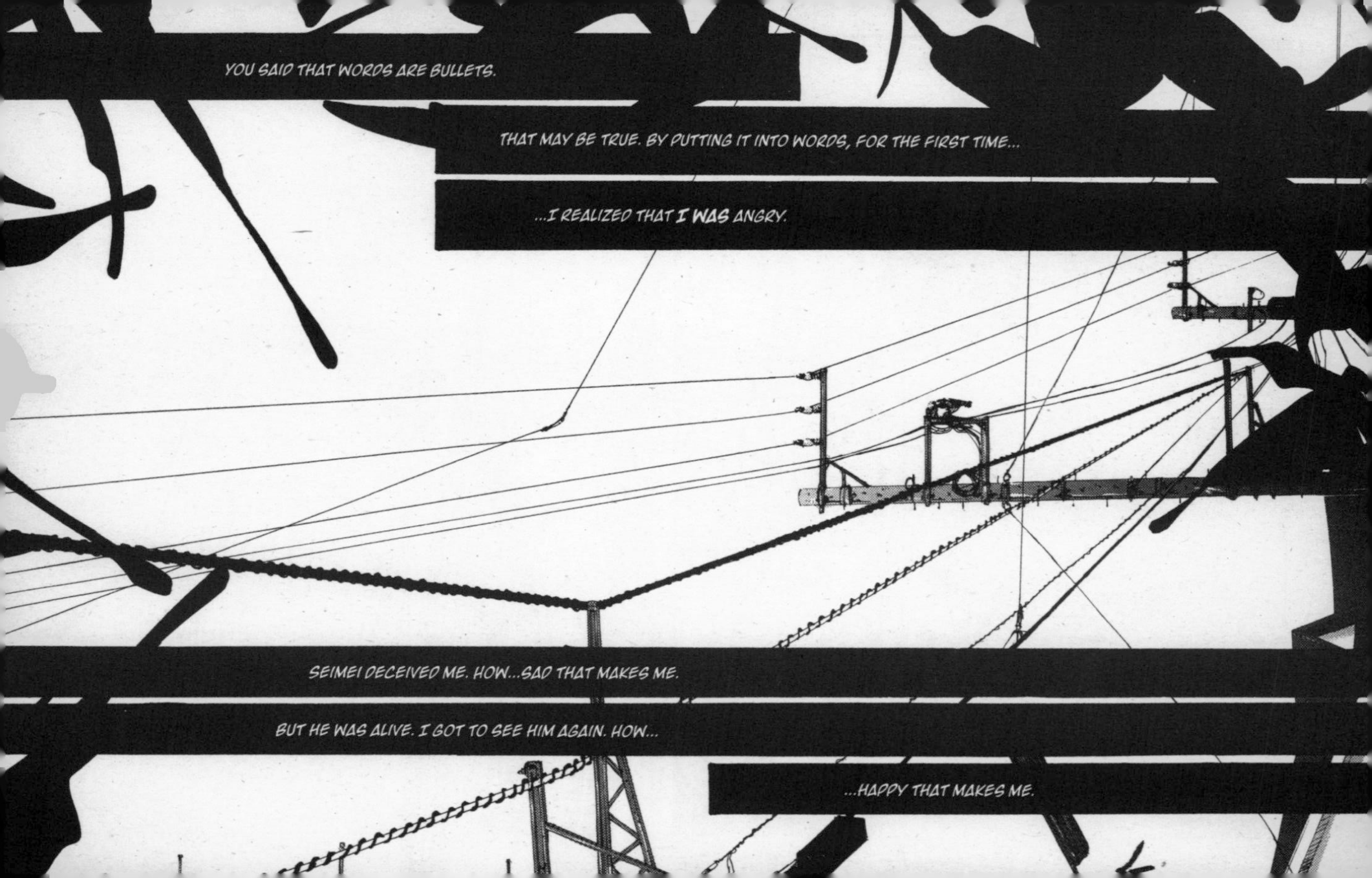
YOU SAID THAT WORDS ARE BULLETS.
THAT MAY BE TRUE. BY PUTTING IT INTO WORDS, FOR THE FIRST TIME...
...I REALIZED THAT I WAS ANGRY.
SEIMEI DECEIVED ME. HOW...SAD THAT MAKES ME.
BUT HE WAS ALIVE. I GOT TO SEE HIM AGAIN. HOW...
...HAPPY THAT MAKES ME.

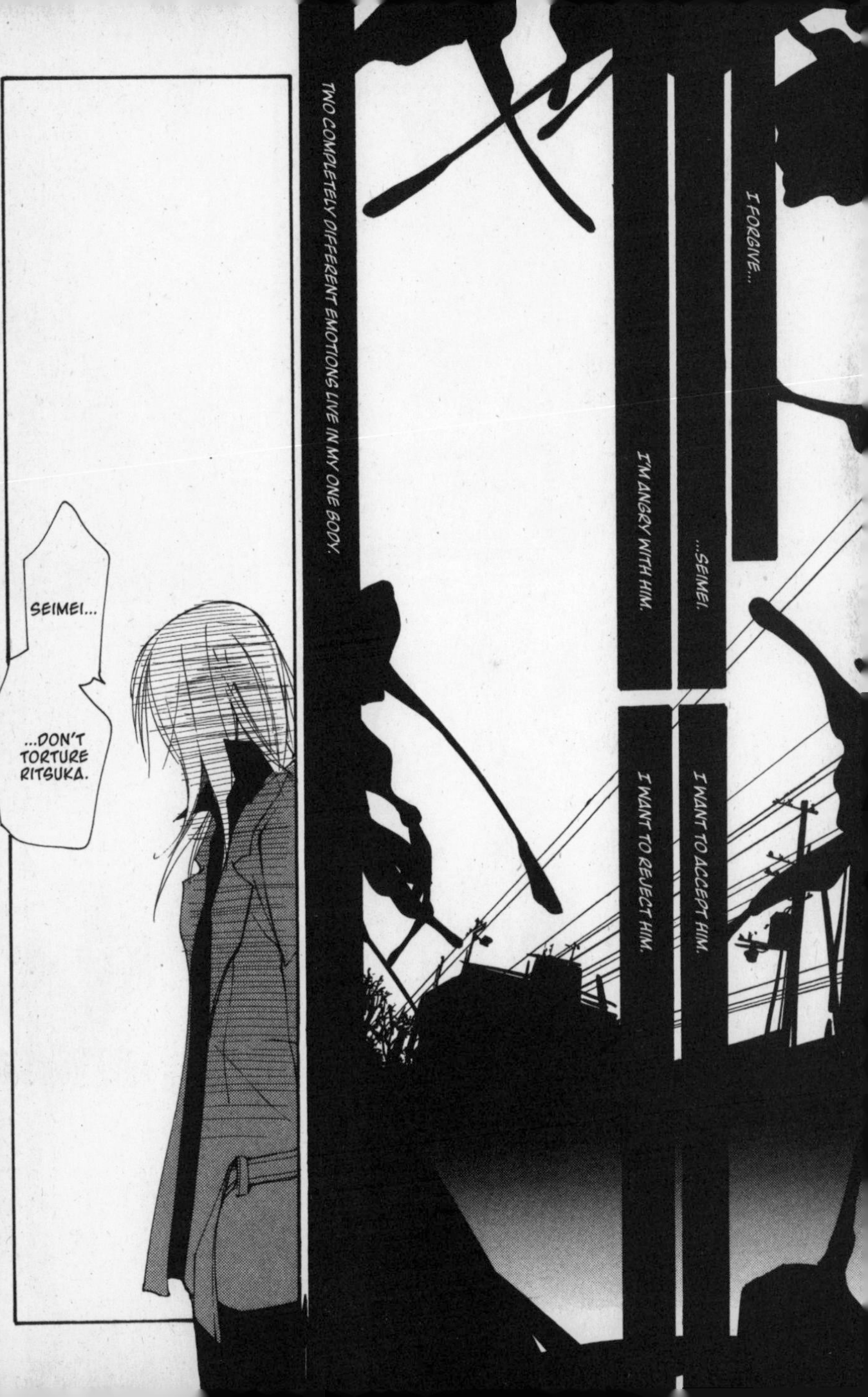
I FORGIVE...
...SEIMEI.
I'M ANGRY WITH HIM.
I WANT TO ACCEPT HIM.
I WANT TO REJECT HIM.
TWO COMPLETELY DIFFERENT EMOTIONS LIVE IN MY ONE BODY.
SEIMEI...
...DON'T TORTURE RITSUKA.

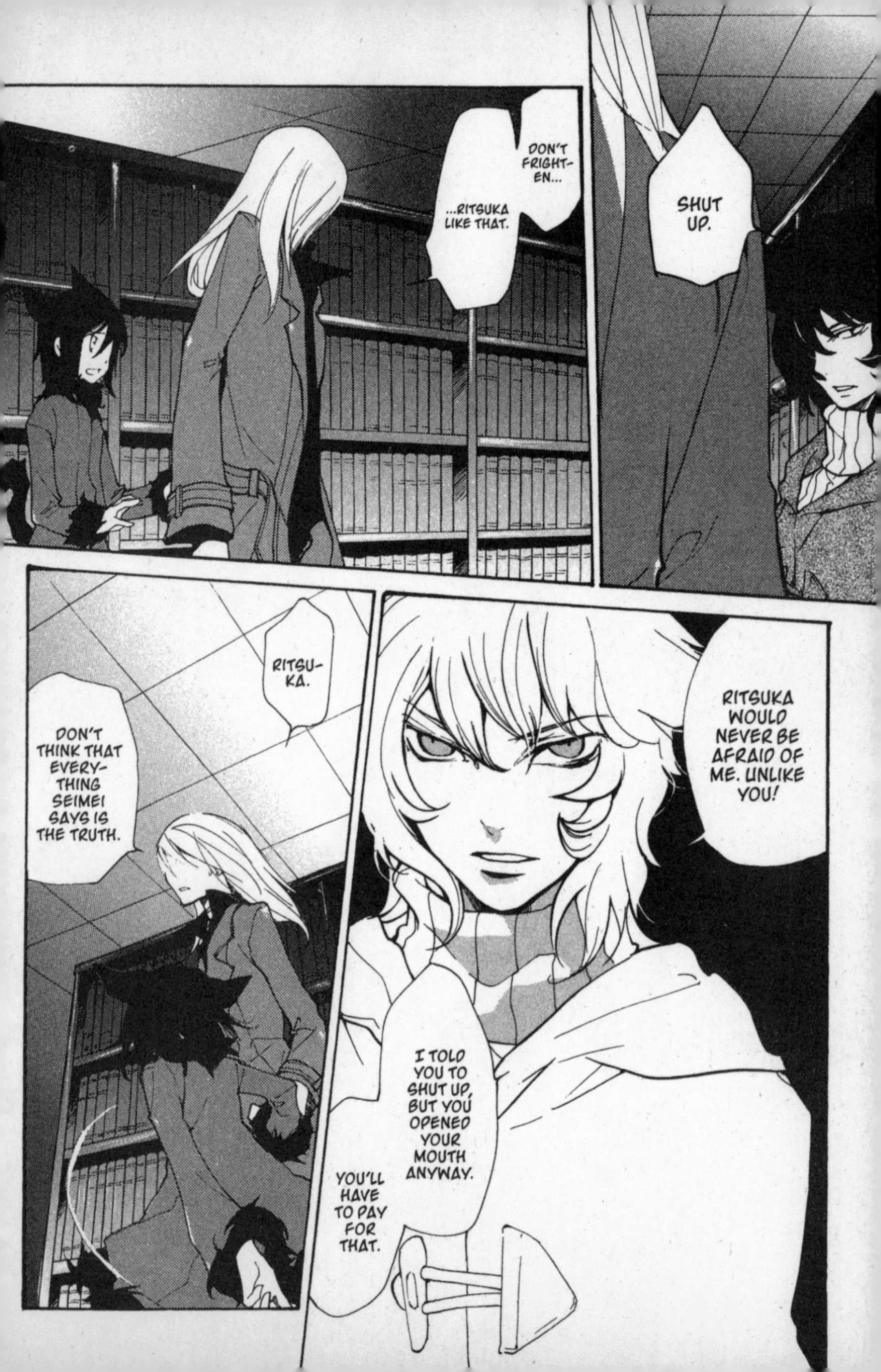
SHUT UP.
DON'T FRIGHT-EN...
...RITSUKA LIKE THAT.
RITSUKA WOULD NEVER BE AFRAID OF ME. UNLIKE YOU!
I TOLD YOU TO SHUT UP, BUT YOU OPENED YOUR MOUTH ANYWAY.
YOU'LL HAVE TO PAY FOR THAT.
RITSU-KA.
DON'T THINK THAT EVERY-THING SEIMEI SAYS IS THE TRUTH.

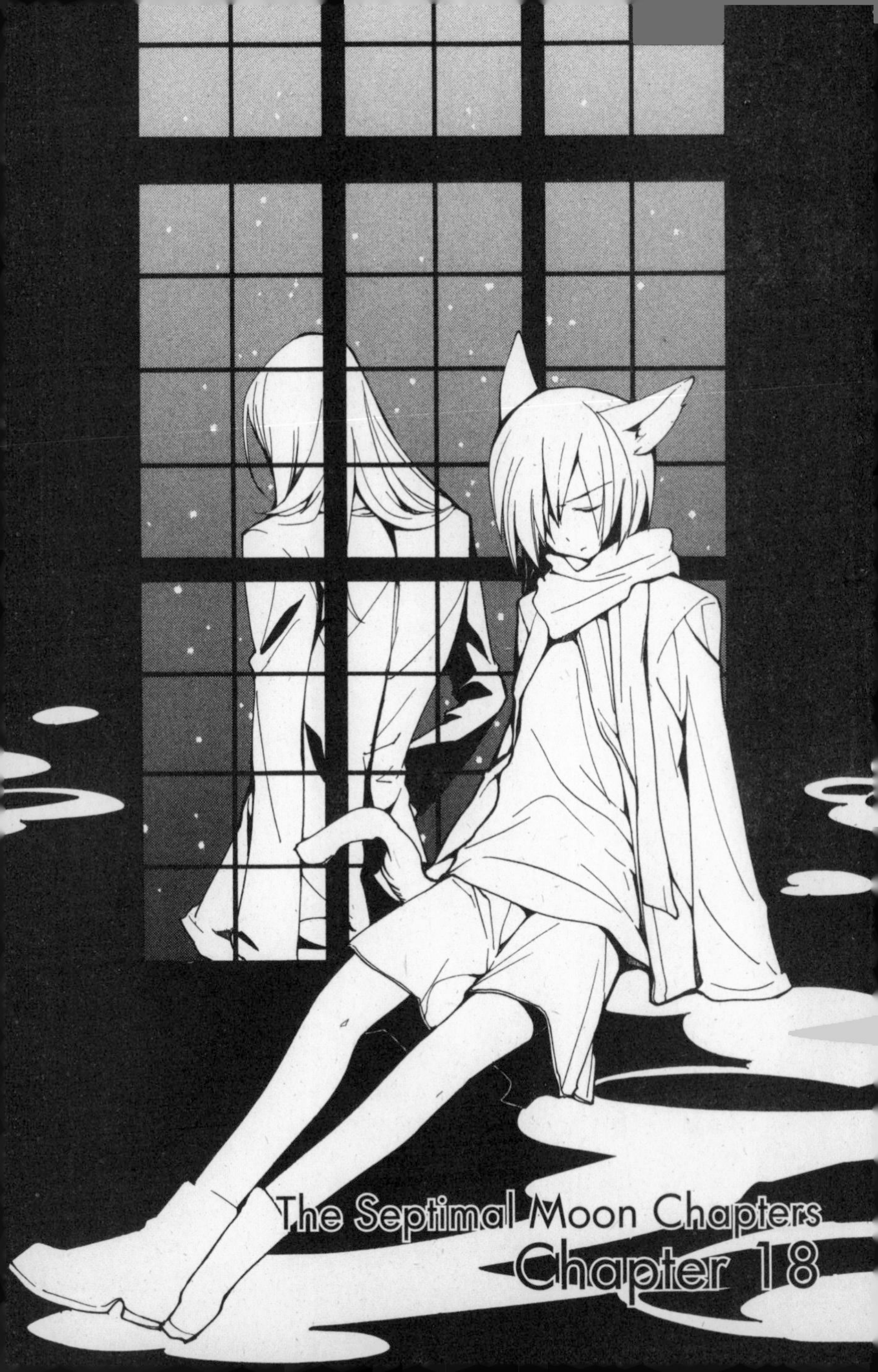
The Septimal Moon Chapters
Chapter 18

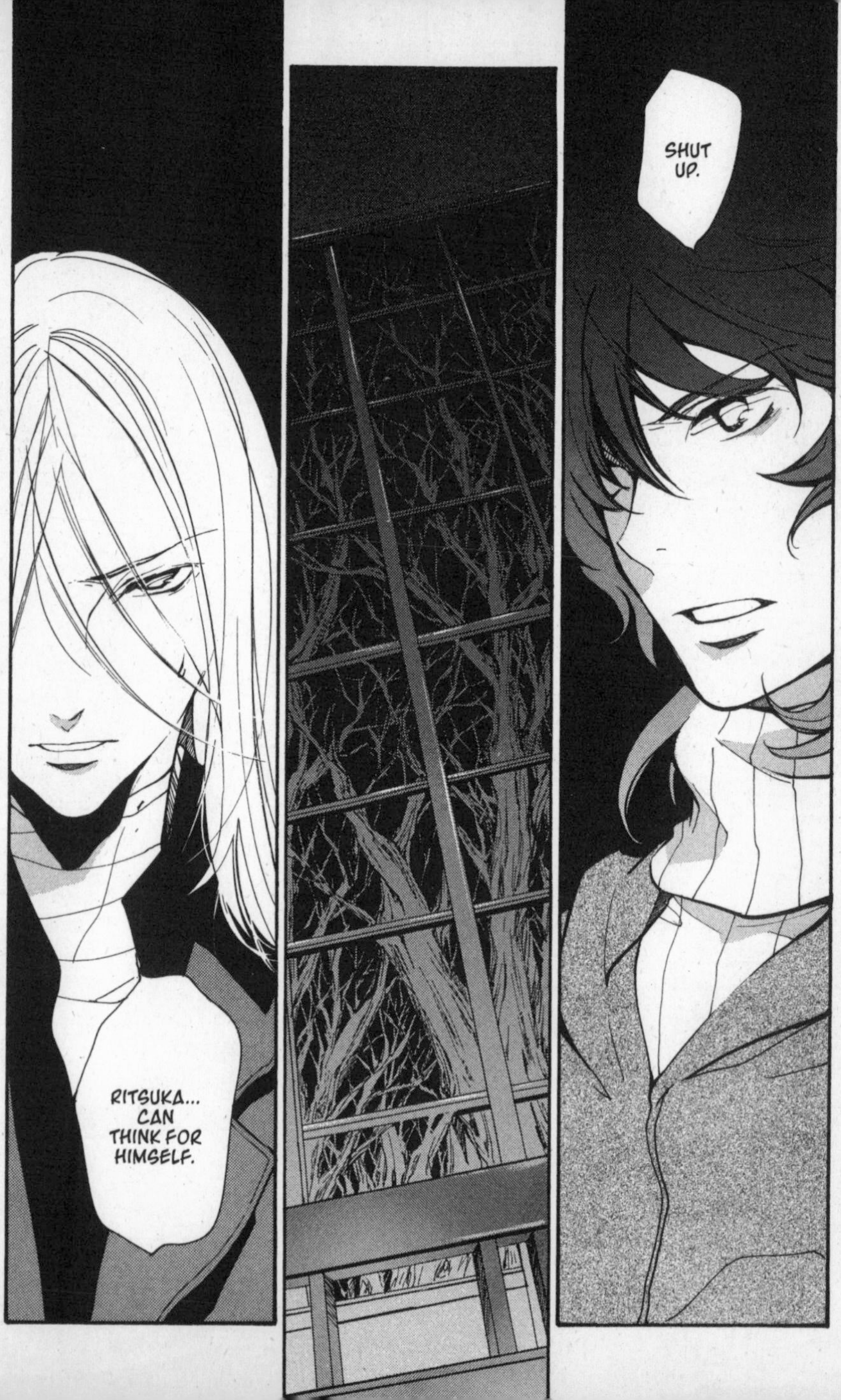
SHUT UP.
RITSUKA... CAN THINK FOR HIMSELF.

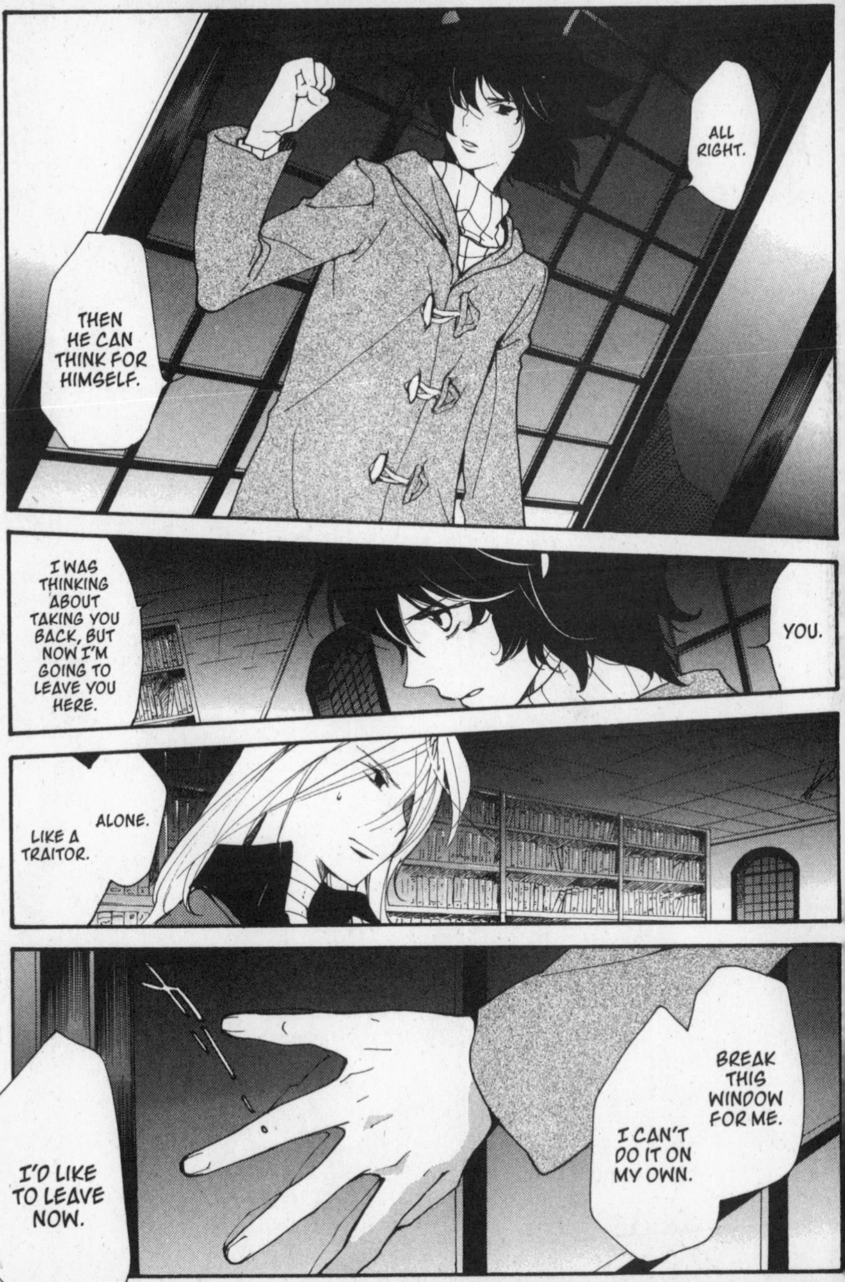
ALL RIGHT.
THEN HE CAN THINK FOR HIMSELF.
YOU.
I WAS THINKING ABOUT TAKING YOU BACK, BUT NOW I'M GOING TO LEAVE YOU HERE.
ALONE.
LIKE A TRAITOR.
BREAK THIS WINDOW FOR ME.
I CAN'T DO IT ON MY OWN.
I'D LIKE TO LEAVE NOW.

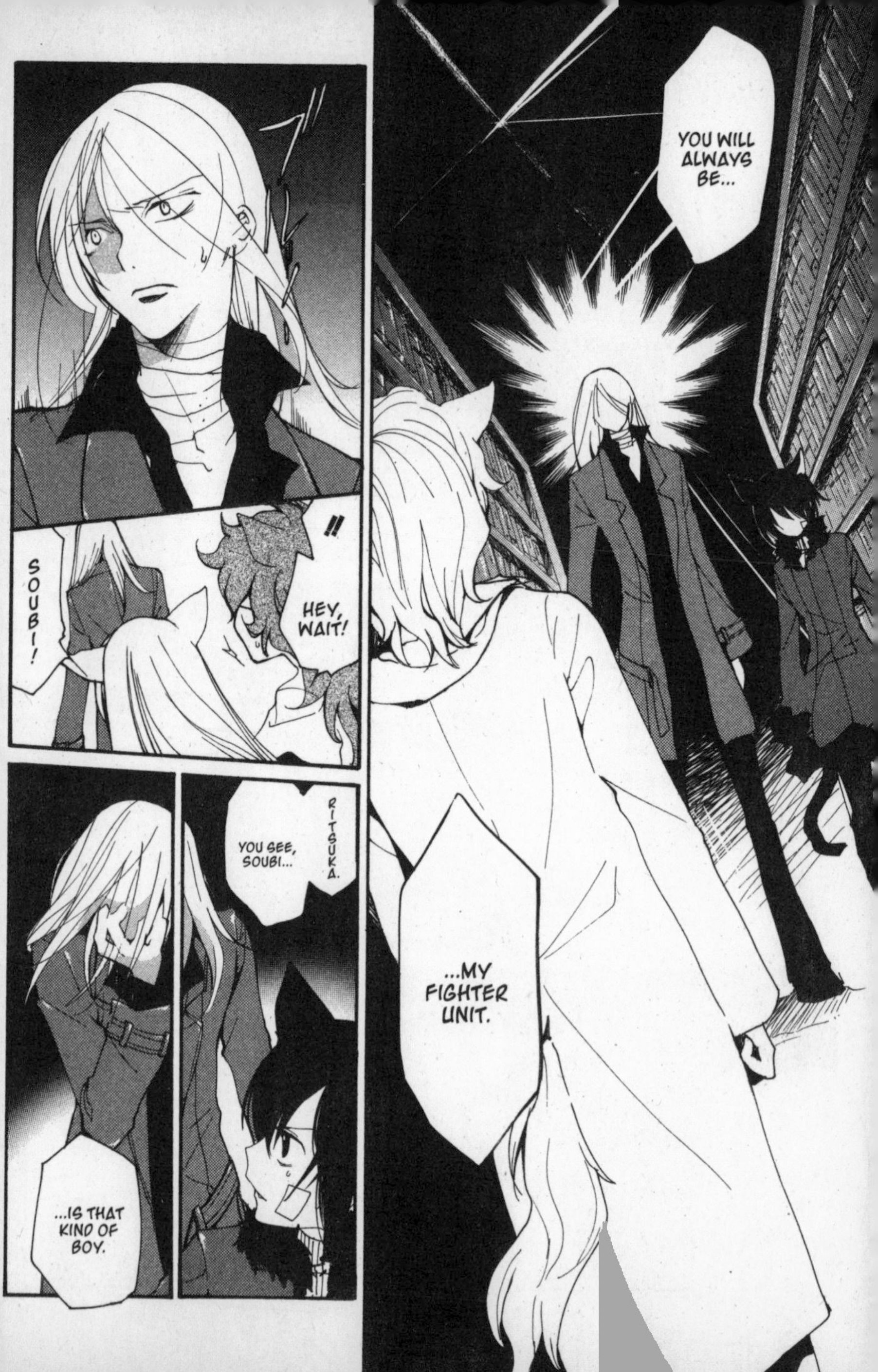
YOU WILL ALWAYS BE...
...MY FIGHTER UNIT.
!!
HEY, WAIT!
SOUBI!
RITSUKA.
YOU SEE, SOUBI...
...IS THAT KIND OF BOY.

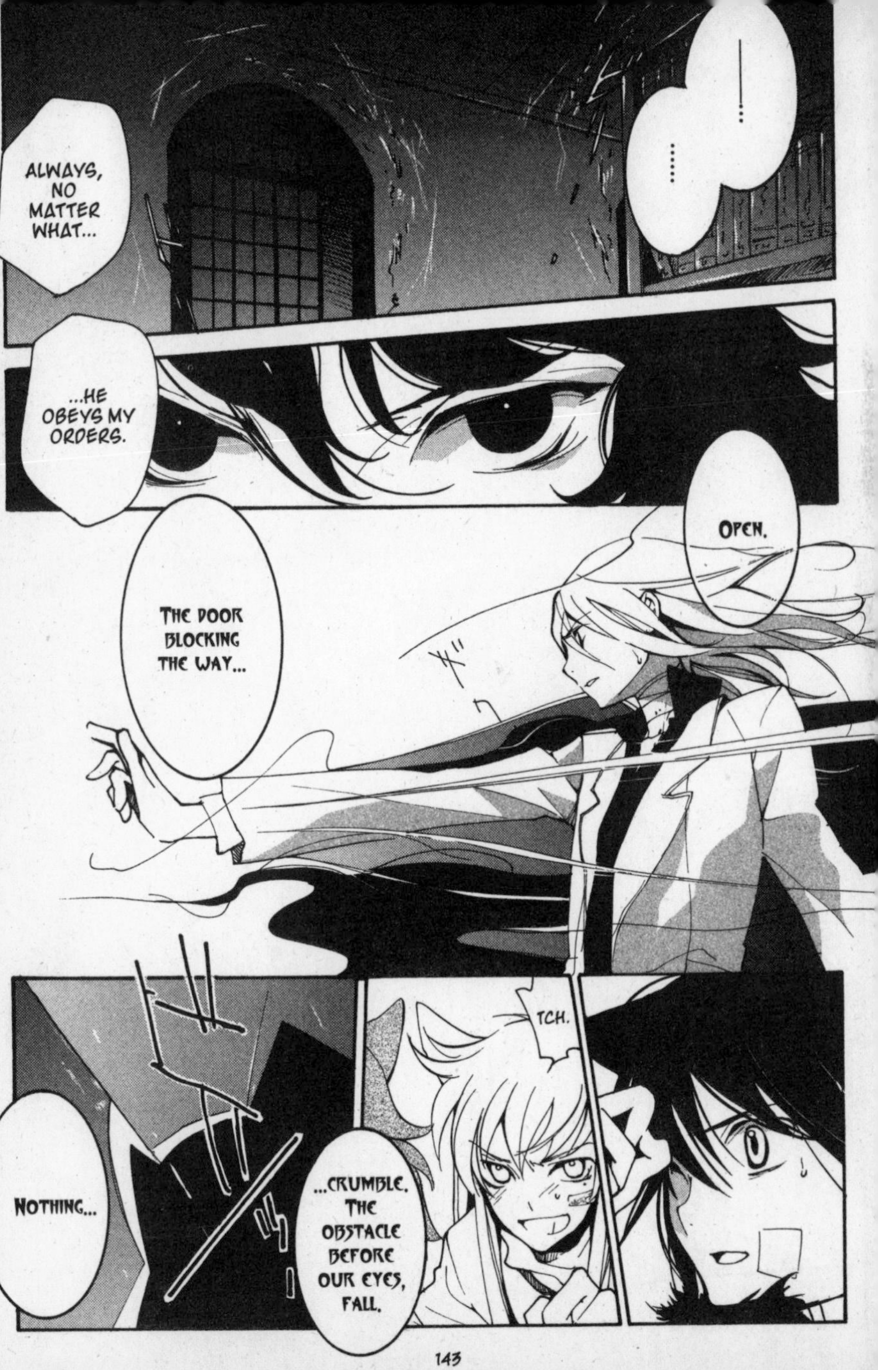
ALWAYS, NO MATTER WHAT...
...HE OBEYS MY ORDERS.
OPEN.
THE DOOR BLOCKING THE WAY...
TCH.
...CRUMBLE. THE OBSTACLE BEFORE OUR EYES, FALL.
NOTHING...

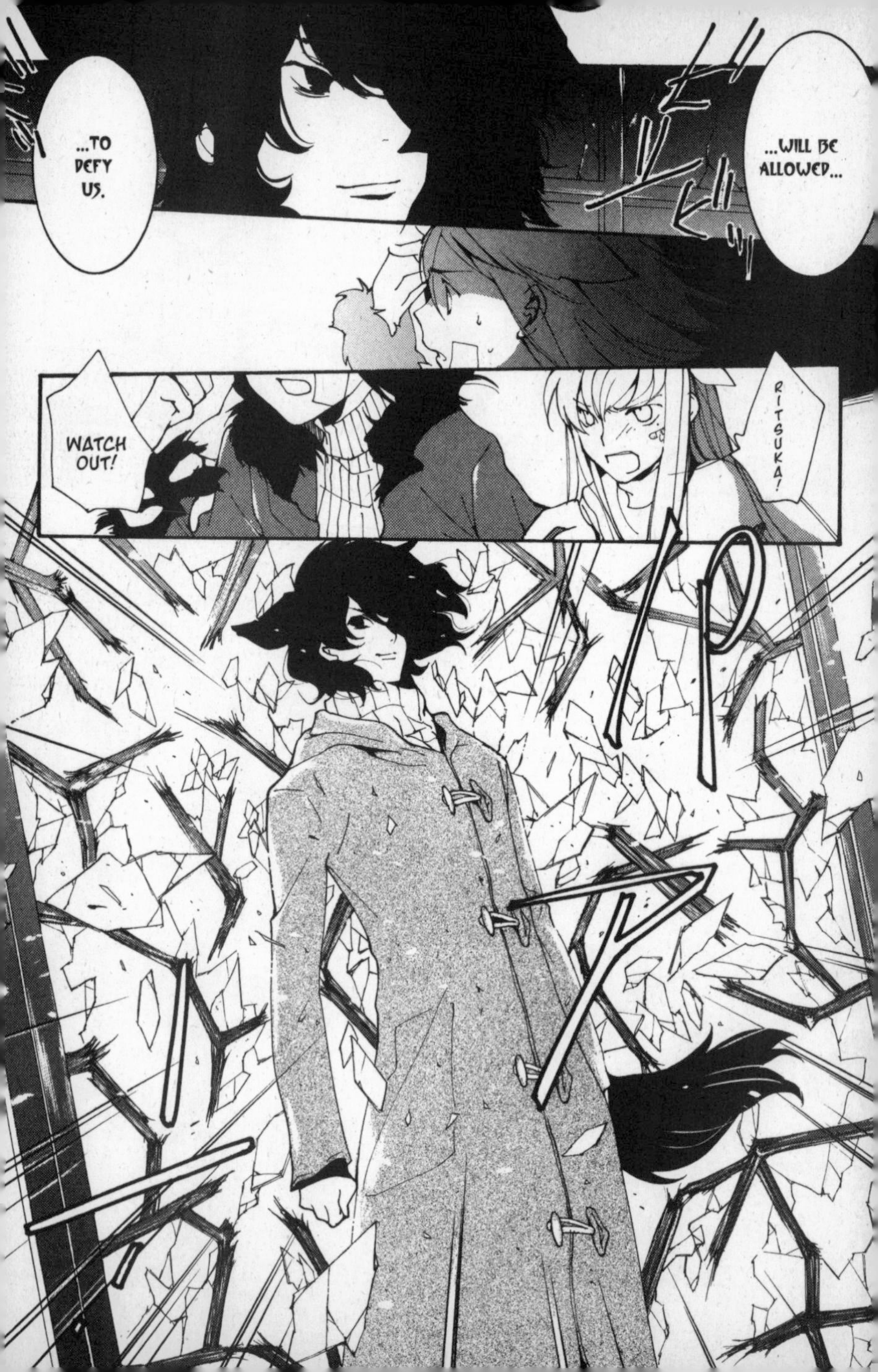
...WILL BE ALLOWED...
...TO DEFY US.
RITSUKA!
WATCH OUT!

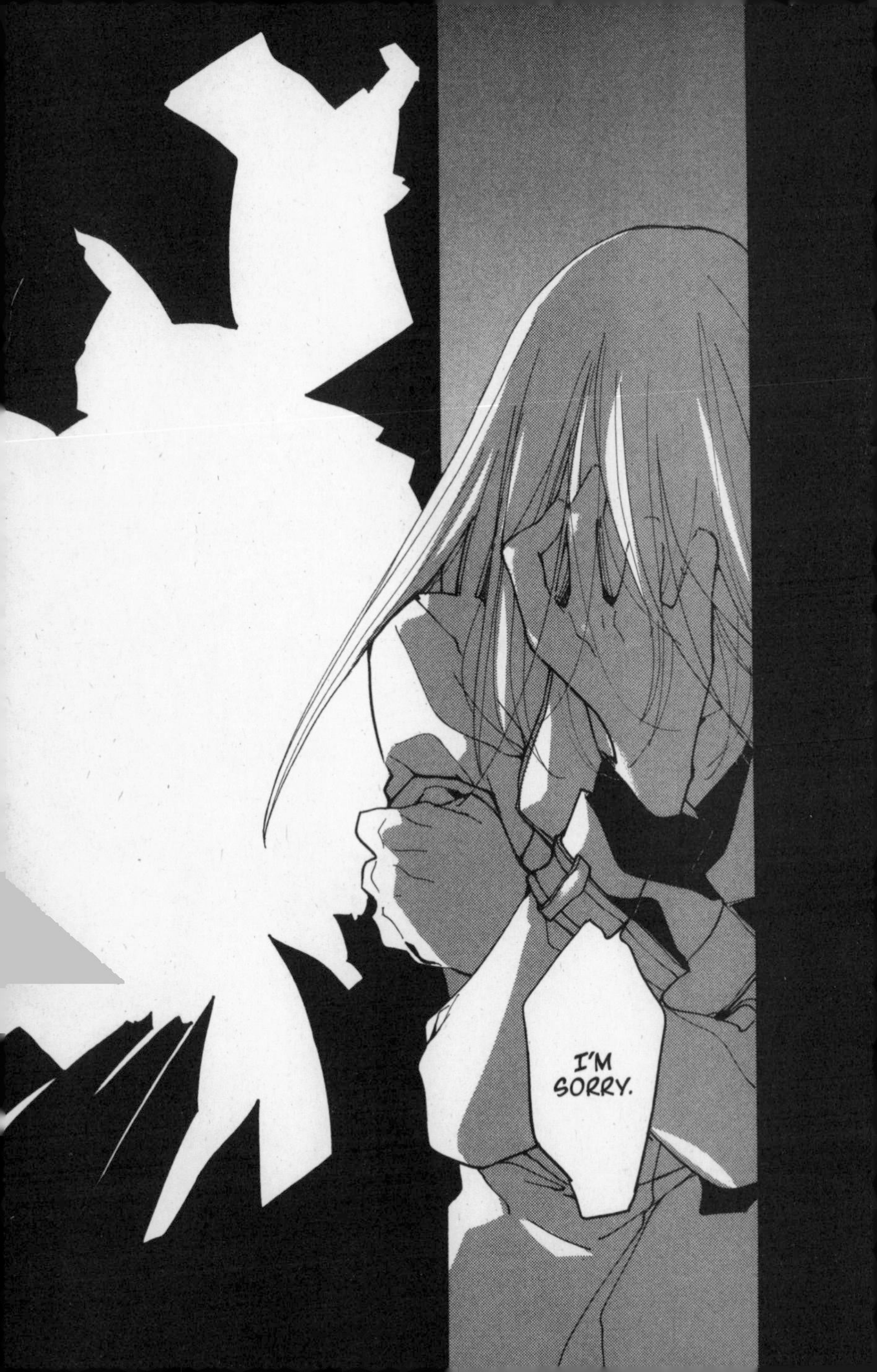
I'M SORRY.

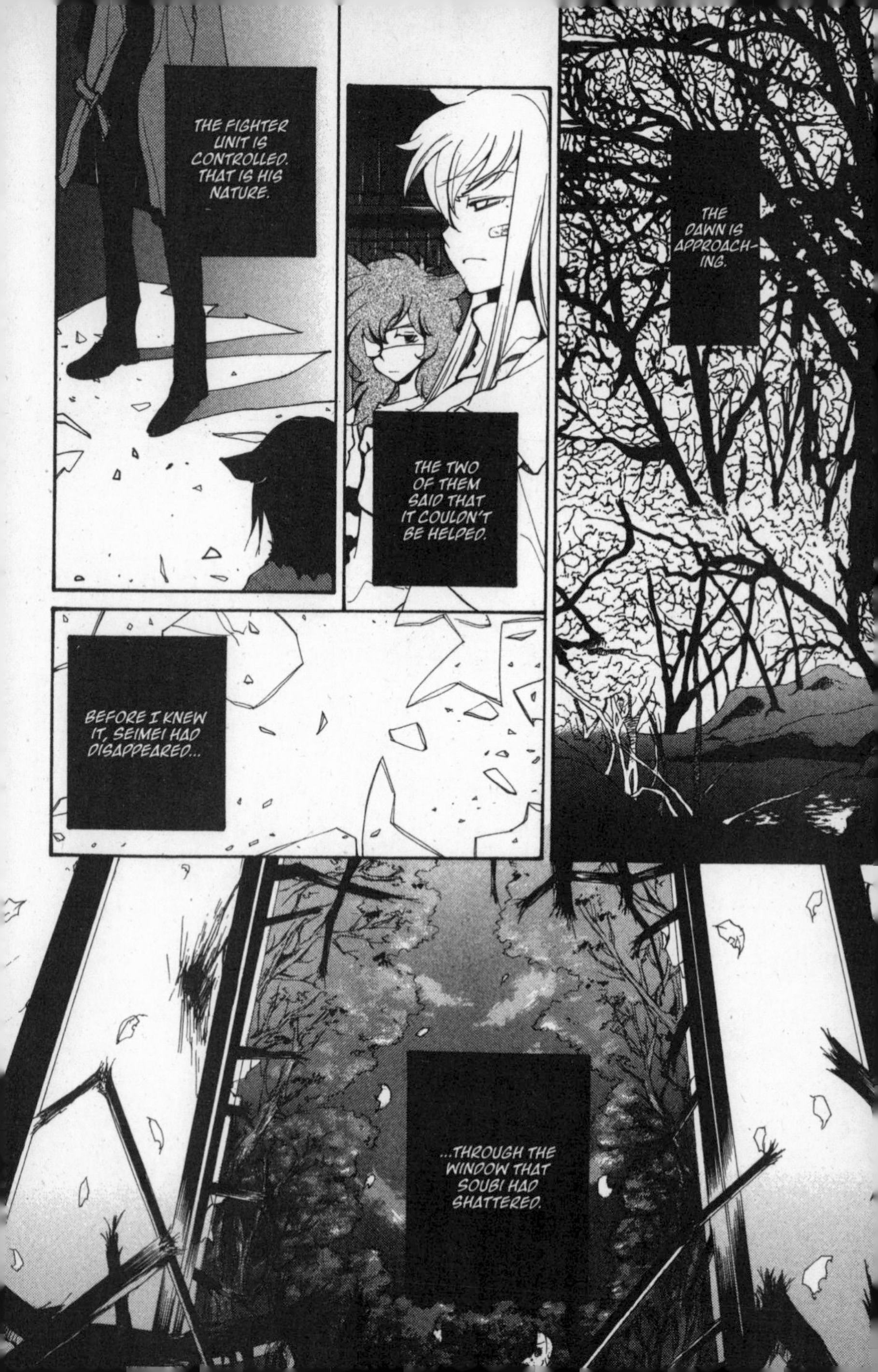
THE DAWN IS APPROACHING.
THE TWO OF THEM SAID THAT IT COULDN'T BE HELPED.
THE FIGHTER UNIT IS CONTROLLED. THAT IS HIS NATURE.
BEFORE I KNEW IT, SEIMEI HAD DISAPPEARED...
...THROUGH THE WINDOW THAT SOUBI HAD SHATTERED.

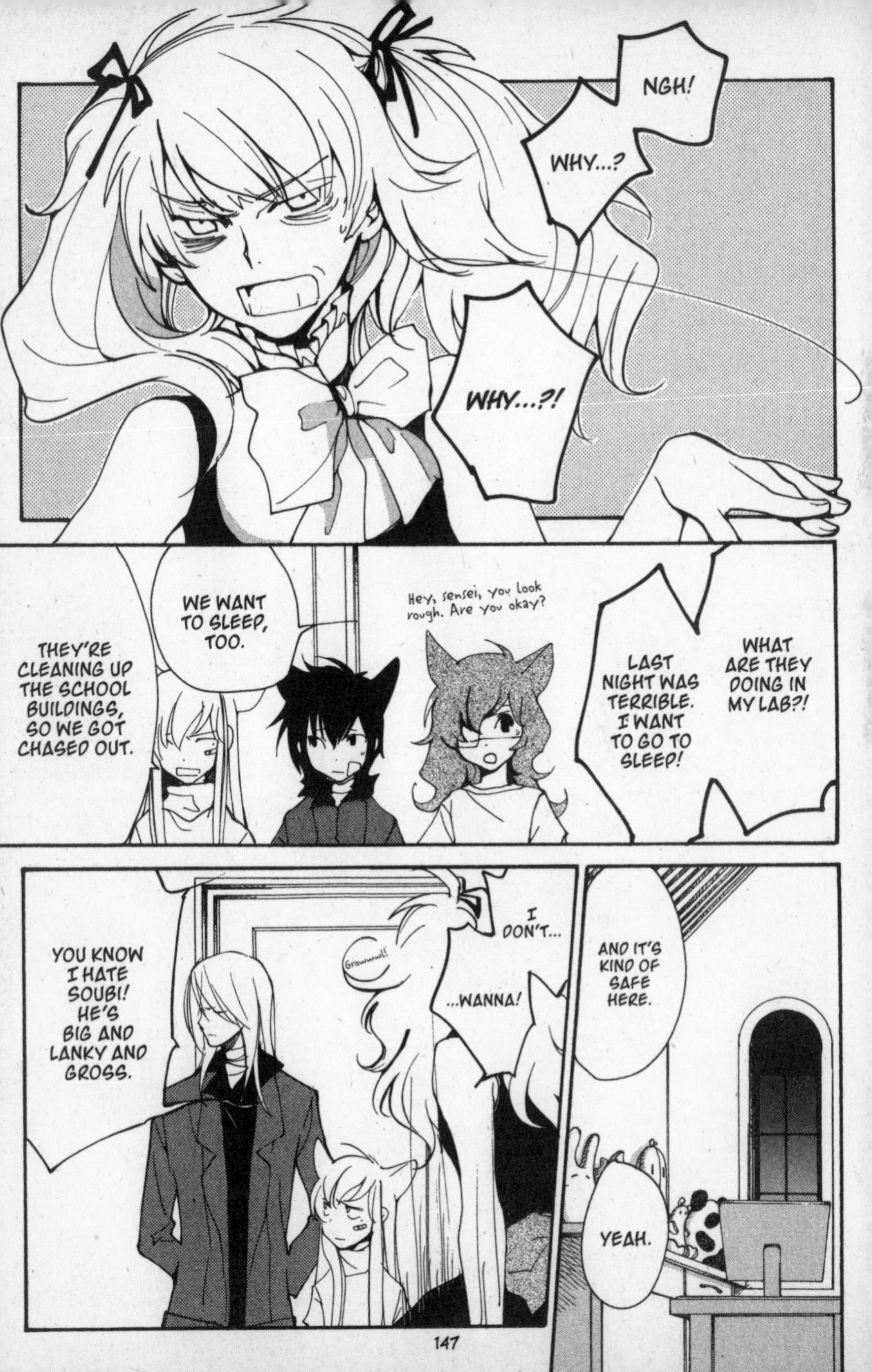
NGH!
WHY...?
WHY...?!
WHAT ARE THEY DOING IN MY LAB?!
LAST NIGHT WAS TERRIBLE. I WANT TO GO TO SLEEP!
Hey, sensei, you look rough. Are you okay?
WE WANT TO SLEEP, TOO.
THEY'RE CLEANING UP THE SCHOOL BUILDINGS, SO WE GOT CHASED OUT.
AND IT'S KIND OF SAFE HERE.
YEAH.
I DON'T...
...WANNA!
Growwwl!
YOU KNOW I HATE SOUBI! HE'S BIG AND LANKY AND GROSS.

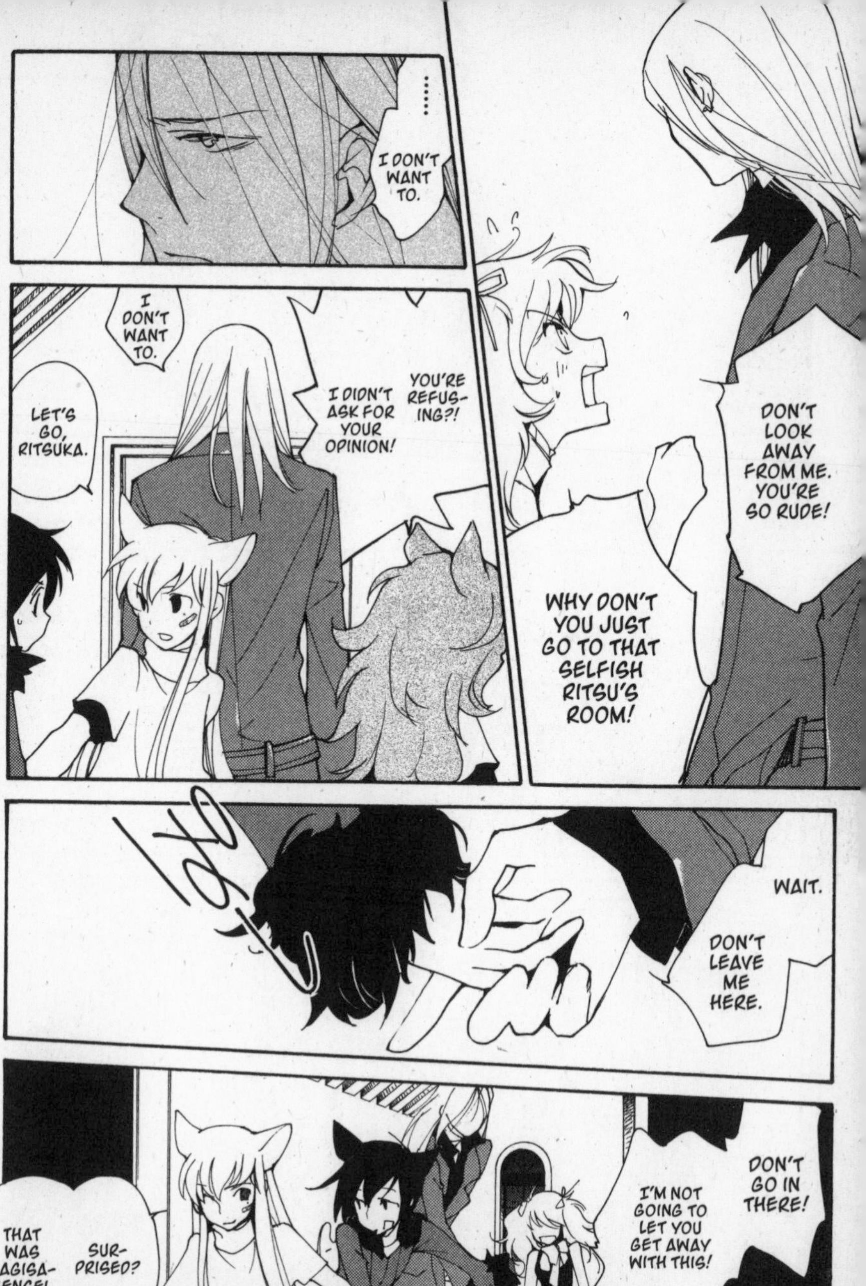

DON'T LOOK AWAY FROM ME. YOU'RE SO RUDE!
WHY DON'T YOU JUST GO TO THAT SELFISH RITSU'S ROOM!
......
I DON'T WANT TO.
YOU'RE REFUSING?!
I DIDN'T ASK FOR YOUR OPINION!
I DON'T WANT TO.
LET'S GO, RITSUKA.
WAIT.
DON'T LEAVE ME HERE.
DON'T GO IN THERE!
I'M NOT GOING TO LET YOU GET AWAY WITH THIS!
SURPRISED?
THAT WAS NAGISA-SENSEI.

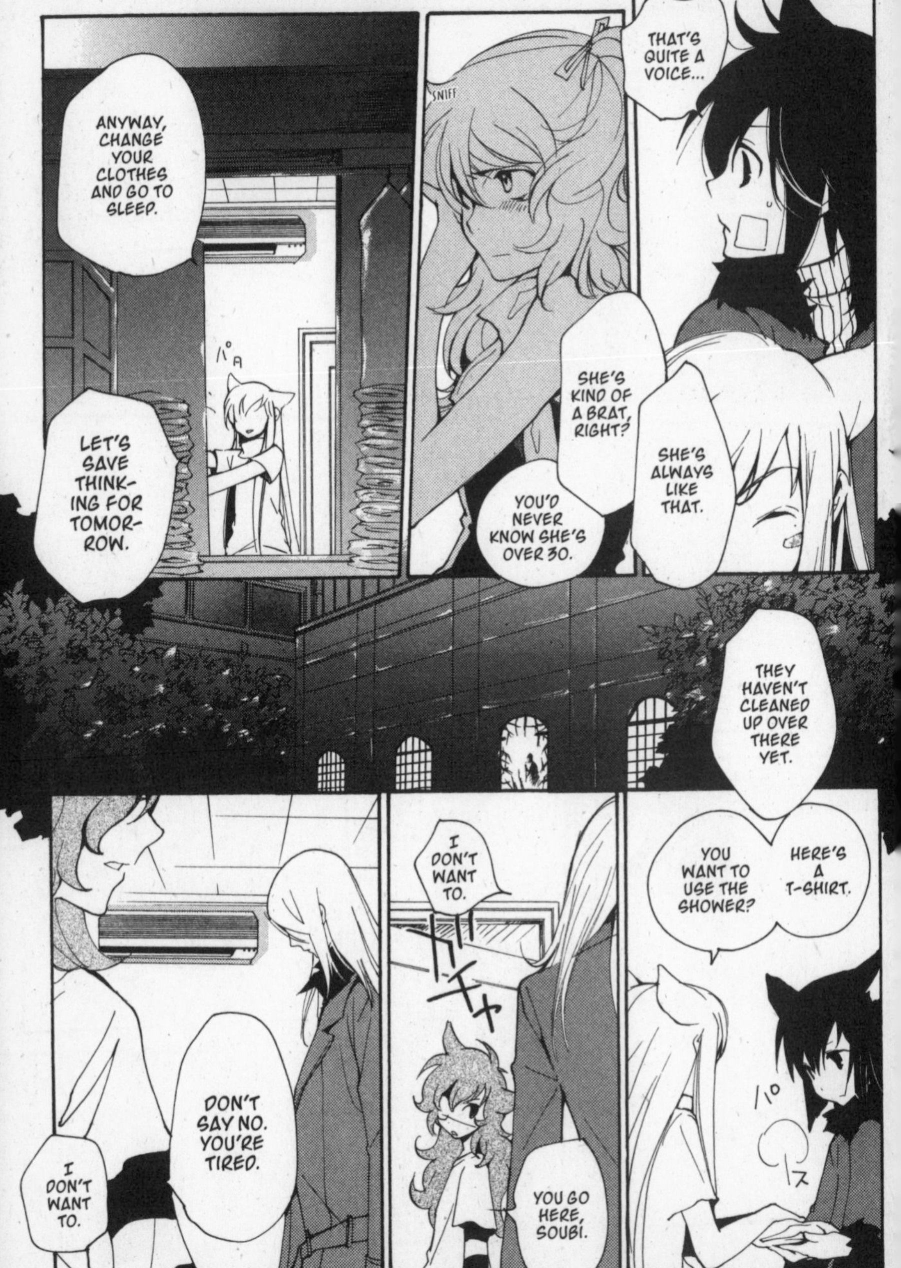
THAT'S QUITE A VOICE...
SNIFF
SHE'S KIND OF A BRAT, RIGHT?
SHE'S ALWAYS LIKE THAT.
YOU'D NEVER KNOW SHE'S OVER 30.
ANYWAY, CHANGE YOUR CLOTHES AND GO TO SLEEP.
パ
LET'S SAVE THINKING FOR TOMORROW.
THEY HAVEN'T CLEANED UP OVER THERE YET.
HERE'S A T-SHIRT.
YOU WANT TO USE THE SHOWER?
パ
I DON'T WANT TO.
YOU GO HERE, SOUBI.
DON'T SAY NO. YOU'RE TIRED.
I DON'T WANT TO.

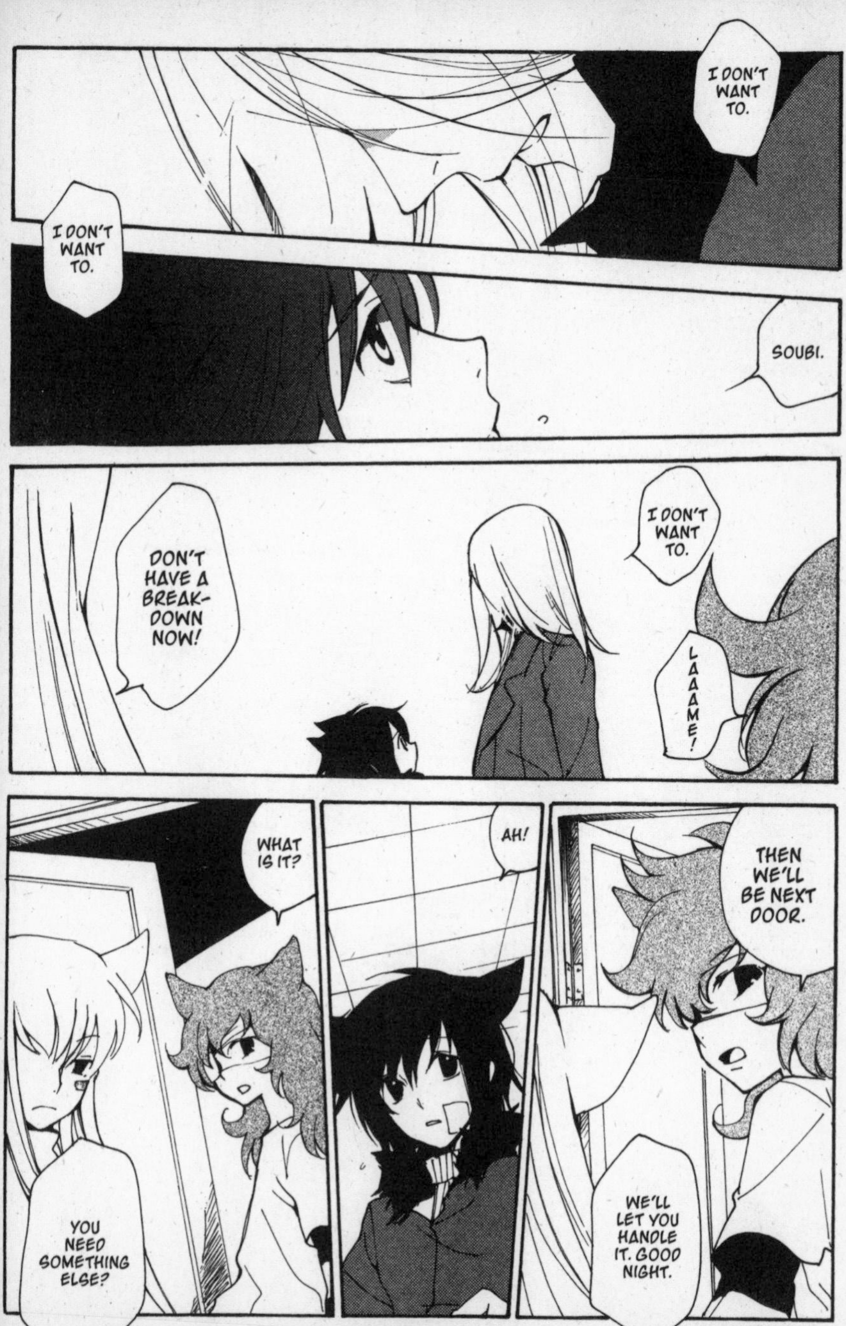
I DON'T WANT TO.
I DON'T WANT TO.
SOUBI.
I DON'T WANT TO.
LAAAME!
DON'T HAVE A BREAK-DOWN NOW!
THEN WE'LL BE NEXT DOOR.
WE'LL LET YOU HANDLE IT. GOOD NIGHT.
AH!
WHAT IS IT?
YOU NEED SOMETHING ELSE?

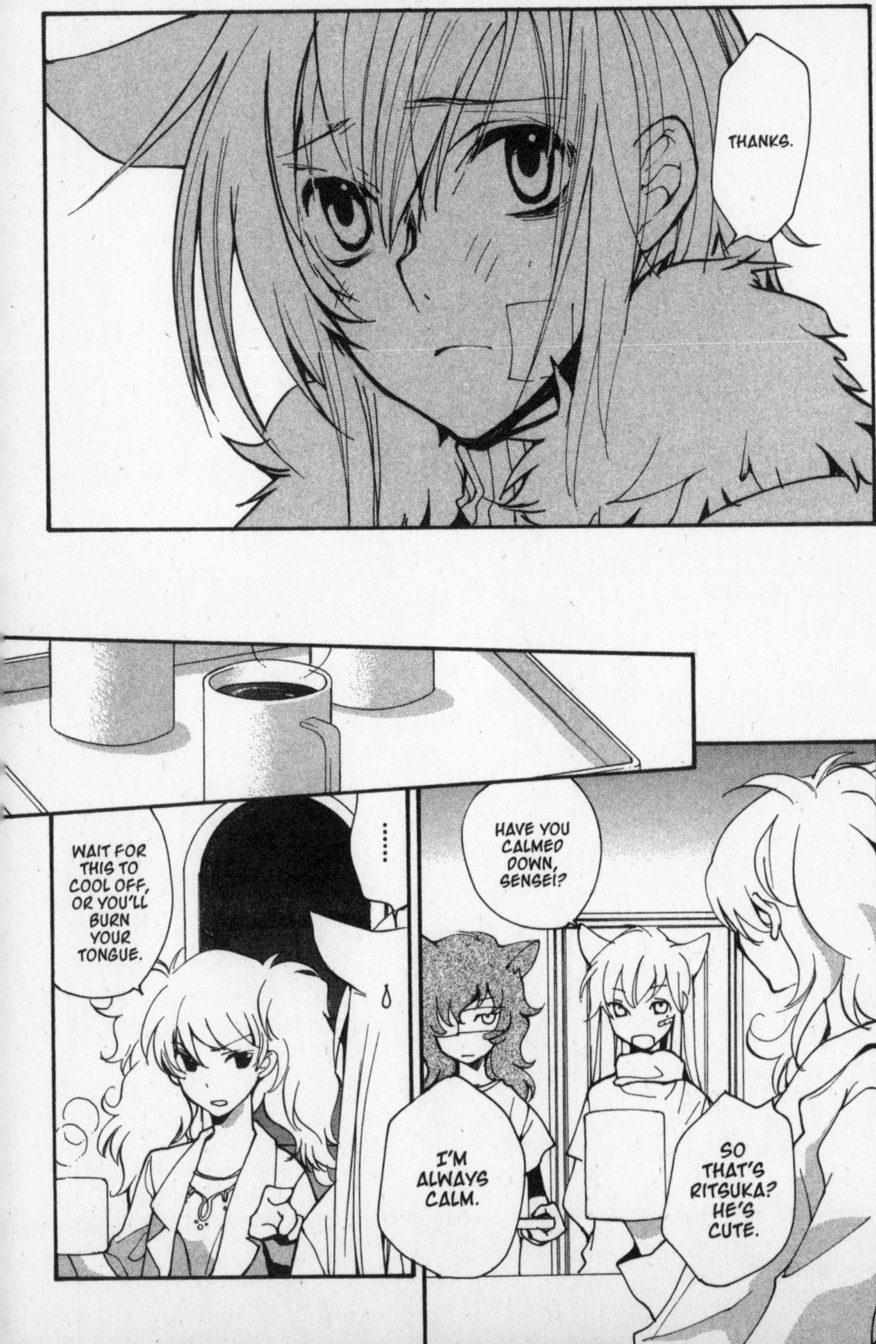
THANKS.
HAVE YOU CALMED DOWN, SENSEI?
SO THAT'S RITSUKA? HE'S CUTE.
I'M ALWAYS CALM.
......
WAIT FOR THIS TO COOL OFF, OR YOU'LL BURN YOUR TONGUE.

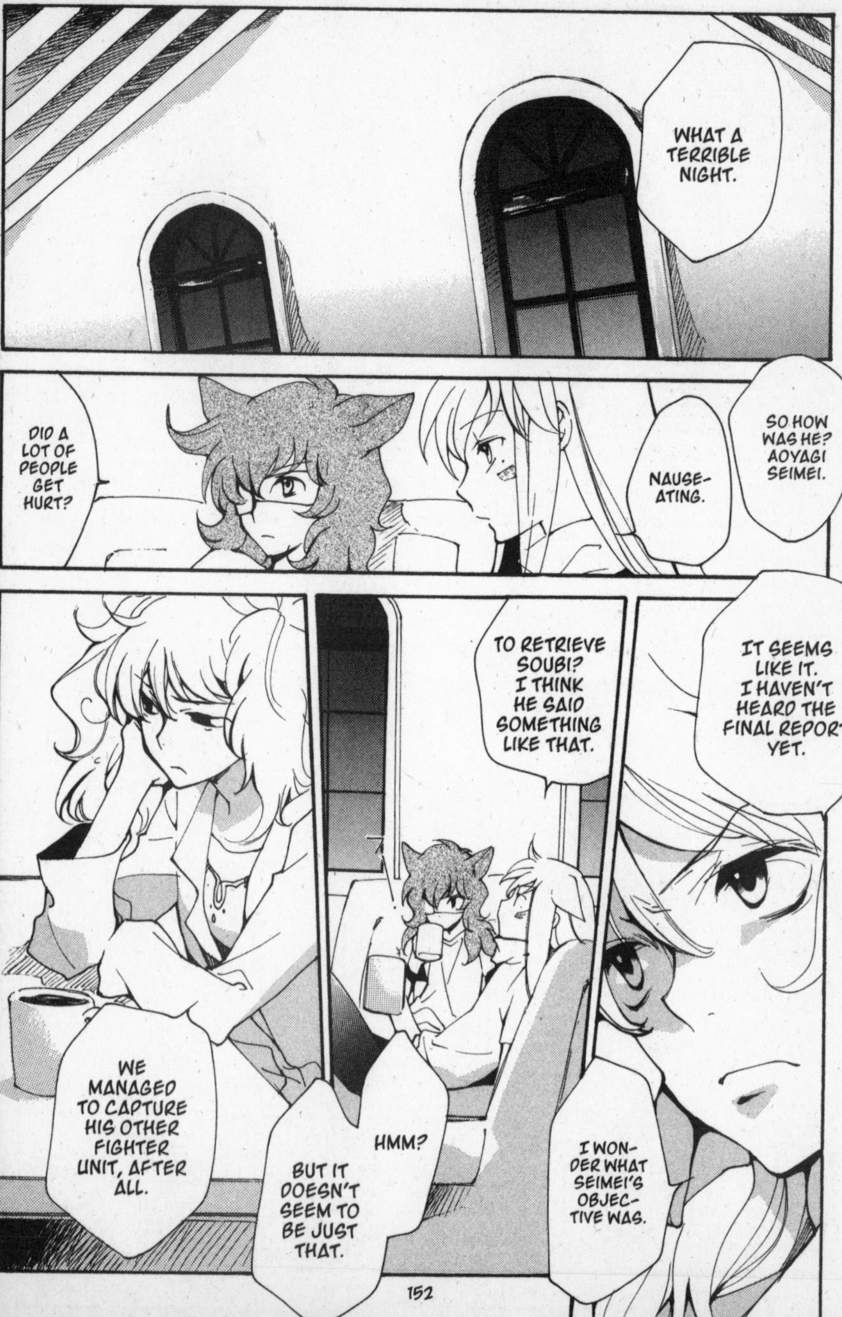
WHAT A TERRIBLE NIGHT.
SO HOW WAS HE? AOYAGI SEIMEI.
NAUSE-ATING.
DID A LOT OF PEOPLE GET HURT?
IT SEEMS LIKE IT. I HAVEN'T HEARD THE FINAL REPORT YET.
I WONDER WHAT SEIMEI'S OBJECTIVE WAS.
TO RETRIEVE SOUBI? I THINK HE SAID SOMETHING LIKE THAT.
WE MANAGED TO CAPTURE HIS OTHER FIGHTER UNIT, AFTER ALL.
HMM?
BUT IT DOESN'T SEEM TO BE JUST THAT.

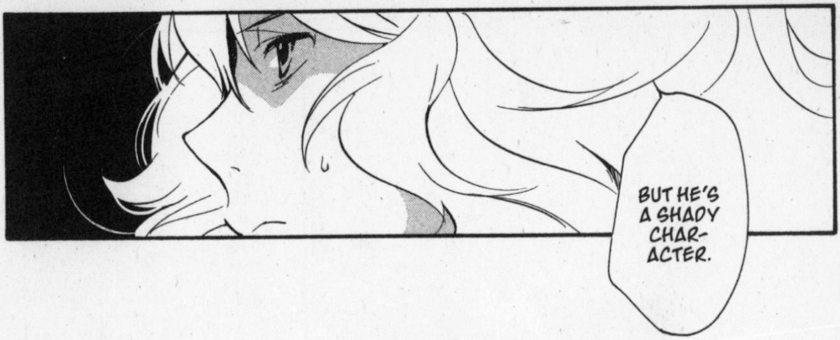
BUT HE'S A SHADY CHAR-ACTER.

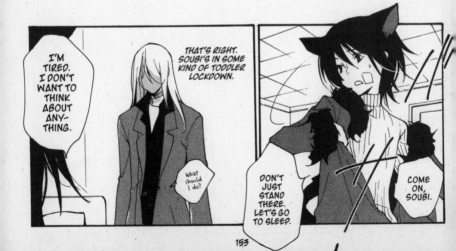

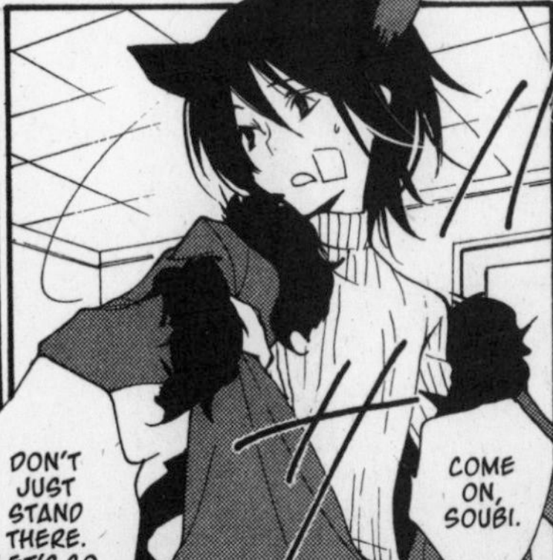
COME ON, SOUBI.
DON'T JUST STAND THERE. LET'S GO TO SLEEP.

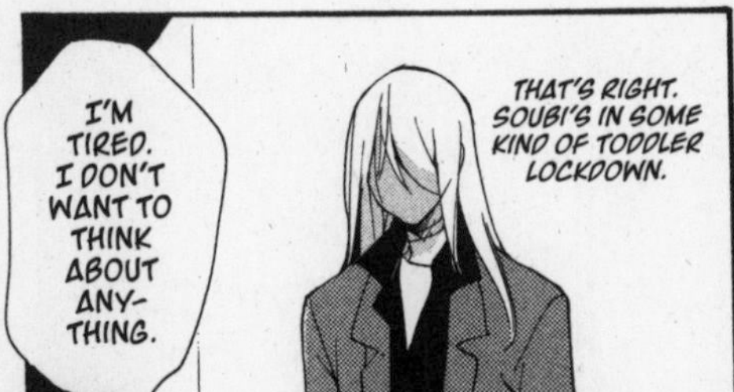
THAT'S RIGHT. SOUBI'S IN SOME KIND OF TODDLER LOCKDOWN.
I'M TIRED. I DON'T WANT TO THINK ABOUT ANY-THING.
What should I do?

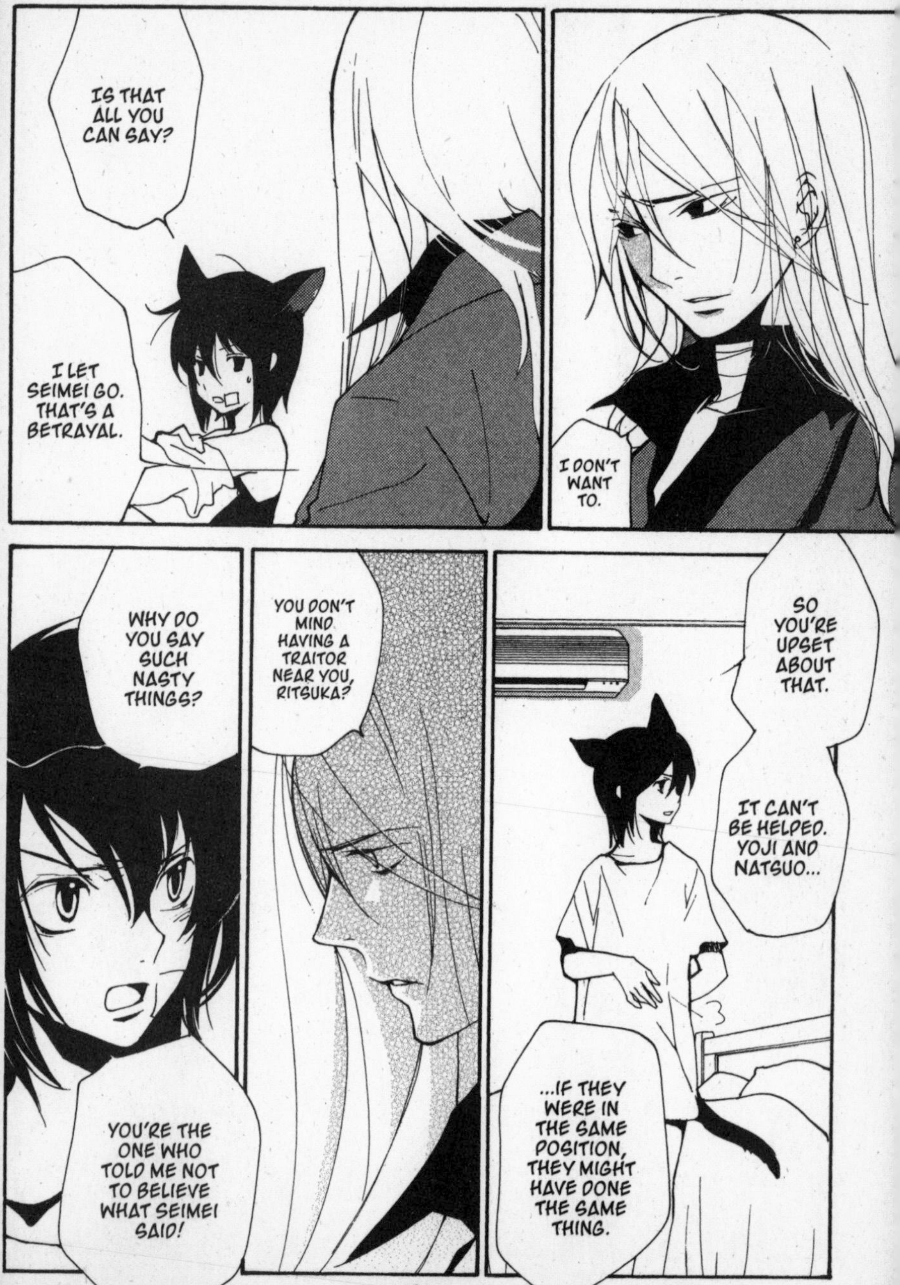
I DON'T WANT TO.
IS THAT ALL YOU CAN SAY?
I LET SEIMEI GO. THAT'S A BETRAYAL.
SO YOU'RE UPSET ABOUT THAT.
IT CAN'T BE HELPED. YOJI AND NATSUO...
...IF THEY WERE IN THE SAME POSITION, THEY MIGHT HAVE DONE THE SAME THING.
YOU DON'T MIND HAVING A TRAITOR NEAR YOU, RITSUKA?
WHY DO YOU SAY SUCH NASTY THINGS?
YOU'RE THE ONE WHO TOLD ME NOT TO BELIEVE WHAT SEIMEI SAID!

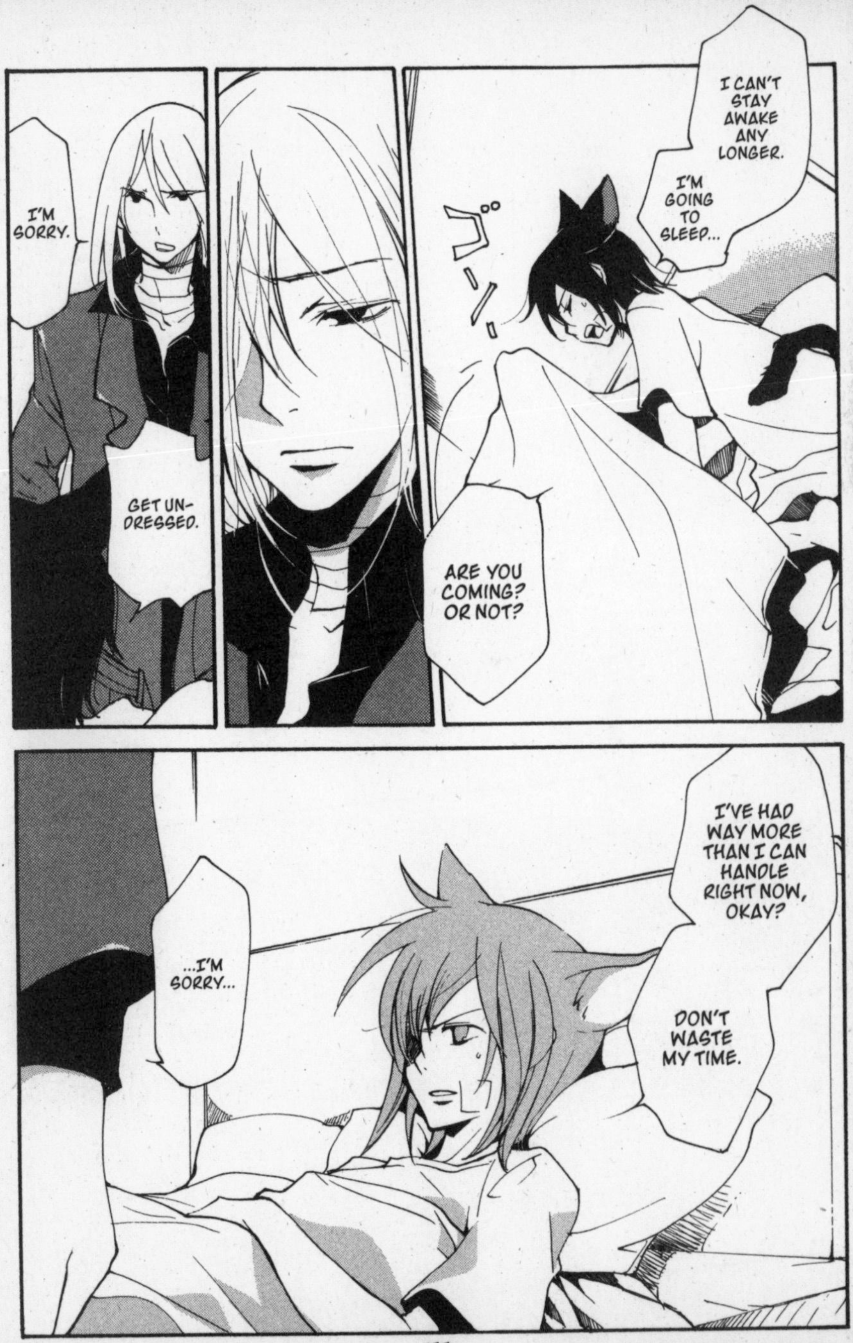
I CAN'T STAY AWAKE ANY LONGER.
I'M GOING TO SLEEP...
ARE YOU COMING? OR NOT?
I'M SORRY.
GET UN-DRESSED.
I'VE HAD WAY MORE THAN I CAN HANDLE RIGHT NOW, OKAY?
DON'T WASTE MY TIME.
...I'M SORRY...

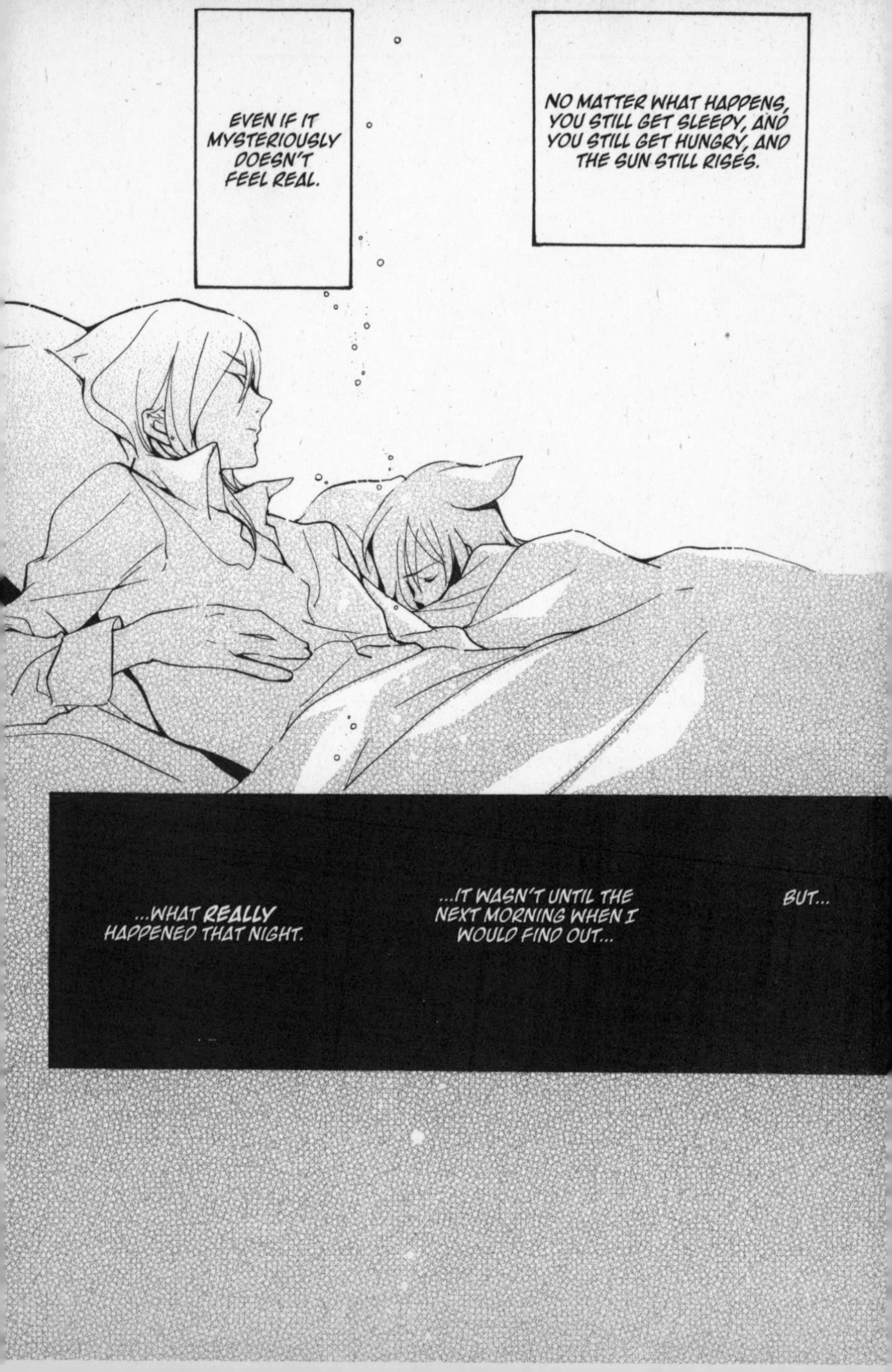
NO MATTER WHAT HAPPENS, YOU STILL GET SLEEPY, AND YOU STILL GET HUNGRY, AND THE SUN STILL RISES.
EVEN IF IT MYSTERIOUSLY DOESN'T FEEL REAL.
BUT...
...IT WASN'T UNTIL THE NEXT MORNING WHEN I WOULD FIND OUT...
...WHAT **REALLY** HAPPENED THAT NIGHT.

An Intermission
Wish Upon A Star

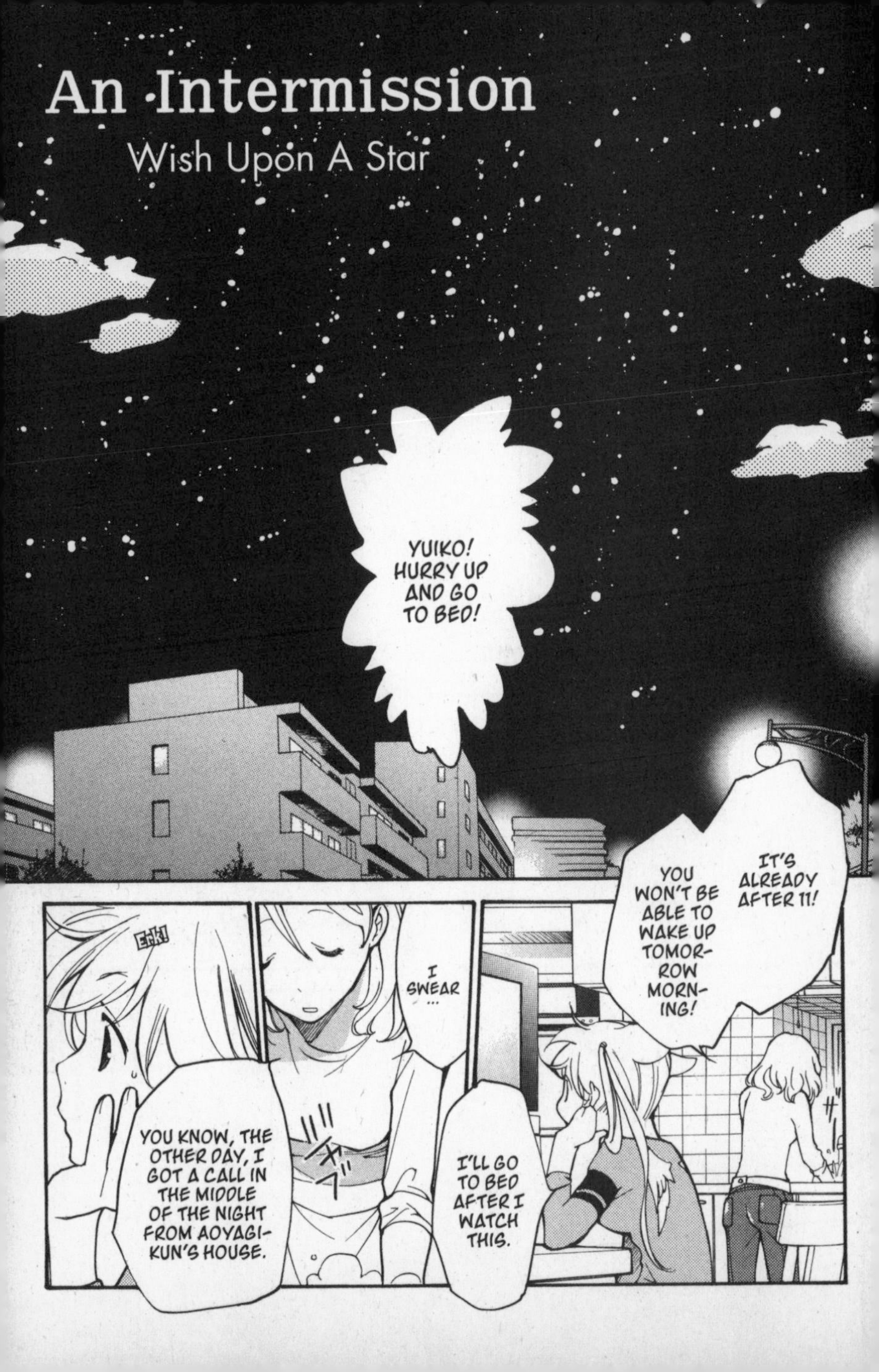
YUIKO! HURRY UP AND GO TO BED!
IT'S ALREADY AFTER 11!
YOU WON'T BE ABLE TO WAKE UP TOMOR-ROW MORN-ING!
I'LL GO TO BED AFTER I WATCH THIS.
I SWEAR ...
EHK!
YOU KNOW, THE OTHER DAY, I GOT A CALL IN THE MIDDLE OF THE NIGHT FROM AOYAGI-KUN'S HOUSE.

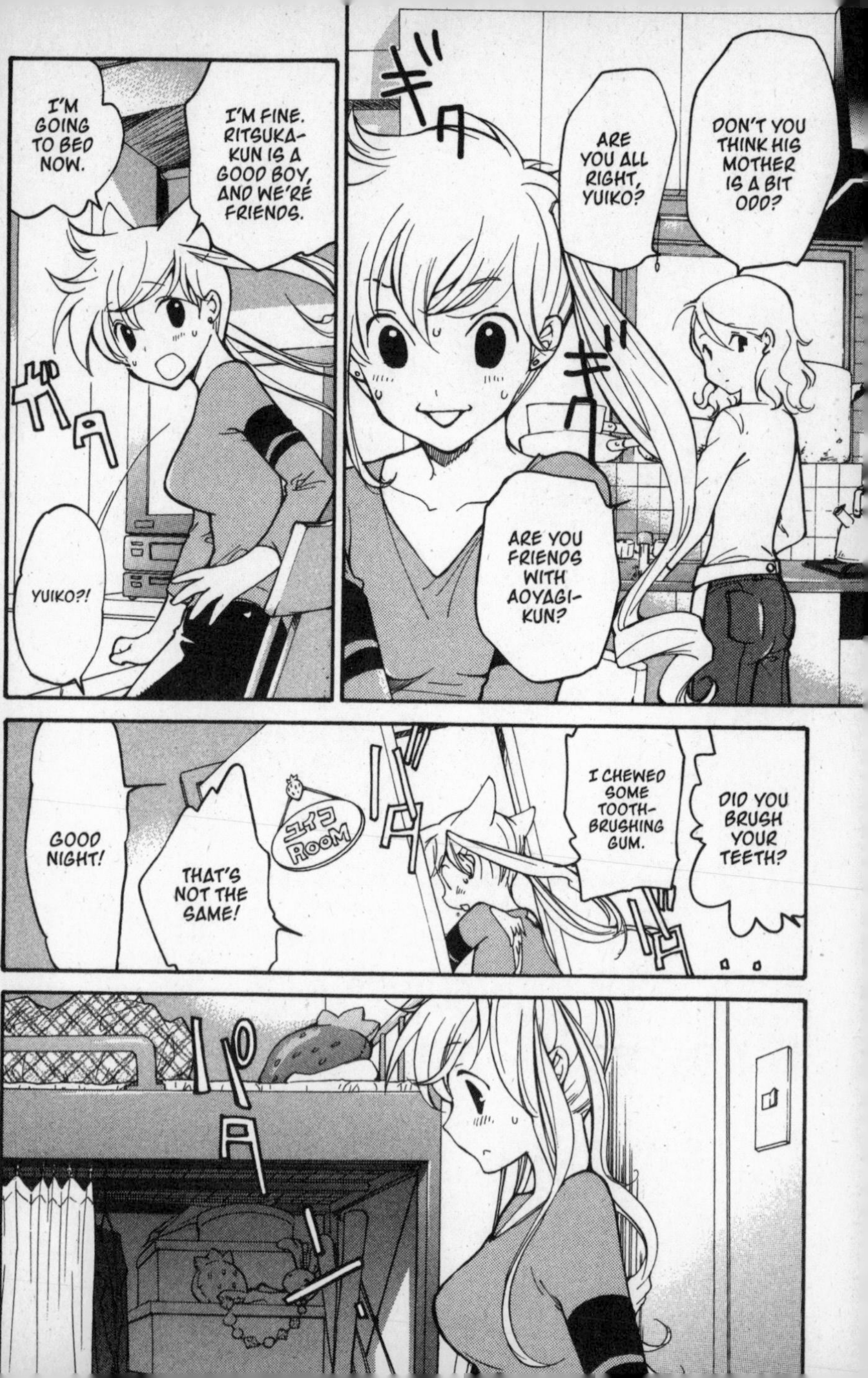
DON'T YOU THINK HIS MOTHER IS A BIT ODD?
ARE YOU ALL RIGHT, YUIKO?
ARE YOU FRIENDS WITH AOYAGI-KUN?
I'M FINE. RITSUKA-KUN IS A GOOD BOY, AND WE'RE FRIENDS.
I'M GOING TO BED NOW.
YUIKO?!
DID YOU BRUSH YOUR TEETH?
I CHEWED SOME TOOTH-BRUSHING GUM.
ユイコ ROOM
THAT'S NOT THE SAME!
GOOD NIGHT!

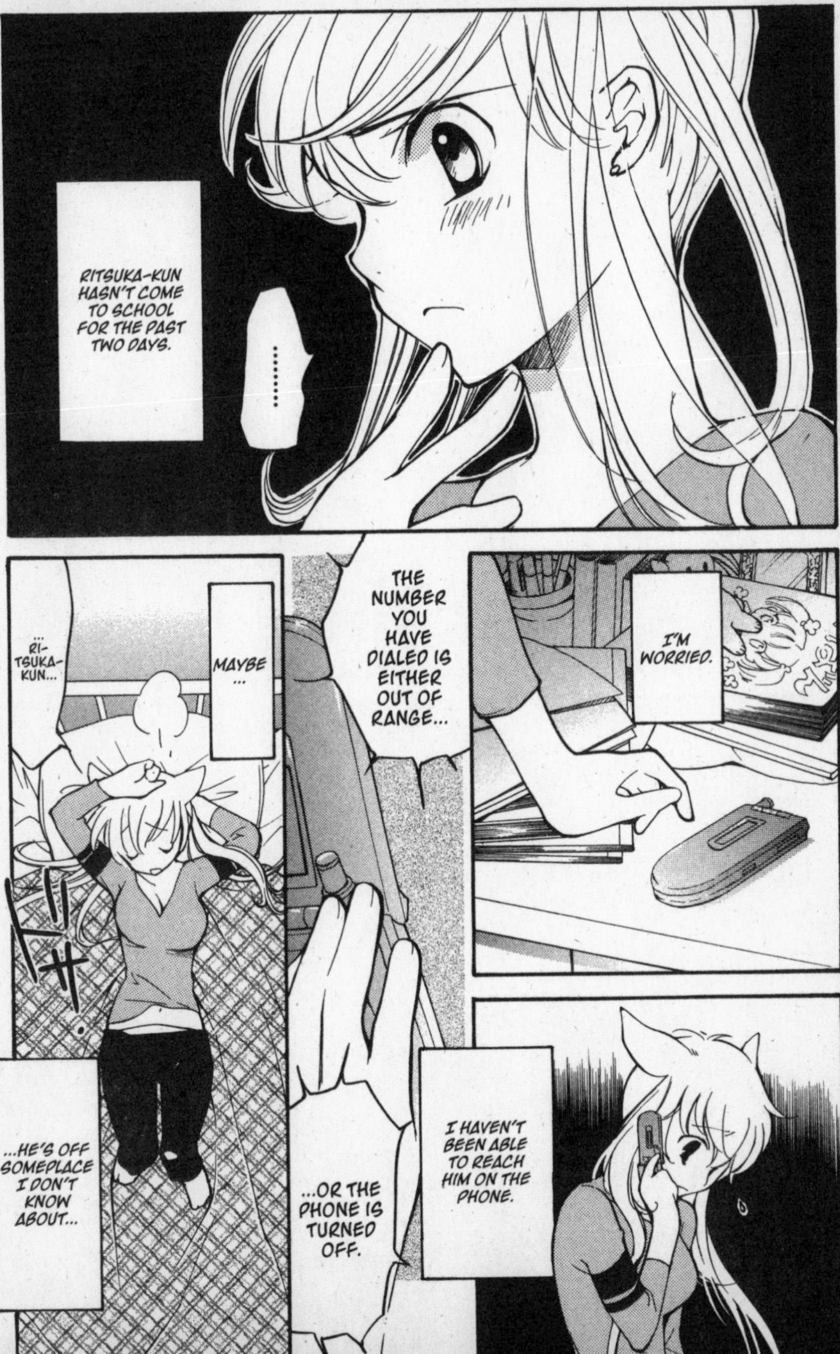
RITSUKA-KUN HASN'T COME TO SCHOOL FOR THE PAST TWO DAYS.
......
I'M WORRIED.
I HAVEN'T BEEN ABLE TO REACH HIM ON THE PHONE.
THE NUMBER YOU HAVE DIALED IS EITHER OUT OF RANGE...
...OR THE PHONE IS TURNED OFF.
MAYBE ...
... RI-TSUKA-KUN...
...HE'S OFF SOMEPLACE I DON'T KNOW ABOUT...

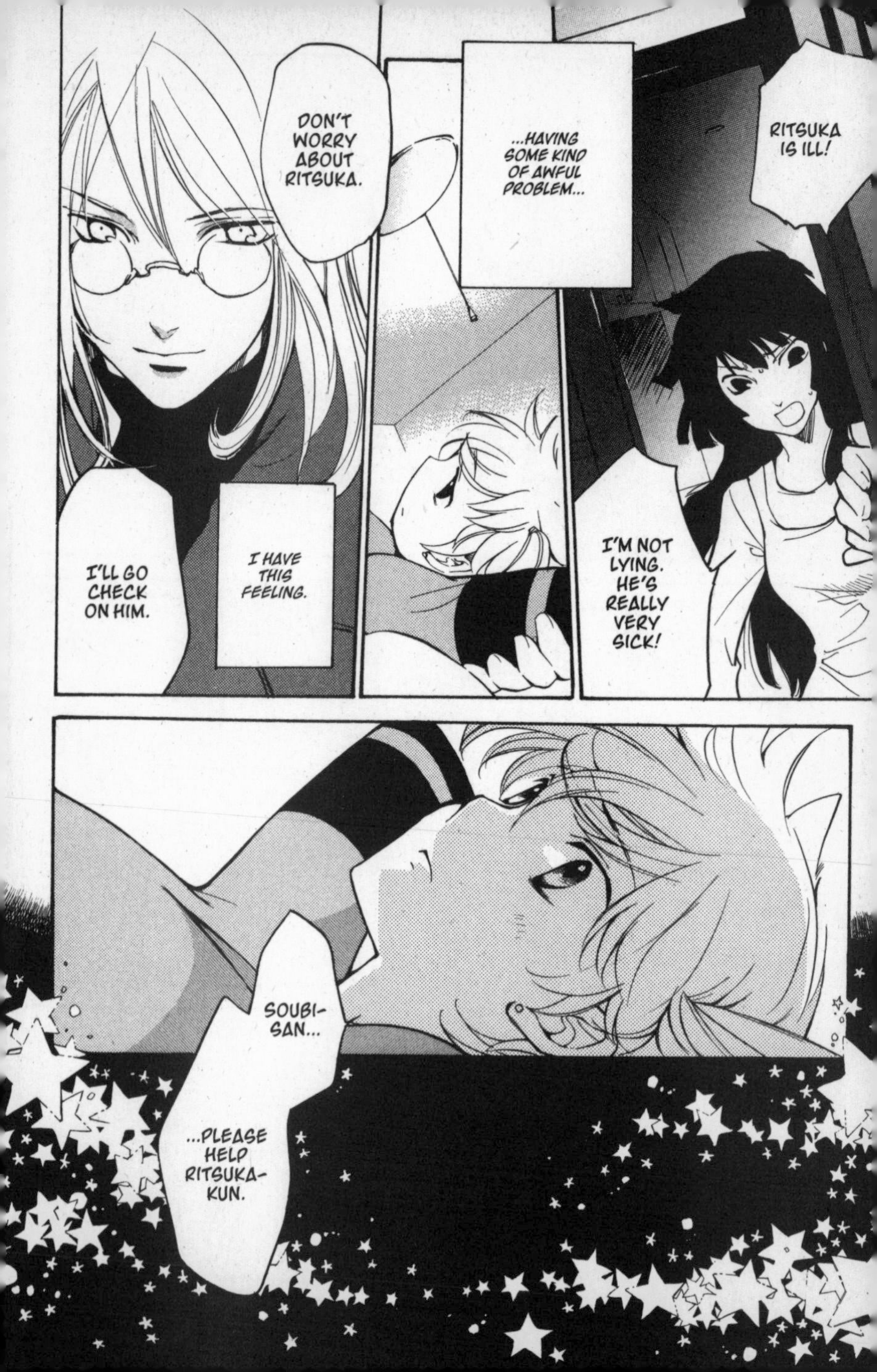
RITSUKA IS ILL!
I'M NOT LYING. HE'S REALLY VERY SICK!
...HAVING SOME KIND OF AWFUL PROBLEM...
DON'T WORRY ABOUT RITSUKA.
I HAVE THIS FEELING.
I'LL GO CHECK ON HIM.
SOUBI-SAN...
...PLEASE HELP RITSUKA-KUN.

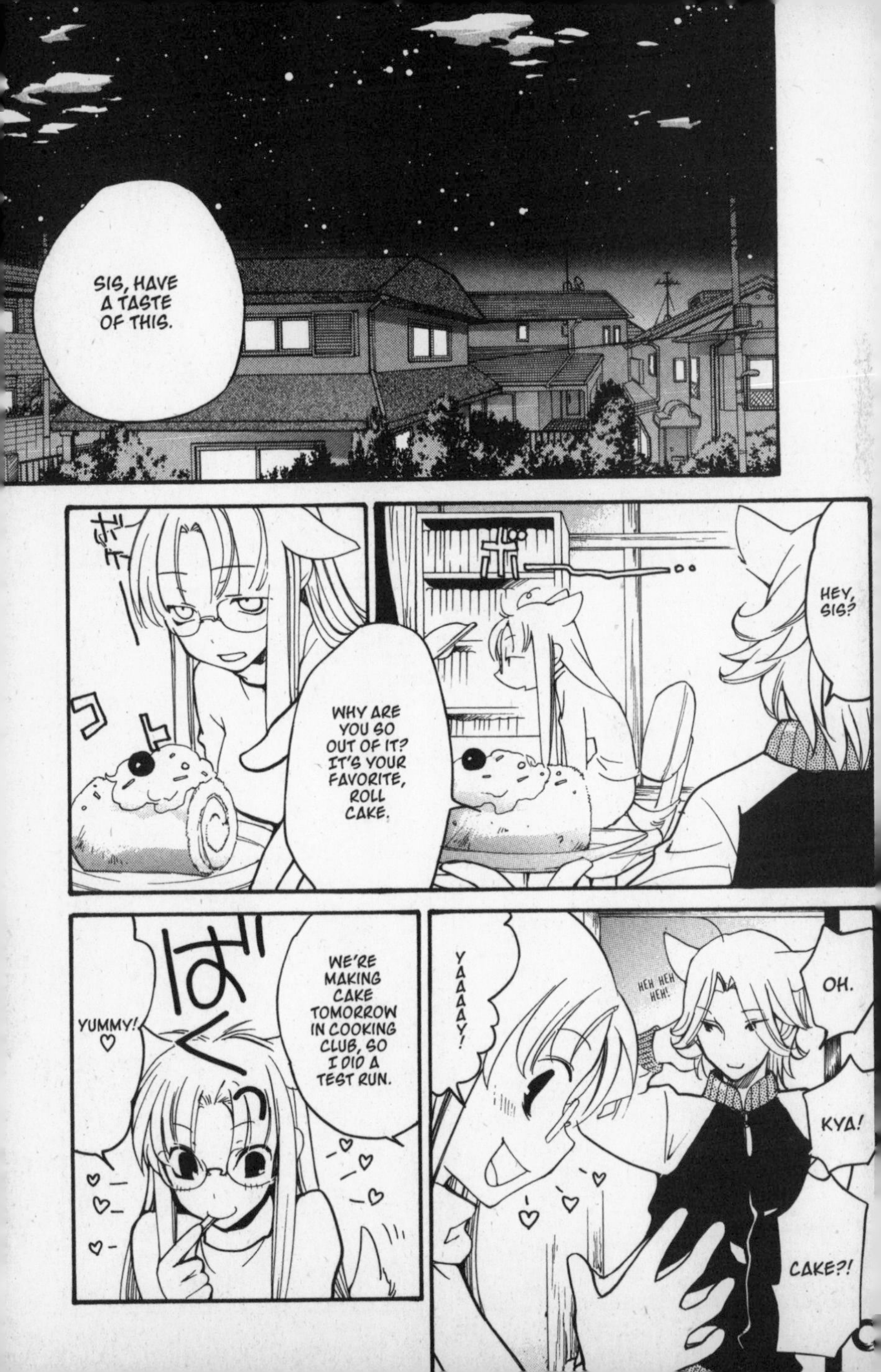
SIS, HAVE A TASTE OF THIS.
HEY, SIS?
WHY ARE YOU SO OUT OF IT? IT'S YOUR FAVORITE, ROLL CAKE.
OH.
KYA!
HEH HEH HEH!
CAKE?!
YAAAAAY!
WE'RE MAKING CAKE TOMORROW IN COOKING CLUB, SO I DID A TEST RUN.
ぱくっ
YUMMY! ♡

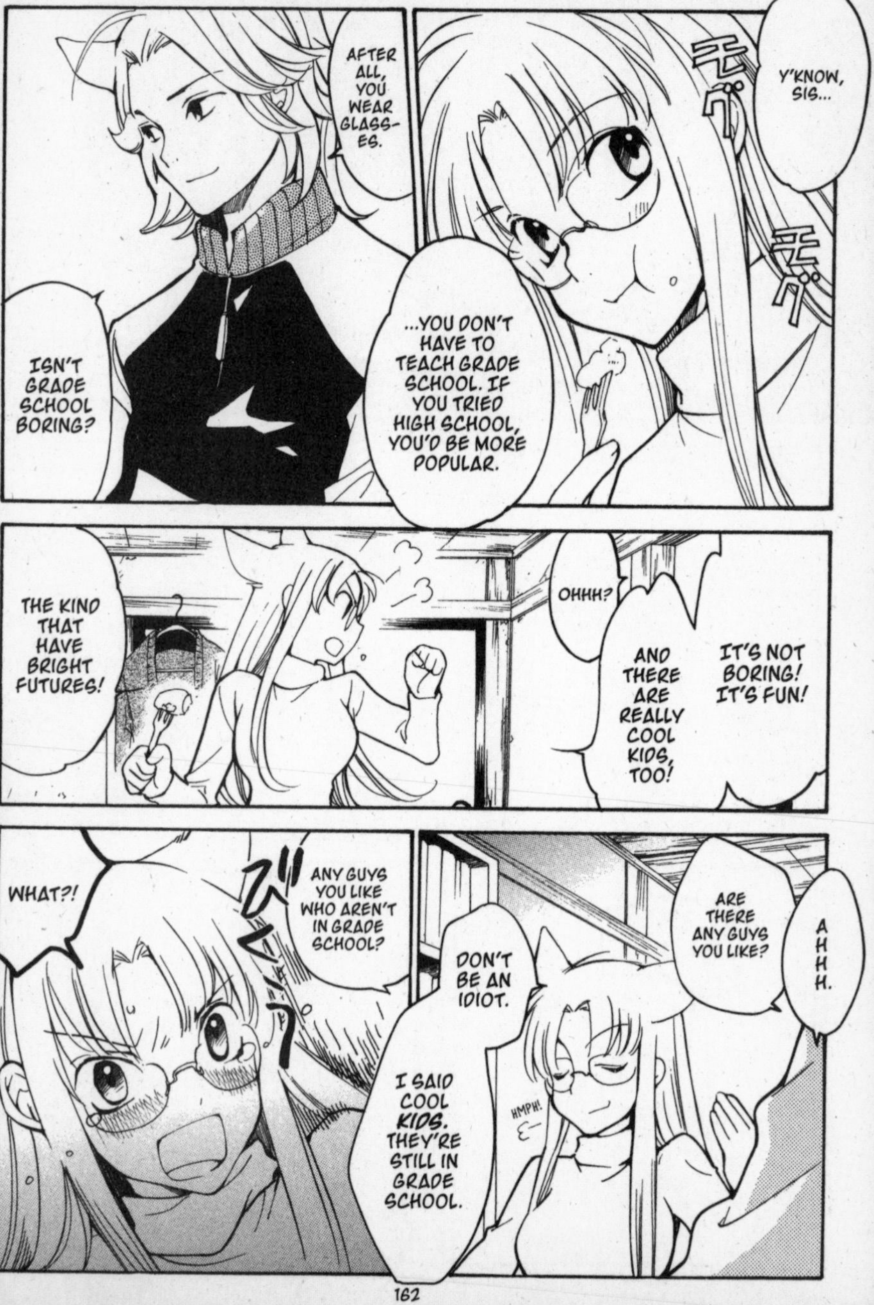
Y'KNOW, SIS...
モグ
モグ
...YOU DON'T HAVE TO TEACH GRADE SCHOOL. IF YOU TRIED HIGH SCHOOL, YOU'D BE MORE POPULAR.
AFTER ALL, YOU WEAR GLASSES.
ISN'T GRADE SCHOOL BORING?
OHHH?
IT'S NOT BORING! IT'S FUN!
AND THERE ARE REALLY COOL KIDS, TOO!
THE KIND THAT HAVE BRIGHT FUTURES!
AHHH.
ARE THERE ANY GUYS YOU LIKE?
DON'T BE AN IDIOT.
HMPH!
I SAID COOL KIDS. THEY'RE STILL IN GRADE SCHOOL.
ANY GUYS YOU LIKE WHO AREN'T IN GRADE SCHOOL?
WHAT?!

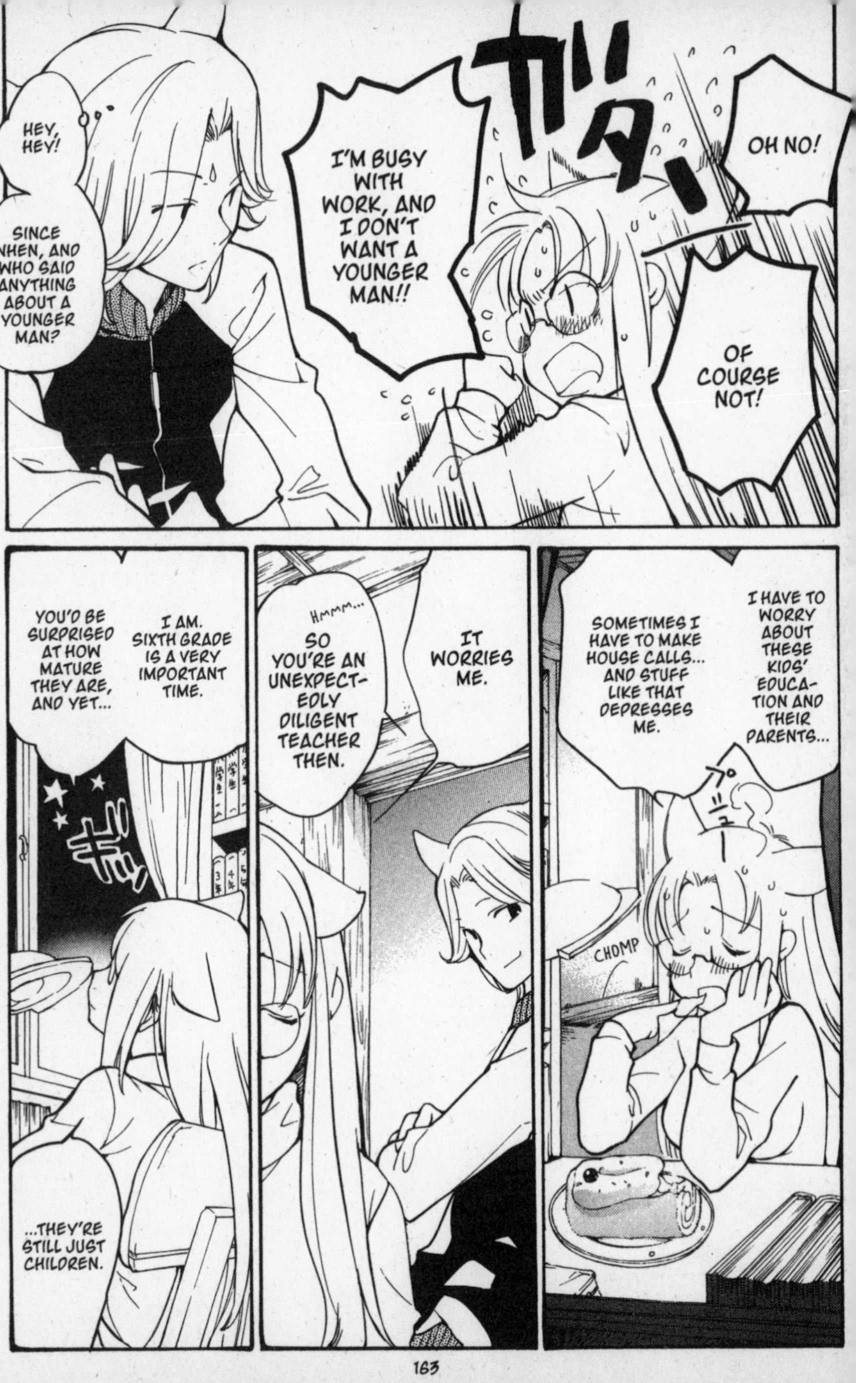
OH NO!
OF COURSE NOT!
I'M BUSY WITH WORK, AND I DON'T WANT A YOUNGER MAN!!
HEY, HEY!
SINCE WHEN, AND WHO SAID ANYTHING ABOUT A YOUNGER MAN?
I HAVE TO WORRY ABOUT THESE KIDS' EDUCATION AND THEIR PARENTS...
SOMETIMES I HAVE TO MAKE HOUSE CALLS... AND STUFF LIKE THAT DEPRESSES ME.
CHOMP
IT WORRIES ME.
HMMM...
SO YOU'RE AN UNEXPECTEDLY DILIGENT TEACHER THEN.
I AM. SIXTH GRADE IS A VERY IMPORTANT TIME.
YOU'D BE SURPRISED AT HOW MATURE THEY ARE, AND YET...
...THEY'RE STILL JUST CHILDREN.

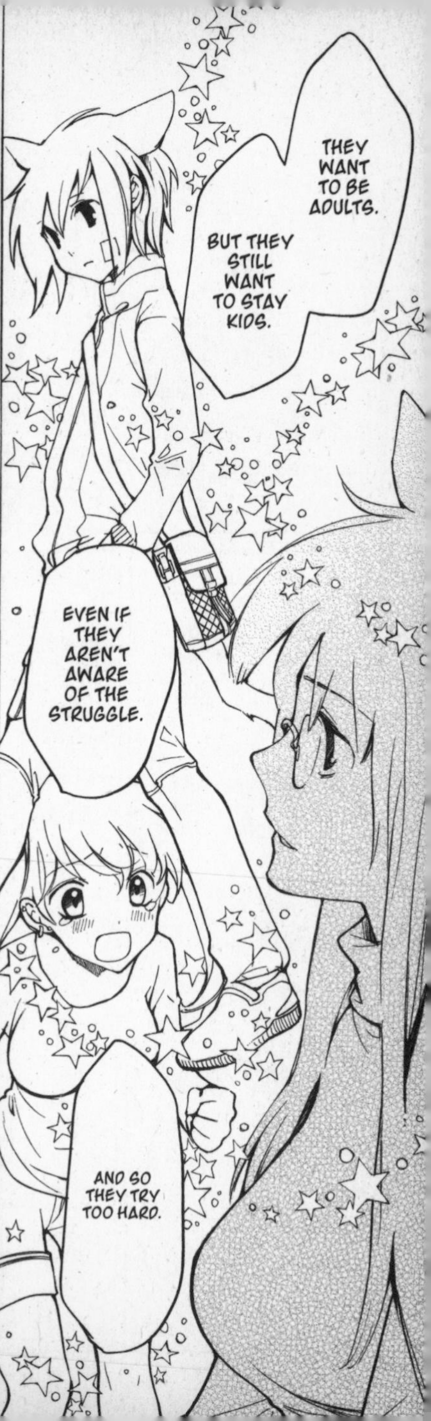
THEY WANT TO BE ADULTS.
BUT THEY STILL WANT TO STAY KIDS.
EVEN IF THEY AREN'T AWARE OF THE STRUGGLE.
AND SO THEY TRY TOO HARD.

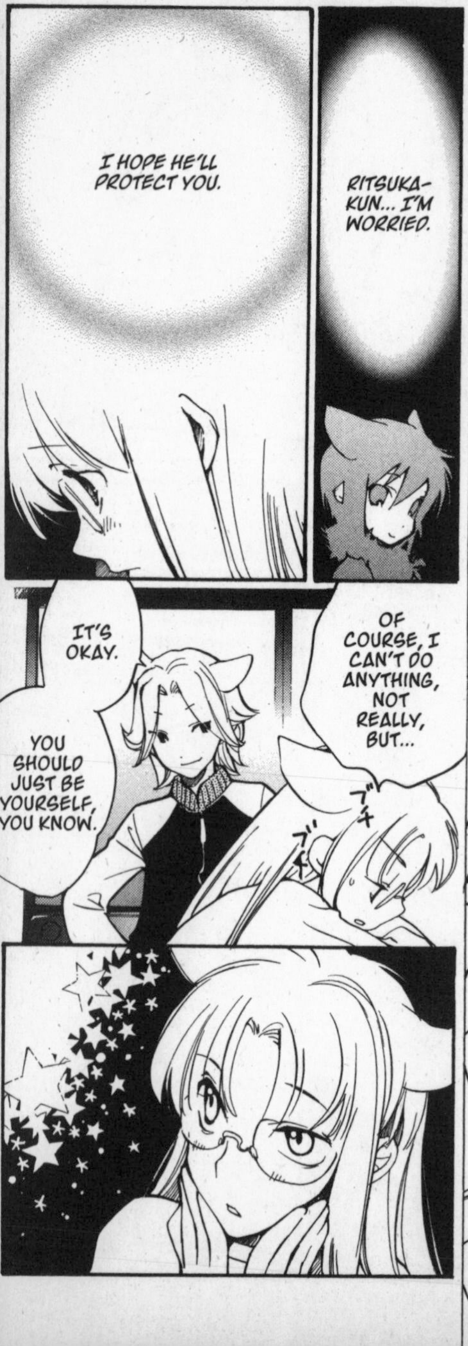
RITSUKA-KUN... I'M WORRIED.
I HOPE HE'LL PROTECT YOU.
OF COURSE, I CAN'T DO ANYTHING, NOT REALLY, BUT...
ブチ
ブチ
IT'S OKAY.
YOU SHOULD JUST BE YOURSELF, YOU KNOW.

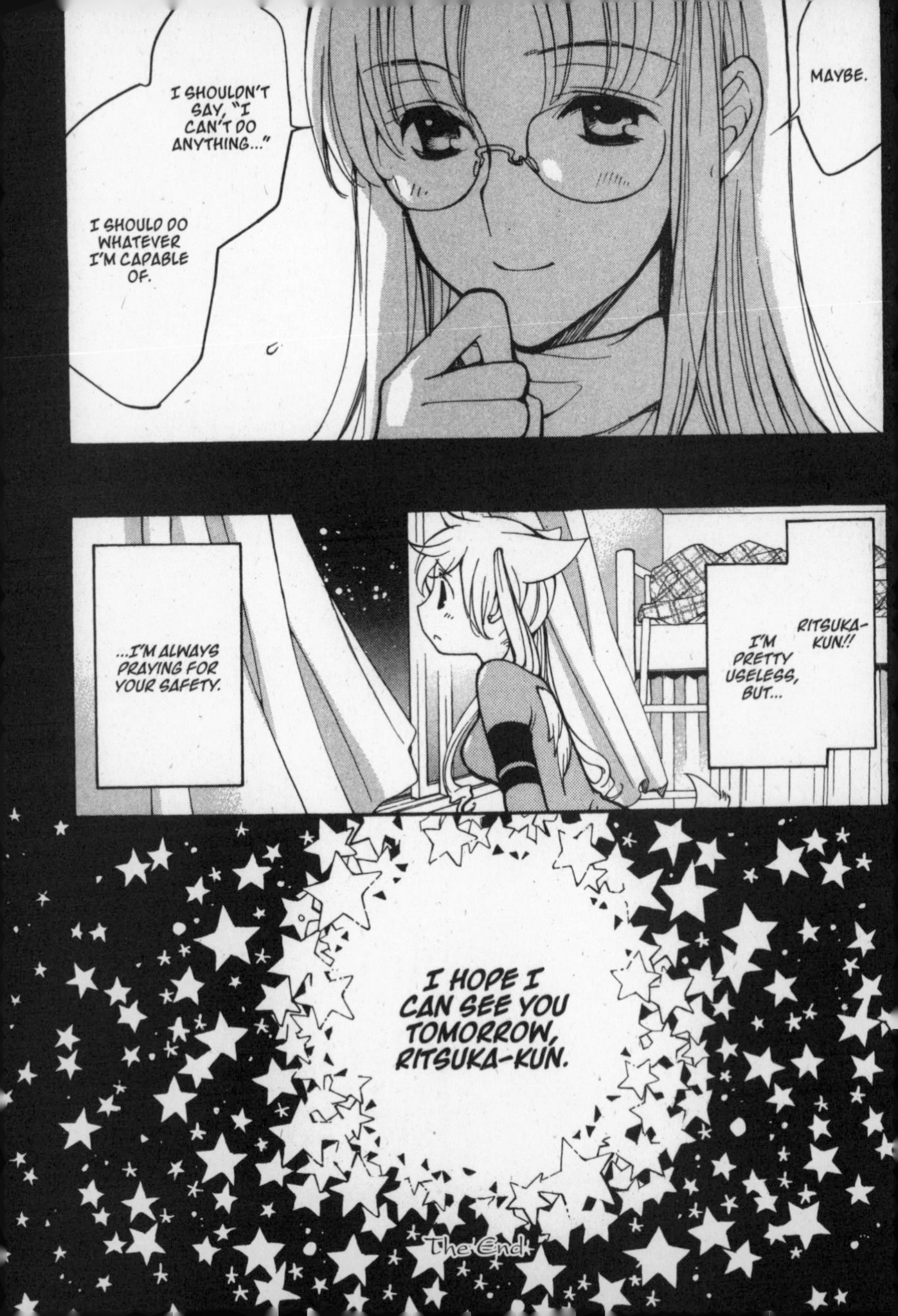
MAYBE.
I SHOULDN'T SAY, "I CAN'T DO ANYTHING..."
I SHOULD DO WHATEVER I'M CAPABLE OF.
RITSUKA-KUN!!
I'M PRETTY USELESS, BUT...
...I'M ALWAYS PRAYING FOR YOUR SAFETY.
I HOPE I CAN SEE YOU TOMORROW, RITSUKA-KUN.
The End

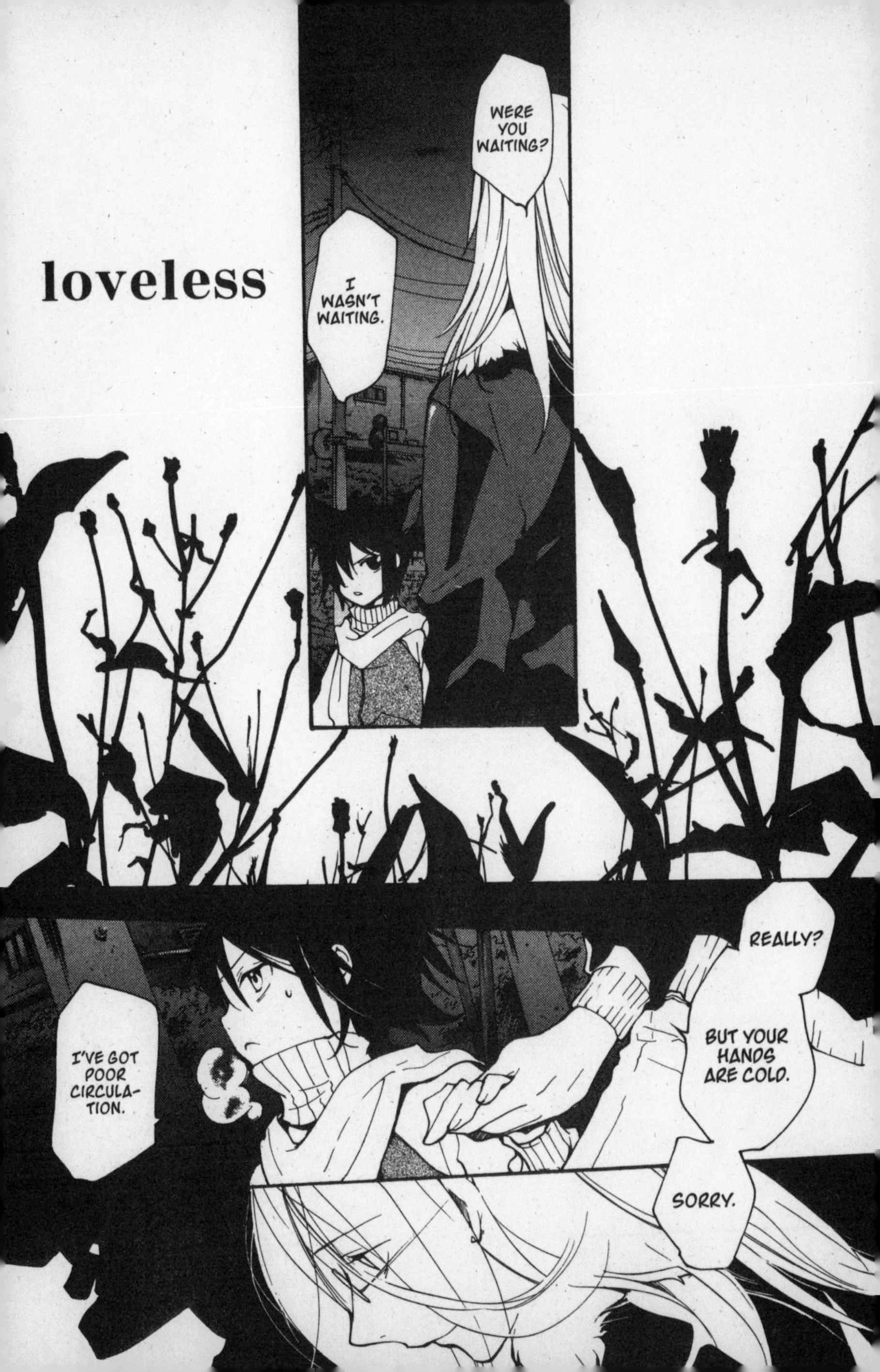
WERE YOU WAITING?
I WASN'T WAITING.
loveless
REALLY?
BUT YOUR HANDS ARE COLD.
I'VE GOT POOR CIRCULA-TION.
SORRY.

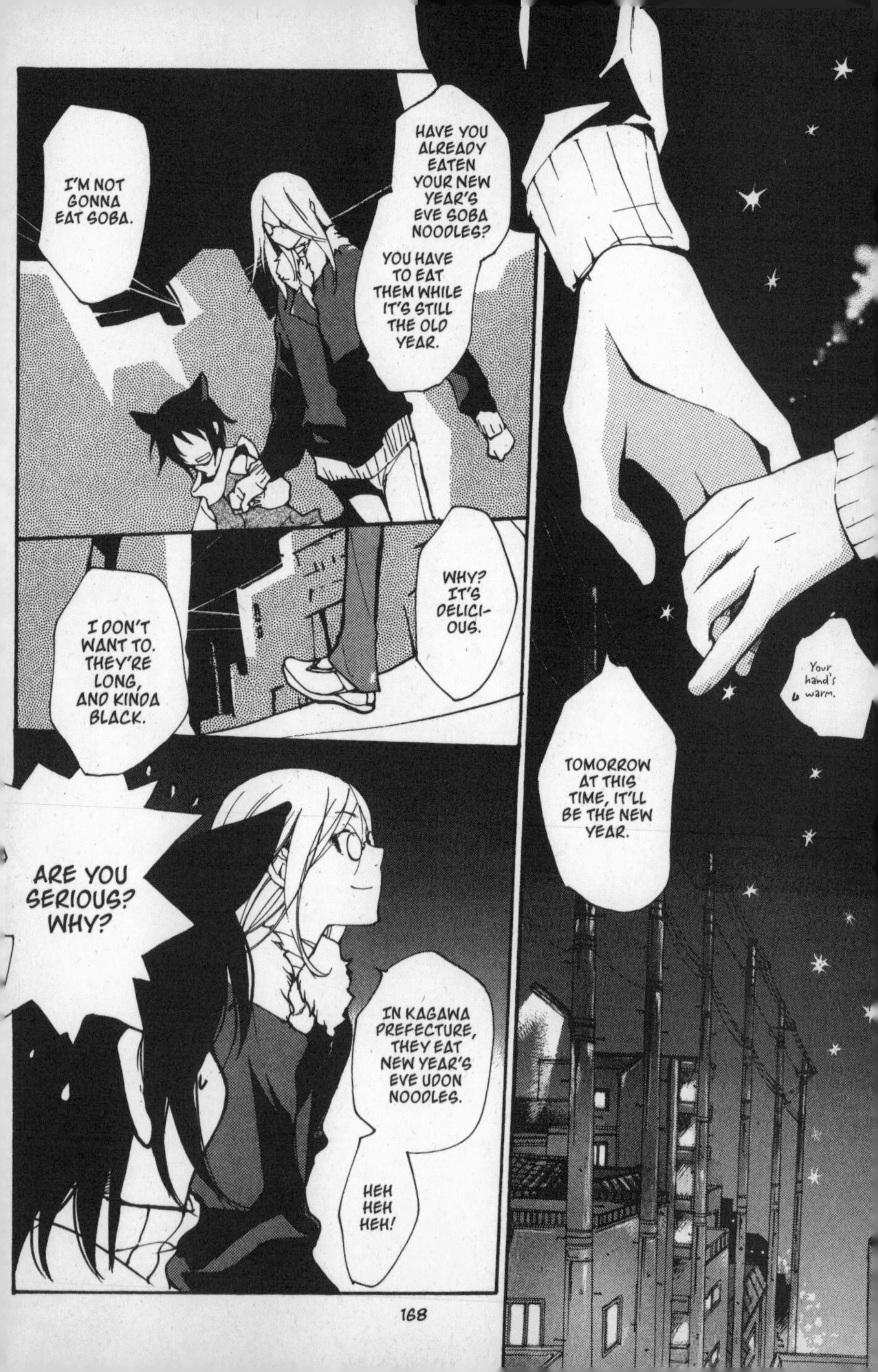
Your hand's warm.
TOMORROW AT THIS TIME, IT'LL BE THE NEW YEAR.
HAVE YOU ALREADY EATEN YOUR NEW YEAR'S EVE SOBA NOODLES?
YOU HAVE TO EAT THEM WHILE IT'S STILL THE OLD YEAR.
I'M NOT GONNA EAT SOBA.
WHY? IT'S DELICI-OUS.
I DON'T WANT TO. THEY'RE LONG, AND KINDA BLACK.
ARE YOU SERIOUS? WHY?
IN KAGAWA PREFECTURE, THEY EAT NEW YEAR'S EVE UDON NOODLES.
HEH HEH HEH!

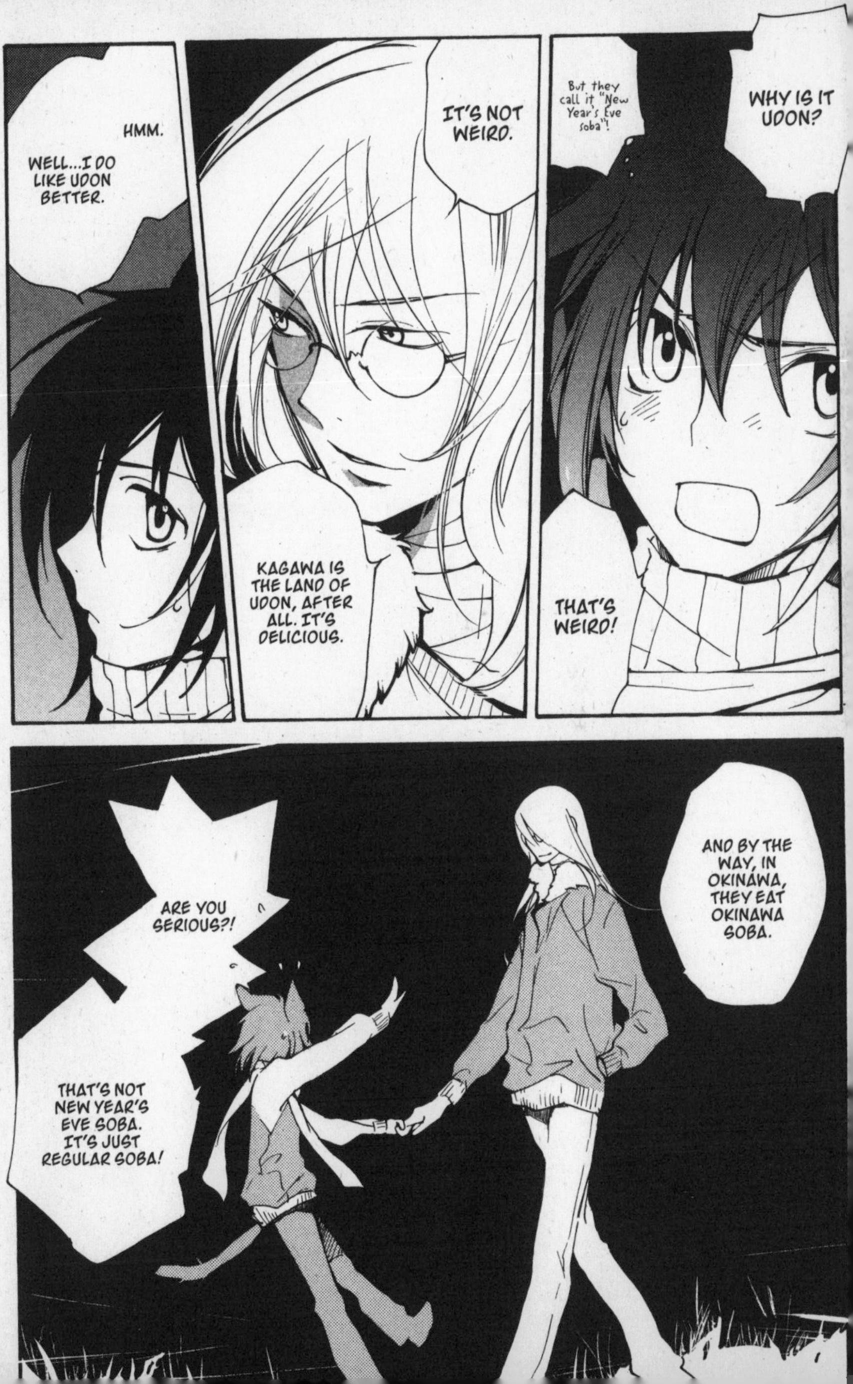
WHY IS IT UDON?
But they call it "New Year's Eve soba"!
THAT'S WEIRD!
IT'S NOT WEIRD.
KAGAWA IS THE LAND OF UDON, AFTER ALL. IT'S DELICIOUS.
HMM.
WELL...I DO LIKE UDON BETTER.
AND BY THE WAY, IN OKINAWA, THEY EAT OKINAWA SOBA.
ARE YOU SERIOUS?!
THAT'S NOT NEW YEAR'S EVE SOBA. IT'S JUST REGULAR SOBA!

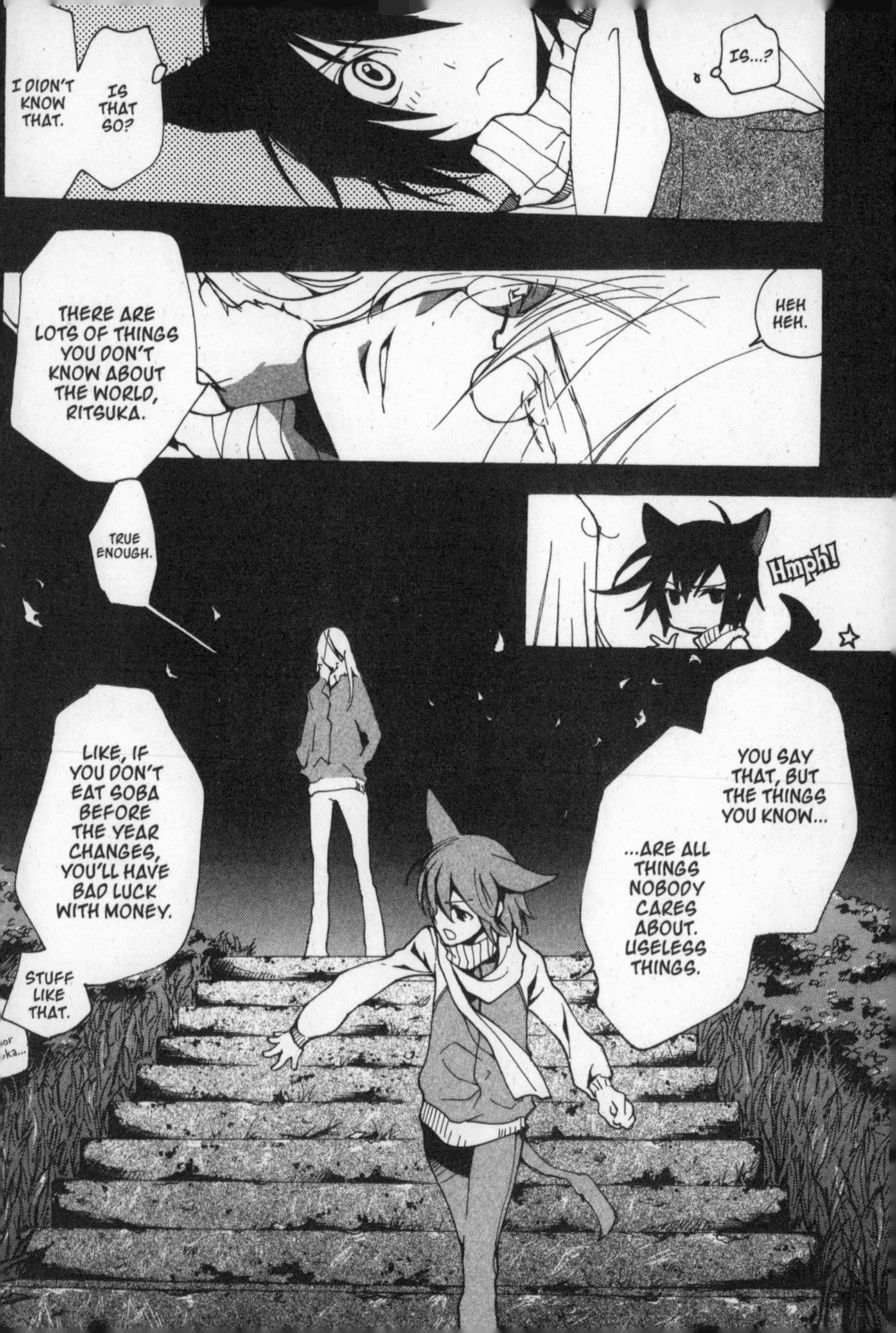
IS...?
IS THAT SO?
I DIDN'T KNOW THAT.
HEH HEH.
THERE ARE LOTS OF THINGS YOU DON'T KNOW ABOUT THE WORLD, RITSUKA.
Hmph!
TRUE ENOUGH.
YOU SAY THAT, BUT THE THINGS YOU KNOW...
...ARE ALL THINGS NOBODY CARES ABOUT. USELESS THINGS.
LIKE, IF YOU DON'T EAT SOBA BEFORE THE YEAR CHANGES, YOU'LL HAVE BAD LUCK WITH MONEY.
STUFF LIKE THAT.

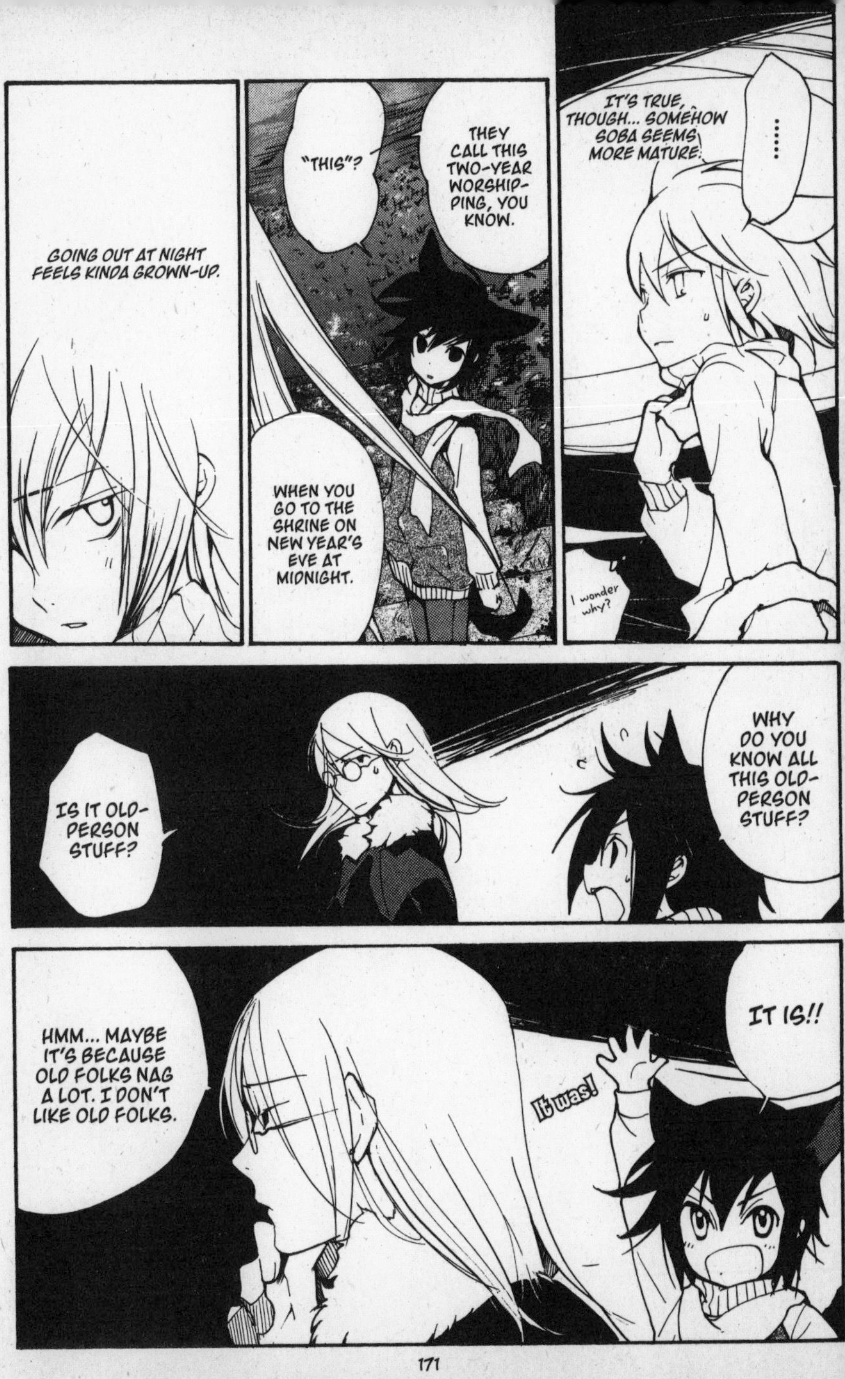
......
IT'S TRUE, THOUGH... SOMEHOW SOBA SEEMS MORE MATURE.
I wonder why?
THEY CALL THIS TWO-YEAR WORSHIP-PING, YOU KNOW.
"THIS"?
WHEN YOU GO TO THE SHRINE ON NEW YEAR'S EVE AT MIDNIGHT.
GOING OUT AT NIGHT FEELS KINDA GROWN-UP.
WHY DO YOU KNOW ALL THIS OLD-PERSON STUFF?
IS IT OLD-PERSON STUFF?
IT IS!!
It was!
HMM... MAYBE IT'S BECAUSE OLD FOLKS NAG A LOT. I DON'T LIKE OLD FOLKS.

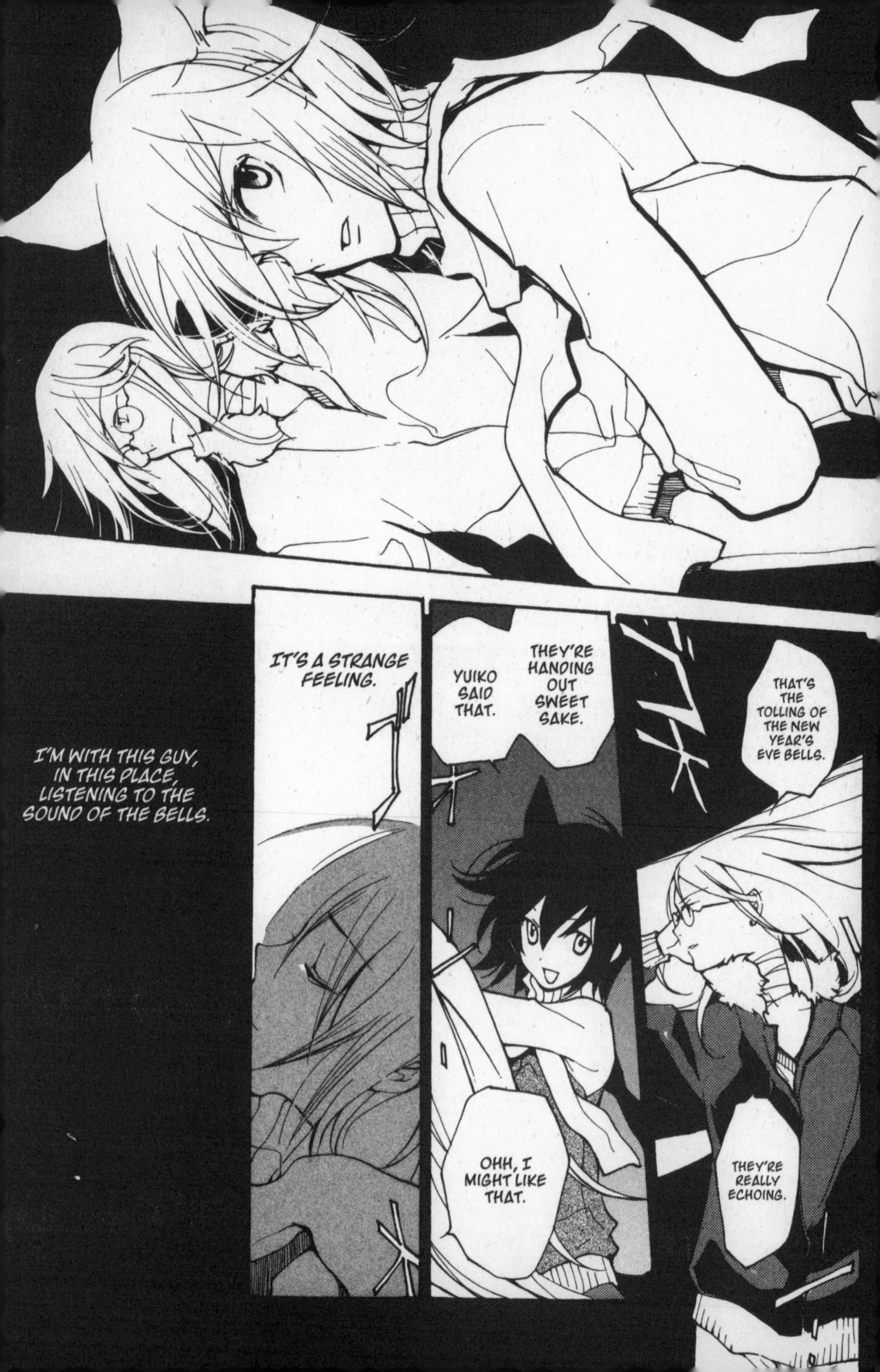
THAT'S THE TOLLING OF THE NEW YEAR'S EVE BELLS.
THEY'RE REALLY ECHOING.
THEY'RE HANDING OUT SWEET SAKE.
YUIKO SAID THAT.
OHH, I MIGHT LIKE THAT.
IT'S A STRANGE FEELING.
I'M WITH THIS GUY, IN THIS PLACE, LISTENING TO THE SOUND OF THE BELLS.

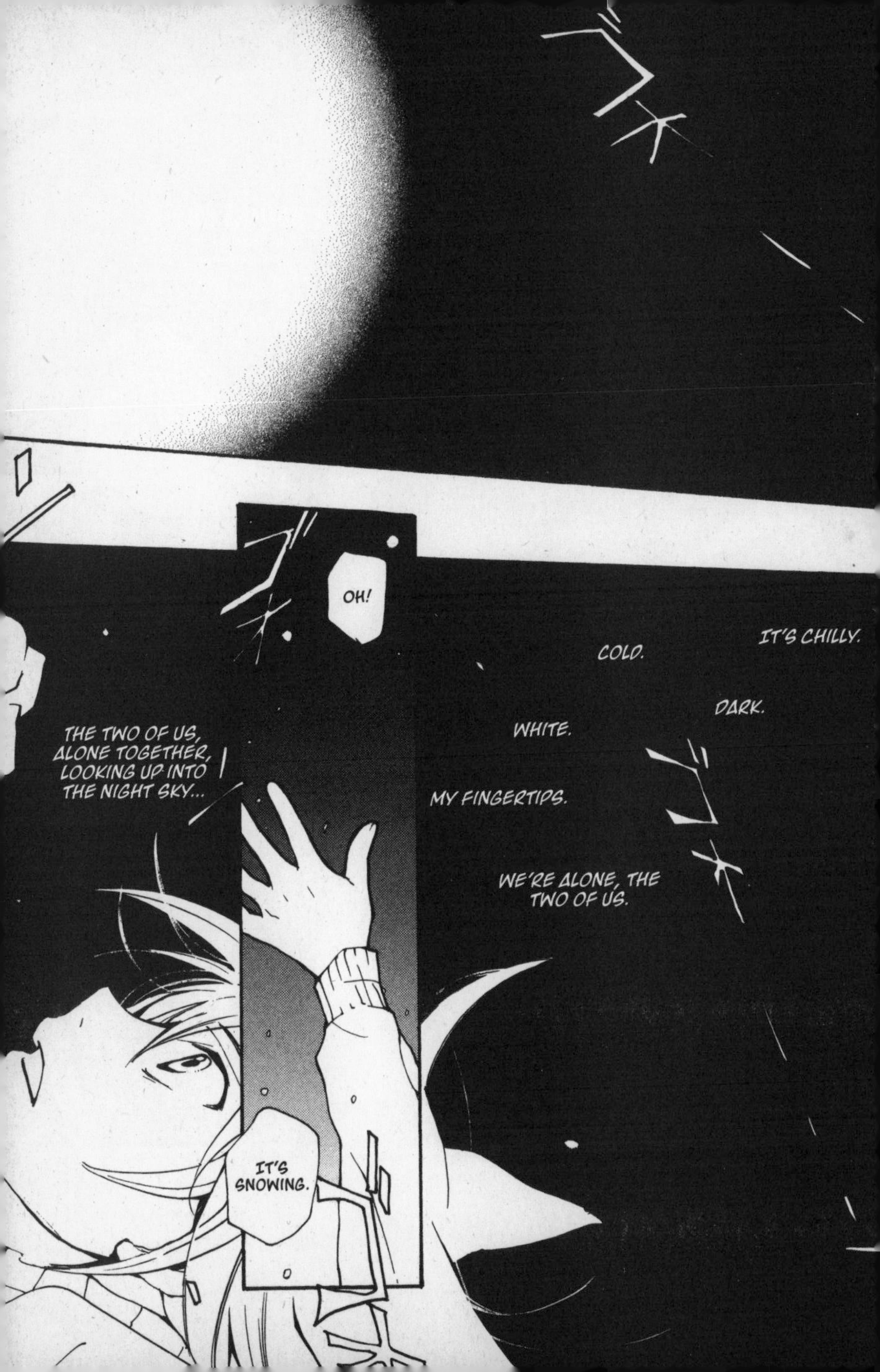
IT'S CHILLY.
COLD.
DARK.
WHITE.
MY FINGERTIPS.
WE'RE ALONE, THE TWO OF US.
OH!
IT'S SNOWING.
THE TWO OF US, ALONE TOGETHER, LOOKING UP INTO THE NIGHT SKY...

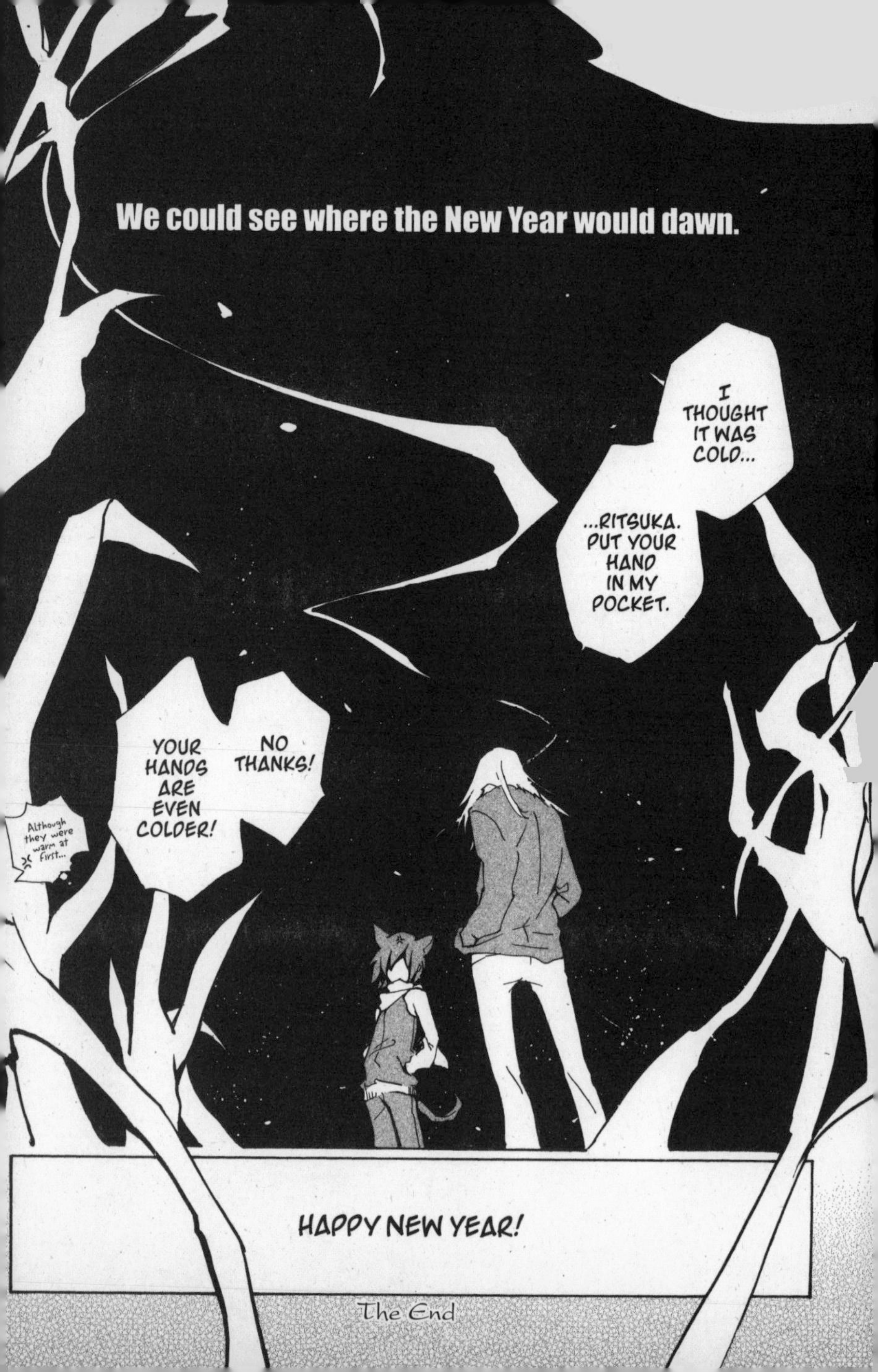
We could see where the New Year would dawn.
I THOUGHT IT WAS COLD...
...RITSUKA. PUT YOUR HAND IN MY POCKET.
NO THANKS!
YOUR HANDS ARE EVEN COLDER!
Although they were warm at first...
HAPPY NEW YEAR!
The End

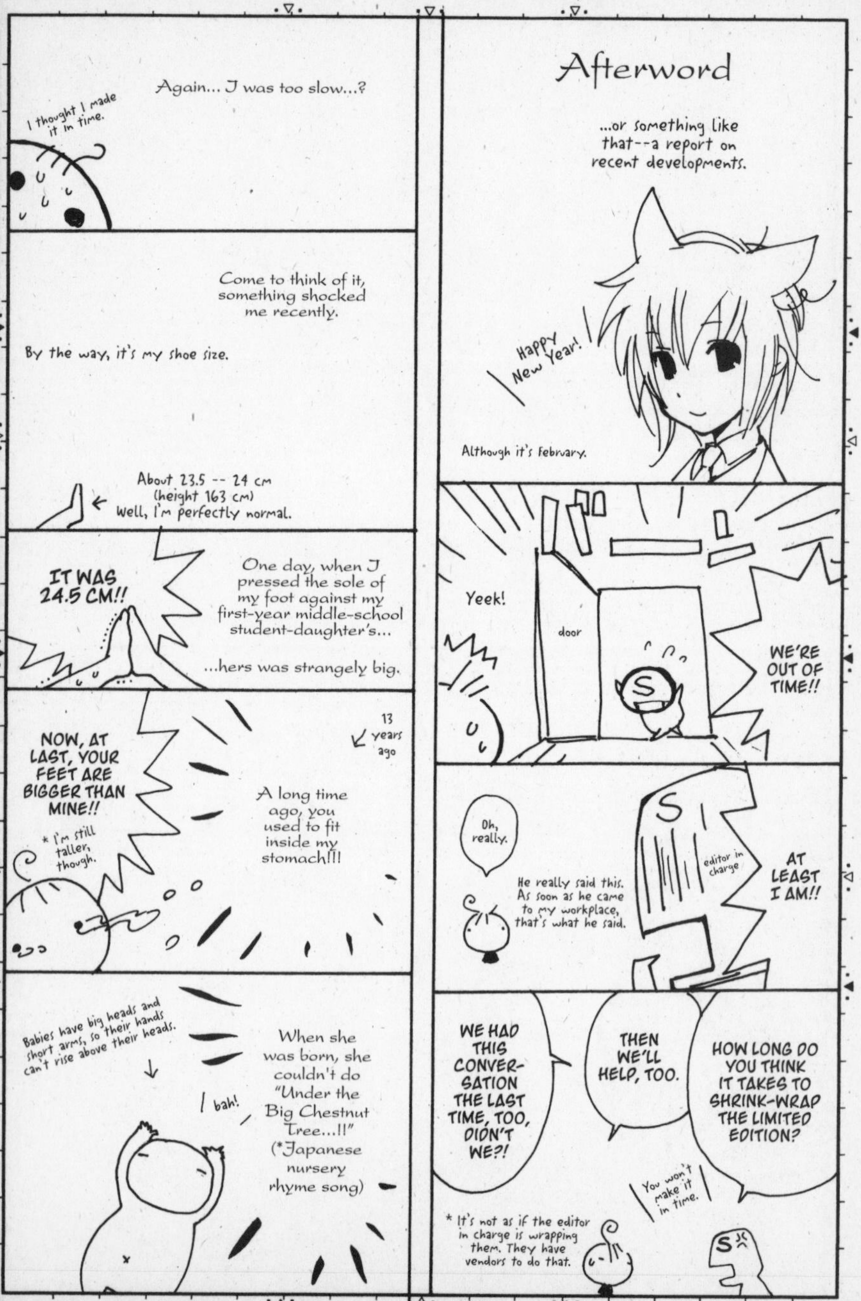
Afterword
...or something like that--a report on recent developments.
Happy New Year!
Although it's February.
WE'RE OUT OF TIME!!
Yeek!
door
AT LEAST I AM!!
editor in charge
Oh, really.
He really said this. As soon as he came to my workplace, that's what he said.
HOW LONG DO YOU THINK IT TAKES TO SHRINK-WRAP THE LIMITED EDITION?
THEN WE'LL HELP, TOO.
WE HAD THIS CONVERSATION THE LAST TIME, TOO, DIDN'T WE?!
You won't make it in time.
* It's not as if the editor in charge is wrapping them. They have vendors to do that.
Again... I was too slow...?
I thought I made it in time.
Come to think of it, something shocked me recently.
By the way, it's my shoe size.
About 23.5 -- 24 cm (height 163 cm) Well, I'm perfectly normal.
One day, when I pressed the sole of my foot against my first-year middle-school student-daughter's...
...hers was strangely big.
IT WAS 24.5 CM!!
13 years ago
A long time ago, you used to fit inside my stomach!!!
NOW, AT LAST, YOUR FEET ARE BIGGER THAN MINE!!
* I'm still taller, though.
When she was born, she couldn't do "Under the Big Chestnut Tree...!!" (*Japanese nursery rhyme song)
bah!
Babies have big heads and short arms, so their hands can't rise above their heads.

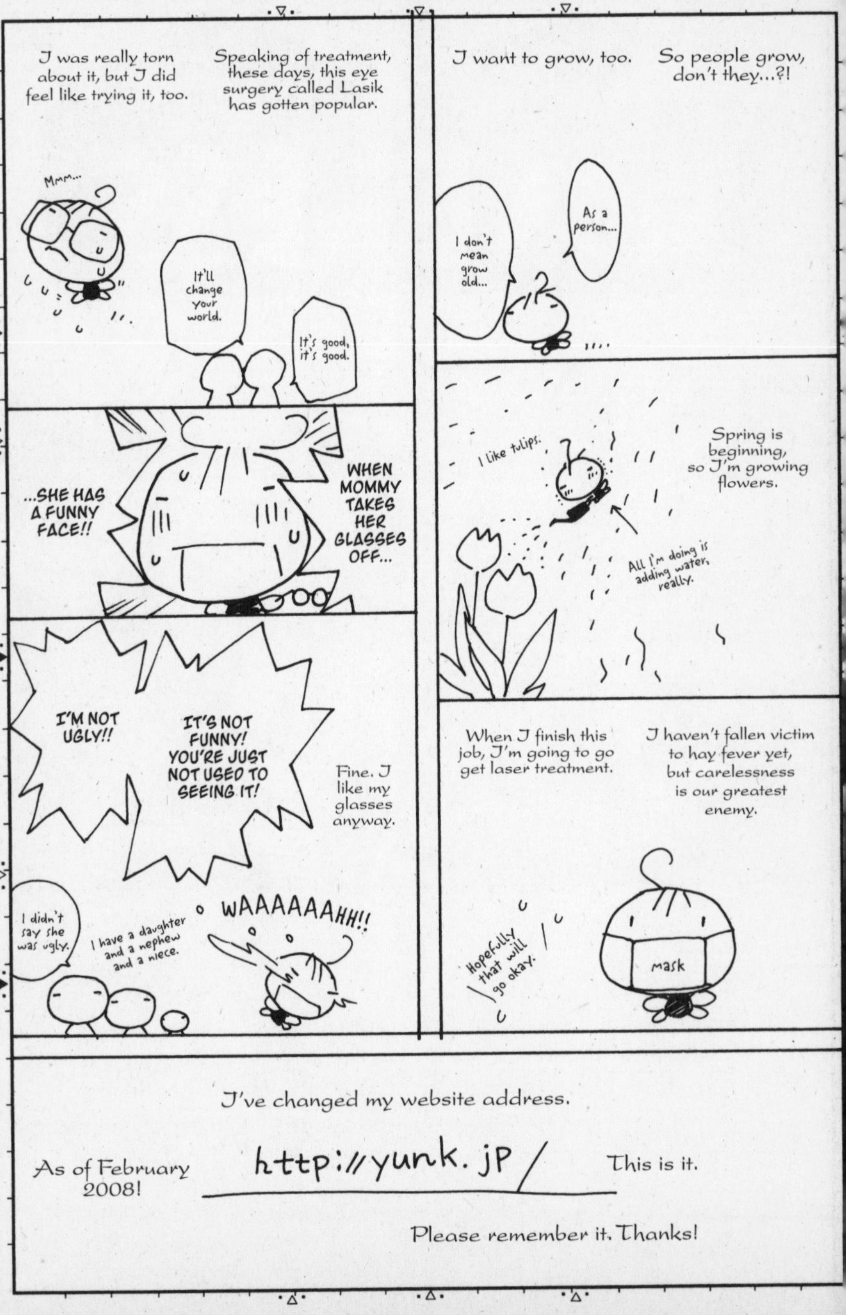
So people grow, don't they...?!
I want to grow, too.
As a person...
I don't mean grow old...
Spring is beginning, so I'm growing flowers.
I like tulips.
All I'm doing is adding water, really.
I haven't fallen victim to hay fever yet, but carelessness is our greatest enemy.
When I finish this job, I'm going to go get laser treatment.
mask
Hopefully that will go okay.
Speaking of treatment, these days, this eye surgery called Lasik has gotten popular.
I was really torn about it, but I did feel like trying it, too.
It's good, it's good.
It'll change your world.
Mmm...
WHEN MOMMY TAKES HER GLASSES OFF...
...SHE HAS A FUNNY FACE!!
Fine. I like my glasses anyway.
IT'S NOT FUNNY! YOU'RE JUST NOT USED TO SEEING IT!
I'M NOT UGLY!!
WAAAAAAHH!!
I have a daughter and a nephew and a niece.
I didn't say she was ugly.
I've changed my website address.
This is it.
http://yunk.jp/
As of February 2008!
Please remember it. Thanks!

In The Next Volume of

LOVELESS

In the aftermath of the battle at the Seven Voices Academy, Soubi and Ritsuka come to a new understanding, and a new level of intimacy. But as the status of the rest of Septimal Moon is revealed, it is soon discovered that Seimei has been very busy indeed...and that when he escaped from Gora, he may have taken Kio with him!

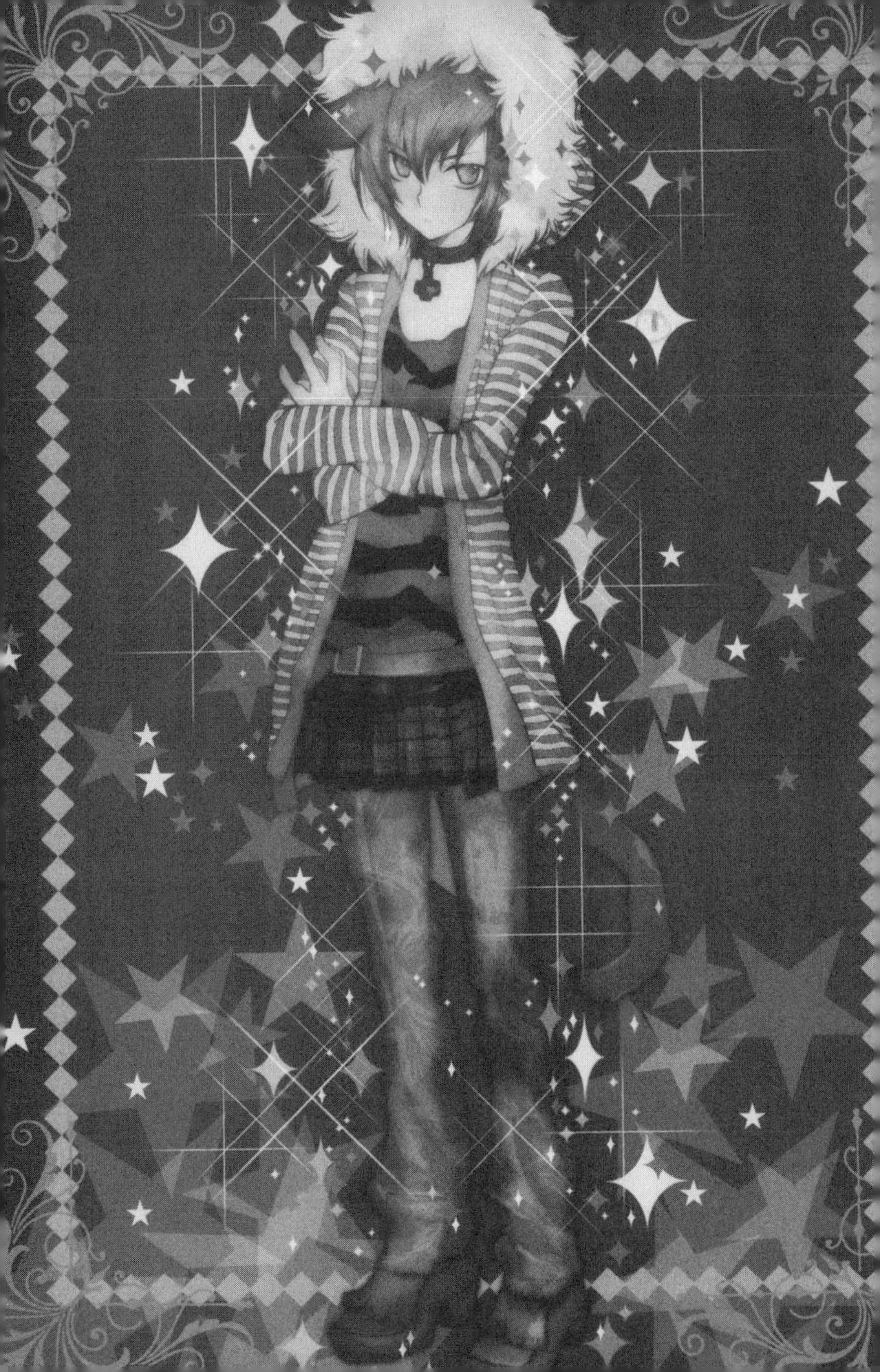

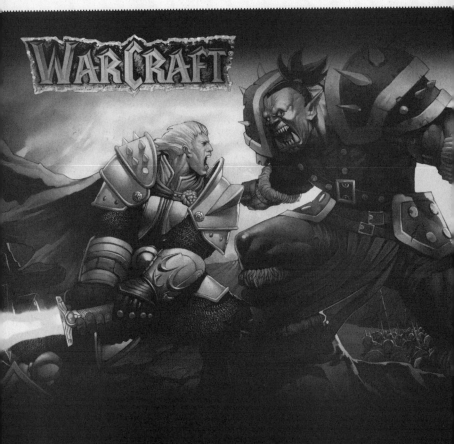

GAKUEN ALICE VOLUME FOUR

Mikan's daring rescue of Natsume has earned her an upgrade to One-star rank!

Mikan's upgrade to One-star rank has come just in time for the School Festival, and it's even more spectacular than Mikan ever dreamed. But what will happen when Mikan and Natsume get locked in the haunted house together?!

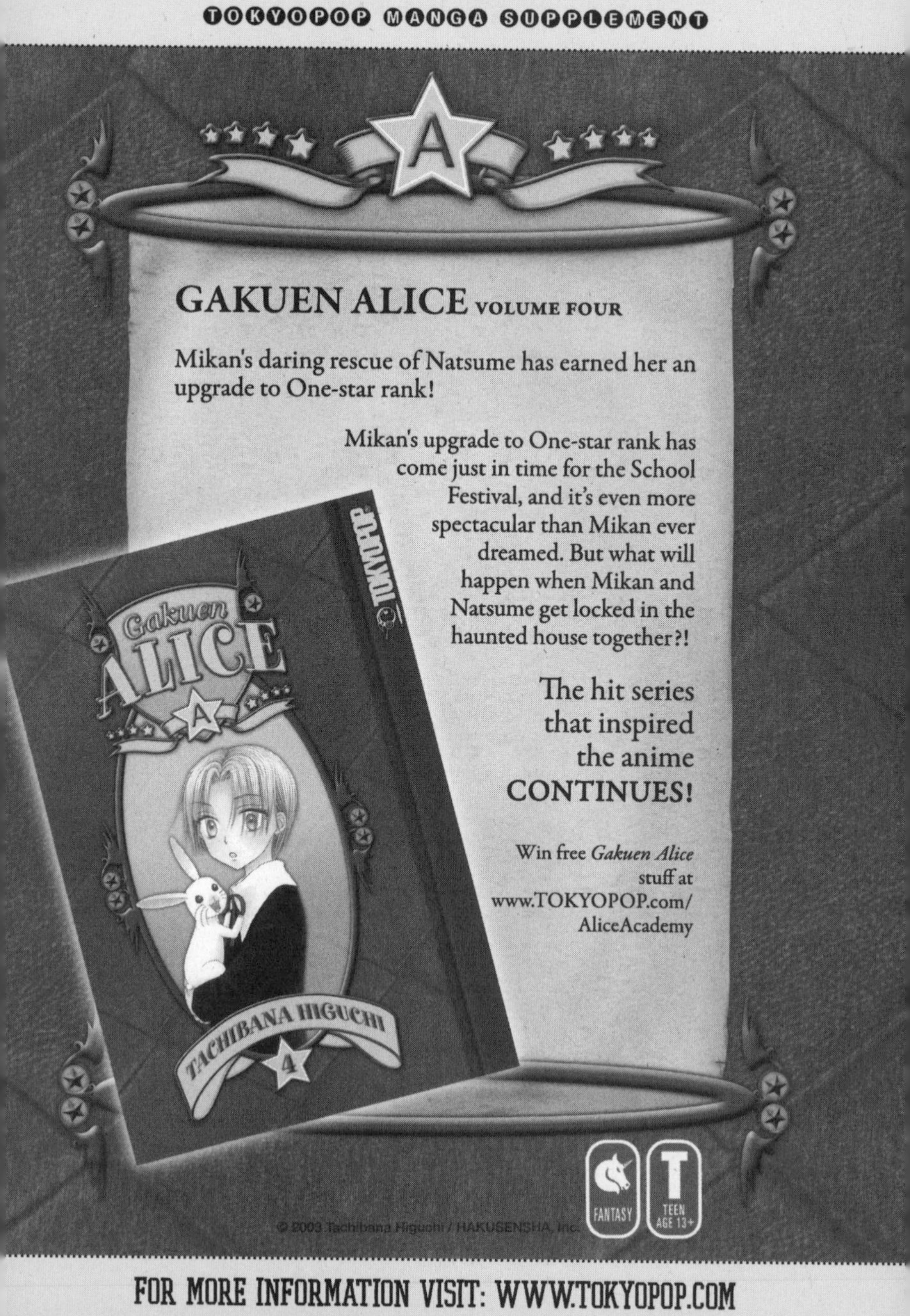
Gakuen
ALICE
TOKYOPOP
TACHIBANA HIGUCHI
4

The hit series that inspired the anime **CONTINUES!**

Win free *Gakuen Alice* stuff at www.TOKYOPOP.com/AliceAcademy

FANTASY

TEEN AGE 13+

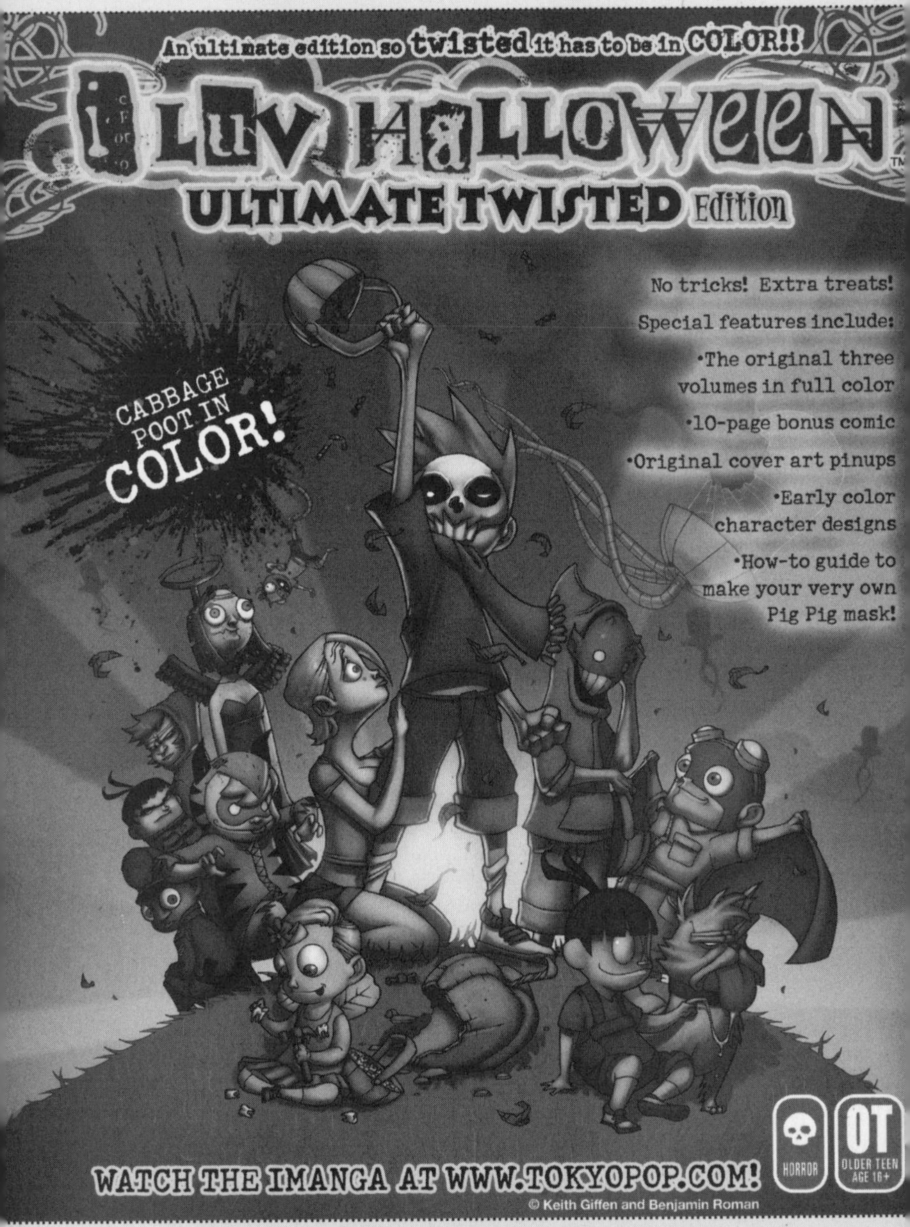
An ultimate edition so twisted it has to be in COLOR!!
I LUV HALLOWEEN™
ULTIMATE TWISTED Edition
No tricks! Extra treats!
Special features include:
•The original three volumes in full color
•10-page bonus comic
•Original cover art pinups
•Early color character designs
•How-to guide to make your very own Pig Pig mask!
CABBAGE POOT IN COLOR!
HORROR
OT
OLDER TEEN AGE 16+
WATCH THE IMANGA AT WWW.TOKYOPOP.COM!
© Keith Giffen and Benjamin Roman

BIZENGHAST
BY M. ALICE LEGROW, NOVEL BY SHAWN THORGERSEN

Not every lost soul is a lost cause

Dinah must fight to keep her sanity and life together, *and* keep all hell from breaking loose in the Mausoleum! The town of Bizenghast holds many secrets, and Dinah will have to grow up and grow strong if she intends to seek out the truth behind the mystery.

FOR MORE INFORMATION VISIT:

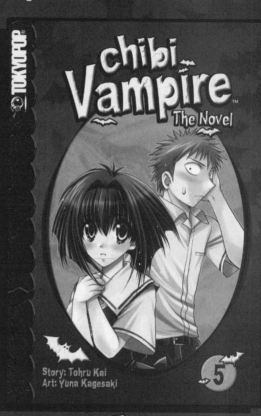

CHIBI VAMPIRE
MANGA BY YUNA KAGESAKI, NOVEL BY TOHRU KAI AND YUNA KAGESAKI

The HILARIOUS adventures of

As Karin and Kenta's official first date continues, Anju shows up to keep an eye on the clumsy couple. When Kenta tells Karin how he really feels, will it destroy their relationship? Also, the new girl in town, Yuriya, begins snooping around in search of vampires. Why is she trying to uncover Karin's identity, and what secrets of her own is she hiding?

chibi Vampire™ Inspired the

FOR MORE INFORMATION VISIT:

STOP!

This is the back of the book.
You wouldn't want to spoil a great ending!

This book is printed "manga-style," in the authentic Japanese right-to-left format. Since none of the artwork has been flipped or altered, readers get to experience the story just as the creator intended. You've been asking for it, so TOKYOPOP® delivered: authentic, hot-off-the-press, and far more fun!

DIRECTIONS

If this is your first time reading manga-style, here's a quick guide to help you understand how it works.

It's easy... just start in the top right panel and follow the numbers. Have fun, and look for more 100% authentic manga from TOKYOPOP®!